the creation of positive, safe, and more equal workplace environments. This book will be useful to organizational management at all levels, organizational trainers, consultants, and students aspiring to these roles."

Joann Keyton, *Distinguished Professor Emerita, North Carolina State University, USA; Principal, Joann Keyton Consulting, Inc*

COMMUNICATION AND ORGANIZATIONAL CHANGEMAKING FOR DIVERSITY, EQUITY, AND INCLUSION

This book explores the opportunities, challenges, and effective approaches to organizational change regarding diversity, equity, inclusion, and belonging.

Featuring application-based case studies and practical guidelines for meaningful organizational change, this book problematizes some of the current DEI initiatives in today's organizations. It examines multiple forms of diversity (e.g., race, age, and mental health) from a variety of perspectives (e.g., leadership and employee), with case studies that demonstrate how changemaking efforts can be reimagined and implemented in better, more nuanced, and more sustainable ways to produce meaningful organizational change. Through these case studies, readers learn from organizations' successes and failures in their attempts to implement DEI practices. Each chapter concludes with explicit practical implications and/or actionable recommendations for organizational changemaking.

This text will make an impactful addition to courses in communication and diversity or organizational communication/change at the advanced undergraduate or graduate level, and will be an essential guide for professionals wishing to lead change in their organizations.

Bobbi J. Van Gilder is an Assistant Professor of Global and Cultural Communication at Suffolk University, USA.

Jasmine T. Austin is an Assistant Professor of Race and Organizational Communication at Texas State University, USA.

Jacqueline S. Bruscella is an Associate Professor of Organizational Communication at the State University of New York at Oneonta, USA.

COMMUNICATION AND ORGANIZATIONAL CHANGEMAKING FOR DIVERSITY, EQUITY, AND INCLUSION

A Case Studies Approach

Edited by Bobbi J. Van Gilder,
Jasmine T. Austin, and
Jacqueline S. Bruscella

Routledge
Taylor & Francis Group

NEW YORK AND LONDON

Designed cover image: sssimone/© Getty Images

First published 2024
by Routledge
605 Third Avenue, New York, NY 10158

and by Routledge
4 Park Square, Milton Park, Abingdon, Oxon, OX14 4RN

Routledge is an imprint of the Taylor & Francis Group, an informa business

Library of Congress Cataloguing-in-Publication Data
Names: Van Gilder, Bobbi J., editor. | Austin, Jasmine T., editor. |
Bruscella, Jaqueline S., editor.
Title: Communication and organizational changemaking for diversity, equity, and inclusion : a case studies approach / edited by Bobbi J. Van Gilder, Jasmine T. Austin and Jaqueline S. Bruscella.
Other titles: Communication and organisational changemaking for diversity, equity, and inclusion
Description: New York, NY : Routledge, 2024. | Includes bibliographical references and index.
Identifiers: LCCN 2023024462 (print) | LCCN 2023024463 (ebook) |
ISBN 9781032367798 (hardback) | ISBN 9781032367774 (paperback) |
ISBN 9781003333746 (ebook)
Classification: LCC HD30.3 .C6396 2024 (print) | LCC HD30.3 (ebook) |
DDC 658.4/5--dc23/eng/20230823
LC record available at https://lccn.loc.gov/2023024462
LC ebook record available at https://lccn.loc.gov/2023024463

ISBN: 978-1-032-36779-8 (hbk)
ISBN: 978-1-032-36777-4 (pbk)
ISBN: 978-1-003-33374-6 (ebk)

DOI: 10.4324/9781003333746

Typeset in Times New Roman
by MPS Limited, Dehradun

CONTENTS

CONTRIBUTORS

Marwa Abdalla, University of California, San Diego

Beauty Fosu Acheampong, University of Georgia

Al Waqqas Al Balushi, Arizona State University

Wilfredo Alvarez, Metropolitan State University of Denver

Greg G. Armfield, New Mexico State University

Jasmine T. Austin, Texas State University

Dawna I. Ballard, The University of Texas

Raymond Blanton, University of the Incarnate Word

Jacqueline S. Bruscella, SUNY Oneonta

Zifei Fay Chen, University of San Francisco

Tianna L. Cobb, Johns Hopkins University

Ignacio F. Cruz, Northwestern University

Elizabeth K. Eger, Texas State University

Kirsten Foot, University of Washington

Diane Forbes Berthoud, University of Maryland, Baltimore

Maria J. Genao-Homs, Hamilton College

Erin E. Gilles, University of Southern Indiana

Angela N. Gist-Mackey, University of Kansas

Lorena Gomez-Barris, University of San Francisco

Elizabeht Hernandez, Independent Scholar

Leandra H. Hernández, University of Utah

Anne P. Hubbell, New Mexico State University

Laura Irwin, University of Washington

Anna Jewell, University of Kansas

Heewon Kim, Arizona State University

Rebecca B. Leach, University of Arkansas

Lore/tta LeMaster, Arizona State University

Joshua H. Miller, Texas State University

Gabriela I. Morales, New Mexico State University

Ashton Mouton, Sam Houston State University

Stevie M. Munz, Utah Valley University

Sidney Murray, University of South Florida

Saleema Mustafa Campbell, Kentucky State University

Alyssa Obradovich, Purdue University

Srividya Ramasubramanian, Syracuse University

Robert J. Razzante, Independent Scholar

Divya S, University of Georgia

Samantha Szczur, Eastern Illinois University

Sachiko Terui, University of Georgia

Cris J. Tietsort, University of Denver

Bobbi J. Van Gilder, Suffolk University

Richard D. Waters, University of San Francisco

Sunshine Webster, Talent Development, Q2

Savaughn E. Williams, University of Kansas

Anna Wolfe, Texas A&M University

Elizabeth Yanas, Texas State University

Alaina C. Zanin, Arizona State University

1

INTRODUCTION

Communication and Organizational Changemaking for Diversity, Equity, and Inclusion

Bobbi J. Van Gilder[1], Jasmine T. Austin[2], and Jacqueline S. Bruscella[3]

[1]*Suffolk University;* [2]*Texas State University;* [3]*SUNY Oneonta*

Rationale

US society has been changing for a long time. For instance, there are growing numbers of people of color, with several states having already obtained majority–minority status (US Census Bureau, 2022). We also have an aging population—by 2035 older adults will outnumber children for the first time in US history (Turner, 2018). Today, immigrants make up nearly 14% of the US population (Ward & Batalova, 2023). One in six Gen Z adults is LGBTQIA+ (Schmidt, 2021). A total of 26% of US adults have some type of disability (CDC, 2018).

These changing demographics have prompted increased demands for equal access and opportunity. And "related fear of lawsuits or boycotts have made difference (usually called 'diversity') a hot topic" (Allen, 2023, p. 6). This has resulted in some positive changes. For example, we have witnessed new legislation to advance the rights of various marginalized groups (e.g., the Americans with Disabilities Act). Furthermore, many organizations have implemented training programs centered on issues of diversity and have made efforts to increase the recruitment and retention of organizational members from diverse backgrounds. But historically, many of these efforts have fallen short, as organizations often do the bare minimum for the sake of their public image, with little *real* change being made to the organizing structures that maintain inequity. Will the changes we are seeing *now* be more impactful or more sustainable than what we have observed in the past?

DOI: 10.4324/9781003333746-1

Socio-Political Context Sparking DEI Initiatives

In 2020, a lot happened that prompted organizations to initiate or renew their commitments to diversity, equity, and inclusion (DEI). On May 25, 2020, George Floyd was murdered by a white police officer, and protests erupted across the country. While this was certainly neither the first instance of police brutality to result in the death of an unarmed Black person nor was it the last, it was the first time in recent history we saw racial justice protests of this magnitude since the civil rights movement.

It is also important to note that these Black Lives Matter protests were taking place during a global pandemic that has now become the deadliest pandemic in US history. With this, we observed a rise in anti-Asian rhetoric and violence against Asians. In 2020, we also observed (and are continuing to observe) an unprecedented number of anti-LGBTQIA+ bills enacted in state legislatures across the country. These are just a few (of many) recent events which have led to DEI-centered change initiatives within and across organizations.

For example, in response to some of the identity-based hate and violence in 2020, many organizations made public statements condemning racism (e.g., the NFL, Uber, PayPal) and other forms of discrimination. Not only did organizations discursively condemn identity-based hate, but many also committed to advance diversity and inclusion initiatives inside and outside of their own organizations. In 2020, it was clear that the masses were angry, energized, and willing to mobilize for the cause, even despite an ongoing pandemic. But, when the energy dies down, how will these organizations be held accountable for their commitments? In other words, how do we ensure DEI practices are more than just empty talk?

Organizational Changemaking

This book emphasizes *organizations*, as organizations are settings where conceptions about identity and difference are learned and experienced (e.g., schools, religious organizations, and places of work). Importantly, they are places where social identities are negotiated and managed, where conflicts related to difference emerge, and where structures are (or can be) disrupted and transformed. Furthermore, we are more likely to communicate *across* difference in organizational settings (Allen, 2023). Most importantly, "Organizations are sites of power dynamics where different groups try to serve their own interests and to access or control resources. They are also critical contexts where advocates for equality and equity can effect social change" (Allen, 2023, p. 12).

Although diversity and inclusion have been studied extensively in organizational settings before, many studies demonstrate a *need* for diversity and inclusion but tend to focus more on barriers (e.g., stereotypes) without shedding light on how organizations are transformed (Wilhoit Larson et al., 2022). Furthermore, as noted by Galliard et al. (2020), "diversity and inclusion are often vaguely intertwined and the underlying emphasis tends to be on representation (diversity) over processes (inclusion)" (p. 266). As such, this book emphasizes DEI changemaking *in practice*.

Summary of Contents

While DEI initiatives have been extensively discussed in existing communication literature from various theoretical perspectives, this book aims to problematize some of the current DEI initiatives by exploring the challenges, failures, opportunities, and effective approaches pertaining to organizational changemaking, specifically regarding DEI and belonging. Chapters in this book interrogate the meaning of diversity and problematize some of the mainstream approaches to DEI work, which often function to preserve dominant cultural norms that serve dominant group members. Most importantly, this book provides application-based case studies and practical guidelines for meaningful organizational changemaking.

This book examines multiple forms of diversity (e.g., race, age, mental health, gender, etc.) from a variety of organizational stakeholder perspectives (i.e., leaders and members). The case studies presented in the book are also diverse, reflecting popular culture, intraorganizational and interorganizational collaboration, and many other interaction contexts. Finally, this book has the explicit goal of embodying DEI work, not just in the content, but in the contributors as well. Authors from academic and practitioner backgrounds featured in this collection approach organizational changemaking from diverse perspectives, using a variety of methodological and theoretical approaches. Through purposeful selection of a diverse body of contributors that reflect the purpose of this book, readers will find this text to be engaging, accessible, and relevant to the racial, ethnic, and cultural diversity in today's world.

Organization of the Book

Our primary aim for this book is to demonstrate ways in which changemaking efforts can be reimagined and implemented in better, more nuanced, and more sustainable ways to produce meaningful change within and across organizations. In doing so, each chapter applies and analyzes a case study pertaining to organizational changemaking. Importantly, each chapter concludes with a set of actionable recommendations that readers can implement in their respective organizations.

We organized the book into three parts: (1) Envisioning more equitable policies and practices, (2) Challenging dominant discourses and fostering inclusive dialogue, and (3) Promoting meaningful and impactful organizational leadership.

Envisioning More Equitable Structures, Policies, and Practices

In the first section of the book, authors problematize current DEI initiatives by addressing structural barriers to organizational changemaking, focusing specifically on communication norms and expectations and, policies and, procedures that guide organizational decision making. For example, several scholars examined problems in hiring practices that can prevent DEI from meaningfully coming to fruition within organizations. Specifically, Ignacio F. Cruz problematizes the use of artificial intelligence (AI) in hiring processes. While AI was introduced into some hiring processes with the explicit aim of reducing implicit biases, AI can often reproduce the problem of bias in hiring when not implemented effectively.

In another chapter, Samantha Szczur and Alyssa Obradovich focus on age discrimination in hiring. While age-blind hiring practices have been implemented in an effort to address this problem, age-blind hiring can/should only function as a *first step*. The authors use a narrative case study to highlight the shortcomings of age-blind hiring practices and offer recommendations for changing organizational culture to enhance age diversity and inclusion.

Joshua H. Miller problematizes communication and professionalism standards, which also influence hiring decisions. As Miller explains, because those with the most power determine what is acceptable (or "good") communication for everybody else, communication policies, norms, and expectations (which guide decision making) are often exclusionary. As such, he argues that the interview process, in particular, should be reimagined.

Other scholars in this section advocate for improved DEI training to promote organizational equity and inclusion. Sachiko Terui, Divya S, and Beauty Fosu, for example, examined diversity and equity in the context of healthcare. Specifically, they examine language discordance as a barrier to health equity. They then offer actionable recommendations for healthcare providers and healthcare organizations that could help them to improve patient care (e.g., training recommendations and technology integration).

In another chapter, Gabriela I. Morales, Anne P. Hubbell, and Greg G. Armfield problematize traditional compliance-based training. They highlight the importance of integrating integrity-based training. They also offer more specific recommendations for impactful DEI training that include needs assessment, goal setting, DEI leadership, and prolonged/ongoing training.

Wilfredo Alvarez and Maria J. Genao-Homs focus on the context of higher education. In their chapter, they reimagine faculty members' roles in shifting higher education organizations, discussing some of the ways that faculty stakeholders could be(come) changemakers. In doing so, they advance strategies that enhance faculty engagement in/with equitable and inclusive practices in higher education. As changemakers themselves, they were able to interweave their own voices and experiences throughout the chapter, illustrating how their recommendations can be enacted in meaningful ways.

Lastly, Erin E. Gilles and Saleema Mustafa Campbell examine Humana, a health insurance company that was recognized by DiversityInc as a Top 50 company. Humana presents a unique case study for analysis because it serves as an exemplar for how DEI can be implemented at every level of an organization. In their chapter, the authors are able to draw from Humana's DEI efforts to develop concrete, actionable recommendations for DEI campaigns that can be adapted to a variety of organizational contexts.

Challenging Dominant Discourses and Fostering Dialogue

In the second section of the book, we include case studies that challenge some of the dominant discourses that shape organizations and organizing practices. Other case studies in this section focus on interpersonal connection, dialogue, and collaboration for changemaking.

In their chapter, Sunshine Webster and Dawna I. Ballard challenge dominant discourses related to "work-life balance." In their case study analysis, the authors illuminate the political dimensions of work-life policies as a function of class, race, and post-industrial capitalism. They advocate for a collaborative approach to scheduling to make work-life policies more equitable.

In another chapter, Heewon Kim and Ashton Mouton examine their own experiences as members of a DEI ad hoc committee to illuminate the ways in which structural tensions constrained decision making and (re)produced whiteness. They then offer actionable recommendations for overcoming these barriers.

Marwa Abdalla analyzes exemplars related to #BeingBlackandMuslim, a social media campaign centering the experiences of Black Muslims, along with organizational discourses responding to racial justice concerns from the Islamic Society of North America (ISNA), a national, historically non-Black Muslim-led institution. The chapter concludes with practical insights on addressing intersectional invisibility in organizational contexts.

Stevie M. Munz, Leandra H. Hernández, and Elizabeht Hernandez examine their own experiences in higher education using an autoethnographic vignette approach. In doing so, they argue that pedagogy and mentorship can serve as mechanisms of organizational changemaking, particularly at predominantly white institutions.

In another chapter, Cris J. Tietsort and Rebecca B. Leach focus on compassion. The authors point out that while compassion at work is essential to employee well-being, those holding traditionally marginalized identities face additional challenges that limit compassion and may even exacerbate their suffering. As such, the authors offer actionable recommendations for the equitable practice of compassion in organizations.

Srividya Ramasubramanian and Anna Wolfe's chapter advocates for a trauma-informed approach for designing action-oriented dialogues for organizational changemaking. The authors offer practical tips and recommendations for designing, hosting, and evaluating dialogues within the context of any organization.

In their chapter, Laura Irwin and Kirsten Foot examined the case of a court-ordered and professionally facilitated mediation between four organizations. In their chapter, they examine how racialized power dynamics ultimately resulted in the failure of the collaborative effort. They provide facilitators of interorganizational and/or multistakeholder collaboration with strategies for both guiding diverse participants through difficult decision-making processes and addressing historic power imbalances by creating ethical communication structures for dialoguing across differences.

Lastly, Raymond Blanton examines the Apple TV+ workplace sitcom, *Ted Lasso*, as a case study for organizational changemaking. He uses the work of bell hooks and encases DEI initiatives into an exploration of belonging, advocating for the implementation of practices that include healing talk, civility, care, and commitment.

Promoting Meaningful and Impactful Organizational Leadership

In the final section of the book, case studies focus on issues of leadership. For instance, Sidney Murray, Elizabeth Yanas, Jasmine T. Austin, and Elizabeth K. Eger use a case study of a gym in Texas that displayed a large LGBTQ+ artifact with the goal of making employees and gym members feel welcomed. Unfortunately, this display had the unintended consequence of outing employees. The authors offer practical recommendations for leadership to improve LGBTQ+ allyship.

In another chapter, Richard D. Waters, Zifei Fay Chen, and Lorena Gomez-Barris examine how DEI efforts often stall once HR-focused DEI training programs are implemented. The authors advocate for a more comprehensive, reflective, and actionable set of proposals during the planning stage. They propose a stage model for organizational changemaking that managers can implement across a variety of organizations.

Robert J. Razzante and Al Waqqas Al Balushi utilize a case study of a healthcare organization to illuminate the shortcomings of some DEI efforts. In doing so, the authors highlight macro-, meso-, and micro-level communicative actions dominant group leaders and colleagues can use for creating an inclusive workplace. Their chapter provides valuable insight into how organizational leaders can better train employees in responding to social injustice in the workplace.

In another chapter, Tianna L. Cobb centers on the experiences of Black women religious leaders to identify organizational changemaking strategies to implement more leadership practices pertaining to, and inclusive of, mental health and illness. As argued by Cobb, because mental health is essential to DEI, it is imperative that organizational leaders apply inclusive mental health and illness leadership strategies.

Diane Forbes Berthoud proposes a changemaking model that centers equity principles, practices, and outcomes to strengthen and enhance leadership for sustainable organizational change. Specifically, she advances the Data, Review, Collective Engagement, and Critical Organizational Praxis (DRCC) model and offers practical guidelines for implementing this model across a variety of organizations.

Angela N. Gist-Mackey, Savaughn E. Williams, and Anna Jewell examine a human service non-profit's organizational culture after a problematic leader retires and a new leader is hired. Their findings demonstrate how the new leadership team worked to rebuild the organizational culture and how they leaned into diversity and inclusion as part of that organizational change effort. The chapter offers practical insights about how to engage in culture audits for organizations, engage in trauma stewardship for non-profit workers in helping professions, and how to lead with humility.

Finally, Alaina C. Zanin and Lore/tta LeMaster's chapter features two interrelated case studies that help to theorize Taylor's (a transgender and genderfluid athlete) experience navigating sports. They offer recommendations for how organizational leaders can articulate new shared values and organizational premises regarding the value of inclusivity, which might contradict or counter legislative policy. They also advocate for organizing new material norms that facilitate inclusivity.

Closing Thoughts

Although the events of 2020 sparked many organizations to take action and create or renew their commitments to DEI, there has also been extensive backlash. Dominant group members who oppose change have taken actions to prevent organizational change efforts. For example, some states have taken legislative action to prevent or reverse policies aimed at improving DEI (e.g., Florida's "Stop Woke Act" and "Don't Say Gay" bill; the criminalization of trans-affirming care). This makes collective changemaking efforts even more crucial. This also means that organizational changemaking must sometimes be executed in defiance of legislative policy. It may require organizational leaders and members to give up some of their benefits in order to achieve larger change (e.g., Disney stripped of some autonomy in Florida). Thus, the chapters presented in this collection aim to not only help situate DEI initiatives at the forefront of organizational changemakers' agendas, but also to offer actionable recommendations and best practices to help see these initiatives through to evoke real change in our organizational experiences.

Author Bios

Bobbi J. Van Gilder, Ph.D., is an Assistant Professor of Global and Cultural Communication at Suffolk University who teaches in both the Communication, Journalism, and Media Department, and in the Women's and Gender Studies program. Her scholarly interests intersect intercultural communication, intergroup communication, and gender and sexuality studies, with specific emphases on identity, difference, and disparities, particularly within organizational contexts. Her research has been published in journals such as the *Journal of International and Intercultural Communication*, the *Journal of Homosexuality*, and *Western Journal of Communication*, among others.

Jasmine T. Austin, Ph.D., is a scholar-activist who promotes social justice, advocacy, decentering colonialism, and (re)centering blackness and marginalized identities. Her two main areas of research are socialization and marginalized identities. This includes theorizing about Black women and examining the impact of early racialized conversations between group members (e.g., supervisor/member, parent/child) on future interactions, experiences, and identity development. She is the lead editor of *Communication Theory: Racially Diverse and Inclusive Perspectives.* https://orcid.org/0000-0002-4131-1273

Jacqueline (Bruscella) Bishop, Ph.D., is an Associate Professor of Communication Studies in the Department of Communication and Media at the State University of New York at Oneonta, where she teaches courses in organizational, professional, and small group communication. Her scholarly interests include the communicative constitution of organizations (CCO), specifically as it relates to organizational culture. Jackie's work has been published in *Communication Monographs*, *Communication Quarterly*, and *Western Journal of Communication*.

References

Allen, B. (2023). *Difference matters: Communicating social identity (third edition)*. Waveland Press, Inc.

CDC (2018). 1 in 4 US adults live with a disability. *Center for Disease Control and Prevention*. Retrieved from: https://www.cdc.gov/media/releases/2018/p0816-disability.html

Galliard, B. M., Davis, S. M., Gibbs, J. L., & Doerfel, M. L. (2020). Organizing as a tension between tradition and innovation: Promoting inclusion in academia. In M. L. Doerfel, & J. L. Gibbs (Eds.), *Organizing inclusion: Moving diversity from demographics to communication processes* (pp. 260–280). Routledge.

Schmidt, S. (2021). 1 in 6 Gen Z adults are LGBT. And this number could continue to grow. *Washington Post*. Retrieved from: https://www.washingtonpost.com/dc-md-va/2021/02/24/gen-z-lgbt/

Turner, A. (2018). Retirees will outnumber children for the first time in US history, report says. *CNBC*. Retrieved from: https://www.cnbc.com/2018/03/14/retirees-will-outnumber-kids-for-the-first-time-in-us-history-report.html

US Census Bureau (2022). *2020 U.S. population more racially, ethnically diverse than in 2010*. Retrieved from: https://www.census.gov/library/stories/2021/08/2020-united-states-population-more-racially-ethnically-diverse-than-2010.html

Ward, N., & Batalova, J. (2023). Frequently Requested Statistics on Immigrants and Immigration in the United States. *Migration Policy Institute*. Retrieved from: https://www.migrationpolicy.org/article/frequently-requested-statistics-immigrants-and-immigration-united-states

Wilhoit Larson, E., Linabary, J. R., & Long, Z. (2022). Communicating inclusion: A review and research agenda on inclusion research in organizational communication. *Annals of the International Communication Association*, *46*(2), 63–90.

PART 1

Envisioning More Equitable Structures, Policies, and Practices

2

FINDING THE RIGHT FIT

Strategies for DEI Sourcing in AI-Driven Recruitment

Ignacio F. Cruz
Northwestern University

Learning Objectives

After reading this chapter, you will:

1 Be able to explain the role of artificial intelligence (AI) technologies within an organization's hiring process.
2 Be able to evaluate the tensions that recruiters face when leveraging algorithmic outputs with diversity and inclusion hiring needs through a case study of AI-driven recruitment.
3 Be able to apply recommendations for executing equity-driven candidate hiring practices focusing on sourcing potential job candidates.

Introduction

Companies are hiring more than ever. Despite the ongoing Great Resignation—a US economic trend where millions of employees across all industries are quitting their jobs in pursuit of better wages, flexible work arrangements, and new career prospects—human resources (HR) departments are struggling to keep up in the race to recruit new talent. Recruitment teams are turning to algorithmic hiring tools to help optimize their workflows to get hiring done quicker and smarter. For example, by automating tasks like finding candidates with specialized credentials, employers can attract, screen, and select job applicants before their competitors.

Aside from supporting processes in recruitment workflows, algorithmic tools are increasingly used by employers to help reduce bias

DOI: 10.4324/9781003333746-3

within hiring and aim to increase diversity standards in their recruitment efforts (Black & van Esch, 2020; Raghavan et al., 2020). Diversity management is often a priority in talent acquisition, but there is little consensus on how to conceptualize, design, train, and deploy effective inclusive practices with artificial intelligence (AI) tools (Cruz, 2021; Köchling & Wehner, 2020; Li et al., 2021). It is important to note that algorithmic tools do not exist in a social vacuum. Communication and management scholarship has long questioned how employees adapt their use of technologies to match individual, group, or organizational demands (Bailey & Leonardi, 2015). Relatedly, organizational norms and policies, alongside personal judgments from HR personnel, often influence the degree to which AI outputs are considered within hiring decisions (Cruz, 2021). This chapter provides an opportunity to examine on-the-ground challenges and tensions faced by HR personnel when using AI-hiring tools during one of the most significant moments in the recruitment process—sourcing, or the act of finding, attracting, and cultivating relationships with prospective candidates for a job position. These tensions provide deeper insight into the considerations and adaptive practices hiring personnel employ when using AI-powered tools.

The Hiring Funnel: How AI Is Used from Application to Hire

AI-driven hiring tools are integrated into several hiring stages within applicant tracking systems that recruitment personnel uses to manage job candidates. The initial hiring process begins with finding and attracting potential candidates to apply for an open position. This stage is referred to as sourcing and involves recruiters working with hiring managers to develop and post a job advertisement, actively searching and attracting potential candidates, and using different forms of predictive analytics to curate a pool of applicants, or what is often referred to as a hiring pipeline. Following the sourcing of candidates, recruiters screen or evaluate candidates for experience, skills, and other relevant characteristics present in a job application against the fit for the position. Given the sheer number of applications per job position, predictive technologies are also readily used during this stage by recruitment personnel. Both in sourcing and screening processes, these tools automate elements of decision-making activities such as ranking data, matching relevant information about candidates for a job, scoring the qualifications of an applicant based on their job application materials, and parsing through job applicant data to narrow down the best candidates for an interview (Bogen & Rieke, 2018). Often, a varied process of interviewing, selecting candidates, and extending job offers concludes the hiring process. In each stage of the hiring process, recruitment personnel often leverage their tools, skills, and expertise to facilitate decision-making processes.

Figure 2.1 shows the four stages of the hiring funnel: sourcing, screening, interviewing, and selecting a job candidate.

FIGURE 2.1 The Hiring Funnel.

The design and use of AI-hiring tools in recruitment require the involvement of an organization and a third-party technology developer. In the context of designing an AI-hiring tool, an organization will identify tasks or processes pertaining to a recruiter's job responsibilities that can be integrated into a workflow for automation (Whittaker et al., 2018). AI-driven hiring tools offer an opportunity to codify expertise possessed by personnel and program it into a set of procedures that transform input data into an output or metric that is useful for determining a candidate's fit or qualification for a position (e.g., a ranking, score, and classification; Kellogg et al., 2020). Table 2.1 outlines the most common applications of AI-driven tools within the hiring funnel, as described by the Center for Democracy and Technology (2021).

Challenges for Integrating AI in Hiring

Existing work examining AI-driven hiring tools has placed focus on how algorithms shape the interplay between personnel workflows and organizational demands (Li et al., 2021; van den Broek, 2019), challenges over the lack of transparency and explainability of technical systems (Köchling & Wehner, 2020), and the lack of industry-wide regulation concerning the widescale development of algorithmic hiring technology (Ajunwa, 2020).

TABLE 2.1 Types of AI Tools Used in the Hiring Funnel

Type of Algorithmic Hiring Tool	Purpose
Sourcing and cultivation	This class of technologies assists in finding, attracting, and engaging with potential job applicants. Sourcing strategies can involve the use of predictive analytics that can filter for the inclusion or exclusion of specific qualities about a prospective candidate, parse and analyze candidate data found in applicant tracking systems, or rank and classify prospective candidate data on job boards like LinkedIn Recruiter. These tools are used to search for qualified job candidates for current or planned job requestions. Cultivation tools also aim to assist recruiters with engagement tasks by automating follow-ups, check-ins, and scheduling.
Resume or document scoring	These tools are designed to scan materials (often resumes or applicant-provided data) submitted by candidates and screen, match, or rank information in an application. Or these tools can screen a document to identify trends, terms, or patterns in applicant data.
Facial and voice expression	These tools analyze data from recorded interviews to process digital facial expressions and emotions, word choices, vocal tone, and quality of an applicant.
Games	These tools analyze data from games played by applicants that often assess skills through simulations of tasks (e.g., measures an applicant's level of coding via a software coding task). Games can also take the form of simulations that can measure an applicant's judgment through vocal, logical, or numerical reasoning.
Trait assessments	Like games, trait assessments are tools that take the form of surveys or tests that applicants take to measure individual-level traits such as personality or ability. Other times, these tools are non-intrusive and use applicant data (e.g., application materials or publicly accessible information about candidates like social media profiles) to measure an applicant's traits.

Table 2.1 outlines a list of common AI-driven hiring tools that was compiled using examples from the Center for Democracy and Technology's *2021 Algorithm-Driven Hiring Tools Report.*

When organizations implement algorithmic predictive tools, employees often encounter mismatches between their expertise and the recommended output from a technology (Li et al., 2021).

While not explicitly studied in the hiring context, Valentine and Hinds (2019) find that employees who are mandated to use predictive tools would ignore the recommendations from an algorithm. The workers often rejected recommendations as they perceived the advice to be inconsistent with their own experience on the job. Similarly, in the field of journalism, writers and legal professionals would ignore risk scores and analytics and not consider them as part of their corpus of data when making data-driven decisions (Christin, 2017). In legal settings, during criminal court proceedings, workers at a county courthouse hid AI-generated recidivism risk scores of defendants in files that were reviewed by pretrial parties and probation officers. These examples highlight the challenges that workers face using and developing trust in AI recommendations.

Recent management and communication scholarship advances a concept called *algoactivism* to describe tactics that employees use to augment or resist the recommendations from algorithms through practical action (Kellogg et al., 2020). While algorithms are used as a technology that enhances employee performance, AI technologies can also open a channel to constrain and nudge the behaviors of the employees who use them. These mechanisms manifest during an employee's interaction with algorithms, and they may amplify how organizational demands and expectations can be incongruent with ways of practice carried out by employees.

Resisting Technology

One way to explain moments of algoactivism—or the behavioral responses of employees attenuating the effect of algorithms in their decisions and overall work (Kellogg et al., 2020)—is to understand the folk theories that users form about the nature of the algorithmic systems that they are tasked to use for work (Christin, 2017; Liao & Tyson, 2021). Christin (2017) speculates that technology users "have distinct algorithmic imaginaries, in the sense that they interpret and make sense of algorithms in different ways" (p. 10). Through persistent use, users come to form opinions and rationalize their experiences using algorithmic tools. Essentially, they create folk theories or understandings about how technologies operate, but they are able to rationalize their theories through specialized tacit and explicit knowledge of job tasks (Devito et al., 2018). Folk theories are a way to make sense of past experiences and can be used as cognitive tools to justify future use of technology (Christin, 2017; Liao & Tyson, 2021).

In the context of hiring, recruiters who review a large number of applications (e.g., high-volume recruiting typically involves 250 or more applications per job posting) often have to make sourcing decisions that consider if a potential job candidate meets certain criteria or proficiencies outlined by a job listing. For example, an applicant that lists specific skills on their job board profiles (e.g., LinkedIn or ZipRecruiter) or application materials will then be evaluated against an algorithmic hiring tool to filter, rank, or predict the likelihood of success for a job (Oberst et al., 2020). However, recruiters tend not to fully accept the recommendations from the algorithms they are mandated to use (Oberst et al., 2020) and, at times, may use strategies to pre-emptively modify or intervene in the overall output of a system (Cruz, 2021). In terms of diversity and inclusive measures for hiring, most HR departments set explicit but loosely enforced goals for diversity for talent acquisition (Rivera, 2012). Recruiters likely face the challenges of attenuating the tension between the scope and capability of the tools they use, alongside the demands from management to reach diversity goals. In turn, the disagreements between algorithms and human workers could result from negotiations over expertise types that lead human recruiters to apply workarounds toward a desired computational result (Cruz, 2021).

The current research about AI use and hiring reveals many unexplored and challenging questions about the ways that hiring personnel engage and interact with algorithmic systems at work. Christin (2017) highlights the importance of work in this area to "study the practices, uses, and implementations surrounding algorithmic technologies. Algorithms may be described as 'revolutionary,' but this kind of discourse is as much prescriptive (algorithms should do all of these things) as it is descriptive ... we need to pay close attention to the actual rather than aspirational practices connected to algorithms" (pp. 11–12). Related to this chapter, I focus on uncovering the strategies that recruiters employ when coordinating action between AI-hiring technologies and the needs of their organization with an implicit focus on issues of diversity and inclusion. The following section details the methods used in this study to examine these foundational tensions during the sourcing and cultivation stages of hiring across a variety of firms.

Methods

To investigate the coordination strategies of hiring personnel within an AI-hiring setting, I conducted interviews with 42 recruitment professionals across 26 industries. Primary data collection for this study lasted ten months, with virtual interviews scheduled in October 2020 and concluding in August 2021. I approached sampling in three ways: (1) through online customer lists of AI tool developers, (2) searches for recruitment personnel with specific recruiter job titles on LinkedIn, and (3) contacting recruiters on groups within social networking sites like Facebook and LinkedIn. A total of 40 interviews were audio recorded and two were accompanied with hand-written notes.

The interview guide comprised of four sections: (1) Warm-up questions to gain background information about the participant's organization and their role (including tasks, responsibilities, affiliation to teams, etc.), (2) Questions related to the participant's perception of technology use across their work processes, with a focus on algorithmic tools, (3) Questions related to specific actions taken when using algorithms, and (4) Individual-level demographic questions about each participant. I analyzed data using a qualitative data analysis approach (Miles et al., 2019) while placing emphasis on coding techniques derived from a constructivist grounded theory approach (Charmaz, 2014) with in-depth, semi-structured interviews as my primary source of data. The following section provides an account of the findings generated by these analyses.

Findings

Recruiters source candidates in a variety of different ways. They often rely on finding candidates through internal company referrals, predictive recommendations for social media, and job boards like LinkedIn Recruiter from social networks, in-person or virtual job fairs and trade events, or from previous job applicants who had previously applied to a position at the organization. Generally, recruiters narrow their searches to match a baseline set by hiring; searches often filter for applicant characteristics like required skills for a job, current type of employment, education level, current location, and expected salary. However, recruiters often use algorithmic sourcing tools to pre-emptively screen candidates for implicit criteria through proxies listed on job boards like LinkedIn or in stored applicant data.

In turn, recruiters use filters as a form of preliminary screening. For example, one of the most common forms of screening involves filtering for explicit criteria like expected compensation. If an applicant indicates their preferred salary to be outside the budget range for a designated position, they are excluded and removed for further consideration. Filtering tactics are often used to "not waste anyone's time when you bring them in for an interview" (referring to recruiter, applicant, or hiring managers, Ashely, a recruiter in Sales, Los Angeles) or to "not include someone that is clearly under or overqualified for a job or someone who just doesn't seem like a good fit from the onset" (Anne, recruiter in Legal, Los Angeles). In general, sourcing candidates allows for the cultivation of an applicant pipeline that eases work demands by reducing the time to fill a position and offers credible candidates for further screening processes.

Sourcing Accelerates Legitimized Screening Processes

Sourcing provides an opportunity for recruiters to exert control over the screening process from an initial stage. Sourcing tools are leveraged to identify promising candidates and encourage or "cultivate" (Andres, recruitment manager in Education based in Brooklyn) them to apply for positions. Roxie, a technical recruiter for a technology firm in Seattle, describes the benefit of sourcing as a "win-win for everyone involved" as this form of preliminary screening refines an applicant pool for relevant skills, experiences, and qualifications that hiring managers rely on when interviewing and selecting potential hires.

I refer to these sourcing strategies as moments of anticipatory expert screening. They represent moments when recruiters exert different forms of expertise to screen candidates before an application process. In addition, applicants are screened in this preliminary stage before they are evaluated against advanced types of screeners. In this study, anticipatory expert screening occurs when recruiters source to match prospective applicants with the demands of the hiring organization by identifying applicants that align with explicit and tacit criteria about the organization.

Using Expertise to Source for Explicit Criteria

Recruiters are tasked to fill requisitions (i.e., open positions) that often require an applicant to possess minimum qualifications for a position. Skills and professional credentials are markers recognized by recruiters to qualify an applicant for a role. Using filters built into their applicant tracking systems or other sourcing software like LinkedIn Recruiter, recruiters input these skills and credentials as filters to identify potential applicants. Victoria, a recruiting coordinator in Legal, based in Denver, provides more detail about this process:

> Although we get so many applications per position, sometimes I feel like I'm a headhunter. Thankfully, I like to think I've gotten pretty good at finding what I need. Right now, I'm working on filling three reqs (requisitions), but the hiring manager wants people who are bilingual in Spanish, live within 20 minutes of the law firm in Downtown, and do personal injury (a type of law specialty). Can you imagine how long that would take if I had to look up every single applicant in the system? I just plug all that into Salesforce, and voila, I reach out to that pipeline and can start on getting those reqs filled.

In this instance, Victoria describes how she begins filling requisitions by using sourcing tools before she posts jobs publicly. Victoria harvests a list of relevant potential applicants and conducts outreach efforts to encourage that specific group of people to apply for open positions. Like Victoria, other recruiters engage in this overt process of sourcing candidates by searching for education qualities, specific technical skills, distance from a location, and employment history. Teddy, an applications recruiter lead in Technology based in Los Angeles, described how he uses a map function in his applicant tracking system, Salesforce, to map applicants' zip codes. If an applicant lived too far from a client's office, he considered that a negative quality when sourcing prospective applicants. Recruiters in these situations often have the discretion to conduct complex searches through in-house applicant tracking systems or third-party job board sites that filter and parse various kinds of applicant data to form assumptions about their fit with a prospective employer. These candidates are integrated into a specialized applicant pipeline, where their application progress is monitored from beginning to end.

Sourcing to Meet Hiring Quotas

Recruiters often receive direct requests from their managers to fulfill certain demographic quotas in their recruitment efforts. Moreover, it is not uncommon for recruiters to be expected to manage racial and gender diversity expectations among applicant pools. However, as US employment laws forbid employers from discriminating against protected classes such as gender and race when hiring, recruiters would often engage in search tactics to identify potential applicants that fit specific racial or gender characteristics. Jessie, a Talent Acquisition Manager in Food and Beverage in Atlanta, describes the degree to which hiring managers at her workplace require minimum quotas for diversity in their hiring process.

> So the AI we use will only reject them (applicants) if they have a GPA lower than 2.5. In fact, if someone applies and has lower than a 2.5, they won't be put into Salesforce and they won't count for goals. On top of that, we also have to meet an internal diversity benchmark. So we have to source a specific number of Latino, African American and Asian American folks. And then we also have a specific breakdown of goals based on race and ethnicity. It is so specific. But that's what the numbers need to be, so I need to make sure my numbers apply (referring to management requesting demographic quotas).

Jessie later goes on to describe how she, like other recruiters, often segments their general applicant pool by identifying racial or gender features of candidates from their LinkedIn profiles or data sources like resumes. Monica, a senior recruiter in finance based in Chicago, shared how she identifies diverse candidates by performing Boolean searches (e.g., a type of search where keywords and operators [AND, OR, NOT] are used to produce refined results) with gender or racial descriptives as proxies for a particular race or gender designation. She details that she typically conducts searches for "Black Management Association" (to identify Black business graduates) or "Women in Business" (to identify college graduates that were women who majored in business). Other recruiters reported how diversity quotas transcend beyond gender or race—searches for first-generation college student status and religious diversity were also reported as criteria for socio-cultural demographics.

Navigating Recruiting Within the Current US Racial Movement

While this study's main findings emphasize how recruiters strategize their technology use, this analysis would be remiss not to make mention of how the current US social climate surrounding race and gender has had implications for the ways the organizations perform talent acquisition initiatives. Across the stages of data coding, I noted how recruitment personnel working in non-profit organizations were more direct and forthright in mentioning diversity and inclusion management. These employees often pointed out that they engage in "mission-aligned" recruiting (Will, External Recruitment Manager in Education, Brooklyn), which refers to how their organizations do not only prioritize diversity in recruiting, but within their organizational mission. For example, organizations that promoted pillars of "impact," "inclusion," "diversity," or "courage" often had their recruiters prioritize job candidates from minoritized demographic backgrounds through self-disclosed characteristics like race, gender, first-generation status, and sexual orientation. Recruiters rely on self-disclosed information from applicant materials, job board profiles, or formerly established rapport with candidates. In contrast, recruiters who work in private industries often explain the challenges in meeting diversity and inclusion expectations. Mel, a Division Director of Recruitment for a Legal Staffing Firm in Los Angeles, comments on the misalignment between the expectations and practices of diversity and inclusion initiatives within recruiting. She adds:

Sometimes we have some managers say they want a diverse hire, and we navigate that carefully based on the company and what they say they want, and what they actually want. It's funny that managers say, 'Oh, we want a diverse hire,' meaning they want someone that doesn't have white skin. But when it comes to diversity of thought, diversity of background, and in all the other senses of the word besides what you look like, they are not as thrilled. They want someone who doesn't look like them, but has been to the same school as them, or has the same life experiences as them, and that's not diverse. So people get caught up, especially nowadays, in diverse hiring—but they're not looking beyond skin tone or gender.

When fulfilling requisitions with specific criteria, recruiters often find themselves in situations where their understanding of an explicit trait differs from that of the manager who decides on the final hiring decision. Recruiters take note of invisible requests or framed suggestions from managers that are unclear or opaque characteristics of applicants that require experts to engage with tacit understandings of their workplace norms, policies, and expectations in order to successfully execute their job search. These forms of invisible requests can be considered a form of tacit knowledge that is coordinated through sourcing tools. This practice of invisible requests within anticipatory expert screening requires recruiters to read between the lines for implicit expectations of their managers when sourcing, screening, and preparing candidates for the selection process.

Sourcing Supports Organizational Needs in Light of Formal Screening Processes

These empirical findings reveal how recruiting decisions are often arbitrary and dependent on the organization, its needs for hiring, and its recruiter's expertise. In the following section, I discuss how these findings relate to how recruiters account for their AI technology use and the overall impact these practices have on our current theoretical and practical considerations of artificial intelligent technology at work.

Discussion

AI-powered hiring tools are useful predictive technologies that can complement the expertise of recruitment personnel during the sourcing stage of the hiring lifecycle. This case study accentuates the complex relationship between recruiters and AI-hiring tools that aid initial hiring decisions. This relationship hinges on how the capabilities of an AI tool are negotiated and accounted for by recruitment personnel who are embedded within organizational social structures of norms, policies, and personal ideologies. Recruiters often manage diversity and inclusion needs by invoking their expertise, sometimes paradoxically, toward effective diversity management and to diffuse institutional biases.

In an attempt to explain processes by which recruiters are attuned to anticipating and diverting algorithmic outcomes, I turn to an evolving yet powerful analytical framework of critical social theory that is gaining momentum within studies of human–computer interaction: intersectionality (Crenshaw, 1989; McDonald & Pan, 2020). Originally coined in the 1980s, stemming from the Black Feminist Thought Movement, intersectionality argues for the inclusion of race, class, gender, nationality, and sexuality, among other identities, as compounds that shape inequality and barriers to power, success, and security (Collins, 2019; Crenshaw, 1989). An intersectional lens to technology practice can be a useful lens to foreground this study's findings, as the concept aids in highlighting how complex, dynamic identities like a job candidate's demographic attributes are often constrained when narrowly evaluated against an organization's hiring needs. When recruiters engage in diversity management of talent, they use specific affordances of algorithmic tools sourcing tools to attract job candidates uniformly. This process of balancing organizational demands with their technology choices reifies potential structural bias within the organization and areas that produce unfairness within the hiring process.

The findings of this study reveal how there are limits to embedding algorithmic tools in hiring processes like sourcing when recruiters attempt to superficially account for multiple dimensions of an applicant's identity as a form of diversity management. This study contextualizes how organizational policies may allow adverse forms of decision making that advance discrimination rather than avoid it. Recruiters in this study often were aware of the predictive outcomes of algorithmic sourcing tools, which enabled them to pre-emptively source candidates that would fit diverse metrics in later screening phases. This form of anticipated sourcing aligns with similar algoactivistic actions that enable employees to augment, resist, or take control of algorithmic outputs (Kellogg et al., 2020).

In this study, the outputs generated by algorithms are used by recruiters to verify and uphold explicit knowledge that is presented in a clear way. This practice is depicted when recruiters source candidates using algorithms that parse and rank specific candidate information such as GPA, employment eligibility, technical skills, and leadership experience. Recruiters can interpret different semantic meanings from applicant data that allow them to coordinate affordances from AI tools to configure future algorithmic evaluations of applicants. In other words, recruiters often use sourcing algorithms to more holistically evaluate and screen candidates before more formal, specific forms of evaluation. This is of interest to note as organizations often legitimize their sourcing processes as objective and accredited through the use of AI-hiring systems. In practice, algorithmic sourcing of applicants can arguably be conceptualized as an organized practice of expert screening involving the use of algorithmic tools and human expertise to complement further predictive analytics used in later screening stages. These forms of AI-employee pairings offer an avenue for deeper theoretical considerations to understanding the interaction between technology use and organizational dynamics that offer practical implications for using emerging technology in hiring.

Practical Applications

Every organization has different needs when it comes to hiring. With the influx of AI-powered tools aiding HR personnel in each stage of hiring, organizational processes at the individual level aptly shape recruitment processes. It is necessary for management to outline specific training and policies for integrating AI-powered tools in HR. Based on the results of this study, I present strategic-level recommendations for practitioners looking for guidance on how to best implement AI tools for equitable and inclusive hiring.

Set Job Requirements Clearly and Hold Them to Your Hiring Plan

Job advertisements that are posted on job boards like LinkedIn, Monster, or Indeed are often the first points of contact that a prospective applicant has with a company. Being mindful of your organization's hiring needs and the ways that you present a job advertisement has the power to influence a person's perception of your organization and the job. For effective sourcing purposes, use language in your job ads that accentuates skills and experience that pertain to the role. This practice helps to ensure that applicants with different forms and levels of experience can relate to the job ad and are not deterred from applying. Moreover, listing only necessary requirements allows recruiters to clearly enforce their sourcing strategies to fit the role. For example, hidden requirements (e.g., seeking candidates with particular communication styles, physical ability, or descriptive traits that measure specific skills like "digital native" are often ageist and deter older candidates from applying to a job; Burn et al., 2022) are unknowingly listed on job ads that can leave out many qualified applicants.

Remove Unconscious Bias in Applicant Materials

Before advanced screening with AI tools, sourcing provides an opportunity for recruitment personnel to review applicant materials to determine a preliminary fit. However, unconscious biases related to hegemonic status markers like an applicant's university, former employer, or leisurely pursuits can leave out competent and qualified individuals. The process of masking a resume—or removing identifying information not related to a candidate's skill set, experiences, or required qualifications—is an effective way to reduce human bias and judgment from superficial markers. This process helps to elevate applicants from untraditional employment paths that may often be overlooked due to arbitrary factors an applicant has no control over (e.g., such as the prestige of their former employers or universities.) Implementing structured evaluation criteria like rubrics during the sourcing process can aid recruiters in searching, attracting, and cultivating qualified applicants.

Update Company-Wide Hiring Goals Frequently to Drive Daily Impact

Organizations collaborate with third-party developers to build, deploy, and update their technology. Because AI-driven recruiting is constantly under development, this research suggests that organizational stakeholders that oversee hiring processes should have clear observable goals from each stage of hiring, sourced from more than one platform, to enable diverse hiring pipelines and update relevant personnel on changing hiring goals. In addition to updating hiring practices and policies, working closely with technology developers to build systems and write code that performs actions directly related to hiring needs can be useful in maintaining clear, observable performance goals for recruitment. Relatedly, hands-on practices like setting up an in-take session between hiring managers and recruiters can ensure all relevant parties involved in hiring for a position are well informed about the goals for an effective hire, acknowledge and remedy any potential areas of bias in the hiring funnel, and practice efficacious implementation of inclusive and equitable standards of practice for their respective organization.

Conclusion

It should be noted that this project does not advocate for or against the use of AI-powered tools in hiring. The goal of this work is to empirically ground the experiences of recruitment personnel within organizations who are instructed to use these emerging forms of technology in addition to their own expertise and judgment. The analyses and findings provide an in-depth explanation of how the use of AI-driven tools can impact the recruitment and hiring goals of an organization. This case study offers technology designers and hiring personnel an account of experiences that help us expand our existing frameworks of technology use toward a more inclusive, substantive, and equitable perspective. Individuals, job applicants in this case, although subjected to analyses performed by AI technologies, are not atomized pieces of data. As organizations integrate AI-driven tools within their hiring processes, more attention and action should be placed on accounting for the varied differences in identities and experiences of applicants as they make their way through the hiring funnel.

Discussion Questions

1 What does inclusivity look like in your department's hiring processes? What are some areas of improvement that can be identified and measured?
2 How do you think your organizational structures (e.g., team dynamics, workplace policies, and norms) may influence the way that technologies are used by you or your colleagues?
3 How can your hiring department audit its hiring performance and ensure optimal fairness through the hiring funnel? How can these processes be revisited and improved?

Author Bio

Ignacio Fernandez Cruz, Ph.D., is an Assistant Professor of Communication in the School of Communication at Northwestern University. His research examines emerging technology at work and the sociotechnical practices between AI tools and their users, focusing on bridging bias within technology use.

References

Ajunwa, I. (2020). The Paradox of Automation as Anti-bias Intervention. *Cardozo Law Review*, *41*(5), 1671–1742. https://cardozolawreview.com/the-paradox-of-automation-as-anti-bias-intervention/

Bailey, D. E., & Leonardi, P. M. (2015). *Technology choices: Why occupations differ in their Embrace of new technology*. Cambridge, MA: MIT Press.

Black, J. S., & van Esch, P. (2020). AI-enabled recruiting: What is it and how should a manager use it? *Business Horizons*, *63*(2), 215–226. 10.1016/j.bushor. 2019.12.001

Bogen, M., & Rieke, A. (2018, December). *Help wanted: An examination of hiring algorithms, equity, and bias*. (Report). Upturn. https://www.upturn.org/reports/2018/hiring-algorithms/

Burn, I., Firoozi, D., Ladd, D., & Neumark, D. (2022). Help really wanted? The Impact of age stereotypes in job ads on applications from older workers (No. W30287). *National Bureau of Economic Research*. DOI: 10.3386/w30287

Center for Democracy & Technology. (2021). *Algorithm-driven hiring tools: Innovative recruitment or expedited disability discrimination?* (Report) https://cdt. org/insights/report-algorithm-driven-hiring-tools-innovative-recruitment-or-expedited-disability-discrimination/

Charmaz, K. (2014). *Constructing grounded theory*. Sage.

Christin, A. (2017). Algorithms in practice: Comparing web journalism and criminal justice. *Big Data & Society, 4*(2), 2053951717718855. 10.1177/205395171771 8855

Collins, P. H. (2019). *Intersectionality as critical social theory*, Duke University Press. https://doi.org/10.1215/9781478007098

Crenshaw, K. (1989). Demarginalizing the Intersection of Race and Sex: A Black Feminist Critique of Antidiscrimination Doctrine, Feminist Theory and Antiracist Politics. *University of Chicago Legal Forum*, 139–167. https://chicagounbound. uchicago.edu/uclf/vol1989/iss1/8

Cruz, I. (2021). *Adjusting the algorithm: How experts intervene in automated hiring decisions* (Doctoral Dissertation). University of Southern California. https://library.usc.edu

DeVito, M. A., Birnholtz, J., Hancock, J. T., French, M., & Liu, S. (2018). How people form folk theories of social media feeds and what it means for how we study self-presentation. In *Proceedings of the 2018 CHI Conference on Human Factors in Computing Systems*, 1–12. 10.1145/3173574.3173694

Kellogg, K. C., Valentine, M. A., & Christin, A. (2020). Algorithms at work: The new contested terrain of control. *Academy of Management Annals, 14*(1), 366–410. 10.5465/annals.2018.0174

Köchling, A., & Wehner, M. C. (2020). Discriminated by an algorithm: A systematic review of discrimination and fairness by algorithmic decision-making in the context of HR recruitment and HR development. *Business Research, 13*(3), 795–848. DOI: 10.1016/j.bushor.2019.12.001

Leonardi, P. M., Barley, W. C., & Woo, D. (2021). Why should I trust your model? How to successfully enroll digital models for innovation. *Innovation*, 1–19. 10.1080/14479338.2021.1873787

Li, L., Lassiter, T., Oh, J., & Lee, M. K. (2021). Algorithmic hiring in practice: Recruiter and HR professional's perspectives on AI use in hiring. In *Proceedings of the AAAI/ACM Conference on Artificial Intelligence, Ethics, and Society (AIES 2021)*. 10.1145/3461702.3462531

Liao, T., & Tyson, O. (2021). "Crystal Is Creepy, but Cool": Mapping folk theories and responses to automated personality recognition algorithms. *Social Media & Society, 7*(2), 20563051211010170. 10.1177/20563051211010170

McDonald, N., & Pan, S. (2020). Intersectional AI: A study of how information science students think about ethics and their impact. In *Proceedings of the ACM on Human-Computer Interaction, (CSCW)*, 1–19. 10.1145/3415218

Miles, M., Huberman, A. M., & Saldaña, J. (2019). *Qualitative data analysis: A methods sourcebook*. SAGE Publications.

Oberst, U., De Quintana, M., Del Cerro, S., & Chamarro, A. (2020). Recruiters prefer expert recommendations over digital hiring algorithms: A choice-based conjoint study in a pre-employment screening scenario. *Management Research Review, 44*(4), 625–641. 10.1108/MRR-06-2020-0356

Raghavan, M., Barocas, S., Kleinberg, J., & Levy, K. (2020). Mitigating bias in algorithmic hiring: Evaluating claims and practices. In *Proceedings of the 2020 Conference on Fairness, Accountability, and Transparency*, 469–481. 10.1145/3351095.3372828

Rivera, L. A. (2012). Hiring as cultural matching: The case of elite professional service firms. *American Sociological Review, 77*(6), 999–1022. 10.1177/0003122412463213

Valentine, M., & Hinds, R. (2019). *Algorithms and the org chart*. Working Paper. Stanford University.

van den Broek, E., Sergeeva, A., & Huysman, M. (2019). Hiring algorithms: An ethnography of fairness in practice. *Fortieth International Conference on Information Systems*, 1–9. https://core.ac.uk/download/pdf/301385085.pdf

Whittaker, M., Crawford, K., & Dobbe, R. (2018). *AI Now Report 2018*. (Report). AI Now. https://ainowinstitute.org/reports.html

3

AGE DISCRIMINATION IN THE WORKPLACE

An Exploration of Age-Blind Hiring Practices

Samantha Szczur[1] *and Alyssa Obradovich*[2]

[1]*Eastern Illinois University;* [2]*Purdue University*

Learning Objectives

After reading this chapter, you will:

1 Understand the changing demographics of the American workplace.
2 Be able to critique Ageism, age diversity, and age discrimination in workplaces.
3 Be able to evaluate the challenges and strengths of age-blind hiring.

Introduction

For some time, the issue of diversity has held high importance for both academics and organizational decision makers. Black Lives Matter, #metoo, and other social movements have inspired cultural narratives regarding diversity, equity, and inclusion (DEI) in organizational life. As such, organizations face an ethical imperative to attend to ways in which an employee base may be diversified. As shifting cultural expectations about increasing organizational difference, DEI has driven diversity initiatives for organizations, these efforts are affirmed and bolstered by the notion that diverse organizations excel in innovation, productivity, recruitment, and retention (Hunt et al., 2014). In other words, diversifying a workforce is assumed to be both ethically and financially sound (Paine, 2003). The cultural and pragmatic imperatives seem clear in suggesting that diverse organizations simultaneously make good business sense while contributing to a more just and equitable society (Jansen et al., 2020; Lasch-Quinn, 2003; Nkomo 1992).

DOI: 10.4324/9781003333746-4

Organizational diversity initiatives have often addressed the pressing issues of race, gender, and sex, attempting to mitigate racist and misogynistic practices and biases within an organization. In recent years, concerns about ageism and age discrimination have come to the fore as organizations confront the evolving age demographics of the United States which contribute to intergenerationally diverse organizations. As Desilver (2016) notes, 18.8% of Americans over the age of 65 are working which suggests that older adults comprise approximately 1 in every 5 American workers. This chapter examines the issues of age diversity and discrimination and recognizes the significance of these issues for both organizations and aging adults. Specifically, we assess organizational efforts to minimize age discrimination by examining blind hiring practices and the (in)efficacy of such efforts. Overall, we problematize the notion that institutional practices alone are enough to adequately minimize age discrimination since the individuals who execute organizational objectives are influenced by social biases and stereotypes about aging individuals and workers.

In the following pages, we discuss why age needs to be included in organizational DEI efforts, we introduce a case study to demonstrate the challenges associated with change efforts designed to eliminate ageism, and we offer suggestions for combatting ageism that are applicable across a variety of organizational contexts.

An Aging Population and an Aging Workforce

The United States is undergoing a significant demographic shift. Our population is greying, a colloquial term for the growing proportion of older adults compared to younger individuals. In short, we have a larger percentage of older adults than we have before (Toossi & Torpey, 2017). This population shift has myriad social, cultural, economic, and organizational implications. Our collective cultural assumptions about age and ability, intelligence, and employment are being challenged as many workplaces experience an intergenerational shift (Trethewey, 2001).

With the greying of the United States, increasing numbers of aging adults seek to remain gainfully employed past the traditional retirement age (Toossi & Torpey, 2017). The US Bureau of Labor Statistics (2017) reports that the numbers and percentages of older workers have been gradually increasing for the past two decades. For example, in 2017, 32% of those aged 65–69 were working and 19% of those aged 70–74 were also employed. In terms of the overall workforce, it is projected that in 2024, 24.8% of the American workforce will be aged 55 and above compared to 13.1% in 2000 (Toossi & Torpey, 2017). People are working longer and postponing retirement for an array of reasons ranging from economic necessity, identity, boredom, a desire for the social interaction a workplace provides, or a combination of these and other factors (Rosa & Hastings, 2016). Regardless of the motivations of aging workers, their continued presence in the workplace has increased the likelihood of intergenerational interactions and considerations at all levels of organizational socialization.

The workplace has long since been recognized as a site with implications far beyond paid labor. Many scholars from an array of disciplines have discussed how difference, and hence, inequity, are woven into, negotiated, and resisted in organizational life. Much of the literature in this area has focused on racial identity (Ashcraft & Allen, 2003; Parker, 2005), sex and gender (Ashcraft, 2005; Mumby, 1998; Trethewey, 1999), and sexuality (Spradlin, 1998; Woog, 2001). This work, written from a critical perspective, recognizes that social ills in the form of prejudice and discrimination will be replicated in the organizational forms we create. Put simply, organizations are social and cultural entities and as such will reflect social and cultural attitudes. Thus, it follows that if we live in a racist, sexist, and ageist (among many other "isms") society, we will create racist, sexist, and ageist organizations. Within the communication studies discipline, only recently have scholars turned their focus to age as an area of difference in organizational life (e.g., Rosa & Hastings, 2016; Szczur, 2019; Trethewey, 2001). Similar to the critically oriented research on race, sex, and gender, organizational scholars focused on the intersection of age and work accept the premise that the master narrative surrounding aging and associated negative stereotypes are inextricable from organizational realities. We see this evidenced through overt, covert, material, symbolic, and sometimes esoteric ways.

Overall, organizations are trying to confront the opportunities and challenges associated with age diversity while aging workers strive to retain dignity and respect in the twilight of their working years. Policy and legislation exist to protect aging workers from potential discrimination. The Age Discrimination in Employment Act (ADEA) of 1967 is, in effect, an extension of both labor law and civil rights legislation (Age Discrimination, n.d.). The ADEA aims to protect individuals over the age of 40 against an array of discriminatory practices regarding employment including hiring, promotion, termination, compensation, and excluding benefits. Congressional findings indicated that older workers were denied employment opportunities based on stereotypes of incompetency related to a worker's age (Age Discrimination, n.d.). As the need to protect older workers was evidenced, policy attempted to forbid discriminatory practices.

Though policy and legislation exist to protect aging workers, the evidence clearly indicates that discriminatory practices remain in place.

The Equal Employment Opportunity Commission (EEOC) reports a steady stream of age discrimination complaints from 1997 to 2021 (Age Discrimination in Employment Act FY 1997–2021, n.d.). In 2019, the EEOC received 15,573 age discrimination complaints which illustrate that age discrimination is a problem, and with increasing numbers of aging workers, the problem persists and can potentially worsen.

Official statistics from government agencies such as the Bureau of Labor Statistics, the EEOC, and the Department of Labor indicate a complex and changing labor market. As stated above, older adults are staying in the workplace past traditional retirement ages for an array of reasons. Hence, the greying of America is evidenced in workplaces. With the cultural drive for productive and cost-efficient organizations, some organizations find older adults to be too expensive or lacking knowledge of contemporary organizational trends (Truxillo et al., 2015). Unfortunately, this manifests in discriminatory practices that exclude aging adults from employment opportunities. Neumark et al. (2017) examined age discrimination in their study in which they fabricated applications and submitted them to job advertisements. The applications were designed to indicate a young, middle aged, or older worker. They submitted over 40,000 applications for more than 13,000 jobs in multiple geographic locations. Their data suggests that young workers were far more likely to receive an invitation to proceed in the interview process. Furthermore, applicants aged 64–66 experienced more discrimination than applicants aged 49–51, suggesting that the older a worker is, the more likely they are to be discriminated against.

Age Diversity in Organizations

Using an array of methodologies and approaches, scholars have demonstrated the ways in which ageism and age inequity are built into organizations. For example, Riach and Kelly (2015) employed the trope of vampirism to argue that older workers are positioned as the monstrous other that must be sacrificed by an organization in order to survive. As such, older workers are conceptualized as expensive leeches on an organization and are thus rendered justifiably expendable. Similarly, in a study of workers at an automotive factory, Zanoni (2011) argued that older workers (along with disabled workers) were repeatedly framed as incapable or reluctant to perform in a "lean" organizational environment that depended on the narratives of speed, youth, and efficiency. In Zanoni's (2011) study, the discursive framing of older adults as slow and ineffective enabled and emboldened management to rid the organization of the "undesirable" aging worker.

Conceptualizations of what it means to age are social and cultural constructions that are created and negotiated via a web of communicative mechanisms. In many facets of life, we construct dominant and widely circulated stories that tailor our attitudes, perceptions, and behaviors. Gullette (1997) identified these stories as "master narratives" which function similarly to ideology and discourse. Master narratives weave together common tropes that offer optimism, pessimism, or both. In terms of aging, Gullette (1997) proposed that within the United States, the master narrative of becoming old is steeped in the notion of decline. More specifically, Americans very much associate aging, and hence older adults, as entering a state of physical and mental deterioration characterized by failings of both body and mind. As such, notions of decrepit bodies and senility largely characterize the master narrative of decline. Furthermore, the master narrative of aging and decline transcends social spheres. Thus, an aging adult is likely to encounter the narrative of decline within personal relationships, in the media, in the workplace, and in other social realms. Of key concern is that master narratives reify the process of aging as one of inevitable decay while oversimplifying the entirety of the experience of older adults. Furthermore, the master narrative of aging highlights negative aspects of growing old with no inclusion of alternative narratives. In other words, a master narrative of aging could easily focus on the wisdom one cultivates over the life course, instead of highlighting the senescence of one's mental and physical capacities.

As noted above, master narratives in general, and master narratives of aging in particular, circulate in many cultural realms. One such arena is of course the workplace. Smith and Dougherty (2012) analyzed the intersections of master narratives of aging and retirement, noting that organizational spaces highlight age differences. Smith and Dougherty (2012) noted the dominant attitudes about aging that circulate throughout organizations are overwhelmingly negative and focus on the overall deterioration of the older worker. Similarly, Trethewey (2001) also built on Gullette's (1997) work and addressed how aging female professionals experience, interpret, and resist the master narrative of decline in their work environments. Trethewey's (2001) interview data suggests that her participants were keenly aware of the assumption that an aging and working woman's body and mind were on the wane. Participants recount instances of overt and covert discrimination at all levels of organizational and working life including affronts to their intelligence, appearance, dress, and demeanor.

In many ways, master narratives rely on stereotypes. Stereotypes are socially created and culturally shared (albeit contested) assumptions about a group of people (Hummert, 1994). Stereotypes can be positive and connote admirable attributes of people. Conversely, stereotypes can also be negative and suggest derogatory characteristics about groups and individuals. Pecchioni and Croghan (2002) discussed both positive and negative stereotypes in their study of young adults and their grandparents. Positive stereotypes include the ideas that older adults are wise, wealthy, caring, devoted, uncomplicated, and experienced. Negative stereotypes include the notion that older adults are grouchy, inflexible, out of touch, senile, decrepit, and unsophisticated. While both positive and negative stereotypes are significant, negative stereotypes have a significant impact on both society and the individual.

Among the strategies organizational practitioners have developed to increase diversity and mitigate the age discrimination that accompanies negative stereotypes of older adults, the practice of blind hiring has recently received increased attention. Although there is a discrepancy regarding the actual origins of the practice, it is agreed that blind hiring began as a means to minimize discrimination in the audition practices of symphony orchestras by holding applicant auditions behind a screen (Orchestrating Equity, n.d.). The practice has evolved and adapted to the digital age and now largely consists of an organization's removal of identifying markers such as one's name, collegiate affiliation, and dates of employment from application materials like cover letters and resumes before they undergo evaluation. Age-blind hiring seeks to eliminate cues indicating how old someone may be. For example, one's college graduation date may be redacted so hiring agents cannot deduce the age of the applicant based on their graduation date. Age-blind hiring certainly seems like a step in the right direction in dealing with age discrimination, but is the practice a cure-all for an organization's ageist ills?

Below, we share a case study intended to illuminate some of the challenges associated with organizational efforts to combat ageism.

Case Study—The Promise and Failure of Age-Blind Hiring

Rashad and Beth work in the human resources wing of a university's fundraising foundation. Rashad and Beth were hired at the same time and a pivotal part of their roles at the foundation has been to develop, implement, and evaluate DEI initiatives regarding recruiting, hiring, and retention practices. They have a lengthy meeting every Wednesday to check in with each other, regarding their ideas, progress, problems, and successes. This particular Wednesday, Beth was feeling noticeably happy with their work.

"Rashad, I mean we are just on fire," Beth said. "We have both been here for about three years and look at all the progress we've made! I can't believe all we have accomplished!"

"You think?" asked Rashad. "I don't know. I guess I don't share your confidence. Maybe I'm being an overachiever, but sometimes I feel like we aren't doing enough."

"Are you kidding?!" replied Beth. "Look at our assessment data. We have greatly increased our racial diversity. Over 50% of new hires are women. We have expanded parental benefits to same-sex and unmarried couples. We have also put pressure on our health insurance provider to offer more trans inclusive healthcare. I'd say that's pretty good! What else do you want?!"

"Well, I know that's a rhetorical question," responded Rashad, "but something has been bothering me the past couple of weeks."

"Oh," said Beth, now suddenly concerned. "What's up? What happened?"

"It's my mom. She has been looking around at different jobs, thinking that it might be time for her to move on to another company. The thing is, no one is calling her back. She has submitted her resume to 20 or so open positions and nothing. Not one word back."

"Okay," said Beth, "well what do you think the problem is?"

"Honestly," said Rashad, "I think people are dismissing her applications because when they see her years of experience across multiple organizations, they think she's 'too old.' And for a lot of organizations, 'too old' means 'too slow,' 'too expensive,' 'too rigid,' and all the other negative stereotypes of older adults. She's only 55, she's incredibly smart, she has so much experience, and no one will call her to even set up an interview? Really?"

"Huh. That's illegal. Can you and your mom prove that they are ignoring her application because of her age?"

"That's the thing," stated Rashad. "No, we can't prove anything. What's even more challenging is that since she doesn't work at these companies, there's absolutely nothing we can do. What would we even say? 'Hey, we can't offer any evidence of this and we know we've never met, but we feel pretty certain that your ageist biases are major obstacles for older adults looking to join your organization.' It's really frustrating. Anyway, it's been bothering me for a lot of reasons and I've been reflecting on our own policies and practices related to age and age diversity."

Beth laughed. "What policies and practices related to age and age diversity?"

"Exactly my point," responded Rashad. "Look around. Almost everyone working here is under 50. Have we been ageist in our recruiting and hiring? I can only speak for myself, but I know I certainly haven't made any concerted effort to hire older adults or generate any kind of intergenerational connection. I never even considered age as an issue related to diversity despite the fact that that's exactly what we were hired to do. Now, watching my mom go through this, I just feel awful."

"You're right," said Beth, as she realized that she and Rashad were both in their late twenties when they were hired for their roles at the foundation. "Wow. That's really bad. I have been so pleased with what we have accomplished that I've totally ignored the age issue. What do you think we should do?"

"I've read about a practice called 'age blind hiring,'" said Rashad. "It's when any age markers or indicators are removed from a resume or any other application materials. For example, we might block out one's graduation year from college. Or, we could eliminate dates all together, even from work history. That way, we can't do any quick math to speculate how old someone is."

"That's really interesting! I love that idea!" said Beth. "We can get going with this right away. We are getting ready to hire someone for the IT position. Maybe this can be a test run to see how this age-blind review process might work?"

"Sounds good," said Rashad. "I'll work out the details and make sure the age indicators have been removed before we review the materials. Then, we can proceed as usual, evaluate the applications, and decide who we want to bring in to interview."

"Great! I'm excited to see how this goes!" stated Beth.

A month went by and gradually applications trickled in for the IT position. Rashad and Beth's co-workers in HR redacted all age-related information and they were ready to begin the review process. They were optimistic and hopeful that they may be one step closer to an even more diverse and inclusive environment. As far as the hiring process, Rashad and Beth would decide upon three of the most qualified candidates to bring in for an interview. Anthony, the IT manager, would interview the candidates with Rashad and Beth, and Anthony would then make the final selection for who would fill the role.

After a few days of review, Rashad and Beth settled on what they deemed three excellent candidates. They found the review process pleasant and were not at all off put by the age redactions. "Rashad," Beth said, "I really think you're onto something here. We should think about how we can do this with other identity markers!"

"Let's not get ahead of ourselves," Rashad said as he chuckled.

The three candidates were notified, and on-site interviews were scheduled. Rashad and Beth were wildly curious about who the candidates were and how the age-blind review impacted the candidate selection if at all. Interviews were scheduled one right after another, with candidate one being interviewed from 9 to 10, candidate two from 10 to 11, and candidate three from 11 to 12. Rashad, Beth, and Anthony were prepared with their interview questions and were anxious to get the process underway.

The first two interviews went incredibly well, and Rashad and Beth were certain that Anthony would have a hard time making the final call. The third interview was shaky. The applicant seemed ill-prepared and responded poorly to a couple of questions. Rashad and Beth were not so humbly pleased with their work. They were certain that their blind review process was going to impact this hire and many hires moving forward.

"Okay, Anthony, who is it going to be?" asked Rashad.

"Easy," responded Anthony. "Kevin. Candidate three."

Rashad and Beth looked at each other incredulously. "Seriously?" they both said in unison. Beth followed, "Why?!"

"I don't know," said Anthony. "I guess he just seemed high-energy and up to date on new technology. The first woman, candidate one, was stuffy and kind of rigid. I can tell by her experience that she's stuck in the stone ages. And the other guy, candidate two, didn't seem very quick. Like he was a slow thinker or something. I just can't have those characteristics in IT. I need an innovative, quick worker that is knowledgeable about current technology. Someone I can teach and train. Not someone already set in their ways."

"Right," said Rashad as he heaved a disappointed sigh. "Someone in their 30s."

Beth looked at Rashad, helplessly shrugged her shoulders and said, "What do we do now?"

Case Study Analysis and Practical Applications

As the literature and case study suggest, the American workplace is changing in parallel to shifts in age demographics. Many workplaces are sites of intergenerational interaction as people from different generational cohorts interact and work toward organizational goals. However, this is not to say that generations exist in some utopic image of egalitarianism and inclusion. As human beings with social and cultural biases, we unfortunately build those biases into our social institutions, and workplace organizations are surely not exempt from ageist practices. At times, despite our efforts and intentions, such as the integration of age-blind hiring, we cannot shake ageist practices. In the following paragraphs, we discuss practical implications of both the previously discussed academic literature and the case study. Our intent is that practitioners can gain insight into ways to move forward in their efforts to establish age-blind hiring practices and minimize age discrimination in general.

The machine metaphor has long since offered the image of an organization as a faceless, soulless composite of hierarchy and policy (Stohl, 1995). Conceptualizing an organization as an amalgam of cogs and gears easily obscures the reality that organizations are fundamentally and inherently human. As such, we put practices in place and expect that their execution be unbiased, neutral, and fair. However, hiding behind the veiled anonymity of the machine stymies our understanding that if organizations are ageist, it is likely because **we** are ageist. Thus, perhaps a solid first step in minimizing age discrimination is abandoning the notion that policies are "blind" while recognizing that human beings, with all their biases and assumptions, are the force that powers the machine. As such, organizations cannot simply throw a new policy or practice at every organizational problem and expect that issue to resolve. True change is far more difficult than that. True change lies in unhinging damaging assumptions about people. True change lies in shifting culture.

"Change the culture" may sound like a convenient chorus and an impossible task, yet that is what must be done. The pressing question is: how? In the case of ageism and ageist practices in organizations, cultural change can come about by fostering new intergenerational relationships and cultivating those that already exist. For example, an organizational mentorship program which links co-workers from different generational cohorts is an excellent way to increase intergenerational understanding. In general, mentoring programs can serve as an effective way to develop relationships that exist within an organization (Bokeno & Gantt, 2000). Reverse mentoring is a relatively well-known practice that connects senior employees with junior employees in the hopes that a mutually beneficial exchange of knowledge may occur (Carruthers, 2022). Furthermore, an effort to ensure that these mentoring relationships are intergenerational has evidenced the promotion of positive attitudes regarding age diversity within organizations (Anderson, 2019). As the mentoring relationship evolves, ideally, all parties interrogate their personally held (yet socially influenced) perceptions about age, youth, older adults, and how they relate to a workplace. As such, employees may consider how both positive and negative stereotypes influence one's interactions with others as well as the general assumptions one has about certain groups of people. Furthermore, in a similar vein, age-diverse committees and work teams can also foster increased inter-generational interaction and understanding. These are just two organizational changes that could go a long way in terms of shifting how age is perceived in an organizational environment. However, radical cultural change does not happen on its own, and organizational decision makers must actively pursue desired outcomes and change. In practice, this means that there must be concerted efforts to move the cultural needle and organizations must be willing to put the necessary resources forward in order to do so.

While this case study illustrates the failure of an organizational practice to increase age diversity, we would be remiss to throw the proverbial baby out with the bathwater. Instead of shrugging our shoulders or turning our backs on processes such as age-blind hiring, perhaps a better approach is to accept it as a step in the right direction, albeit an imperfect step. If age redaction has been effective in getting more older adults to the interview stage, that is a victory of sorts. Then, the focus shifts to ways in which we can halt age discrimination once people get to the interview stage. Ideally, if the aforementioned strategies of intergenerational mentoring and team building are effective, older employees will be seen as an asset and not a liability.

Or, and perhaps maybe even more effective, organizations can prioritize hiring older adults by taking intentional steps to audit the age diversity of employees and increase that diversity as needed. For example, organizational leaders could survey their employees to identify whether or not age diversity is adequately represented within their organization. If not, they may need to take steps to engage in age-*conscious* recruitment and retention efforts (as opposed to age-*blind* efforts).

Moreover, intergenerational hiring committees could also be effective in mitigating age biases. Many researchers have emphasized the importance of diversifying hiring committees to ensure more equitable hiring practices and to enhance organizational diversity (Anderson, 2019) yet most of this work has focused only on gender and race. Intergenerational hiring committees are also important, as intergenerational dialogue within hiring committees may help to illuminate ageist biases, thus reducing the influence of ageist stereotypes in the collaborative decision-making process.

Growing pains are inevitable, but a cynical dismissal of all efforts at inclusion certainly gets us no closer to an equitable organization or an equitable society.

Conclusion

As the complexity of the American workplace continues to change, age diversity and discrimination are coming to the fore. In order to seriously address the problem of ageism, new organizational policies should be considered, but deeper cultural changes are necessary in order to exact significant change. The execution of age-blind hiring practices may be imperfect; however, age-blind hiring practices can be used as a jumping-off point to interrogate related practices and to implement new practices that contribute to more age diverse and inclusive organizations.

Discussion Questions

1 What are the positive and negative age stereotypes you see at play in the case study?
2 How do we see cultural bias outweigh organizational policy in the case study?
3 How has your organization dealt with age bias and discrimination in the hiring process? Do you have any further recommendations for Rashad and Beth as to what they should do next?

Author Bios

Samantha Szczur, Ph.D., is a Full Professor at Eastern Illinois University. Broadly speaking, she is interested in the cultural politics of workplace organizations. Her research is critically oriented and has examined issues of gender, race, and age related to work and organizations.

Alyssa Obradovich, ABD, is a dual-title PhD candidate in Communication Studies and Gerontology at Purdue University. She currently works as a communication practitioner at the University of Illinois Foundation. Her research is applied in nature and seeks to offer real-world solutions to real-world issues.

References

Age discrimination. (n.d.). Retrieved from https://www.dol.gov/general/topic/discrimination/agedisc

Age discrimination in employment Act. (n.d.). Retrieved from https://www.eeoc.gov/eeoc/statistics/enforcement/adea.cfm.

Age discrimination in employment Act FY 1997–2021. (n.d.) Retrieved from https://www.eeoc.gov/data/age-discrimination-employment-act-charges-filed-eeoc-includes-concurrent-charges-title-vii-ada

Anderson, G. (2019). Mentorship and the value of a multigenerational workplace. Retrieved from https://www.aarp.org/research/topics/economics/info-2019/multigenerational-work-mentorship.html.

Ashcraft, K. (2005). Resistance through consent? Occupational identity, organizational form, and the maintenance of masculinity among commercial airline pilots. *Management Communication Quarterly, 19*, 67–90.

Ashcraft, K., & Allen, B. (2003). The racial foundation of organizational communication. *Communication Theory, 13*, 5–38.

Bokeno, R., & Gantt, V. (2000). Dialogic mentoring: Core relationships for organizational learning. *Management Communication Quarterly, 14*(2), 237–270. doi:10.1177/0893318900142002

Carruthers, R. (2022). Reverse mentoring: Connecting a multi-generation workplace. Retrieved from https://www.togetherplatform.com/blog/reverse-mentoring-the-future-of-work.

Desilver, D. (2016). More older Americans are working, and working more, than they used to. Retrieved from https://www.pewresearch.org/fact-tank/2016/06/20/more-older-americans-are-working-and-working-more-than-they-used-to/

Gullette, M. M. (1997). *Declining to decline: Cultural combat and the politics of midlife*. University Press of Virginia.

Hummert, M. L. (1994). Stereotypes of the elderly and patronizing speech. In M. L. Hummert, J. M. Wiemann, & J. F. Nussbaum (Eds.), *Interpersonal communication in older adulthood: Interdisciplinary research* (pp. 162–184). Newbury Park, CA: Sage.

Hunt, V., Layton, D., & Prince, S. (2014). *Diversity matters*. New York, NY: McKinsey.

Jansen, W. S., Meeussen, L., Jetten, J., & Ellemers, N. (2020). Negotiating inclusion: Revealing the dynamic interplay between individual and group inclusion goals. *European Journal of Social Psychology, 50*(3), 520–533. 10.1002/ejsp.2633

Lasch-Quinn, E. (2003). *Race experts: How racial etiquette, sensitivity training, and new age therapy hijacked the civil rights revolution*. New York, NY: Norton.

Mumby, D. (1998). Organizing men: Power, discourse, and the social construction of masculinity(s) in the workplace. *Communication Theory, 8*, 164–183.

Neumark, D., Burn, I., & Button, P. (2017). *Age discrimination and hiring of older workers*. Retrieved from https://www.frbsf.org/economic-research/publications/economic-letter/2017/february/age-discrimination-and-hiring-of-older-workers/.

Nkomo, S. (1992). The emperor has no clothes: Rewriting race in organizations. *Academy of Management Review, 17*, 487–513.

Orchestrating equity. (n.d.) Retrieved from https://www.fairhire.org/quest/orchestrating-equity-a-brief-history-into-blind-hiring/.

Paine, L. (2003). *Value shift: Why companies must merge social and financial imperatives to achieve superior performance*. New York, NY: McGraw-Hill.

Parker, P. (2005). *Race, gender and leadership: Re-envisioning organizational leadership from the perspectives of African American women executives*. Mahwah, NJ: Lawrence Erlbaum.

Pecchioni, L., & Croghan, J. (2002). Young adults' stereotypes of older adults with their grandparents as the targets. *Journal of Communication, 52*(4), 715–730.

Riach, K., & Kelly, S. (2015). The need for fresh blood: Understanding organizational age inequality through a vampiric lens. *Organization, 22*(3), 287–305. doi:10.1177/1350508413508999

Rosa, N., & Hastings, S. (2016). Managers making sense of millennials: Perceptions of a generational cohort. *Qualitative Research Reports in Communication, 17*(1), 52–59. 10.1080/17459435.2015.1088895

Smith, F., & Dougherty, D. (2012). Revealing a master narrative: Discourses of retirement throughout the working life cycle. *Management Communication Quarterly, 26*(3), 453–478. doi:10.1177/0893318912438687

Spradlin, A. (1998). The price of "passing": A lesbian perspective on authenticity in organizations. *Management Communication Quarterly, 11*, 598–605.

Stohl, C. (1995). *Organizational communication: Connectedness in action*. London: Sage.

Szczur, S. (2019). Mobile millennials: Plugged in but left out? In S. Smith (Ed.), *Recruitment, retention, and engagement of a millennial workforce* (pp. 147–162). Lexington Books.

Toossi, M., & Torpey, E. (2017, May). *Older workers: Labor force trends and career options*. Retrieved from https://www.bls.gov/careeroutlook/2017/article/older-workers.htm.

Trethewey, A. (1999). Disciplined bodies: Women's embodied identities at work. *Organization Studies, 20*, 423–450.

Trethewey, A. (2001). Reproducing and resisting the master narrative of decline: Midlife professional women's experiences of aging. *Management Communication Quarterly, 15*(2), 183–226. doi: 10.1177/0893318901152002

Truxillo, D., Cadiz, D., & Hammer, L. (2015). Supporting the aging workforce: A review and recommendations for workplace intervention research. *Annual Review of Organizational Psychology and Organizational Behavior, 2*, 351–381. doi: 10.1146

Woog, D. (2001). *Gay men, straight jobs*. New York, NY: Alyson Books.

Zanoni, P. (2011). Diversity in the lean automobile factory: Doing class through gender, disability and age. *Organization, 18*(1), 105–127. doi: 10.1177/135050841 0378216

4

AGAINST PROFESSIONALISM AND "GOOD" COMMUNICATION

Transforming Exclusionary Assumptions in Interviews and Beyond

Joshua H. Miller

Texas State University

Learning Objectives

After reading this chapter, you will:

1 Identify exclusionary assumptions about communication that persist in organizations.
2 Critique discourses that promote exclusion based on harmful assumptions about communication.
3 Reassess organizational norms around communication and create alternative means of assessing communication.

Introduction

As society continues to grapple with questions of injustice and exclusion, organizations must make a choice: join the cause of justice or maintain the oppressive structures of the status quo. Unfortunately, too many organizations maintain oppression even when they ostensibly claim that their aim is to join the cause of justice. Challenging oppression involves much more than hoisting a rainbow flag during June, stating Black Lives Matter on one's website, or declaring that immigrants are welcome in your home, organization, or community. Organizations must transform many of their assumptions and practices to promote inclusion and justice. Specifically, without fundamentally *unlearning* standards of professionalism and "good" communication, the organization may simply make an oppressive institution or system look "kinder and gentler and better without actually changing much at all" (Chávez, 2015, p. 166).

DOI: 10.4324/9781003333746-5

When organizations only focus on diversity and inclusion, their efforts will likely fall short and, worse, reinforce marginalization. Scholars have repeatedly emphasized this point, highlighting the dangers of a surface-level focus on diversity. First, promoting diversity can tokenize marginalized people, requiring them to perform additional and inequitable labor to help secure the organization's image; the additional labor enables increased mental stress and burnout among marginalized people (Duncan, 2014). Second, because "diversity provides a way of talking about difference without talking about inequality" (Moore & Bell, 2011, p. 600), an organization's emphasis on diversity can obscure systematic exclusions, such as lack of pay equity, implicit bias of customers, or toxic workplace environments. This is because diversity discourses often "individuate difference and to conceal the continuation of systematic inequalities" (Ahmed, 2007, p. 236). Diversity discourses allow organizations to focus on surface-level optics without asking fundamental questions about organizational culture and marginalization within it (Bell & Hartmann, 2007; Cisneros & Nakayama, 2015; Hikido & Murray, 2016). Third, the celebration of diversity can accompany assimilationist discourses that reify the norms of the dominant group and simultaneously displace the views of those on the margins (Bell & Hartmann, 2007; Jenkins, 2014). Organizations may invite historically marginalized individuals into the organization so long as they learn its normative customs, rules, and norms. Fourth, an emphasis on only diversity or inclusion can undermine efforts to dismantle structural racism and oppression; promoting diversity alone does not necessarily enable transformation. Simply, organizations can frame their diversity and inclusion efforts as enough change, which curtails the need to further discuss issues of inequality (Chávez, 2015; Moore & Bell, 2011; Sugino, 2020). Thus, organizations that only aim for diversity can fail to challenge oppression and promote transformation.

As such, organizations must ask tough questions about their willingness to alter their assumptions about professionalism and what constitutes "good" communication as they pursue diversity, inclusion, equity, justice, and transformation. Failing to question standards of professionalism and "good" communication only serves to reinforce ableism, sexism, racism, classism, homophobia, and cisnormativity. To advance this argument, I first provide an overview of the academic literature on how a focus on diversity can reinforce oppression. I show how seemingly neutral concepts like professionalism, merit, and civility can maintain injustice to emphasize how organizations must rethink these concepts to cultivate inclusion. Then, I analyze how advice for job interviewees circulates exclusionary assumptions that illustrate the potential consequences of assumptions about professionalism. Discourses around job interviews and professionalism constitute a way organizations, especially leaders of organizations, may unknowingly perpetuate exclusion even when they claim to support inclusion.

Exclusion, Professionalism, and "Good" Communication

To cultivate transformation and justice, organizational leaders must rethink "good" communication and professionalism. Here, I view "good" communication as communication that follows normative assumptions for what interactants would likely view as persuasive and, in places of work, professional. The problems rest in how normative assumptions about how one should communicate rely on exclusionary and ableist assumptions, including (1) maintaining eye contact, (2) speaking clearly and concisely, (3) using appropriate hand gestures, and (4) controlling body movements (Moe, 2012; Tigert & Miller, 2021). Bodies and minds work differently. By defining certain people's bodily and/or cognitive abilities as preferred or persuasive, society perpetuates ableism. Price (2011), for instance, illuminates how ableism persists in language in higher education and, we can infer, how the language would perpetuate exclusionary beliefs in other organizations. Price attends to "rationality," "presence," "participation," "productivity," "collegiality," and "coherence" (p. 5), arguing that these common discourses exclude those with what she terms mental disabilities. She asks a series of questions to promote reflection about how these terms can marginalize: "What does 'participation' in a class mean for a student who is undergoing a deep depression and cannot get out of bed?" (p. 5). She continues,

> What about a student on the autism spectrum who has difficulty apprehending the subtle social cues that govern classroom participation, the difference between 'showing engagement' and 'dominating the conversation,' the sorts of spontaneous oral performances that are considered 'smart'? What does 'collegiality' mean for a faculty member who has these same difficulties? (p. 6)

Price's questions reveal how much of the language surrounding academic performance contains ableist assumptions that further marginalize people with disabilities. Of course, these same discourses persist in many organizations where people, especially organization leaders, want others to be present, participate, produce, and be collegial. To account for the exclusionary assumptions underlying these discourses, people in organizations must reconsider how they assess others' communication practices.

In addition, organizational leaders must recognize "professionalism as a form of discourse that privileges some, disenfranchises others, and provides an unwritten form of organizational control" (Ferguson & Dougherty, 2022, p. 5). Professional standards reinforce exclusionary assumptions about race, gender, sexuality, ableism, age, and class. Professionalism generally centers on normative expectations about how people should act, behave, think, and look. Such expectations privilege dominant members of society (e.g., white, cisgender, straight, and able-bodied men). For example, because of exclusionary logics rooted in professionalism about how one should communicate, Black individuals, as well as other people of color and/or immigrants, may opt to code switch to maintain their image as a professional. These individuals change their behaviors and how they speak to assimilate into the dominant culture of the organization (Ferguson & Dougherty, 2022, p. 7). Think about the recent discussions of natural hair as another example. The efforts to pass CROWN acts, which would prohibit race-based hair discrimination, respond to the exclusionary belief that certain forms of natural hair are unprofessional. People attempt to justify discrimination by invoking professionalism as a critical value for an organization. In addition, discourses of professionalism also enable people to avoid difficult questions about sexuality, which reinforces cisnormativity—societal norms that privilege those who identify with their assigned sex at birth—and heteronormativity (Samek & Donofrio, 2013). As such, organizations must question assumptions about professionalism to ensure inclusion and justice.

Like professionalism, other discourses that may initially seem neutral buttress marginalization. These discourses include (1) civility, (2) merit, and (3) neutrality. These discourses often interweave as people claim professionals should be civil, have merit, and/or remain impartial in their decision-making. First, organizational leaders must recognize that efforts to promote civility, or politeness, are not neutral. Alongside professionalism, calls for civility occur inequitably and often discipline or silence those on the margins, especially women of color (Calafell, 2020; Duncan, 2014; Lozano-Reich & Cloud, 2009). Colleagues appeal to civility or frame others as uncivil to undermine the credibility of those on the margins and prevent efforts to transform an organization (Calafell, 2020). The promotion of civility works "to insulate white fragility through appeals to language and scholarship that protects whites from racial discomfort" (Báez & Ore, 2018, p. 331). Norms around civility furthermore encourage individuals on the margins to remain silent or hide their justified emotions when they experience discrimination or navigate discriminatory situations (Sowards, 2020). Politeness works to obfuscate questions about power imbalances and unequitable practices (Corrigan & Vats, 2020).

Second, organizational leaders must understand that merit is not an objective or neutral concept. By invoking merit, people can generally sidestep questions of structural inequality and focus on individual actions; doing so ignores the ongoing problems of marginalization produced by structures, not individual actions. People who invoke merit generally assume that "measure of competence or 'merit' developed by white elite institutions are valid and complete measures," when research repeatedly shows many of these metrics contain cultural biases (Moore & Bell, 2011, p. 611). Thus, someone's merit might be decided based on a standardized test score even when the test was biased. Moreover, those with power can invoke merit to diminish the contributions of those who have been historically excluded. For instance, they may discount a law student of color by positioning the student as an affirmative action hire (Moore & Bell, 2011). In this way, people may place diversity and merit at odds with each other (Calafell, 2020). Scholars have illustrated the ways success becomes "measured by one party pleasing the other" rather than by "some objective, empirical standard" (Wilson & Ono, 2021, p. 176; also see, Corrigan & Vats, 2020), illustrating the "subjective" nature of merit. That is, because those with power in the organization can determine merit, raises, and promotions, those with less power remain incentivized to befriend and please those with power—a subjective and ableist metric for evaluation. Such a dynamic reinforces the status quo's power relationships and creates inequity.

Third, organizational leaders should remain cautious about when they and others invoke neutrality or claim they are impartial. When people claim impartiality or neutrality, they cover their own personal investments in the topic under discussion. Like appeals to merit, neutrality allows leaders and other organizational members to obscure their privilege and minimize structural oppressions (Gent, 2017). Writing about controversies over homeless bill of rights, for example, Gent (2017) emphasized that "in practice, neutrality is anything but neutral. A lack of engagement with difference tends to cause publics to uphold the power relations of the status quo" (p. 237). Scholars have furthermore connected the interrelated discourses of neutrality, merit, and professionalism. In the field of rhetorical criticism, for example, scholars highlighted how writing styles that attempted to maintain an image of neutrality ultimately downplayed the inherently ideological and political nature of scholarship itself. The perceived objectivity of the analysis helps cultivate authority and credence for the analysis through the view that the scholarship follows professional standards (Shugart, 2003).

These connected discourses occur in basic organizational decisions, like hiring. Imagine a meeting where colleagues are discussing a hiring decision. One individual emphasizes that they want to impartially assess the credentials of each candidate. Another colleague mentions that they desire to hire the candidate that will be the most collegial and professional. Although this conversation might seem neutral, scholars continue to show that it is not. The following analysis unpacks this claim to show how hiring decisions and the interview process can remain riddled with exclusionary assumptions.

In what follows, I analyze a dozen, largely popular press, articles that provide advice for interviewees for a job to illustrate the connection between standards for professionalism, as illustrated by the advice for interviewees, and exclusion. To find the articles, I completed several simple "Google" searches with search terms related to advice for interviewing, such as "interview tips." The articles enable me to assess the norms and assumptions that continue to circulate about interviewing. The articles serve as "representative anecdotes" from which we can learn about broader discourses and assumptions related to professionalism (Brummett, 1984). Analyzing the interview advice serves as window from which we can observe the circulation of larger societal assumptions about professionalism and "good" communication. Much of the advice I analyze remains commonplace and useful for helping someone receive a job offer. That is the problem. Exclusionary assumptions continue to circulate in ways that reinforce the marginalization of those who have been historically excluded. The analysis demonstrates how normative expectations around eye contact, dress, food and drink, nonverbal communication, controlling emotions, clarity, and focus maintain exclusion and marginalization.

Interviewing and Exclusionary Assumptions

Articles that provide advice to job interviewees circulated exclusionary logics that maintain marginalization. Although I analyzed advice for interviewees, the analysis reveals assumptions about professionalism that apply to anyone in an organization as well. When members of organizations expect interviewees to follow that advice, they further perpetuate oppression even when ostensibly committed to diversity and inclusion.

Eye Contact as Exclusionary

First, advice articles frequently encouraged interviewees to "remember to maintain eye contact" ("21 Job Interview Tips"), "make eye contact" ("20 Tips"), and "maintain eye contact with the interviewer" (Doyle, 2022, February 24). Another article reinforces the negative association between lack of eye contact and being viewed as trustworthy: "avoiding eye contact entirely comes across as untrustworthy and distant—it could make it seem like your answers are dishonest" (Burry, 2022).

Doyle (2021) echoed the concerns about eye contact and honesty: "if the person is not looking you in the eye, he or she might be uncomfortable or hiding the truth." The view that eye contact matters or should matter perpetuates exclusionary norms. Simply, not everyone can give eye contact in the same way that others can. First, as research continually shows the importance of eye contact, research has also demonstrated that blind individuals "cannot see and make any eye contact in blind-sighted conversations" and "experience communication breakdown in conversation scenarios, which leads to feelings of social isolation and low self-confidence" (Qiu et al., 2020, p. 839). Second, individuals living with autism differ from those not living with autism in terms of eye contact and eye gaze (Frazier et al., 2017). When making eye contact, people living with autism may experience negative emotional reactions, increased stress and social anxiety, or sensory overload (Trevisan et al., 2017). Third, culture shapes how people gaze and maintain (or do not maintain) eye contact (Senju et al., 2012). By privileging one's own culture's norms about eye contact, interviewers can marginalize other cultures and their norms. Thus, interviewers should not demand eye contact or form conclusions about applicants based on the lack of eye contact. Interviewers could also ask applicants what type of interview they would prefer.

Professional Dress as Exclusionary

Second, much interviewing advice emphasized professional and appropriate dress, which perpetuates sexism and classism. According to one advice article, interviewees should not "forget the little things—shine your shoes, make sure your nails are clean and tidy, and check your clothes for holes, stains, pet hair and loose threads" ("21 Job Interview Tips", 2022). Another article concurs, "It's essential to take particular care with your appearance during a job interview. The candidate dressed in a suit and tie, or dress and heels, will usually make a much better impression than the candidate dressed in jeans and speakers" (Doyle, 2022, March 21). The article continues, "this means a suit and tie for men and a pantsuit or skirt and blouse for women" (Doyle, 2022). Sexism persists when "men" and "women"—note how the discourse reinforces the gender binary—must wear different attire to portray themselves as professional. These pieces of advice also discourage wearing cultural attire; unfortunately, this advice could reinforce assimilation as interviewees are encouraged to dress to the norm of the organization.

Classism persists when organizations assess candidates based on pro-fessional attire. Suits, ties, polished dress shoes, heels, and dresses all cost money. In 2020, 37.2 million people lived in poverty in the United States, which represented an increase over the previous year (United States Census Bureau, 2022). With people experiencing rampant poverty, encouraging that they have expensive clothing to acquire a job perpetuates exclusion and maintains classism. Imagine someone experiencing homelessness and the difficulty they will likely experience trying to procure a clean and tidy suit or dress to wear for an interview. Assumptions about professional dress place these people in an incredibly precarious position: needing a job to afford dress clothes and needing dress clothes to get a job.

Organizations may approach this problem by working to equip interviewees with professional clothing, enabling those interviewees to assimilate into a workplace culture. For example, many universities offer career closets that allow students to dress in a manner that allows them to meet potential employers' classist assumptions of what they are looking for in potential employees while simultaneously leaving that classist assumption in place and unquestioned (i.e., professional clothes are expensive and presenting one as "professional" requires the financial means to do so). Although career closets help marginalized individuals navigate the exclusionary assumptions, organizations should not require expensive or normative dress from interviewees or use clothing in their assessment of candidates. Organizations may even encourage candidates to "come as they are" to reduce the influence of classism in the hiring process.

Food, Drink, and Ableism

Third, subtle forms of ableism can endure when people make recommendations about what interviewees should bring to their interview. One advice article paid particular attention to food and drink, recommending that interviewees do not have either with them. The author wrote, "Not only is it unprofessional to enter with a drink, but during your interview, you should be focused on the task at hand" (Doyle, 2019). The author continued to highlight the risks of bringing food or drink to an interview,

> Having a drink in front of you creates the opportunity for distraction—fiddling with the cup, or missing a question while taking a sip, for example. And although it may be a relatively unlikely possibility, bringing a drink into your interview also gives way to other unsightly accidents—like spilling the drink on the desk, on you, or even your interviewer!
>
> (Doyle)

By foregrounding the risks of having food or drink as universal, the author delegitimates a subtle strategy that interviewees, especially those with diabetes, might use. Having a drink or snack can be a critical strategy for those with diabetes to manage their blood sugar. For instance, during her confirmation process, now Justice Sonia Sotomayor used this strategy and had Sprite with her as she answered Senators' questions (Bennett, 2018). The assumption that thinking about food or drink during an interview would be a distraction privileges those who do not have to worry about their health or, in this case, their blood sugar level. Viewing having a quick drink as unprofessional marginalizes people with diabetes as they work to manage their diagnosis. Thus, interviewers, at the very least, should be open to and not assess interviewees drinking or eating happens during the interview. Organizations might also try to offer candidates snacks, water, and/or coffee to those being interviewed.

Nonverbal Communication and Exclusion

Fourth, many articles emphasized the significance of nonverbal communication, but recommendations about body language and posture reinforce ableist assumptions that inclusive organizations must avoid. Doyle (2021) wrote that "your body language, eye contact, hand gestures, and tone of voice all color the message you are trying to convey." Another article concurred, "the wrong body language can send the wrong signal and sour how you're perceived" (Burry, 2022). One article provided specific advice such as "no slumping. Keep your back straight. Lean forward slightly to indicate interest. Do not recline back into the chair fully; this can make you seem bored and disengaged" (Burry). Another article agreed: "Sit or stand tall with your shoulders back" ("21 Job Interview Tips", 2022). Yet, those with ankylosing spondylitis, a type of arthritis, or scoliosis will not and cannot maintain a straight back. Those living with back pain, a pinched nerve, arthritis, or a host of other diagnoses may feel pain or discomfort from leaning forward or not reclining in the chair. If interviewers associate these types of body language with boredom, then they would be reinforcing ableist assumptions in their organizations.

Articles promoted two other forms of nonverbal communication—the handshake and the smile. Like other forms of body language, the assumption that an interviewee can deliver a "good" handshake or smile maintains ableism. According to advice articles, one should start the interview with "a handshake and a smile" and end the process by leaving "quickly and courteously with a handshake and a smile" ("Tips for a Successful Interview", 2022). Another article recommended that interviewees "look the person in the eye and smile. A good handshake should be firm but not crush the other person's fingers" ("21 Job Interview Tips", 2022). The interviewee should also "display confident body language and a smile throughout" ("21 Job Interview Tips"). Accordingly, interviewees should "give a firm handshake" ("20 Tips," 2022). Encouraging handshakes and smiling maintains ableism. Those experiencing carpel tunnel syndrome or arthritis may feel pain or discomfort when trying to provide a firm handshake. Those living with multiple sclerosis, Parkinson's, or amyotrophic lateral sclerosis (ALA) may struggle to control their arms and hands in ways that enable them to shake hands (Moe, 2012). People living with obsessive-compulsive disorder may fear or dislike needing the provide a handshake. Smiling may be more difficult for (1) those who live with Bell's palsy or other causes of facial paralysis or (2) those who may lack a normative "beautiful" smile due to lack of dental care. Thus, even in their simple assumptions about greeting others, people may subtly reinforce ableism. Thus, interviewers should reflect on their assumptions about ableism and not evaluate interviewee's posture. Interviewers, if comfortable with handshakes themselves, should also wait for candidates to offer a handshake.

Assessing "Nervousness" as Exclusionary

Sixth, interview advice often privileges people who are not expressing anxiety, depression, or other mental health challenges. Privilege related to mental health manifests in recommendations about controlling one's emotions. One article provided a list of specific behaviors to avoid: "if you're a nail-biter, knuckle-cracker, hair-twirler, or leg-tapper, don't allow these habits to make an appearance during the interview. All will appear unprofessional and convey nerves" (Burry, 2022). Another article provided the suggestion to ask for a moment to pause to gather oneself if expressing anxiety but also invoked a negative connection between anxiety and performance: "Recruiters will appreciate your ability to stay calm under pressure instead of fumbling" (Laker et al., 2021). Those living with anxiety disorders or post-traumatic stress may find it difficult to avoid behaviors associated with anxiety or nervousness, especially in comparison to interviewees who do not live with anxiety and stress. Some anxiety might only be managed via medication—medication that might only be accessible with the health insurance afforded by a job. In addition, interview advice emphasized the significance of positivity. For instance, one article argued, "Showing positivity with a smile and upbeat body language can help keep the interview light and constructive" ("21 Job Interview Tips", 2022). Another author stated, "you need to stay upbeat and enthusiastic through it all" (Doyle, 2022, February 24). Still another encouraged interviewees to "think positive. No one likes a complainer, so don't dwell on negative experiences during an interview" and to "come in with energy and enthusiasm" ("20 Tips," 2022). Such advice privileges those living without depression, post-traumatic stress, and/or thyroid conditions. Those who recently experienced workplace bullying and/or a toxic workplace may also find it more difficult to remain positive in these interviews because of the mental consequences of working in such an environment (Prevost & Hunt, 2018). Thus, advice around controlling emotions further marginalizes those experiencing mental health conditions or other health challenges that influence mood. As such, interviewers should refrain from assessing or judging a candidate based on habits that could manifest because of anxiety. In addition, organizations might consider proactively offering ALL candidates information about health benefits, including mental health benefits, as part of the interview process.

Articulation, Presence, and Exclusion

Finally, when interviewers assess candidates based on how articulate or present the candidates are, those interviewers reinforce exclusionary assumptions. Advice focused on clarity of expression, conciseness, being smooth, and being present. For example, one author wrote, "Keep your answers succinct, to-the-point and focused and don't ramble—simply answer the question" (Doyle, 2019). Another author concurred but also emphasized the importance of being smooth and articulate:

> It's one thing to come prepared with a mental answer to a question like, 'Why should we hire you?' It's another challenge entirely to say it out loud in a confident and convincing way. The first time you try it, you'll sound garbled and confused, no matter how clear your thoughts are in your own mind! Do it another 10 times, and you'll sound a lot smoother and more articulate.
>
> ("20 Tips", 2021)

The advice and those interviewers who expect concise and clear answers privilege neurotypical ways of thinking and communicating. First, as Price (2011) highlighted, not everyone's brains operate in ways that enable the linear logics that clear and concise answers may require. Second, a whole host of people, such as those who have a stutter, may never achieve the smoothness or "good" articulation that others view as important. Therefore, the expectation that interviewees remain concise and clear negates people who are neurodiverse and people with disabilities.

When stressing the significance of clear and smooth communication, advice givers also highlighted focus and presence as critical factors for successful interviewees, which further perpetuates neurotypical privilege.

For example, authors indicated that "of the 72% of job candidates we observed who did not bag offers, the majority (around 80%) appeared to be distracted, failed to engage their recruiter in a meaningful way, or seemed as they were reading from a script" (Laker et al., 2021). Still another articulate suggested, "Don't let yourself zone out during an interview. Make sure you are well-rested, alert, and prepared. Getting distracted and missing a question looks bad on your part" (Doyle, 2019). The ability to stay focused is a form of privilege. People living with attention-deficit/hyperactivity disorder or post-traumatic stress disorder may struggle to maintain the level of attention that individuals who do not share those diagnoses. Because depression, anxiety, chronic pain, or chronic illness can manifest in brain fog, the demand to maintain focus and express oneself clearly further marginalizes people with these diagnoses. Interviewers should plan sufficient time for interviews to allow for moments of "zoning out" or distraction.

Concluding Recommendations

I conclude by providing a few recommendations about how organizations might use the insights provided by the analysis. Most basically, the analysis demonstrates that organizations should not only focus on interviewing more diverse candidates but reassess and transform the interview process. First, members of organizations must *unlearn* assumptions about professionalism and "good" communication. Many of the exclusionary assumptions highlighted in the analysis remain the norm. To produce inclusion and justice, people must continually question the assumptions they have about how someone should communicate and how they define professionalism. Organizations should require ongoing implicit bias training, which will help people notice and be more aware of their own biases. Organizations should also develop transparent evaluation standards, provided to all candidates, that avoid criteria related to professionalism and "good" communication. Organizations should continually question their practices and assumptions and whether the dominant groups' norms are viewed as universal. For example, different cultures define "on time" differently, so interviewers should not discount a candidate for "being late" without assessing their assumptions about what "on time" means (Jenkins, 2014).

As a part of this effort, people must continually reflect upon whether they really remain as committed to inclusion as they publicly profess it. If an organizational leader will not hire someone experiencing homelessness, then that organization is not interested in inclusion. If an organizational leader is worried that customers will complain that a gay man acts to femininely, then that organization is not interested in inclusion. If an organizational leader is not interested in offering a job to someone experiencing severe depression which makes it difficult for them to maintain a professional look, that organization is not interested in inclusion. Thus, organizational leaders must commit themselves to an *ongoing* process where they question their assumptions about professionalism.

Organizational leaders must assess the organization's value hierarchies. Many organizations may claim that they support inclusion but also value reputation, professionalism, efficiency, and profit. When reflecting on one's value hierarchies, organizational leaders should ask which of these values come first, second, third, and so on. Organizations must anticipate that these values will conflict from time to time. When that occurs, will diversity, inclusion, and justice fall by the wayside as the organization pursues its other values? Remember that it costs money to ensure that the organization is accessible. The organization must have ramps and elevators to every part of the building, and those ramps and elevators must be easy to find and work well. The organization might be tempted to view itself as less efficient when it hires people living with obsessive-compulsive disorder or attention-deficit/hyperactivity disorder. Organizational leaders might fear that the organization's bottom line will be threatened if it focuses too much on inclusion and justice. The preceding analysis demonstrates that other values like professionalism can undermine one's commitment to inclusion. Thus, to claim inclusion as a value, organizations must place it at the top of their value hierarchy.

Those with privilege may be unwilling to expend energy and effort to create change in an organization even when they claim they support diversity and inclusion. It is easy to use exclusionary logic to dismiss an applicant based on their appearance, and it is easy to forget that judging someone based on their appearance might be promoting classist, sexist, racist, and other discriminatory ideologies. Changing how people respond when an interviewee shows up in ripped jeans, ensuring no one assesses that candidate based on their clothing, is difficult. What is difficult is committing to refraining from comments about professionalism or merit when assessing candidates or current employees. What is difficult is continually questioning one's assumptions about eye contact, dress, nonverbal communication, clarity, focus, and professionalism. What is difficult is requiring everyone in the organization to take implicit bias training. What is difficult is defending a member of the organization, especially when doing so may result in the loss of a client. So, what should organizations do to foster inclusion and justice? Take the difficult route.

Discussion Questions

1 Think about the last time that you have been involved in the hiring process. By what standards did you assume applicants would be assessed? In what ways did these standards reinforce or challenge exclusionary assumptions about professionalism or "good" communication?
2 In this chapter, you learned about exclusionary assumptions about professionalism and "good" communication circulate in advice about interviewing. In what other contexts have you observed these exclusionary assumptions in an organization?
3 How do you plan on applying the analysis provided by this chapter to your own organization? How do you plan to learn more about exclusionary assumptions about professionalism and "good" communication in the future?

Author Bio

Joshua H. Miller is an Assistant Professor at Texas State University. His research focuses on how marginalized communities and people use rhetoric to inspire shared action, build and maintain community, and promote social change. He teaches courses on rhetoric, diversity, LGBTQ+ advocacy, and political communication.

References

20 Tips for Great Job Interviews. (2021). Experis: ManpowerGroup. Retrieved July 26, 2022, from https://www.experis.com/en/insights/articles/2021/05/25/20-tips-for-great-job-interviews
21 Job Interview Tips: How to Make a Great Impression. (June 10, 2022). Indeed. Retrieved July 20, 2022, from https://www.indeed.com/career-advice/interviewing/job-interview-tips-how-to-make-a-great-impression
Ahmed, S. (2007). The language of diversity. *Ethnic and Racial Studies*, *30*(2), 235–256. 10.1080/01419870601143927
Báez, K. L., & Ore, E. (2018). The moral imperative of race for rhetorical studies: on civility and walking-in-white in academe. *Communication and Critical/Cultural Studies*, 15 (4), 331–336. 10.1080/14791420.2018.1533989
Bell, J. M., & Hartmann, D. (2007). Diversity in everyday discourse: The cultural ambiguities and consequences of "happy talk". *American Sociological Review*, *72*(6), 895–914. 10.1177/000312240707200603
Bennett, J. A. (2018). Containing Sotomayor: Rhetorics of personal restraint, judicial prudence, and diabetes management. *Quarterly Journal of Speech*, *104*(3), 257–278. 10.1080/00335630.2018.1486033
Brummett, B. (1984). Burke's representative anecdote as a method in media criticism. *Critical Studies in Mass Communication*, *1*, 161–176. doi:10.1080/1529503 8409360027

Burry, M. (2022, January 20). *Body language tips for your next job interview.* The Balance Careers. https://www.thebalancecareers.com/body-language-tips-for-your-next-job-interview-2060576

Calafell, B. M. (2020). Cisnormativity, whiteness, and the fear of contagion in academia. *QED: A Journal in GLBTQ Worldmaking, 7*(1), 68–74. https://www.muse.jhu.edu/article/754455

Chávez, K. R. (2015). Beyond inclusion: Rethinking rhetoric's historical narrative. *Quarterly Journal of Speech, 101*(1), 162–172. 10.1080/00335630.2015.994908

Cisneros, J. D., & Nakayama, T. K. (2015). New media, old racisms: Twitter, Miss America, and cultural logics of race. *Journal of International and Intercultural Communication, 8*(2), 108–127. 10.1080/17513057.2015.1025328

Corrigan, L. M., & Vats, A. (2020). The structural whiteness of academic patronage. *Communication and Critical/Cultural Studies, 17*(2), 220–227. 10.1080/14791420.2020.1770824

Doyle, A. (2019, November 20). *10 easy-to-make job interview mistakes.* The Balance Careers. https://www.thebalancecareers.com/most-common-interview-mistakes-2061111

Doyle, A. (2021, March 13). *Communication skills for workplace success.* The Balance Careers. https://www.thebalancecareers.com/communication-skills-list-2063779

Doyle, A. (2022, February 24). *Job interview tips that will help you get hired.* The Balance Careers. https://www.thebalancecareers.com/top-interview-tips-2058577

Doyle, A. (2022, March 21). *How to dress for a job interview.* The Balance Careers. https://www.thebalancecareers.com/how-to-dress-for-an-interview-2061163

Duncan, P. (2014). Hot commodities, cheap labor: Women of color in the academy. *Frontiers: A Journal of Women Studies, 35*(3), 39–63. 10.5250/fronjwomestud.35.3.0039

Ferguson Jr., M. W., & Dougherty, D. S. (2022). The paradox of the black professional: Whitewashing blackness through professionalism. *Management Communication Quarterly, 36*(1), 3–29. 10.1177/08933189211019751

Frazier, T. W., Strauss, M., Klingemier, E. W., Zetzer, E. E., Hardon, A. Y., Eng, C., & Youngstrom, E. A. (2017). A meta-analysis of gaze differences to social and nonsocial information between individuals with and without autism. *Journal of the American Academy of Child & Adolescent Psychiatry, 56*(7), 546–555. 10.1016/j.jaac.2017.05.005

Gent, W. 2017. When homelessness become a 'luxury': Neutrality as an obstacle to counterpublic rights claims. *Quarterly Journal of Speech, 103*(3), 230–250. 10.1080/00335630.2017.1321133

Hikido, H., & Murray, S. B. (2016). Whitened rainbows: How white college students protect whiteness through diversity discourses. *Race Ethnicity and Education, 19*(2), 389–411. 10.1080/13613324.2015.1025736

Jenkins, J. J. (2014). A "community" of discipline: The paradox of diversity within an intercultural church. *Western Journal of Communication, 78*(2), 134–154. 10.1080/10570314.2013.845793

Laker, B., Godley, W., Kudret, S., & Trehan, R. (2021, March 9). *4 Tips to Nail a Virtual Job Interview*. Harvard Business Review. https://hbr.org/2021/03/4-tips-to-nail-a-virtual-job-interview

Lozano-Reich, N. M., & Cloud, D. L. (2009). The uncivil tongue: Invitational rhetoric and the problem of inequality. *Western Journal of Communication, 73*(2), 220–226. 10.1080/10570310902856105

Moe, P. W. (2012). Revealing rather than concealing disability: The rhetoric of Parkinson's advocacy Michael J. Fox. *Rhetoric Review, 31*(4), 443–460. 10.1080/07350198.2012.711200

Moore, W. L., & Bell, J. M. (2011). Maneuvers of whiteness: "Diversity" as a mechanism of retrenchment in the affirmative action discourse. *Critical Sociology, 37*(5), 597–613. 10.1177/0896920510380066

Prevost, C., & Hunt, E. (2018). Bullying and mobbing in academe: A literature review. *European Scientific Journal, 14*(8), 1–15. 10.19044/esj.2018.v14n8p1

Price, M. (2011). *Mad at school: Rhetorics of mental disability and academic life*. Ann Arbor: The University of Michigan Press.

Qiu, S., Hu, J., Han, T., Osawa, H., & Rauterberg, M. (2020). Social glasses: Simulating interactive gaze for visually impaired people in face-to-face communication. *International Journal of Human-Computer Interaction, 36*(9), 839–855. 10.1080/10447318.2019.1696513

Samek, A. A., & Donofrio, T. A. (2013). "Academic drag" and the performance of the critical personae: An exchange on sexuality, politics, and identity in the academy. *Women's Studies in Communication, 36*(1), 28–55. 10.1080/07491409.2012.754388

Senju, A., Vernetti, A., Kikuchi, Y., Akechi, H., Hasegawa, T., & Johnson, M. H. (2012). Cultural background modulates how we look at other persons' gaze. *International Journal of Behavioral Development, 37*(2), 131–136. 10.1177/0165025412465360

Shugart, H. A. (2003). An appropriating aesthetic: Reproducing power in the discourse of critical scholarship. *Communication Theory, 13*(3), 275–303. 10.1111/j.1468-2885.2003.tb00293.x

Sowards, S. K. (2020). Constant civility as corrosion of the soul: Surviving through and beyond the politics of politeness. *Communication and Critical/Cultural Studies, 17*(4), 395–400. 10.1080/14791420.2020.1829661

Sugino, C. M. (2020). Multicultural incorporation in Donald Trump's political rhetoric. *Southern Communication Journal, 85*(3), 191–202. 10.1080/1041794X.2020.1780301

Tigert, M. K., & Miller, J. H. (2021). Ableism in the classroom: Teaching accessibility and ethos by analyzing rubrics. *Communication Teacher*. 10.1080/17404622.2021.2006254

Tips for a Successful Interview. (2022). University of North Georgia. Retrieved July 20, 2022, from https://ung.edu/career-services/online-career-resources/interview-well/tips-for-a-successful-interview.php

Trevisan, D. A., Roberts, N., Lin, C., & Birmingham, E. (2017). How do adults and teens with self-declared Austin Spectrum Disorder experience eye contact? A qualitative analysis of first-hand accounts. *PLoS One, 12*(11), 1–22.

United States Census Bureau. (2022, January 21). *National poverty in America awareness month: January 2022.* https://www.census.gov/newsroom/stories/poverty-awareness-month.html#:~:text=Highlights%2C%20Poverty%3A,and%20Table%20B%2D4)

Wilson, K. H., & Ono, K. A. (2021). Creating equitable opportunities: The thoughts of two administrator rhetoricians. *Rhetoric & Public Affairs, 24*(1), 169–190. https://www.muse.jhu.edu/article/803157

5

LANGUAGE-DISCORDANCE AS A BARRIER TO HEALTH EQUITY

Identifying Inclusive Practices in Health Organizations from Patients' Perspectives

Sachiko Terui, Divya S, and Beauty Fosu Acheampong
University of Georgia

Learning Objectives

After reading this chapter, you will:

1 Be able to describe language-discordant patients as a unique, challenged population.
2 Be able to categorize the ways language barriers affect one's health and experiences in healthcare from patients' perspectives.
3 Be able to identify possible approaches to reduce adverse influences of language barriers.

Introduction

More than 20% of the registered US population speak languages other than English at home (The United States Census Bureau, 2022), which can be higher with undocumented individuals. Research supports a strong correlation between language barriers and health disparities (Al Shamsi et al., 2020). Language barriers affect access, utilization, and quality of healthcare (Terui, 2017). The purpose of this study is twofold. First, we examine healthcare barriers affecting language-discordant individuals. Second, we identify/propose inclusive and equitable health communication practices for DEI changemaking.

Individuals face language barriers when their primary language does not match the dominant language spoken in their living environment. Language barriers in healthcare settings are defined as:

DOI: 10.4324/9781003333746-6

Language-based obstacles to successful access to medical treatment, especially in emergency situations, and to effective interaction with medical providers when discussing and negotiating possible healthcare treatment. From the perspective of medical providers, language barriers can have visible consequences (e.g., clinical results) and invisible consequences (e.g., avoidance of/hesitation for following up visit) for patients' health management.

(Terui, 2016, p. 208)

Healthcare for patients with language barriers cannot be effectively delivered in the same ways as for patients with language proficiency, attributable at least partly to the unique challenges related to their language barriers (Bischoff, 2012). Language-discordant individuals are less likely to utilize primary care and preventive services (Betancourt et al., 2012). They are less likely to understand the recommended procedures, adhere to medical recommendations, and return for follow-up appointments (Fernandez et al., 2011; Flores, 2006). Moreover, they are less likely to have health insurance compared with individuals with language proficiency after adjusting for demographic factors (Pérez-Escamilla et al., 2010). These contribute to higher rates of emergency room visits and delayed diagnoses.

Difficulties in describing themselves and their symptoms negatively affect their experiences and health: patients with language barriers are more likely to receive inappropriate amounts of medication and face drug complications (Bischoff, 2012). They also tend to experience a higher risk for hospitalization, have longer stays, and face 15–25% higher readmission rates in 30 days compared with individuals with language proficiency (Betancourt et al., 2012). Moreover, they tend to experience delays in receiving surgeries, an increased risk of misdiagnoses and inappropriate treatment, and a higher risk of surgical infections (Divi et al., 2007). Such difficulties are also associated with the use of more diagnostic tests and invasive procedures (Timmins, 2002). Unnecessary examinations place excessive financial burdens on patients, while too few examinations may contribute to overlooking possible symptoms.

Language barriers negatively influence patient satisfaction with patient–provider interactions, treatments, completeness of care, courtesy and respect, explanation of treatments, and discharge instructions (Fernandez et al., 2011). Their satisfaction rate decreases when patients do not use a medical interpreter (Ngo-Metzger et al., 2009). Because communication is the core of patient–provider interactions, individuals with language barriers inherently lack access to therapeutic aspects of their relationship with their healthcare providers (Timmins, 2002).

To help address health disparities, the Office of Minority Health at the US Department of Health and Human Services (USDHHS) published the National Standards for Culturally and Linguistically Appropriate Services in Health and Health Care (CLAS Standards) in 2000. The Standards were revised in subsequent years to include a more nuanced, detailed set of action steps and recommendations addressing organizational and structural assistance for providing culturally and linguistically appropriate care, language-related support, and organizational quality improvement efforts. CLAS Standards in healthcare guide healthcare organizations to "provide effective, equitable, understandable and respectful quality care and services that are responsive to diverse cultural health beliefs and practices, preferred languages, health literacy and other communication needs" (USDHHS, 2020).

In the CLAS Standards, the section on organizational and structural assistance contains three mandates addressing the importance of recruiting and maintaining workers in health and healthcare organizations to be responsive to the population they serve, while training workers in health and healthcare organizations to be culturally competent. The area of language-related support, containing four requirements, states that health and healthcare organizations offer professional interpreting services and plain language to patients for free to avoid the negative consequences of using ad hoc interpreters. The organizational quality improvement efforts include seven mandates emphasizing the strategies and assessment to hold themselves accountable toward the CLAS Standards (USDHHS, 2020).

Many health and healthcare organizations made efforts to follow this requirement to improve the quality of care among patients with various backgrounds. Despite such efforts, numerous health and healthcare organizations failed to integrate the CLAS Standards into their policies and practices partially because healthcare providers and staff were not fully aware of the CLAS Standards and how to implement them in their practice (Barksdale et al., 2017). Examining the effects of language barriers from patients' perspectives can provide important insights into how health organizations assist language-discordant patients and comply with the CLAS Standards. Accordingly, we examine the following research question: how do language barriers place challenges for language-discordant individuals in the healthcare system and health organizations?

Methods

The authors examined narratives collected through semi-structured, in-depth interviews with 30 language-discordant individuals in the United States. Participants are from ten non-English speaking countries

(China, Japan, Korea, Italy, Venezuela, Bangladesh, India, Vietnam, Taiwan, and Norway). The initials of participants' pseudonyms match the initials of their home countries' names (i.e., Callie is from China). The narrative approach (Fisher, 1987) along with the grounded theory analysis (Charmaz, 2006) were employed. Japanese and English languages were used for data collection. Two participants (Jake and James) used Japanese in interviews, and others used English. More than 25 hours of interview data were collected and transcribed verbatim. Interviews conducted in Japanese were first analyzed in Japanese before translating into English to preserve the cultural context, ensuring minimal distortions and lost meanings in the translation processes (Squires, 2009). All authors conducted open coding independently and then combined themes. Disagreements were dissolved through discussions.

Results

Language barriers place challenges by "reducing individuals' access to the healthcare system" and "reducing the quality of patient-provider interactions." Below, we discuss each theme with corresponding subthemes in detail. While these themes are conceptually distinct, they are not mutually exclusive.

Language Barriers Reduce Individuals' Access to the Healthcare System

Language barriers present an additional challenge for language-discordant individuals when trying to access and utilize available healthcare due to the following reasons.

Scepticism and Distrust

Participants explained it was more convenient to use their native language when looking for ways to initiate medical treatment. These individuals navigate the medical systems based on information obtained from their own networks. Callie reflected, "I basically chat online, using Chinese, and chat and type the symptoms to find out what I should do. It's easy and fast." Such interactions are helpful when evaluating and considering various suggestions to access healthcare. However, when information is largely negative, these strategies may hinder access when needed.

Some participants expressed skepticism about medical advice or exorbitant bills. Participants indicated that they could have misunderstood their provider's intentions due to language issues, but to be on the safer side, they formed a sense of distrust toward certain medical advice provided to them. In elaborating on the reason why she does not want to see a doctor, Callie mentioned, "You don't know how much benefit the doctor gets from treating a patient or from insurance company. Like in the US, those kind of providers recommended some optional product ... but it could be for some sort of incentives."

Even when individuals have positive perceptions about the US health-care system, hearing negative experiences from people in their network can prompt questioning of previous experiences. Callie hesitated to visit hospitals/clinics because of what she heard from her Chinese friends. Callie said, "the doctor did a very roughly check-up ... and the doctor gave him painkillers. I don't think it's helpful ... after the painkiller is gone, the effect is gone. Many examples like this, when he told me that case, I hesitate [to see a doctor]."

Vulnerability and Discomfort

When participants perceive possibilities of interactions with other people reduce their positive social value in the process of accessing healthcare, it reduces the likelihood they will initiate medical treatment or attend follow-up visits. These participants' narratives show that they are aware of negative perceptions attached to language-discordant patients. Brent described the reasons he hesitates to go to a hospital:

> There are some occasions when I could get some negative expressions from not only health professionals, maybe also from the people seeking for the doctors ... I feel like they were not happy with me or they didn't like me, ... I won't go to the hospital until and unless it's emergency. I try to avoid going to the hospitals. I don't want to be, you know, humiliated ... because of my language or anything.

Despite having access to healthcare, many language-discordant participants would rather avoid utilizing it due to such distrust and vulnerability. Many choose to rely on their social network or self-medicate instead. While these are alternatives that could help reduce short-term minor health issues, inaccurate self-medication or misconstrued health advice from lay persons could lead to detrimental health consequences.

Additional Effort Required for Using Healthcare System

Many participants noted that they would avoid using the healthcare system as much as they possible due to the aforementioned reasons. However, language barriers can place challenges even when they are willing to use the system. An appointment is required in many hospitals and clinics. Some participants found it challenging to make an appointment via telephone. Cooper said, "I really don't want to make an appointment with my phone." By believing that every language-related challenge can be solved with a dictionary, Cooper stated, "As long as I have a dictionary, everything will be fine. If I don't understand what they are saying, I will just ask them to put the words on my phone, so I can translate it. If I don't know the words, I will put the Chinese words on my phone and show the translations to them."

Cooper's preference is the result of his previous experience in making an appointment. "I want face-to-face communication, so I came [to the student health center] to make an appointment. It takes a little bit more time than making a phone call, but it makes things clearer." When asked if he had sought help to make an appointment, he said, "Nah, I can do it by myself. It's not that troublesome." Cooper's strategy, however, does add extra time to accessing healthcare; making appointments in person is clearly a bigger burden in terms of time and transportation than making a phone call.

Language Barriers Reduce the Quality of Patient's Interaction with Healthcare Providers

Beyond access to healthcare, language barriers reduce the quality of patient–provider interactions due to the challenges in identity management, information exchange, and relationship building.

Identity Management

Individuals learn desirable behaviors in their host societies through daily interaction and attempt to perform these identities in patient–provider interaction. Despite their attempts, language barriers sometimes prevent these individuals from asserting desirable identities as (a) active, engaging patients and (b) respected, independent patients.

Identities as Active, Engaging Patients

Participants indicated their involvement in patient–physician interaction affects the quality of care they receive. Despite their desire, patient concerns derived from language barriers reduced their abilities to assert their identities as fully active and engaging patients. Charles shared his concerns about the possible negative influences of "being cumbersome" in patient–provider interaction. Charles said,

We have just a limited number of specialists and even more limited number of specialists who participate in health insurance plan. We don't have too many choices … concern is whether their attitude will influence their behavior later on. If he or she thinks I am trouble, will he or she treat me in the future appropriately? Or [will] he or she just [say], "I just want to get rid of him as soon as possible. I will just give … him [the] minimum amount of care and even lessen the standard."

Despite his high language proficiency in communicating his ideas and preferences in detail, Charles was unsure what would be regarded as patient-appropriate engagement, while simultaneously reducing the possibility of annoying healthcare professionals.

Another concern shared by participants is that their limited language proficiency contributes to unwanted consequences. The participants worried if being active and engaging patients might result in making more mistakes in explaining their symptoms, which they suggest contributes to unexpected, and often negative, influences on treatment types and diagnoses. Kandy shared her hesitation to talk with her medical providers actively:

I'm worried what I'm saying could make a problem, like a one mistake or some words, it could affect … my financial and then, my diagnosis … I know my English is not perfect … If I say something wrong, they gonna give me some medicine which I am not supposed to take, like those kinds of situations.

Being restricted by these concerns, many participants said that they often do not actively share their perspectives about symptoms or ask detailed questions.

Identities as Respected, Independent Patients

Many participants shared their frustrations and struggles with being unable to communicate as clearly as they do in their own languages. Some participants said that they lack confidence related strongly to their limited language proficiency. Kedric shared his perspectives: "Sometimes, I feel afraid when I speak in English. They might not understand what I am saying. It sometimes makes me feel … no confidence."

Corresponding with the impressions they have gathered through social interaction, participants' narratives demonstrated their perceptions that their limited language proficiency contributed to their being seen as less respected and independent in patient–provider interaction. The shared concerns are that language barriers cast the language-discordant patients as incompetent and allow medical providers to take advantage of patients.

Callie stated the importance of being prepared to share concerns and symptoms before going to see a doctor, demonstrating her desire to present herself as responsible and independent. Callie said, "if you are a foreigner come from other countries and not familiar with the system, I think you should do some research. ... it's not saving your own time, it's saving other people's time. At least you need to know how to explain your symptoms and nature." Callie believes that taking a long time to explain symptoms and concerns uses up other people's time, and doing so may result in less opportunity for her to be treated equally as individuals with language proficiency.

Some participants believe that language barriers allow providers to take advantage of the patients. Chaz shared his tips for visiting a doctor:

Try to be more critical, ... suspect some of the action taken by the doctor if it is completely necessary. Sometimes they may take advantage of you because you are from a different country, or you may not know the language well. You may not [use] the terminology well, so they may provide you some extra care (chuckles) and extra services that are unnecessary.

By describing patients with language barriers as "soft targets" who are easy to take advantage of, Chaz expressed his distrust toward providers and the implications that language barriers make individuals look inferior to those with language proficiency. The language-discordant patient might not fully comprehend the provider's intentions and could misinterpret or be skeptical about additional health advice or medication provided. This could lead to individuals taking health advice lightly, potentially resulting in large oversights that could be harmful to one's health.

Despite these negative connotations attached to language barriers, some participants voluntarily accept less independent identities to achieve other goals. Describing his general experiences of visiting hospitals in the United States, Knight said, "I think here is more like ... if English [is] my first language, I might think that you know, hey 'don't ask any more questions, ... I wanna make it quick,' ... As a foreigner, I like it here. They, they treat me like ... a little baby." While Knight accepts the dependent role in patient–provider interactions, it later appears to be a strategy to reduce his uncertainty in the process of receiving medical treatment. Knight reframed his language barriers and less independent identity as an additional resource to be an active and engaging patient. When asked if he feels comfortable about being treated like a baby, Knight said, "It's true.

I don't know anything in the medical field. Whenever I ask questions, they tell me everything in detail ... I can ask questions anytime."

Reduced Effectiveness in Information Exchange

Most participants identified the process of exchanging information with providers as challenging. Three subthemes emerged: individuals confront challenges in exchanging information because of (a) assumptions about language proficiency, (b) unfamiliar contexts, and (c) normative practices from home countries.

Assumptions about Language Proficiency

Disfluency and accent can signal one's non-native status, and native-speaking individuals sometimes make accommodations in their communicative styles to facilitate conversations. However, detecting disfluencies and accents does not always prompt native-speaking providers to alter their communicative styles. Having an accent is sometimes not enough to label or treat individuals as having language barriers. People sometimes presume and expect sociolinguistic skills along with language proficiency. Isabelle, for example, does not perceive any trouble communicating in English. When asked if she has difficulties with her language skills, she said,

> Well, not really ... Since you show a certain proficiency in the language, then, there is the assumption that you understand the system. You can't speak the language if you have not been exposed to whatever system we are talking about ... What if I ... have not been exposed or I don't remember, or I'm not sure if it works that way anymore, but there is the assumption that ... if you speak the language, then you should know this, so let's move on.

Failing to accommodate language-discordant patients based on perceived language proficiency could reflect healthcare providers' respect for these language-discordant patients or their positive intentions to treat these individuals as equal to patients with language proficiency. However, as the narrative from Knight demonstrated, some of the participants expressed appreciation for being treated as foreigners who are unfamiliar with sociolinguistic skills in the host society, especially when these participants face anxiety and uncertainty in healthcare situations.

Individuals' physical and psychological state can affect their language proficiency. Ken said, "If I am really sleepy or sick, I cannot understand what they are talking about." Claudia echoed, "I felt like what I was saying didn't make sense to them because I was too upset." Given these situations, language barriers can create additional challenges for individuals to manage health even though they typically perceive themselves as fluent.

Presuming individuals are equipped with sociolinguistic skills, healthcare providers may miss the opportunity to provide important, but common, information. Such presumptions can create additional challenges if these individuals—both patients and medical providers—are not aware of the need to ask questions or do not know which questions to ask.

Interaction in Unfamiliar Contexts

Participants frequently attributed challenges in interacting with medical providers to unfamiliar terms and uncommon vocabularies. The commonly shared challenges are (a) the inability to find words to explain one's conditions ("some words, I didn't know how to say it in English," Corwin); and (b) the unusual conditions in which patients have to communicate in their non-native languages ("I felt a little bit of trouble describing what I encountered … because that sort of thing has … never happened to me," Claudia). All participants shared this apparent challenge attributed to language barriers. Participants' narratives illustrate that individuals' abilities to express themselves (i.e., share their symptoms) do not always mean that these individuals exchange information successfully. The concerns and symptoms they express can be different from what they experience because vocabulary in healthcare is often *studied* rather than *acquired*. Individuals study words by using dictionaries or by hearing the definition/explanation from someone. They consciously make attempts to match these definitions/explanations with their experiences. The attempts are not always successful, so individuals correct their understandings when opportunities arise. Such conscious efforts differentiate a studied language and an acquired language.

Valerie commented, "I understand a lot, and I can talk about it, but I don't know exactly if that's the word [to describe my symptoms]." The narrative from Valerie indicates the possibility that patients and providers have different interpretations and understandings of symptoms, even when these patients' descriptions make perfect sense to the providers. The impact of the possible misunderstandings created by such subtle nuances in the meanings can be small. However, these possible misunderstandings can influence the quality of care as well as patients' satisfaction.

Normative Practice from Home Countries

Language-discordant patients must adopt different communicative styles for successful patient–provider interaction. When conversations take unexpected directions, language barriers frequently affect one's performance partially because individuals are unfamiliar with creating utterances in those ways. Virginia and Vallen noted that in Venezuela, people often talk about many different things with their doctors. Vallen described the normative patient–provider interactions in Venezuela as "very unstructured," saying, "the doctors are the ones to pick up cues from these stories [on various topics] and to make a decision on what is related to my situation and symptoms." Because of this normative belief, Virginia and Vallen found it difficult to provide the needed information to the doctor. Virginia said, "'What are your symptoms?' They ask this kind of question. It's very, very specific for specific things … it's very framed and very specific for what you are going to do with the doctor." Virginia felt the pressure to provide specific and concise answers to the doctors, so she forgot about other information to deliver. The pressure may be even greater when these individuals face an elevated level of uncertainty/anxiety about their symptoms.

Additionally, efforts to produce concise and accurate statements can create challenges in patient–provider interaction. In some Asian countries, stoicism and calmness are perceived as virtues that come with respect and better treatment. Participants' narratives illustrate that such stoicism and calmness can carry different meanings in the United States. Valerie had pneumonia and headed to an ER. Acknowledging that talking with too much emotion is not well perceived in Vietnam, she said,

> It's important to explain as much as you can about what you are having problems with, and try to let them know that you are really sick, that you really (laughs) need help … Whenever I am alone, even when I'm tired, I will still kind of keep it inside, and I try to talk and … pay attention [to] my word choice so that they can understand, and they can give me proper treatment quickly. But sometimes they feel that you are really calm, so you are not really seriously sick. I was really suffering at that time.

By following the normative practice from the home country, Valerie attempted to make the patient–provider communication as smooth as possible. However, her calmness and careful word choices were seen by ER staff as indicative of less severe symptoms.

Building and Strengthening Relationships

Patients tend to put higher regard and trust toward providers who put in the effort to establish patient–provider rapport and treat them like a close friend or family member (Fisher et al., 2018). However, due to language barriers, many participants felt that this relationship rarely gets established. They mentioned that they were treated differently because of how they spoke. The reported differences were mainly related to non-verbal behaviors. The differences can be quite subtle, but affect the ways patients perceive patient–provider interaction. Colby expressed that her experience with her provider was very cold and authoritative, "I think the way she spoke to me ... and she was very authoritative. She was not friendly at all. Cold."

Rapport is an important quality determining the overall quality of patient–provider interactions and satisfaction toward the health treatment. The participant felt uncomfortable and afraid in an already vulnerable and uncertainty-provoking medical environment as indicated from, "Because she made me feel scared? Afraid, a little bit ... I just feel uncomfortable. Yeah, I was just trying to have a general check, but you know, the way she spoke to me, sounds like, I have some issue, so-" Although it was just a general check, language barriers reduced the opportunity for the patient to develop rapport with the provider.

Participants mentioned that because they were unable to express themselves clearly and/or effectively, some providers were impatient and would not actively listen to their issues. Jake said, "I can see they are feeling 'oh no, we have a cumbersome patient' based on their facial expressions." Some participants who were from more collectivist cultures had reservations about re-emphasizing their health issues for fear of offending or irritating their medical provider. Brent said, "I had some hesitation because I said, 'Well, if I ask this question again, maybe he or she might be, uh, disturbed or angry with me,' but a little I thought, 'Well, if I want to know the information, required information I have to ask.' So, initially I have hesitations."

Participants had to use alternative and less effective methods to communicate their pain and put in extra effort to convince providers that treatments were necessary. When patients do not feel welcomed by providers, both the quality of the exchanged information and patient satisfaction levels can be negatively affected. Language barriers contribute to challenges in building relationships with providers partially because non-native individuals perceive alienation in interpersonal interaction. Perceived alienation not only negatively affects patients with language barriers from building relationships with their medical providers, but it also reduces their willingness to return for follow-up treatments or to access healthcare if other symptoms develop.

Practical Applications

As evidenced by our data, language barriers create many challenges for language-discordant individuals navigating the US healthcare system. As such, we recommend several inclusive and equitable health communication practices for healthcare providers and healthcare organizations that could help to improve the healthcare experience (and health equity) for language-discordant individuals.

Accessible Resources

First, by following the CLAS Standards, larger health organizations place some signs describing language services in their lobbies, making the language services available *after* these language-discordant patients take the first step in seeking/receiving health treatment. So, having access to linguistic support to make and prepare for appointments could be helpful *prior to* health visits. As such, we recommend that healthcare organizations make resources available and easily accessible to patients prior to their visits by presenting information about these resources in multiple languages on their home pages and providing an option to receive services in other languages. If patients must go through multiple web pages to get the information using English, the resources are not accessible. Healthcare providers can also remind the patients about the free resources because not every patient notices the signs about language services or is aware of the resources.

Technology Integration

The use of technology could help overcome language challenges between patients and providers, as expressed by Cooper above. Although the use of professional translators or interpreters is recommended, they are not necessarily well-utilized resources (Hsieh, 2015). The use of translation applications (e.g., Care to Translate) could help to bridge this gap and enhance patient–provider interaction and overall healthcare experience and improve patient safety (Al Shamsi et al., 2020). Such resources can be integrated into healthcare websites, healthcare applications, and other healthcare tools that are already available to patients. It is tempting for healthcare providers to use their foreign language skills (i.e., medical Spanish), and it may help build a rapport in patient–provider relationships. However, it is not recommended to rely on one's foreign language skills to assist patients because of the translation errors and associated negative health consequences for patients (Flores et al., 2012).

Trained Medical Interpreters

It is important to note that languages are tightly intertwined with cultures. To enhance the quality of care and experiences in the healthcare system for language-discordant patients, it is important to address both language and cultural barriers simultaneously (Schouten et al., 2020). Besides the use and development of mobile applications that can address cultural aspects of healthcare (i.e., "Options" in COMFORT Communication App), promoting the use of trained medical interpreters is one of the strategies to increase language-discordant patients' experiences and health outcomes (Flores et al., 2012). Medical interpreters can help reduce cultural barriers, be patient advocates, clarify medical information, and assist medical providers in diagnosing patients (Hsieh, 2007). Language preferences and needs of medical interpreters could be asked in the initial encounter, preferably when patients are making an appointment or providers confirming the appointment with patients.

Accessible Active Listening and Language Use by the Provider

The challenge of language barriers accompanied by the sterile and intimidating hospital setting could make patients feel increasingly fearful and anxious. Being patient and actively listening to patients could provide a more welcoming environment. Listening to patients carefully, providing them room to voice their concerns, and not degrading them due to language and cultural challenges could ease tensions and create more effective health communication.

Furthermore, healthcare providers can place more emphasis on *plain language* and provide further explanations about treatment and procedures to reduce misunderstandings in language-discordant patient–provider interactions. Chaz expressed this sentiment during the interview when asked what could be done better by providers in the healthcare setting. He mentioned, "[the doctor] say, 'Okay, since you are from the foreign country, you may not know this term very well. Let me explain you further.'" Such a small remark can reflect medical providers' thoughtfulness and care without offending language-discordant patients' confidence, while avoiding the presumption that these patients have acquired certain sociolinguistic skills. To be inclusive, it is important for healthcare providers to be aware that language proficiency levels fluctuate depending on one's physical and psychological state, and language proficiency does not ensure adequate personal health literacy (Leyva et al., 2005), which entails one's "abilities to find, understand, and use information and services to inform health-related decisions and actions for themselves and others" (Healthy People 2030, 2022, para. 3).

Conclusion

This chapter addressed the ways patients perceive how language barriers affect their health and their experiences in US health organizations. Language barriers can affect both access to and process in healthcare. Although language barriers are not simple barriers to overcome, knowing how individuals with language barriers perceive the challenges can provide helpful insights into the strategies for healthcare providers and health organizations to take for minimizing the negative impacts and promoting health equity.

Discussion Questions

1 What are three ways language-discordance affects health equity?
2 Considering the uncertainty and stress associated with an initial healthcare encounter, come up with three communication behaviors that healthcare providers could employ to create a welcoming environment for language-discordant patients.
3 If you were tasked with improving the patient experience within your organization, what practices would you implement and why?

Author Bios

Sachiko Terui (Ph.D., University of Oklahoma) is an Assistant Professor in the Department of Communication Studies at the University of Georgia. Her research addresses communicative challenges pertaining to linguistic and cultural aspects of health and health management, communication interventions, health literacy, and health disparities experienced among marginalized and underserved populations.

Divya S (MA, University of Miami) is a second-year Ph.D. student in the Department of Communication Studies at the University of Georgia. Her research involves digital health interventions, entertainment education, and health disparities. Her recent research examined how chatbots could provide a safe platform for young adults' sexual health queries.

Beauty Acheampong (MA, Ohio University) is a second-year Ph.D. student in the Department of Communication Studies at the University of

Georgia. She hopes that her research on mental health from a non-western perspective will inform practice and policy on culturally appropriate interventions for African women at home and abroad.

References

Al Shamsi, H., Almutairi, A. G., Al Mashrafi, S., & Al Kalbani, T. (2020). Implications of language barriers for healthcare: A systematic review. *Oman Medical Journal*, *35*(2), e122. 10.5001/omj.2020.40

Barksdale, C. L., Rodick, W. H., 3rd, Hopson, R., Kenyon, J., Green, K., & Jacobs, C. G. (2017). Literature review of the National CLAS Standards: Policy and practical implications in reducing health disparities. *J Racial Ethn Health Disparities*, *4*(4), 632–647. 10.1007/s40615-016-0267-3

Betancourt, J. R., Renfrew, M., Green, A., Lopez, L., & Wasserman, M. (2012). Improving patient safety systems for patients with limited English proficiency: A guide for hospitals. *Agency for Healthcare Research and Quality*. Retrieved April 2 from https://www.ahrq.gov/sites/default/files/publications/files/lepguide.pdf

Bischoff, A. (2012). Do language barriers increase inequalities? Do interpreters decrease inequalities? In D. Ingleby, A. Chiarenza, W. Devillé, & I. Kotsioni (Eds.), *Inequalities in health care for migrants and ethnic minorities* (Vol. 2, pp. 128–143). Garant.

Charmaz, K. (2006). *Constructing grounded theory: A practical guide through qualitative analysis*. Sage.

Divi, C., Koss, R. G., Schmaltz, S. P., & Loeb, J. M. (2007). Language proficiency and adverse events in US hospitals: A pilot study. *International Journal for Quality in Health Care*, *19*(2), 60–67. 10.1093/intqhc/mzl069

Fernandez, A., Schillinger, D., Warton, E. M., Adler, N., Moffet, H., Schenker, Y., Salgado, M. V., Ahmed, A., & Karter, A. (2011). Language barriers, physician-patient language concordance, and glycemic control among insured Latinos with diabetes: The Diabetes Study of Northern California (DISTANCE). *Journal of General Internal Medicine*, *26*(2), 170–176. 10.1007/s11606-010-1507-6

Fisher, C. L., Ledford, C. J., Moss, D. A., & Crawford, P. (2018). Physician communication to enhance patient acupuncture engagement in family medicine. *Journal of Health Communication*, *23*(5), 422–429. 10.1080/10810730.2018.1458924

Fisher, W. R. (1987). *Human communication as narration: Toward a philosophy of reason, value, and action*. University of South Carolina Press.

Flores, G. (2006). Language barriers to health care in the United States. *New England Journal of Medicine*, *355*(3), 229–231. doi:10.1056/NEJMp058316

Flores, G., Abreu, M., Barone, C. P., Bachur, R., & Lin, H. (2012). Errors of medical interpretation and their potential clinical consequences: A comparison of professional versus ad hoc versus no interpreters [Comparative Study Research Support, U.S. Gov't, P.H.S.]. *Annals of Emergency Medicine*, *60*(5), 545–553. 10.1016/j.annemergmed.2012.01.025

Healthy People 2030. (2022). Health literacy in Healthy People 2030. *U.S. Department of Health and Human Services.* Retrieved April 20 from https://health.gov/healthypeople/priority-areas/health-literacy-healthy-people-2030

Hsieh, E. (2007). Interpreters as co-diagnosticians: Overlapping roles and services between providers and interpreters. *Social Science & Medicine, 64*(4), 924–937. 10.1016/j.socscimed.2006.10.015

Hsieh, E. (2015). Not just "getting by": Factors influencing providers' choice of interpreters. *Journal of General Internal Medicine, 30*(1), 75–82. 10.1007/s11606-014-3066-8

Leyva, M., Sharif, I., & Ozuah, P. O. (2005). Health literacy among Spanish-speaking Latino parents with limited English proficiency. *Ambulatory Pediatrics, 5*(1), 56–59. 10.1367/A04-093R.1

Ngo-Metzger, Q., Sorkin, D. H., & Phillips, R. S. (2009). Healthcare experiences of limited English-proficient Asian American patients: A cross-sectional mail survey. *The Patient: Patient-Centered Outcomes Research, 2*(2), 113–120. 10.2165/01312067-200902020-00007

Pérez-Escamilla, R., Garcia, J., & Song, D. (2010). Health care access among Hispanic immigrants: ¿Alguien está escuchando? [Is anybody listening?]. *NAPA Bulletin, 34*(1), 47–67. 10.1111/j.1556-4797.2010.01051.x

Schouten, B. C., Cox, A., Duran, G., Kerremans, K., Banning, L. K., Lahdidioui, A., van den Muijsenbergh, M., Schinkel, S., Sungur, H., Suurmond, J., Zendedel, R., & Krystallidou, D. (2020). Mitigating language and cultural barriers in healthcare communication: Toward a holistic approach. *Patient Education and Counseling, 103*(12), 2604–2608. 10.1016/j.pec.2020.05.001

Squires, A. (2009). Methodological challenges in cross-language qualitative research: A research review [Research Support, N.I.H., Extramural Review]. *International Journal of Nursing Studies, 46*(2), 277–287. 10.1016/j.ijnurstu.2008.08.006

Terui, S. (2016). *Cross-cultural comparisons on pathways between language barriers and health disparities* [Doctoral dissertation, The University of Oklahoma]. ProQuest Dissertations & Theses Full Text. http://search.proquest.com.ezproxy.lib.ou.edu/docview/608827269?accountid=12964

Terui, S. (2017). Conceptualizing the pathways and processes between language barriers and health disparities: Review, synthesis, and extension. *Journal of Immigrant and Minority Health*, 1–10. 10.1007/s10903-015-0322-x

The United States Department of Health & Human Services. (2020). *National CLAS standards.* https://thinkculturalhealth.hhs.gov/clas

The United States Census Bureau. (2022). *QuickFacts.* Retrieved July 1 from https://www.census.gov/quickfacts/fact/table/US/PST045221

Timmins, C. L. (2002). The impact of language barriers on the health care of Latinos in the United States: A review of the literature and guidelines for practice. *J Midwifery Womens Health, 47*(2), 80–96. 10.1016/s1526-9523(02)00218-0

6

TAKING ACTION TO INCREASE DIVERSITY AND INCLUSION IN THE WORKPLACE

Integrity- and Compliance-Based Training as a Foundation for Training in Organizations

Gabriela I. Morales, Anne P. Hubbell, and Greg G. Armfield

New Mexico State University

Learning Objectives

After reading this chapter, you will:

1 Understand the history of DEI training.
2 Be able to evaluate compliance-based and integrity-based training approaches.
3 Be able to review and break down best practices for DEI organizational training.
4 Be able to apply and justify best practices, e.g., adding integrity-based organizational training to compliance-based training programs.

Introduction

The first equal employment opportunity (EEO) legislation in the United States (US) was introduced by Congress in 1943. In 1948, President Truman signed executive order 9981 requiring equal treatment, opportunity, and desegregation of the armed services. However, 9981 did not expressly outlaw segregation (McCormick, 2007). Social and political unrest in the 1960s; including the civil rights movement, women's movement, anti-Vietnam war protests, and Tommy Smith and John Carlos protesting racial inequality from atop the Olympic Podium; along with societal changes, such as school integration forced from *Brown* v. *Board* in 1951, resulted in stronger equal rights legislation. Further legislation introduced in the 1960s had an enduring impact when

DOI: 10.4324/9781003333746-7

President Kennedy signed the Equal Pay Act in 1963 (Equal Employment Opportunity Commission, n.d.-b). This brought about the creation of the US Equal Opportunity Commission (EEOC) in 1965. It took several years until the EEOC had the power to hold organizations accountable for discrimination, but in 1972, the EEOC could actively file suits against organizations based on discrimination claims from employees and potential employees (Equal Employment Opportunity Commission, n.d.-c).

As a result, organizations in the 1970s needed to respond to EEOC claims to not lose significant amounts of money due to claims or complaints. This, in part, led to organizations initiating diversity training. Still, training was often compliance- or rule-based and designed to create awareness of racial differences in an increasingly diverse workforce (Vaughen, 2007). By the 1980s and 1990s, organizations primarily used compliance-based training to protect against or settle legal action as organizations were attempting to avoid losing money from EEOC claims. However, since the 1990s, the realization that diversity and diversity training can positively influence the bottom line has taken hold in organizations (Vaughen, 2007). In the past three decades, leading organizations, such as Accenture, Hilton, JPMorgan Chase, and Marriott, have embraced diversity, equity, and inclusion (DEI) training, including supporting domestic partner benefits and LGBTQ+ employee rights (DiversityInc Top 50, n.d.).

As US organizational cultures progressed, management scholars' discussions also evolved from a human relations approach of encouraging employee participation through showing concern, even fake concern, for associates in the 1920s–1950s to a human resources approach emphasizing employee involvement, the importance of associates being viewed as resources, to present day cultural intelligence (Kramer & Bisel, 2020). Research also shows inclusive leaders who understand cultural differences and similarities exist, value cultural differences, and work to expand their knowledge about cultural differences (Allen, 2017). Furthermore, leaders who practice cultural intelligence are more aware that ethnocentric tendencies impact their attitudes and actions (Allen, 2017).

Despite advances in cultural intelligence practices in organizations, DEI is a buzzword thrown around without context for many organizations. DEI is often used interchangeably when they represent distinctly different ideals. Understanding these concepts means understanding each idea for what it represents *individually*. According to the eXtension Foundation Impact Collaborative, DEI concepts (Diversity, Equity, and Inclusion, 2022a) are defined as follows:

Diversity: the presence of differences that may include race, gender, religion, sexual orientation, ethnicity, nationality, socioeconomic status, language, (dis)ability, age, religious commitment, or political perspective.

Equity: promoting justice, impartiality, and fairness within the procedures, processes, and distribution of resources by institutions or systems. Tackling equity issues requires an understanding of the root causes of outcome disparities within our society.

Inclusion: an outcome to ensure those that are diverse feel and/or are welcomed. Inclusion outcomes are met when you, your institution, and your program are truly inviting to all. To the degree to which diverse individuals can participate fully in the decision-making processes and development opportunities within an organization or group (para. 1–3).

Collectively, these concepts are "actions taken to establish awareness and transform mindsets, behaviors, and practices to create and sustain a diverse, equitable, and inclusive environment" (Diversity Equity, and Inclusion, 2022b, para. 4). Although some organizations have marketed their commitment to DEI, they have not done much to put DEI into actionable plans. Organizational costs could be significant when an organization has not embraced changing its corporate culture to demonstrate a commitment to DEI. Mediation settlements from discrimination claims filed through the EEOC rose from $333.2 million in 2020 to $350.7 million in 2021 (Bayt, 2022). DEI efforts can support growth in an organization, while the lack of such actions can result in significant losses. To mitigate potential costs, many scholars have provided experiences and guidance to integrate DEI into organizational cultures.

DEI Efforts in Organizations: Compliance- and Integrity-Based Training

Organizations often use training to inform employees of acceptable behaviors in the workplace. The two primary methods of training are compliance-based and ethics- or integrity-based. The most common form of training, *compliance-based training,* often consists of legal requirements, rules, policies, inappropriate practices, or behaviors organizational members should avoid. Compliance training focuses on a code of conduct: once individuals know what they should not do (e.g., sexual harassment, "don't do it" scenarios), they will not enact illegal or discriminatory behaviors. Such training is based on social exchange theory (SET) as created by Homans (1961). The idea behind Homan's SET is individuals will do what is in their best interest. This understanding of SET is based on one's perception of costs and rewards. If a behavior will benefit an individual and the costs do not outweigh the perceived reward, an individual is more likely to enact the behavior which will be rewarded (Homans, 1961).

Homans's (1961) perception of SET was based on a rigid behavioristic prediction of human choices. When this perception of SET is applied to organizations, individuals who act appropriately get to keep their jobs and/ or get promoted. Thus, individuals benefit from doing what an organization tells them is appropriate and inappropriate. Organizations whose employees act "appropriately" stand to continue to make money, have a good reputation, and maintain their organizational productivity goals. The organization also benefits by providing information on unacceptable behaviors to avoid lawsuits, EEOC claims and dispute resolutions, and employee turnover. Compliance training offers something positive for both the organization and the individual.

Compliance training is suitable for communicating expectations regarding what not to do but does not necessarily help employees know how to perform better, show respect for others, and develop cultural awareness and competence. Compliance-based training is still necessary for organizations, but when done alone as the only means of DEI training, it is considered the "low road" in training (Menzel, 2015, p. 351).

Organizations are now incorporating *integrity-based ethics training* along with compliance training. Often integrity-based training is called *ethics-* or *values-based training*. Both work toward organizational members learning more about their own implicit biases and/or prejudices. Integrity-based training is based on SET but more from the perspective of Blau (1964), who expanded on Homan's (1961) SET. Blau looked at SET from a relational perspective. Specifically "relationships that are based on trust and unspecified obligations" (Nachmias et al., 2022, p. 295). Through this relational perspective, Blau (1964) focused on the reciprocal and interpersonal nature of SET, including variables common to interpersonal relationships, like trust. Expanding this to organizations, trust in a company and among organizational members is considered one of the most important variables related to the smooth functioning of an organization. In contrast, the lack of trust has been linked to antisocial and hostile behaviors among organizational members (Chory & Hubbell, 2008).

SET has been employed in human resource research to encourage diversity and inclusion practices in organizations (Ashikali & Groeneveld, 2015). SET is particularly relevant to training and improving employee knowledge as "diversity management outcomes depend on the effect of employees' perceptions of diversity management on their attitudes and behavior" (Ashikali & Groeneveld, 2015, p. 758). Applying SET in this manner centers on developing positive relationships in organizations and using policies and training to improve diversity and inclusion in organizations (Nachmias et al., 2022). SET motivates individuals and organizations to participate in DEI training—mutual self-benefit.

Integrity-based training applies SET from Blau's relational perspective (1964) with a focus on employees treating each other with respect. To accomplish this, integrity-based training allows employees to examine their own implicit biases and prejudices to understand how their behaviors may reflect long-held beliefs they do not consciously realize they carry into interactions with colleagues (Bunnis, 2021a, 2021b).

Schein (2010) calls these core beliefs, which drive much of our behavior, assumptions about the world, or worldview. Integrity- or value-based training helps individuals understand how their core beliefs, whether consciously or subconsciously, can induce microaggressions or other discriminatory behaviors. Microaggressions, called *micro* for being "small slights" (Hubbell & Armfield, 2022, p. 29), include "everyday verbal, nonverbal, and environmental slights, snubs, or insults, whether intentional or unintentional, that communicate hostile, derogatory, or negative messages to target persons solely on their marginalized group membership" (Sue, 2010, p. 3). Often an organizational member may commit a microaggression against another organizational member and claim it was not intentional and meant no harm. Even without intent, damage is done, and as often individuals suffer a myriad of microaggressions, not just one, this can lead to a workplace being considered hostile and potentially leading to lawsuits and/or EEOC complaints. Integrity-based training can help individuals access and understand their biases and prejudices and create more respectful communication and behaviors while interacting with organizational members. By embracing integrity-based training, in addition to compliance-based training, organizations can create and implement more effective DEI training programs.

DEI Training Programs

Training programs are a common component of any organizational culture. From orientation to compliance training, employers and employees understand these elements as integral to the start and continuation of many work positions. However, training is perceived as just another task to complete—with no applicable content that makes an employee feel compelled to engage with provided information (Paskoff, 2022).

With efforts to increase DEI among organizations, training programs have recently expanded to include elements that focus on DEI. The current political and social justice climate in the US calls for DEI to be taken seriously and for organizations to become increasingly aware of the need to include training in their organizational structure. According to Holder (2018), employers are looking for DEI training for its leadership and describes "the key to successful DEI training, at this moment, is to strive to reach the audience 'where they are at'" (p. 8).

Compliance training is still needed to inform organizational members of (un)acceptable behaviors and often is required of organizations through lawsuits or EEOC complaints. But it is not enough to change an organization's culture from one where someone must complain to be seen to an organizational culture where individuals are valued, celebrated, and treated with respect by other members. The best way to change organizational culture is through integrity-based training where introspection and understanding of one's biases and prejudices can occur, while developing a better understanding of others' individual lived experiences. Examples of how integrity-based DEI training changes organizations are discussed next.

Examples and Impact of Integrity-Based Training

Treviño et al. (1999) surveyed more than 10,000 employees at six large US companies regarding what works in terms of improving organizational ethical/compliance climates. They found "a values-based cultural approach to ethics/compliance management works best" as it promotes employees "who are aware of ethics and compliance issues, who seek advice within the organization, and who are willing to deliver bad news to their managers or report ethical/legal violations" (p. 149). Some of the largest corporations like JPMorgan Chase and Goldman Sachs demonstrate companies that see value in diversity and inclusion training and continue to invest time, energy, and money into such efforts. JPMorgan Chase (2020) recently committed $30 billion to racial equity programs. Goldman Sachs and other DEI leading organizations partnered with Black women-led organizations to create One Million Black Women, an investment initiative that "commit[s] $10 billion in direct investment capital and $100 million in philanthropic support to address the dual disproportionate gender and racial biases that Black women have faced for generations" ($10 Billion, 2022, para. 1).

The Canadian healthcare organization William Osler Health System also champions DEI compliance training stating, "From a staff perspective, staff training and education focused on DEI versus diversity alone within Osler is beginning to transform the work and team environment and, in turn, positively impact the patient experience" (Gill et al., 2018, p. 196). In Osler's DEI training development, the organization encourages creating safe spaces for their employees to share experiences. Gill mentions, "Stories shared by colleagues have invoked compassion, empathy, and understanding" (p. 197). Integrity-based training at Osler took the form of crucial conversations held among organizational members in safe spaces.

In another health organization, the Mayo Clinic, a year-long assessment of their DEI efforts of their diversity and inclusion task force involved using anonymous "free text comments" on DEI issues they experienced (Enders et al., 2020). The components of their assessment included three items: 1) Recruitment, 2) Culture, and 3) Promotion (Enders et al., 2020). Some of the elements within *recruitment* focused on recruiting a diverse population to be part of this assessment. *Culture* included a focus on leadership training to equip organizational members to address issues that stem from the "hierarchical nature of leadership" and "nudges" or use "subtle prompts or shifts in design that enable or discourage a given behavior" (p. 3) to encourage "appropriate behavior at the moment the behavior occurs [and] is more likely to achieve our goals" (p. 3). Specifically, they looked at *nudges* in the context of diversity and inclusion, which "may serve to raise awareness of unconscious biases or even change organizational processes" (p. 3). Finally, *promotion* included "readiness with regard to their planned path to promotion," providing those who need assistance with mentoring (p. 4). In addition, a blinded promotion review for all junior staff was included. Employees showed the highest support for the blinded promotion reviews and items focused on DEI training. Nudges, however, were not well supported. One interesting finding was that while nudges were not nearly as supported by white, non-Latinx staff members, minority groups welcomed supportive nudges and blinded reviews (Enders et al., 2020).

These studies provide insight into integrity-based DEI efforts in organizations. It is important to highlight that each organization needs to do a thorough assessment of its particular needs. This has become even more important with the civil unrest the US has experienced in recent years, such as the murders of George Floyd, Breonna Taylor, Ahmaud Abery, Dreasjon Reed, McHale Rose, Sean Monterrosa, and many others; the Portland Trump Caravan; the Atlanta mass shooting that targeted three spas; or the mass Walmart shooting in El Paso, TX, among other events. Focusing on DEI has become a priority among organizations (Diversity Equity and Inclusion, 2022b). Integrity-based DEI efforts should not be thought of as a tool kit that is disseminated once. DEI training is a long-term commitment where organizations should address ongoing social and cultural change. The following section will provide some suggestions for DEI training and workshops.

What Can Be Included in DEI Integrity-Based Training

What are the must-haves for DEI training? While there is no one-size-fits-all answer, it must be acknowledged that various efforts have been created to address issues of DEI in organizations.

Structurally speaking, workplaces around the US have "become microcosms that reflect pervasive inequities and gaps found in the culture at large, and the intersections of different systems of oppression (e.g., sexism, racism) result in different disparities even among the marginalized" (Wong, 2019, p. 26). Furthermore, Garibay (2014) argues workplaces have been created to purposely exclude those considered marginalized (e.g., women, people of color and/or with disabilities, LGBTQ+ identities, and religious minorities). There is a need to understand the problems individuals experience within organizational structures, starting with *implicit bias.*

According to the National Education Association Center for Social Justice (NEA, 2021), implicit bias is defined as:

> a mental process that stimulates negative attitudes about people who are not members of one's own "in-group." Implicit bias leads to discrimination against people who are not members of one's racial group. Implicit bias operates in what researchers call our "implicit mind," the part of the brain that we commonly call the "subconscious" or the "unconscious." This means that implicit bias can operate in an individual's mind without a conscious awareness of this process (para. 2).

Implicit biases are often considered the cause of microaggressions. Most often, microaggressions go unnoticed, eventually causing issues within an organization. It is crucial to acknowledge microaggressions take place in organizations across the country and around the world. Microaggressions cannot simply be categorized as *overreactions* to something someone said or did to another person. Constant exposure to microaggressions can harm employees, their morale, and their willingness to remain with the organization.

According to Garibay (2014), microaggressions can encompass race, disability, gender, and sexual orientation, among others. While Garibay's work focuses on educational settings, microaggressions occur in all workplace settings and provide examples of *hidden messages.* For example, when it comes to race, Garibay provides the following example, "A white student clutches her or his backpack tightly as a Black or Latino student passes her or him" (p. 11). The hidden message is "You and your group are criminals or dangerous" (p. 11).

Recommendations for DEI Training

Diversity and inclusion training can help with employee morale and provide a space for underrepresented groups to feel heard and valued (Fernandes, 2022). Here, we will detail strategies organizations can utilize and implement with the support of leadership and the organization.

Recommendation 1: Think beyond the Toolkit

SET (Blau, 1964) can help understand why individuals change their behavior and how to encourage meaningful change. According to SET, individuals will seek to stay in relationships and situations where they perceive greater benefits than costs. By focusing on SET theory, organizations will focus less on DEI training as merely a *toolkit*.

An overreliance on toolkits results in a static DEI approach, as what works for one organization will automatically work at another. Using a toolkit, or what has been used by other organizations, can be a start for how to think about DEI training. But, just doing what another organization has done is akin to thinking that DEI issues can be "fixed" through a prescription or a one-size-fits-all formula for every organization.

That said, compliance programs can easily be designed from existing toolkits. DEI compliance training is often focused on the legal expectations of an organization. For example, do not treat people in a discriminatory way. These types of toolkits are transferable across companies. Compliance training is helpful for organizational members to understand federal laws and consequences. Here, however, the recommendation is for changing the organizational culture to one of inclusion and respect, which requires compliance training coupled with integrity-based training.

Recommendation 2: Encourage DEI Reflection and Dialogue

As discussed above, understanding implicit biases; the definitions of DEI; and providing a safe space for employees and leaders to reflect on their own biases and prejudices is vital to creating a culturally open and respectful organizational culture. Examples of these types of programs include reflective exercises where individuals dive into their own beliefs in conversation with others (Bunniss, 2021a, 2021b) and the use of instruments like the Harvard Implicit Bias test through Project Implicit, 2011). Project Implicit includes online questionnaires so individuals can better understand their own implicit biases regarding "race, gender, sexual orientation" (para. 1), among other topics, including attitudes toward individuals with disabilities. Once individuals complete the questionnaire, they should be encouraged to discuss what they learned, why they feel they may hold a bias toward some groups, and encouraged to share their lived experiences that may have led to these biases. For example, an individual may have grown up in a family that displayed prejudice toward Black Americans and may have turned away from these attitudes as an adult. However, some biases may still exist as their basic values or assumptions. Engaging in this process will help a person realize these assumptions continue to influence their behavior. It is crucial that tools like the implicit bias questionnaire not be used in isolation. They should be part of a toolbox and an opportunity for reflection and connection to how bias influences behaviors.

Integrity-based training should also include examples of issues like microaggressions and, where possible, encourage organizational participants to share when they have experienced these actions in the organization. For example, if an individual with a mental health diagnosis has been told they were "too emotional" over something that happened, it could be a microaggression regarding their mental health. Furthermore, if they identify as a woman, it may be the result of biases toward women and/or individuals with mental illnesses. Without understanding how these small slights impact another individual, organizational employees cannot know how language and judgments may seem benign but can originate from their implicit biases and lack of knowledge.

When conducting conversations like these, it can be challenging to keep the conversation from going to a point where negative experiences can take over the training. To prevent this, trainers can demonstrate ways of showing support for the individual sharing their experience while moving to how that individual wishes they had been treated. For example, a trainer should encourage all to hear the person relaying their experience and when the individual is done sharing, kindly tell them something like, "I see you." Then pause to let others share the same type of statement, should they wish. This could be followed by a question like, "How would you have liked to have been treated? How can we do better?" Another method can be to take a few minutes to reflect through journaling or writing their thoughts down on what was just presented to them. In this collective effort, the trainer or facilitator can collect reflections and share them anonymously with the group to engage in conversations about what can be done about the situation. What is essential in these conversations is that the trainer can use them to emphasize how we have to hear each other and try to be better at perspective-taking to communicate with more respect for each other. This is just one example of how to run a conversation like this, but anyone who does this type of training must receive extensive training on how to manage these conversations.

Recommendation 3: Establish Organizational DEI Teams and Identify Goals

The first step in this process is establishing a committee that can focus on building the organization's DEI efforts. Recruiting members for this committee should be a process that includes everyone within the organization, making it clear that everyone from all organizational levels needs to be invested, especially leadership. Leadership within organizations needs "to demonstrate the willingness [to participate in DEI training] and really model that inclusive, equitable behavior" (Colvin, 2022, para. 19). This process should not be taken lightly. Whoever becomes part of this committee needs to truly represent the organization's employee population. However, do not resort to tokenism or adding more work to already overworked and underpaid minority employees.

Once the committee is established, the first task is to thoroughly understand DEI, starting with the definitions of these terms, implicit bias, and microaggression. During this stage, it is recommended that questions be free of judgment. According to Fernandes (2022), "Establishing a diversity and inclusion program for your organization starts with developing a clear, detailed definition of what the program should entail" (para. 10). Thinking about the organization's DEI integration and defining the organization's goals is necessary (Kirkpatrick & Kirkpatrick, 2021, para. 4). Suggested questions to start thinking about are: 1) What does the organization hope to accomplish by including DEI training?; 2) What long-term efforts should be put into place to continue revisiting DEI training?; 3) How can the organization provide a safe place for employees to talk about topics like implicit bias and microaggressions?; 4) How will these results change the organizational culture and structure?; and 5) How will success be measured? What are the benchmarks and expectations of training?

Recommendation 4: Assess the Organization's Needs

Every organization will have its unique challenges that need to be addressed through DEI training. Because of this that DEI efforts need to incorporate employee feedback and feel safe doing so. Enders et al. (2020) describe their method, "Through a year-long process, the task force utilized anonymous free text comments from members of the Department of HSR on DEI issues they had faced" (p. 2). Others, like Georgetown University's National Center for Cultural Competence, offer recommendations for consideration when thinking about assessment:

1 Self-assessment is a strengths-based model.

2 A safe and non-judgmental environment is essential to the self-assessment process.

3 Self-assessment ensures the meaningful involvement of consumers, community stakeholders, and key constituency groups.

4 The results of the self-assessment are used to enhance and build capacity.

5 Diverse dissemination strategies are essential to the self-assessment process (Goode et al., 2002, p. 2).

The continuity of this assessment is crucial, and its accompanying training should be envisioned as a long-term effort. This leads us to our final strategy, the length of training programs.

Recommendation 5: Prolong DEI Training

According to Dobbin and Kalev (2016), diversity training "rarely lasts beyond a day or two, and several studies suggest that it can activate bias or spark backlash. Nonetheless, nearly half of the midsize companies use it, as do nearly all *Fortune* 500" (para. 7). This is one of the pitfalls when planning DEI training. Thinking of this type of training as a one-time fix does not present enough time to process the content; it inadvertently suggests to employees that this is not something the organization is 100% invested in. According to Bezrukova et al. (2016), in their meta-analysis of diversity training, they found a "strong and significant relationship between the length of diversity training and effect sizes suggesting that diversity programs that are *longer* tend to be more effective" (p. 1244). This is because "longer programs provide more opportunities for contact" (p. 1244).

The goal of compliance programs, according to the US Office of Inspector General, is to develop and implement a regular educational training program for all employees and a compliance officer who is responsible for the training, so all employees know about and observe relevant Federal and State laws and standards (Bower, 2011). DEI training, notably the addition of integrity-based training in organizations, is expensive and potentially time-consuming, so often, such training may only occur once a year. The critical element of such training is based on assessments of the organization and where training is most needed, implemented every year without fail.

Conclusion

Too often, organizations limit training on DEI to slides with a quiz or a toolkit that includes a few things done at another organization that seemed to work. Organizations need to continually assess what is happening internally and create, with employee input, methods to encourage critical conversations and self-reflection to constantly improve how individuals in the organization treat each other.

Compliance training or basic DEI training completed in most organizations is vital in teaching organizational members what is and is not acceptable. However, organizations must go beyond this to make meaningful changes in the organizational culture. To do this organizations must engage in integrity training to help organizational members access their own biases and prejudices and provide a safe space to examine and learn from others about microaggressions. Organizations must continuously monitor and develop DEI training to make these changes.

Finally, training, of any sort, must include organizational leadership, and leaders should exemplify diversity and inclusion in their attitudes, behaviors, and hiring decisions. If an organization ultimately "buys into" DEI training and the work it takes to change the organizational culture to be truly inclusive, this will be seen in those leading the company.

In this chapter, we examined how integrity-based training from the perspective of SET and goal-setting theories can help organizations create better DEI training and improve organizational culture to one with fewer EEOC complaints, better profitability, and become an inclusive and respectful organization. Training is one method toward improving the inclusivity of organizations and, if done well, can communicate to organizational members that the organization values them.

Discussion Questions

1 Consider your own implicit biases and discuss them as a group. For example, have you ever addressed a woman you just met as "Mrs." instead of "Ms." or "Dr.?" Talk about what each of these could mean to a woman, especially a woman who has achieved the role of Dr. and/or is not married. How could it be considered offensive or a microaggression? Discuss how organizations can be impacted through loss of productivity in a situation like this—how would the person being treated dismissively see their value in the organization? Would they want to leave the organization?

2 Think about an organization you are a part of. Where do you think they could do a better job with DEI training? If you were the consultant for that organization, what would you suggest it do to assess organizational issues concerning violations of DEI? What goals could be set at the end of the DEI training?

3 Discuss a time when you experienced some sort of compliance training, even if it was to tell you how to do a job. What was good about that training, and what was missing? How could an integrity-based training model have improved that training? How would you improve inclusion and the organizational culture if you were to lead this training?

Author Bios

Gabriela I. Morales (Ph.D. University of New Mexico) is an Assistant Professor in the Department of Communication Studies at New Mexico State University. Her research focuses on health disparities, intersections of culture and health, minoritized populations' health-related narratives, as well as diversity, equity, and inclusion in educational and healthcare contexts.

Anne P. Hubbell (Ph.D. Michigan State University) is a Professor in the Department of Communication Studies at New Mexico State University. Her research focuses on trust and ethical leadership, mental health, invisible disabilities, and improving cancer screening among underrepresented populations.

Greg G. Armfield (Ph.D., University of Missouri-Columbia) is a Professor and Department Head in the Department of Communication Studies at New Mexico State University. His research explores organizational culture and communication and sport. He has published two books about ESPN with Peter Lang and an Introduction to Human Communication textbook with Kendall Hunt.

References

$10 billion in direct capital investment. (2022). *Goldman Sachs*. https://www.goldmansachs.com/our-commitments/sustainability/one-million-black-women/

Allen, B. J. (2017). Women as inclusive leaders: Intersectionality matters. In C. M. Cunningham, H. M. Crandall, & A. M. Dare (Eds.). *Gender, communication, and the leadership gap* (pp. 13–23). Information Age Publishing, Inc.

Ashikali, T., & Groeneveld, S. (2015). DM in public organizations and its effect on employees' affective commitment: The role of transformational leadership and the inclusiveness of the organizational culture. *Review of Public Personnel Administration, 35*(2), 146–168. 10.1177/0734371X13511088

Bayt, K. S. (2022). EEOC roundup: Top 5 takeaways for employers on the 2021 enforcement and litigation statistics. *The National Law Review, XII*(327). https://www.natlawreview.com/article/eeoc-roundup-top-5-takeaways-employers-2021-enforcement-and-litigation-statistics

Bezrukova, K., Spell, C. S., Perry, J. L., & Jehn, K. A. (2016). A meta-analytical integration of over 40 years of research on diversity training evolution. *Psychological Bulletin, 142*(11). 1227–1274. 10.1037/bul0000067

Blau, P. M. (1964). *Exchange and power in social life*. John Wiley & Sons.

Bower, J. (2011). How effective is your compliance training? *Journal of Health Care Compliance*, *13*(6), 37–40.

Bunniss, S. (2021a). Making courageous conversation in healthcare (part I): Designing and evaluating values based reflective practice® training for healthcare professionals in Scotland. *Health and Social Care Chaplaincy*, *9*(2), 242–257. 10.1558/hscc.40701

Bunniss, S. (2021b). Making courageous conversation in healthcare (part II): Exploring the impact of values based reflective practice® on professional practice. *Health and Social Care Chaplaincy*, *9*(2), 258–277. 10.1558/hscc.40702

Chory, R. M., & Hubbell, A. P. (2008). Organizational justice and managerial trust as predictors of antisocial employee responses. *Communication Quarterly*, *56*, 357–375. 10.1080/01463370802448121

Colvin, C. (2022). *The dual imperative in DEI for trainers and leaders.* HR Dive. https://www.hrdive.com/news/maria-morukian-dei-for-trainers/618492/

Diversity, equity, and inclusion: A professional development offering of the eXtension Foundation Impact Collaborative. (2022a). eXtension Foundation Impact Collaborative. https://dei.extension.org/

Diversity equity, and inclusion: Why it matters. (2022b). St. Bonaventure University Online. https://online.sbu.edu/news/why-dei-matters

DiversityInc Top 50 Lists Since 2001. (n.d.). DiversityInc. https://www.diversityinc.com/diversityinc-top-50-lists-since-2001/

Dobbin, F., & Kalev, A. (2016). Why diversity programs fail. *Harvard Business Review.* https://hbr.org/2016/07/why-diversity-programs-fail

Equal Employment Opportunity Commission. (n.d.-b). *The equal pay act.* U.S. Equal Employment Opportunity Commission (EEOC). https://www.eeoc.gov/statutes/equal-pay-act-1963

Equal Employment Opportunity Commission. (n.d.-c). *Timeline of the Important EEOC Events.* (n.d.). U.S. Equal Employment Opportunity Commission (EEOC). https://www.eeoc.gov/youth/timeline-important-eeoc-events

Enders, F. T., Golembiewski, E. H. Pacheco-Spann, L. M., Allyse, M., Mielke, M. M., & Balls-Berry, J. E. (2020). Building a framework for inclusion in health services research: Development of and pre-implementation faculty and staff attitudes towards the Diversity, Equity, and Inclusion (DEI) plan at Mayo Clinic. *Journal of Clinical and Translational Science*, *5*(1), E88. doi:10.1017/cts.2020.575

Fernandes, P. (2022). *Creating a diversity and inclusion training program.* Business News Daily. https://www.businessnewsdaily.com/9782-diversity-training.html

Garibay, J. (2014). *Diversity in the classroom.* UCLA Diversity & Faculty Development. https://equity.ucla.edu/wp-content/uploads/2016/06/Diversityin theClassroom2014Web.pdf

Gill, G. K., McNally, M. J., & Berman, V. (2018). Effective diversity, equity, and inclusion practices. *Healthcare Management Forum*, *31*(5). 196–199. 10.1177/0840470418773785

Goode, T. W., Jones, W., & Mason, J. (2002). *A guide to planning and implementing cultural competence organizational self-assessment.* National Center for Cultural Competence, Georgetown University Child Development Center University Center for Excellence in Developmental Disabilities. https://nccc.georgetown.edu/documents/ncccorgselfassess.pdf

Holder, L. (2018). A paradigm shift in race consciousness drives the growing demand for diversity, equity, and inclusion consultation. https://static1.squarespace.com/static/5f25d9603966632bfcc18474/t/5f6bff2c8b0e0d7a10857f4f/1600913197749/Paradigm+Shift+Article%281%29.pdf

Homans, G. C. (1961). *Social behaviour: Its elementary forms.* Harcourt, Brace & World.

Hubbell, A., & Armfield, G. G. (2022). Relationship quality matters: LMX and mental health in the workplace. In J. Kahlow (Ed.). *Cases on organizational communication and understanding understudied groups.* IGI Global.

JPMorgan Chase commits $30 billion to advance racial equity. (2020). JPMorgan Chase & Co. https://www.jpmorganchase.com/news-stories/jpmc-commits-30-billion-to-advance-racial-equity

Kirkpatrick, J. D., & Kirkpatrick, W. (2021). Stumped on how to measure DEI training? Association for Talent Development. https://www.td.org/magazines/td-magazine/stumped-on-how-to-measure-dei-training

Kramer, M. W., & Bisel, R. S. (2020). *Organizational communication: A lifespan approach.* (2nd ed.). Oxford.

McCormick, K. (2007). The evolution of workplace diversity. *The Houston Lawyer, 10.*

Menzel, D. C. (2015). Research on ethics and integrity in public administration: Moving forward, looking back. *Public Integrity, 17,* 343–370. 10.1080/10999922.2015.1060824

Nachmias, S., Mitsakis, F. V., Aravopoulou, E., Rees, C. J., & Kouki, A. (2022). Line managers' perceptions of diversity management: Insights from a social exchange theory perspective. *Employee Relations: The International Journal, 44*(2), 294–318. 10.1108/ER-12-2019-0484

NEA (2021). *Implicit bias, microaggressions, and stereotypes resources.* National Education Association Center for Social Justice. https://www.nea.org/resource-library/implicit-bias-microaggressions-and-stereotypes-resources

Paskoff, S. (2022). *Compliance training must do these 3 things to drive culture change.* Training Industry. https://trainingindustry.com/articles/compliance/compliance-training-must-do-these-3-things-to-drive-culture-change/

Project Implicit. (2011). Preliminary Information. https://implicit.harvard.edu/implicit/takeatest.html

Schein, E. H. (2010). *Organizational culture and leadership* (4th ed.). Jossey-Bass.

Sue, D. W. (2010). *Microaggressions in everyday life: Race, gender, and sexual orientation.* John Wiley & Sons Inc.

Treviño, L. K., Weaver, G. R., Gibson, D. G., & Toffler, B. L. (1999). Managing ethics and legal compliance: What works and what hurts. *California Management Review, 41*(2), 131–151. 10.2307/41165990

Vaughen, B. E. (2007). The history of diversity training & its pioneers. *Strategic Diversity & Inclusion Management Magazine, 1*(1), 11–16. https://diversityofficermagazine.com/diversity-inclusion/the-history-of-diversity-training-its-pioneers/

Wong, C. (2019). Changing organizational culture: From embedded bias to equity & inclusion. *Professional Safety, 64*(8), 26–30. https://www.assp.org/docs/default-source/psj-articles/f1_0819.pdf?sfvrsn=0

7

REIMAGINING FACULTY←→ INSTITUTIONAL ENGAGEMENT WITH EQUITABLE AND INCLUSIVE PRACTICES TO FOSTER MEANINGFUL ORGANIZATIONAL CHANGEMAKING IN HIGHER EDUCATION

Wilfredo Alvarez[1] *and Maria J. Genao-Homs*[2]

[1]*Metropolitan State University of Denver;* [2]*Hamilton College*

Learning Objectives

After reading this chapter, you will:

1 Understand structural changes taking place in higher education pertaining to student demographics, needs, teaching, and learning.
2 Be able to identify specific teaching practices that respond to current higher education changes.
3 Establish a conceptual foundation to understand institutional support services that advance inclusive teaching practices.

Introduction

According to Forde and Carpenter (2020), "Faculty developers have a unique opportunity to reframe education to respond to the challenges of redesigning instruction with a particular focus on replacing traditional pedagogical frameworks that have not been effective for all students, especially historically underserved students with new inclusive pedagogies" (p. 1). Faculty developers are the stakeholders primarily responsible for developing and implementing curricula in higher education organizations. As a result of the present dynamic challenges in higher education—for example, the influx of first-generation students—this stakeholder group has a vital responsibility to respond to these changes in innovative ways. Given this backdrop, in this chapter, we respond to Forde and Carpenter's (2020) call to action by providing practical recommendations based on

DOI: 10.4324/9781003333746-8

our research and professional experiences as teachers, scholars, and administrators in higher education. We emphasize three primary themes to structure our narrative: first, we discuss some of the ways that higher education should develop targeted strategies to socialize faculty members to build their capacity to apply inclusive teaching practices. Second, we advance approaches pertaining to faculty members' engagement with inclusive pedagogical practices, and their imperative nature in today's rapidly changing higher education environment (Aragón et al., 2017; Seemiller & Grace, 2018). Third, we discuss the need for faculty members to understand and use, and for institutions to provide, student support resources to enhance inclusive practices (Cisneros & Rivarola, 2020). Throughout this chapter, we highlight practical recommendations that advance those efforts.

Case Study: Organizational Changemaking in Contemporary Higher Education

US society and higher education in particular are experiencing major structural changes (Alvarez, 2022; Putnam, 2020; Williams et al., 2005). To respond to those changes effectively, organizations need engaged and innovative changemakers. For example, today's higher education environment could be characterized as a space of tensions seeking resolutions; one of those tensions is the divergence between "traditional pedagogical frameworks" (Forde & Carpenter, 2020, p. 1) and new modes of instructional design and implementation (Tobin & Behling, 2018). We believe this tension represents a conflict between a social system's (higher education) desire for homeostasis and the pull of chaotic and complex change. In reference to this conflict, Coser (1957) observed, "conflict ... prevents the ossification of the social system by exerting pressure for innovation and creativity" (p. 197). Furthermore, Coser (1957) added that "social arrangements which have become habitual and totally patterned are subject to the blight of ritualism ... so that their habitual training becomes an incapacity to adjust to new conditions" (p. 199). We concur with Coser, and in this chapter, we outline some reasons why certain actions are necessary to respond to the changes currently taking place in higher education—specifically, as it pertains to faculty stakeholders' teaching processes.

Organizational change is partially the byproduct of interdependence within and between complex systems (Aschaffenburg & Maas, 1997). Considering this central dynamic, we seek to (re)envision higher education organizations and faculty stakeholders' relationship. To achieve this goal, according to Williams et al. (2005), "[t]he task, then, becomes identifying how to create powerful enough organizational learning so that deep and transformational change occurs" (p. 11). This is also what these authors call "second-order change," which is "deeper [and] deals with core values and norms and is more systemic and enduring" (p. 10). As a result, to help reimagine faculty members' role in shifting higher education organizations, we propose that: a) higher education expand and focus faculty members' socialization processes with particular attention to inclusive practices; b) faculty remain actively engaged with inclusive practices in their pedagogy by collaborating closely with the instructional design staff and learning about educational frameworks like Universal Design (Burgstahler, 2020); and c) faculty stay up-to-date with knowledge and information about best inclusive practices for student support services (Behling & Linder, 2017; Lombardi et al., 2018). We believe that embracing these strategic approaches denotes a devoted partnership between faculty and institutions at the service of student development. Nevertheless, for these strategies to be effective, both faculty stakeholders and higher education institutions must be engaged with each other and committed to the shared goal of supporting today's students' changing needs.

Student demographics on college campuses are changing rapidly and thus there are emerging complex needs among these new student populations. The Brookings Institution reports that "over 40% of entering students are first-gen, as are about one-third of graduating students" (Startz, para. 3) and this student segment faces significant challenges due to a lack of social and cultural capital (Alvarez, in press). This does not mean these students are not intellectually capable of managing the academic rigor, but they are at a disadvantage because they do not know how to navigate the modern college campus in order to be as successful as their non-first-generation peers (Alvarez, in press). Research shows that for first-generation, low-income, and historically underserved students supportive faculty members are by far more consequential than "student success coaches" (Alvarez & De Walt, 2022). These are institutionally assigned academic advisors who help students navigate course registration and curricular requirements (Gasman et al., 2017). Given these dynamic changes, it is imperative that faculty stakeholders adapt their teaching practices to meet today's students' needs. This chapter offers some ideas for how faculty could approach their vital organizational role in more inclusive ways. The remainder of the chapter outlines our recommendations for how faculty members can achieve this goal.

Faculty Stakeholders as Organizational Changemakers

As explained by Ryder et al. (2016), "Faculty members influence the climate for learning through multiple mechanisms at multiple levels: setting institutional academic policies, structuring curricula, and decid[ing] what to teach and how to design opportunities for learning in the classroom" (p. 348). This is important. And, as teachers, scholars, and practitioners, we welcome the opportunity to engage in this conversation about organizational change-making related to the faculty role and diversity, equity, and inclusion. Primarily, we are interested in engaging discussions about the current challenges higher education faces. Therefore, in this chapter, we grapple with the overarching question: In what innovative ways could faculty stakeholders re-envision their pedagogical practices to advance organizational changemaking in contemporary higher education? To this end, the methods we suggest should be part of a multiprong effort to ensure that "inclusion and excellence are inseparable and mutually reinforcing" (Williams et al., 2005, p. 9). Overall, we believe that a reimagining of the faculty role improves the overall student, and faculty, experience, which can engender consequential organizational changemaking. In addition, the approaches we present in this chapter can help faculty innovate how they communicatively enact their role. A focus on faculty members is essential because this is a core stakeholder group that can influence the organization's functioning, especially as it pertains to student development (Hurtado, 2007; Pascarella & Terenzini, 2005). Ryder et al. (2016) capture the faculty's significance to higher education institutions:

> Faculty members have long been considered primary socializing agents in higher education … as they set and deliver the curriculum, advance knowledge through research and scholarship, and engage the campus and community through service. Through this intellectual leadership, faculty members influence student learning and development, including students' openness to diversity and challenge. (p. 339)

In the following pages, we propose reconsidering some key aspects of the faculty role. A caveat is that this goal is closely linked to institutions' willingness and ability to invest resources to support faculty stakeholders. We start with some ideas for rethinking faculty socialization processes.

Reimagining Faculty Socialization Processes

To our knowledge, there is no gold standard format for higher education institutions to follow regarding effective faculty orientation programs.

Oftentimes, this is a one-time institutional requirement. We believe higher education would benefit greatly from the strategic redesign of faculty socialization processes. From implementing well-developed and targeted orientation programs to expansive professional development opportunities (Forde & Carpenter, 2020), higher education should advance its efforts to prepare today's faculty to teach more inclusively (Bryson et al., 2020). For example, faculty orientation programs should be more longitudinal and immersive, and include robust information about student support resources. In addition, institutions should design comprehensive professional development opportunities to encourage faculty to advance their pedagogical practices. Professional development opportunities directly connected to innovative and inclusive teaching practices should be incorporated into tenure and promotion decisions, and for nontenure line faculty, there should be incentives built into professional advancement. This initiative could be a collaboration between Academic Affairs, Student Affairs, the Center for Teaching and Learning, and Human Resources. This collaboration could be spearheaded by a standing working group chaired by an appointed member of Academic Affairs in a service capacity. The collaborators would have an active role in developing and implementing the orientation curriculum. These efforts are especially significant in the face of a more diverse faculty joining the academy (Alvarez & De Walt, 2022).

Faculty Identity

The professoriate is becoming increasingly diverse as we see higher numbers of nonwhite, first-generation, undocumented, and queer-identified doctoral students graduating with aspirations to join the academy (NCES, 2019). Ignoring the experiences that faculty with historically marginalized identities encounter along the route to becoming faculty does not help them feel connected (Alvarez et al., 2016). And, these experiences do not evaporate as new people enter the faculty ranks (Alvarez & De Walt, 2022). On the contrary, these experiences continue with higher stakes (Councilor, 2022). Therefore, higher education institutions must consider how they onboard, and recruit and retain, diverse faculty members.

Faculty orientation programs should connect new faculty to the campus community over the course of the faculty member's first *and* second year—not just the typical three to five days prior to the start of their first academic term. Part of the reason for this recommendation is that new faculty are already dealing with information overload as they attempt to get settled into a new life. To unpack so much information in a few days and expect the person to absorb and apply, it might be somewhat unrealistic and even futile in the long term. According to Gómez (2009), part of the reason for this haste is that organizations tend to view time as a scarce resource, which affects the formal structures that they create to socialize and retain new organizational members. In contrast, incorporating a prolonged orientation curriculum that allows new faculty time to process and apply the new knowledge as they move through their broader socialization experience is more in line with what researchers have found regarding the early stages of socialization (Van Maanen & Schein, 1979). This early stage of organizational socialization produces a high degree of tension as the newcomer attempts to integrate into the organization. For instance, Woodrow and Guest (2020) posit that "socialization has been characterized as a time of insecurity, during which newcomers attempt to cope with and reduce stressful uncertainty" (p. 111).

Given this heightened period of psychological and physiological stress, we believe it is useful to expand the timeframe over which new faculty learn to adapt to the institution. This is especially important for people in historically marginalized groups, such as first-generation, racial minorities, LGBTQ+, and/or immigrant faculty, as they cope with particular challenges such as fear of belonging and acceptance, implicit bias behaviors, and microaggressions (Allen, 2023; McDonald & Mitra, 2019). Additionally, there is experiential variance between someone who recently finished graduate school and a more experienced faculty member. Thus, newly minted graduates and more experienced faculty should have programs tailored to their specific needs. A collaborative team made up of Academic Affairs, Center for Teaching and Learning, Student Affairs, and Human Resources should determine which strategies fit their specific culture and needs, but this is an important distinction regarding how new faculty are socialized. Several key stakeholders should be a part of this process: engaged faculty mentors, and staff members who will collaborate with new faculty to help them navigate academia's waters in those initial years—particularly, staff members who are knowledgeable about inclusive practices; for example, instructional design and accessibility services staff (Richardson et al., 2019).

Faculty Mentors

Faculty orientation programs should equip faculty mentors with the competencies to support incoming faculty (Johnson, 2015). Institutions should train faculty mentors on matters related to implicit bias, systemic inequities in higher education (and their institution in particular), and inclusive teaching practices. In addition, faculty mentors should be people who have a deeper understanding of key campus resources such as student support services, including, but not limited to counseling services, financial aid, enrichment programs, and accessibility. As a result, at the end of this immersive faculty orientation program, incoming faculty should have a thorough understanding of these resources' primary functions. This type of orientation program's implementation should result in less non-white faculty attrition; it also communicates to all faculty that the institution is serious about the inclusion and retention (Haynes & Tuitt, 2020) of historically excluded people. To be effective, this must be a collaborative process that galvanizes the institution's human capital and other resources to create a culture of communal support. In sum, this is an effort that requires "all hands on deck."

Coalition-Building

As an administrator whose work focuses on addressing institutional inequities that disproportionately impact students with historically marginalized identities (i.e., nonwhite, undocumented, Pell-eligible, trans*, etc.), coalition-building is critical to my (Genao-Homs) work. As a Dean of Students for Diversity and Inclusion, I am aware of the relationship between leadership and employee role performance. My professional experience and research indicate that faculty-staff coalitions are critical to developing stakeholders' ability to understand and practice inclusivity. Consequently, as Marchiondo et al. (2021) observe, "Given the role of leaders in shaping employee perceptions ... academic leaders' diversity-related attitudes are apt to proximally shape faculty's perceptions of bias—and distally, then, faculty endorsement of diversity" (p. 4). This observation captures accurately some of the dynamics I experience when I attempt to work with my faculty colleagues to guide them in the process of embracing and applying inclusive practices.

In my experience, faculty members contact me regularly to seek guidance on available institutional resources to support students in their classes. Over the years, I noticed that when I get more opportunities to inform faculty on available DEI resources, they contact me less frequently. For this reason, after serving at various types of institutions, I am constantly advocating for invitations to present to faculty at their orientations or in general assembly meetings. Interestingly, sometimes I receive pushback to my outreach, which varies from dismissals to organizers yielding a handful of minutes to cover complex topics such as the experiences of first-generation students and hidden curricula (these are unspoken rules and implicit expectations in educational environments) (McNair et al., 2020). Overall, I agree with Furst and Cable (2008) when they posit that "managers must be able to 'unfreeze' employee beliefs that the status quo is acceptable and motivate the employees to make the desired changes" (p. 453). To this end, I learned that the extent to which I can get faculty buy-in pertaining to diversity and equity matters determines how effective we all can be to advance inclusive practices (Bryson et al., 2020). Taken together, in my professional experiences, the concept of coalition-building is vital to produce collaborations that lead to more inclusive strategies concerning the faculty's pedagogical practices.

Lastly, new faculty should develop greater knowledge about navigating the campus culture.

This is important because faculty members have the privilege of routinely interfacing with students as their captive audience (i.e., students must attend classes). For instance, faculty members could be critical in identifying students in crisis. To prepare for those circumstances, faculty could receive gatekeeper training (this is a type of training designed to identify students who might be dealing with suicidal ideation) as part of their orientation program (Holmes et al., 2021). Based on our professional experiences, engaging with these topics does not occur in depth. Anecdotally, we find that they are often omitted or significantly condensed. In sum, we believe these foci are critical to encouraging faculty members' more meaningful pedagogical engagement with students.

Reimagining Faculty Pedagogical Practices

According to Forde and Carpenter (2020), "Historically, some of the earliest research to revise the classroom instruction was based on increasing the multicultural understandings of all the students from culturally and linguistically diverse backgrounds" (pp. 1–2) (Ladson-Billings, 1994; Banks & McGee, 1996). Given the current institutional changes taking place (e.g., increasing student diversity), the need for faculty to adapt their teaching practices to today's institutional needs cannot be overemphasized. Consequently, we believe that every member of a college campus community has a responsibility to practice equity and inclusion within their spheres of influence (McNair et al., 2020). Faculty have a unique opportunity to engage with students during the most vulnerable time in their college career—their time in the classroom.

The power dynamic in the classroom context is inherently imbalanced as students look up to their teachers not only for acquiring knowledge in a specific subject matter, but also as informal mentors (Gasman et al., 2017). As demographics on college campuses continue to change, the needs of students also change, and it is important for faculty to understand *who* they are teaching (NCES, 2019; Richards et al., 2007). This context makes it imperative for faculty stakeholders to be well prepared and engaged in innovative pedagogical practices to work effectively with the latest college student generations (Ryder et al., 2016).

Storytelling

The use of personal anecdotes gives students a window into their teachers' humanity. Thus, the use of storytelling, telling personal and other people's stories, is an effective strategy to make the classroom space more inclusive and inviting of everyone's stories. Faculty members were once college students themselves. As such, they faced obstacles along the path to the front of the classroom. Storytelling is a high-impact strategy to develop connections with students (Landrum et al., 2019). This does not mean that faculty must share every detail of their life, and it also does not mean that we only share stories that are drama filled or have a happy ending. That is not real life. Students benefit from hearing authentic stories that speak to times when their teacher made mistakes and also stories of triumphs as well as mundane details about study habits, setbacks, and other experiences that facilitate relatability between teachers and students. It is important to note that some of these strategies are within faculty members' control. However, the institution should also demonstrate that it is invested in supporting faculty teaching development.

Teaching and Learning Centers

Higher education organizations should build and maintain professional resources to support pedagogy. A well-equipped Teaching and Learning Center (TLC) represents this type of support. This unit is typically staffed with at least one instructional design expert, and additional staff responsible for technological support related to pedagogy. Those employees support faculty with building and navigating their Learning Management Systems (LMS) websites or "shells," designing online courses, and developing effective face-to-face and online teaching strategies. Additionally, the TLC leads workshops and training programs to support faculty teaching through innovative frameworks such as Universal Design for Learning (UDL) to promote inclusive teaching (Tobin & Behling, 2018). Teaching workshops should be available throughout the year and address various aspects of effective teaching including managing classroom dynamics, applying innovative technologies, and incorporating experiential learning activities.

This Center could also be a space where faculty come together to meet other faculty from across academic disciplines. Such spaces are key to maintaining faculty connections with each other, and, potentially, fostering community and belonging (Gigliotti & Ruben, 2017). In sum, a well-resourced TLC is an essential academic support unit in a higher education institution because it supports and advances faculty members' ability to create and develop effective, and inclusive, pedagogical practices. This is vital to meet the needs of today's college students. Furthermore, TLCs are responsible for coordinating events that promote effective teaching. For example, the TLC at my institution (Alvarez) organizes a welcome-back event every fall semester. This event brings together faculty across campus who present and share ideas about innovative teaching practices. Many of the ideas faculty share relate to the theme of best teaching practices for inclusive excellence.

Creating Space for Best Practices

Another key aspect that we believe is fundamental to being an effective teacher in the modern higher education environment is creating spaces to communicate about best practices. When faculty share best practices, they provide useful information to others, but also receive feedback on their pedagogy. This approach helps faculty colleagues remain engaged with each other and also provides insights and perspectives to keep their teaching fresh as they gain a window view into other people's cutting-edge practices. This creates a feedback loop that prevents faculty teaching practices from becoming ossified as it could be the case if they remain insular and closed off to other people's observations of their teaching. This requires faculty and institutions to adjust at the micro and macro levels and to work in tandem to support the student experience in and out of the classroom.

Reimagining Faculty Engagement with Student Support Resources

Today's college experience includes an emergent group of support systems necessary to help students move through this process's transformational rigors (Cisneros & Raviola, 2020). As a result, faculty members' role performance would be enhanced by their ability to remain connected to those emergent and established support systems. For example, higher education organizations are cultivating their capacity to support students who come from families that did not attend college—i.e., first-generation college students. This particular type of student is representative of the major changes currently underway in higher education (NCES, 2019) as the number of first-generation college students is growing rapidly (Startz, 2022). Thus, institutions must demonstrate the ability to support those students if they are to remain viable and thrive into the future.

It is important to note that the extent to which faculty engage with student support resources represents an interdependent relationship between the faculty member and the institution—that is, institutions must create the conditions to support and encourage faculty's ability to stay current with those institutional resources.

Most contemporary higher education institutions provide student support services—e.g., accessibility services. To be engaged changemakers, faculty stakeholders should possess the knowledge necessary to access, explain, and share the student services—including their function, location, contact information (e.g., office extension), etc.—available. On any given day, it is likely that faculty will find themselves in a situation where this information will be useful, and perhaps critical, to a student. Furthermore, to take it one step further, faculty should become acquainted with at least one key person in those student support offices. This allows for a tactical hand-off of students in need of support directly to someone in those offices rather than sending them on a scavenger hunt. In sum, faculty members do not need to be experts, but should be relationally connected and knowledgeable enough to make links between students' needs and the campus' strategic resources to support those needs.

Student support services professionals have plenty of opportunities for committee work that could use faculty expertise. Nevertheless, for faculty to be more motivated and involved on these committees, institutional structures driven by strategic administrative action and reconfigured faculty members' role enactment must coalesce to revise what counts as meaningful "service" in the modern academy. Some actions that provide new types of opportunities for what counts as meaningful service include expanding the service expectation so that service related to students' co-curricular activities carries greater weight than it typically does in relation to traditional academic affairs-related service such as serving on faculty senate committees (Smith & Williams, 2007). This reconfiguring would be beneficial because serving on student affairs-related committees directly connects faculty with other colleagues across campus (e.g., Directors of student support services like the counseling center and the center for multicultural affairs) while indirectly connecting them with those critical campus resources.

Student affairs-related service committees can range the gamut in terms of their purpose, and faculty engagement on those committees will make them stronger teachers and advocates for students. We believe that this type of faculty professional development experience is beneficial to the primary organizational stakeholders, including faculty members themselves, students, and staff. The institutional service revision we propose here is also significant because, historically, many faculty members are perceived as distant from non-academic matters (Moore & Ward, 2010). However, it is also important to observe that there is some variability when it comes to norms and expectations regarding who participates on service committees (Hanasono et al., 2019). For instance, due to their hypervisibility in academia, faculty from racially marginalized groups often engage in what is called "invisible labor," and end up doing much more unrewarded service compared to their white counterparts (Carson et al., 2019), which leads to an uneven distribution of labor concerning service work (Patton et al., 2010). These dynamics shape the extent to which faculty members, but those from marginalized members in particular, engage in student affairs-related service activities. Overall, we believe that more engagement in student affairs committees opens the door for faculty-staff collaborations and also communicates that faculty are committed to being part of the overall student experience, including curricular and co-curricular activities.

Lastly, a collaborative partnership between academic affairs and student affairs to advocate for the importance of faculty members hearing from student support areas would be beneficial to student success (Smith & Williams, 2007). For instance, inviting campus leaders like the director of multicultural affairs to present or provide updates in spaces where faculty congregates (e.g., faculty senate meetings) is an effective inclusion strategy (Stewart, 2016). Staff members responsible for leading areas like the health center, accessibility, counseling services, and the multicultural center are eager to present the services available. Overall, faculty members should advocate for and share information about campus resources. Faculty members, especially those with tenure, influence, and senior status, should use their institutional capital to support students in various ways, including being more tuned in to the student experience beyond the classroom. We believe these activities are necessary to bring about organizational changemaking in contemporary higher education.

Practical Applications

In this chapter, we have asked that readers reimagine faculty members' role in shifting higher education organizations. We have shared actionable recommendations, along with personal examples, that faculty can feasibly apply within their own institutions. Although these actionable recommendations are specific to the context of higher education, we believe many of these suggestions could be creatively adapted to other types of organizations as well. As such, we encourage faculty as well as other types of organizational changemakers to adapt the recommendations above to their own unique organizational contexts.

Conclusion

Contemporary higher education is undergoing unprecedented changes (Bok, 2015). From demographic to technological transformation, today's social environment faces significant challenges that directly affect higher education. Consequently, stakeholders, like faculty, must demonstrate that they are responding to these challenges in intentional and effective ways. This step is vital and "among the most important civic outcomes of college if higher education is to successfully prepare students for active citizenship in our society" (Ryder et al., 2016, p. 339). For instance, higher education "leaders agree that valuing inclusive excellence is a priority under the diversity, equity, and inclusion umbrella, but have difficulty realigning their priorities, policies, and budgets" (Forde & Carpenter, 2020, p. 4). Therefore, in this chapter, we offered practical recommendations that equip faculty stakeholders with the tools necessary to be on the front-line of inclusive practices to meet the challenges created by contemporary social and institutional transformations as well as college students' shifting needs. To close, for higher education organizations to be able to respond to today's multifaceted and dynamic changes, it is imperative for faculty stakeholders to be(come) changemakers.

Discussion Questions

1 In what ways are current structural changes in higher education challenging faculty members to adapt their teaching to more inclusive practices?
2 What is the relationship between this new generation of college students' needs and the demands to modify our teaching practices to meet those needs?
3 What should be the role of technology to support more inclusive ways of teaching in contemporary higher education?

Author Bios

Wilfredo Alvarez (he/him) is an Assistant Professor of Communication Studies at Metropolitan State University of Denver. His teaching and research focus on communication issues related to social identity (e.g., race, social class, and immigration). He is interested in how communication practices create, maintain, and challenge systems of oppression, discrimination, and inequity.

Maria J. Genao-Homs (she/her) is the Associate Dean for Diversity and Inclusion at Hamilton College. She serves as an advocate for students from historically marginalized identities by leading the development of a vision, strategy, and accompanying initiatives to encourage a systemic and inclusive campus culture that celebrates and respects the unique qualities of all its members.

References

Allen, B. J. (2023). *Difference matters: Communicating social identity* (3rd ed.). Waveland Press.

Alvarez, W. (2022). Teaching in higher education as a nonnative English-speaking immigrant. In W. Alvarez, & P. S. De Walt (Eds.), *Voicing diverse teaching experiences, approaches, and perspectives in higher education* (pp.1–24). IGI Global. 10.4018/978-1-7998-9000-3.ch001

Alvarez, W. (in press). My pre-first-gen success story: Navigating college pre and post acceptance as a nonwhite/nonnative English-speaking immigrant. In G. Pacheco, Jr. (Ed.), *First-gen stories for success*. Kendall Hunt.

Alvarez, W., & De Walt, P. S. (Eds.) (2022). *Voicing diverse teaching experiences, approaches, and perspectives in higher education*. IGI Global. 10.4018/978-1-7998-9000-3

Alvarez, W., De Walt, P. S., Genao-Homs, M. J., & Yun, J. (2016). Multidisciplinary graduate student alliance: Crafting a diverse peer-mentoring network within and beyond a predominantly white institution. In B. G. Johannessen (Ed.), *Global mentoring networks: Politics, policies, and practices* (pp. 127–154). Springer. 10.1007/978-3-319-27508-6_8

Aragón, O. R., Dovidio, J. F., & Graham, M. J. (2017). Colorblind and multicultural ideologies are associated with faculty adoption of inclusive teaching practices. *Journal of Diversity in Higher Education, 10*(3), 201–215. 10.1037/dhe0000026

Aschaffenburg, K., & Maas, I. (1997). Cultural and educational careers: The dynamics of social reproduction. *American Sociological Review, 62*, 573–587. 10.2307/2657427

Banks, J. A., & McGee, C. A. (1996). The intergroup education movement. In J. A. Banks (Ed.), *Multicultural education, transformative knowledge, and action: Historical and contemporary perspectives* (pp. 251–277). Teachers College Press.

Behling, K. T., & Linder, K. E. (2017). Collaborations between centers for teaching and learning and offices of disability services: Current partnerships and perceived challenges. *Journal of Postsecondary Education and Disability, 30*(1), 5–15. https://eric.ed.gov/?id=EJ1144608

Bok, D. (2015). *Higher education in America*. Princeton University Press.

Burgstahler, S. (2020). *Creating inclusive learning opportunities in higher education: A universal design toolkit*. Harvard Education Press.

Bryson, B. S., Masland, L., & Colby, S. (2020). Strategic faculty development: Fostering buy-in for inclusive excellence in teaching. *The Journal of Faculty Development, 34*(3), 107–116. https://link.gale.com/apps/doc/A651906896/AONE?u=nysl_oweb&sid=googleScholar&xid=6f2496c2

Carson, T. L., Aguilera, A., Brown, S. D., Peña, J., Butler, A., Dulin, A., ... & Cené, C. W. (2019). A seat at the table: Strategic engagement in service activities for early career faculty from underrepresented groups in the academy. *Journal of the Association of American Medical Colleges*, *94*(8), 1089–1093. 10.1097/acm.0000000000002603

Cisneros, J., & Rivarola, A. R. R. (2020). Undocumented student resource centers. *Journal of College Student Development*, *61*(5), 658–662. 10.1353/csd.2020.0064

Coser, L. A. (1957). Social conflict and the theory of social change. *The British Journal of Sociology*, *8*(3), 197–207. 10.2307/586859

Councilor, K. C. (2022). Transformational pedagogy, or teaching while trans. In W. Alvarez, & P. S. De Walt (Eds.), *Voicing diverse teaching experiences, approaches, and perspectives in higher education* (pp. 28–38). IGI Global. 10.4018/978-1-7998-9000-3.ch003

Forde, T., & Carpenter, R. (2020). Situating inclusive excellence in faculty development programs and practices. *Journal of Faculty Development*, *34*(3), 1–5. https://link.gale.com/apps/doc/A651906895/AONE?u=nysl_oweb&sid=googleScholar&xid=ca14bafd

Furst, S. A., & Cable, D. M. (2008). Employee resistance to organizational change: Managerial influence tactics and leader–member exchange. *Journal of Applied Psychology*, *93*(2), 453–462. 10.1037/00219010.93.2.453

Gasman, M., Nguyen, T. H., Conrad, C. F., Lundberg, T., & Commodore, F. (2017). Black male success in STEM: A case study of Morehouse College. *Journal of Diversity in Higher Education*, *10*(2), 181–200. 10.1037/dhe0000013

Gigliotti, R. A., & Ruben, B. D. (2017). Preparing higher education leaders: A conceptual, strategic, and operational approach. *Journal of Leadership Education*, *16*(1), 96–114. 10.12806/V16/I1/T1

Gómez, L. F. (2009). Time to socialize: Organizational socialization structures and temporality. *The Journal of Business Communication*, *46*(2), 179–207. 10.1177/0021943608328077

Hanasono, L. K., Broido, E. M., Yacobucci, M. M., Root, K. V., Peña, S., & O'Neil, D. A. (2019). Secret service: Revealing gender biases in the visibility and value of faculty service. *Journal of Diversity in Higher Education*, *12*(1), 85–98. 10.1037/dhe0000081

Haynes, C., & Tuitt, F. (2020). Weighing the risks: The impact of campus racial climate on faculty engagement with inclusive excellence. *Journal of the Professoriate*, *11*(2), 31–58. https://caarpweb.org/wp-content/uploads/2021/01/Weighing-the-Risk_Haynes_Tuitt_11_2.pdf

Holmes, G., Clacy, A., Hermens, D. F., & Lagopoulos, J. (2021). The long-term efficacy of suicide prevention gatekeeper training: A systematic review. *Archives of Suicide Research*, *25*(2), 177–207. 10.1080/13811118.2019.1690608

Hurtado, S. (2007). Linking diversity with educational and civic missions of higher education. *The Review of Higher Education*, *30*(1), 185–196. 10.1353/rhe.2006.0070

Johnson, W. B. (2015). *On being a mentor: A guide for higher education faculty* (2nd Edition). 10.4324/9781315669120

Ladson-Billings, G. (1994). *The dreamkeepers.* Jossey-Bass.

Landrum, R. E., Brakke, K., & McCarthy, M. A. (2019). The pedagogical power of storytelling. *Scholarship of Teaching and Learning in Psychology, 5*(3), 247–253. 10.1037/stl0000152

Lombardi, A., McGuire, J. M., & Tarconish, E. (2018). Promoting inclusive teaching among college faculty: A framework for disability service providers. *Journal of Postsecondary Education and Disability, 31*(4), 397–413. https://files.eric.ed.gov/fulltext/EJ1214261.pdf

Marchiondo, L. A., Verney, S. P., & Venner, K. L. (2021). Academic leaders' diversity attitudes: Their role in predicting faculty support for institutional diversity. *Journal of Diversity in Higher Education.* Advance online publication. 10.1037/dhe0000333

McDonald, J., & Mitra, R. (Eds.) (2019). *Movements in organizational communication research.* Routledge. 10.4324/9780203730089

McNair, T. B., Bensimon, E. M., & Malcom-Piqueux, L. (2020). *From equity talk to equity walk: Expanding practitioner knowledge for racial justice in higher education.* John Wiley & Sons. 10.1002/9781119428725

Moore, T. L., & Ward, K. (2010). Institutionalizing faculty engagement through research, teaching, and service at research universities. *Michigan Journal of Community Service Learning, 17*(1), 44–58.

National Center for Education Statistics [NCES]. (2019). *Digest of education statistics.* https://nces.ed.gov/programs/digest

Pascarella, E. T., & Terenzini, P. T. (2005). *How college affects students (Vol. 2): A third decade of research.* Jossey-Bass.

Patton, L. D., Shahjahan, R. A., & Osei-Kofi, N. (2010). Introduction to the emergent approaches to diversity and social justice in higher education special issue. *Equity & Excellence in Education, 43*(3), 265–278. 10.1080/10665684.2010.496692

Putnam, R. D. (2020). *The upswing: How America came together a century ago and how We can do it again.* Simon and Schuster.

Richards, H. V., Brown, A. F., & Forde, T. B. (2007). Addressing diversity in schools: Culturally responsive pedagogy. *Teaching Exceptional Children, 39*(3), 64–68. 10.1177/004005990703900310

Richardson, J. C., Ashby, I., Alshammari, A. N., Cheng, Z., Johnson, B. S., Krause, T. S., ... & Wang, H. (2019). Faculty and instructional designers on building successful collaborative relationships. *Educational Technology Research and Development, 67*(4), 855–880. 10.1007/s11423-018-9636-4

Ryder, A. J., Reason, R. D., Mitchell, J. J., Gillon, K., & Hemer, K. M. (2016). Climate for learning and students' openness to diversity and challenge: A critical role for faculty. *Journal of Diversity in Higher Education, 9*(4), 339–352. 10.1037/a0039766

Seemiller, C., & Grace, M. (2018). *Generation Z: A century in the making.* Routledge. 10.4324/9780429442476

Smith, B. L., & Williams, L. B. (Eds.) (2007). Academic and student affairs: Fostering student success. *Learning communities and student affairs: Partnering for powerful learning.* NASPA. https://www.naspa.org/book/learning-communities-and-student-affairs-partnering-for-powerful-learning

Startz, D. (2022, April 25). First generation college students face unique challenges. *The Brookings Institution.* https://www.brookings.edu/blog/brown-center-chalkboard/2022/04/25/first-generation-college-students-face-unique-challenges/

Stewart, D. L. (2016). It matters who leads them: Connecting leadership in multicultural affairs to student learning and development. *About Campus, 21*(1), 21–28. 10.1002/abc.21227

Tobin, T. J., & Behling, K. T. (2018). *Reach everyone, teach everyone: Universal Design for Learning in higher education.* West Virginia University Press. https://wvupressonline.com/node/757

Van Maanen, J., & Schein, E. H. (1979). Toward a theory of organizational socialization. In B. M. Staw (Ed.), *Research in organizational behavior* (pp. 209–264). JAI Press.

Williams, D. A., Berger, J. B., & McClendon, S. A. (2005). *Toward a model of inclusive excellence and change in postsecondary institutions.* Association of American Colleges and Universities. https://operations.du.edu/sites/default/files/2020-04/model-of-inclusive-excellence.pdf

Woodrow, C., & Guest, D. E. (2020). Pathways through organizational socialization: A longitudinal qualitative study based on the psychological contract. *Journal of Occupational and Organizational Psychology, 93*(1), 110–133. 10.1111/joop.12285

8

BEYOND PERFORMATIVE ALLYSHIP

Moving from Intention to Action in Diversity, Equity, and Inclusion Initiatives

Erin E. Gilles[1] and Saleema Mustafa Campbell[2]
[1]*University of Southern Indiana;* [2]*Collaborative Center for Literacy Development, Kentucky State University*

Learning Objectives

After reading this chapter, you will:

1 Understand tokenism, performative allyship, and wage gaps, and how these concepts may limit career advancement.
2 Critique the information about Humana's diversity, equity, and inclusion (DEI) policies and assess how they compare to your workplace policies and environment.
3 Identify best practices in DEI and learn how they may apply to your workplace.

Introduction

In the aftermath of the racial uprisings in the summer of 2020, many US organizations and companies committed to implementing or increasing their diversity, equity, and inclusion (DEI) initiatives. Many of these organizations articulated desires to lessen cultural trauma, cultivate safe spaces for their employees, and manifest organizational changes through heightened engagement and learning opportunities. American corporations and organizations began to examine themselves through the lenses of institutional bias, disparity, and inequality. This was exacerbated by the heightened stress caused by the global pandemic, which had a greater impact on women and people of color in the workplace (Roberts et al., 2020).

DOI: 10.4324/9781003333746-9

This chapter will examine Humana, which ranks 40 on the Fortune 500 list (Fortune, 2022). In addition, it is recognized by DiversityInc as a Top 50 company, considered a "Best Place to work" in 2019 (Humana, 2021, para. 13), and is Kentucky's largest company. With its wide-ranging commitment to making meaningful organizational and societal change, Humana provides a unique exemplar for analysis. Humana's DEI strategies and initiatives, as noted in its 2019 Diversity and Inclusion Report (Humana, 2020), offer useful guidelines for other organizations hoping to initiate and improve equity and inclusion programs within and across their various enterprises.

Today, most companies and their executives understand the benefits and potential gains associated with having a diverse workforce. Creating a working environment where employees feel valued can be a daunting endeavor. Still, forward-thinking CEOs recognize the rewards of these initiatives. Consequently, in 2017, more than 2,200 CEOs and presidents began "pledging to ACT ON [emphasis in original] supporting a more inclusive workplace for employees, communities, and society at large" (CEO Action, 2022). Humana's CEO, Bruce Broussard, was among this consortium of enterprising leaders. Broussard and the other CEOs were committing to advancing diversity and inclusion in the workplace by building collaborative learning communities which could help increase information exchanges, establish mentoring/mentee relationships among the CEOs and presidents, and expand access to useful resources, techniques, and tools in DEI advancement for their respective companies. In Humana's 2019 Diversity and Inclusion Report, the company's efforts to foster change in its workplace diversity and experience were highlighted. The document opens with the following commitment to diversity statement:

> Our associates' vast experiences and perceptions – your unique characteristics, backgrounds and beliefs – drive the groundbreaking, strategic thinking that gives Humana its competitive edge in a diverse marketplace. Our approach fosters innovative thinking and creativity, expands insights and generates better business outcomes. At Humana, we strive to create an inclusive culture and meaningful work environment where our associates feel welcome and safe to be their true selves. Through Humana's inclusive environment, we support and encourage our people to maximize their potential and bring their A-game to work every day. We see the diversity within our own organization as an asset toward the innovation we need to better serve our members. Humana embraces the diversity of the communities we serve, and we reflect that in our commitment to our people.
>
> (Humana, 2020, Caring for Each Other section)

Following this declaration, the report outlines the scope of Humana's DEI initiative campaign. It appears to involve a public acknowledgment of the company's commitment to pay equity, performance-based incentives, a non-discrimination, and equal employment opportunity policy, along with advocates who help to enforce the policy, a promotion of its "authentic dialogue" and unconscious bias training, details regarding its commitment to gender equality in the workplace, executive and employee inclusion and diversity councils, Network Resource Groups, mentorship opportunities, diversity recruitment and talent acquisition programs, investment in diverse-owned businesses, and community outreach programs (Humana, 2020, Associate Experience section).

Even with this extensive display of institutional effort backing its DEI campaign, progress is not a foregone conclusion. Humana should use metrics that document demographic changes and surveys that gauge employee sentiments and perspectives to help determine if meaningful changes have occurred in this workplace community. Correspondingly, Humana's 2019 Diversity and Inclusion Report (the version made publicly accessible) does not include details about its data collection and evaluation process. Ultimately, the data gathered from the aforementioned surveys and reports are essential to inform the focus of a DEI campaign and measure progress. Companies with genuine intentions of creating inclusive, equitable, and diverse workplace environments need to be proactive, solutions oriented, and consciously reflective when engaging in DEI campaigns if they intend to achieve any measure of long-term success and progress. More importantly, positive changes in workplace environments have the potential to ignite larger societal changes. Thus, companies and their corporate leadership teams should be dedicated stakeholders in these DEI initiatives because they have the power and influence to serve their workplace and global communities. Removing small barriers to equitable access and increasing inclusion in the workplace could provide models for removing barriers in other societal spaces. In this chapter, we will first highlight the common pitfalls to avoid and best practices to implement when engaging in efforts to strengthen workplace communities through DEI initiatives. Using Humana as a case study, we will then discuss the implementation possibilities of its campaign as outlined in two of its D&I reports. Inevitably, what this assessment will reveal is that the robustness of a company's commitment to its DEI campaign will have the most significant influence on the campaign's success. Regardless of the institution or type of DEI initiative, substantial change is born of dedication, engagement, reflection, and effective response.

DEI Pitfalls

Before detailing best practices for DEI initiatives, it is crucial to examine the characteristics of DEI pitfalls to which even well-intentioned organizations and companies can fall victim. Primarily, the common behaviors that cultivate a climate of intolerance include: treating minority employees as tokens, engaging in performative allyship, and/or participating in disingenuous virtue signaling. These concepts and practices, which are described in greater detail below, can derail the most seemingly benevolent DEI campaigns.

Tokenism

This term refers to the ongoing, distinct status given to those with a particular and easily discernible group identification, such as classifications based on one's racial or gender identity. Tokenized individuals are those who are in a noticeable minority among a majority group, which can be isolating and have negative emotional consequences (Niemann, 2016). Tokenism has been studied since the 1960s, and those who have been ascribed token status face the undue burden of representing their group due to their scarcity and the obviousness of their membership. "They can never be just another member while their category is so rare; they will always be a hyphenated member, as in 'woman-engineer' or 'male-nurse' or 'black-physician'" (Kanter, 1977, p. 968). Tokenism is sometimes referred to as hypervisibility, because the tokenized individual's identity is reduced to their group membership. This increases vulnerability, as any mistakes made by a member of the tokenized group will only serve to reinforce negative stereotypes (Buchanan & Settles, 2019).

When it comes to creating a work environment that supports diversity, King et al. (2010) suggest that context matters. For instance, they write that "a woman's perceptions of the gendered nature of her organization's policies, procedures, and events (i.e., the psychological climate of gender inequity) [function] as a critical indicator of her interpretation of the work context" (p. 483). In a three-part study of women working in various professions across social classes, this study found that women generally agreed that they were tokens in the workplace and that their workplaces were negative environments of gender inequity. In some cases, tokenism can stifle career aspirations. According to Nielsen and Madsen (2019), tokenized women experienced diminished managerial aspirations, but the same was not true of tokenized men. In addition, they found that many tokenized women were often employed in trajectories with high managerial ambitions, but their token status consistently dampened these aspirations.

Performative Allyship

Also called optical allyship or performative activism, performative refers to acts of allegiance with disadvantaged groups that are less about support and solidarity and more about increased social status or good optics for the "ally" (Hassan, 2021). For example, taking to social media to align with causes or writing flashy press releases about corporate activity can stifle the voices of the oppressed and take attention away from the true work of activism. Increasingly savvy and vocal audiences are more willing than ever to criticize brands and influencers whose cause-related posts lack substance, are mere reposts of others' activist posts, or lack any authentic engagement with the cause (Wellman, 2022).

Yuan (2020) found that Black employees, regardless of employment sector, indicated that companies routinely fail to back up their corporate rhetoric about racial equity. "They say their companies speak out in support of racial equality but don't hire black executives, pay black employees equally, listen to their concerns regarding discrimination, or were completely silent about racism up until now" (para. 2). Research on DEI-based leadership engagement has shown that executives, who are predominately white, are often depicted as racially neutral (Liu & Baker, 2016).

Disingenuous Virtue Signaling

Sometimes called moral grandstanding, virtue signaling refers to the practice of "making a contribution to moral discourse that aims to convince others that one is 'morally respectable'" (Tosi & Warmke, 2016, p. 199). Virtue signaling is not entirely negative, as it can drive people to activism, raise awareness and unity around social causes, and create the political pressure needed for reform. Yet, the danger in virtue signaling is when it is disingenuous—or when it becomes more about the signaler than the cause. In such cases, the motives may be any combination of the following: to create positive goodwill for the signaler, to align the signaler with the right side of an issue, or to simply recognize the signaler as being a part of the cause. With virtue signaling, the goal is rarely to conduct genuine and intentional activism.

This is further complicated when such contributions are made by white business leaders; there is the potential to fall into the pitfalls of positioning themselves as the saviors or white knights of helpless minorities (Liu & Baker, 2016). Additionally, white business leaders are rarely described with any acknowledgment of ethnicity, which perpetuates whiteness as the default or neutral racial status. It is not uncommon to read of Black business owners supporting Black business communities, but similar language is often avoided with white business owners, which reinforces their normative position (Liu & Baker, 2016).

Microaggressions

Different from the bold acts of hate speech and overt racism, micro-aggressions are more akin to sandpaper than a sledgehammer. Affecting people of color and those in minority groups based on other factors, such as sexual orientation, gender identity, ability, and so forth, "microaggressions are brief, everyday exchanges that send denigrating messages" (Sue et al., 2007, p. 273). Microaggressions can cause many emotions, including feelings of anger, sadness, shame, or embarrassment (Wang et al., 2011). Furthermore, one study found that workplace microaggressions led to LGBT employees' reports of: feeling offended, experiencing a negative impact on coworker relationships, and decreasing job satisfaction, productivity, and retention rates (Galupo & Resnick, 2016). There is still a lot of work and research needed on how to reduce microaggressions in the workplace, but increasing visibility of the problem is a step in the right direction. One study showed that among Black college faculty, educational attainment, economic status, and marital status were not indicative of a decrease in the amount of race-based microaggressions they experienced (DeCuir-Gunby & Gunby, 2016). The cumulative effect of racism has been shown to negatively impact health outcomes, which creates race-based health disparities (Simons et al., 2021). Internalizing anger caused by racism can activate the body's stress response, which exacerbates the aging process and initiates disease progression (McKenna et al., 2021).

In some cases, microaggressions may be used by groups in power to maintain the status quo and keep those in the minority "in their place" (Berdahl & Min, 2012). When employees adopt a mindset of "color-blindness," this can actually exacerbate the occurrence of microaggressions because those individuals are less critical about their own behaviors toward minority coworkers (Kim et al., 2019). Furthermore, this same study indicated that the detrimental effects of microaggressions were less likely to be perceived by whites who rated higher in color-blindness. It is important to note that the term color-blindness is often misunderstood. It is not the inability for one to see another's color or ethnicity, rather it refers to the ideological premise that no race or ethnic group has any inherent superiority (Doane, 2017). However, the concept of color-blindness does allow room for the acceptance that structural forces both perpetuate racism and foster inequality.

Practical Applications

Humana's DEI campaign illustrates a very intentional plan to create positive changes in its workplace environment. Intentionality is the first step in developing practices that can help to achieve this goal. Many companies succumb to the pitfalls of DEI programming because they lack genuine commitment at the onset of their campaigns. There is no one specific process that will work for all, but it is important to focus on the end results. Elevating underrepresented groups and establishing equitable means of closing opportunity gaps in the workplace should be key aspirations. When companies embrace DEI, they can improve their public and consumer perception and increase loyalty among their employees. However, these initiatives cannot be merely symbolic or performative. Companies must do the hard work of convincing all members of their working communities that DEI initiatives are valuable endeavors, as well as the continuous work of assessing the effectiveness of these initiatives. In this section, we include a few best practices or essential characteristics of successful DEI campaigns.

Professional Development and Training

Employee investment is an important element of a successful DEI program, as well as a definitive best practice. It is a critical strategy for maximizing employee retention. When companies offer employees professional development opportunities and training, they are prioritizing them and highlighting their value to their companies. Increased engagement is a positive consequence of this level of employee investment. By improving their competencies and job-related skills, employees are offered a form of empowerment, which can lead to greater job performance and satisfaction. When organizations have control over the content of the training or professional development programs they offer, they can contribute directly to both the culture of their organization and the broader culture. As a result, "providers [of continuing education] do not only respond to societal developments, they are also active members and shapers of societies" (Egetenmeyer et al., 2019, p. 20).

Ultimately when you train current employees versus hiring new employees, you create more efficient pathways to meet the company's needs and those of the employees. Therefore, this will increase the diversity in the candidacy pool throughout the management pipeline. However, with these added opportunities for training and professional development, companies must be prepared to provide their employees with prospects for advancement. Failure to provide these opportunities will limit pathways for advancement and signal performative allyship to employees. Too often companies boast of varied training and professional development opportunities that are not rooted in a desire to maximize employee potential and progress employee advancement. When companies have clear and expansive pathways for advancement by which many employees can benefit, the overall workplace culture can be strengthened. It is essential to use metrics that can demonstrate the success and expanse of these options for advancement (Desimone, 2011). For example, in Humana's 2019 Diversity and Inclusion Report, the company's efforts to promote unconscious bias training (a method of addressing microaggressions) and activate diversity recruitment and talent acquisition programs are well documented, but pathways to train and advance current employees were not detailed (Humana, 2020, Unconscious Bias Training section). These avenues may exist outside of the DEI initiative, and specifically detailing these kinds of opportunities in a DEI report demonstrates that the company views them as DEI best practices and integral tools to improving workplace culture.

Mentorship

Other forms of professional development that companies should activate conspicuously are mentorships. Companies can be very complex and challenging organizations to navigate. Mentors can help more junior employees glean the best ways to progress in their working environments by offering tips, guidance, and other perspectives. This aid can assist mentees to understand how to best showcase their strengths and maximize their career opportunities. With the tools of constructive criticism and an accessible support network, employees with mentors will feel empowered and better equipped to navigate their workplaces. This can have a direct impact on employee development and employee satisfaction.

In Humana's 2019 Diversity and Inclusion Report, the company's "culture of mentorship," which involves established mechanisms to request a mentee or to arrange an individual or group mentorship, is on display. It defines mentorship "as a short-term, time-bound relationship between two people for the purposes of growing themselves or their careers in navigating the workplace or their fields" (Humana, 2020, A Culture of Mentorship section). The report also highlights the company's podcast *Mentoring Matters*, which appears to promote different employee perspectives on mentorship. More importantly, the report articulates Humana's reverence for mentorship; it states "we see mentoring at Humana as an essential development tool for us to Thrive Together, sharing skills and knowledge so we can all succeed. Our commitment to mentoring feeds the successful future of Humana" (Humana, 2020, A Culture of Mentorship section). The report also offers the company's goals and data that tracks its progress on this front: "As with anything important, we must track our progress. Our goal is for 22 percent of people leaders and senior management to track their mentorships by 2020, and right now we're at 19 percent" (Humana, 2020, A Culture of Mentorship section). The inclusion of this information is essential because it demonstrates that the company not only understands that DEI-related goal setting is important, but that success can be explained in quantifiable terms. However, it is not revealed how they determine this particular mentoring goal and how mentoring will affect progressive workplace changes. This is a salient qualitative component that, if stated in this kind of public space as well as privately, could help to dispel concerns of virtue signaling and performative allyship. Employees want professional development and mentorship opportunities that are rooted in tangible workplace advancements. It is important for companies to articulate these kinds of intentions because these programs are most effective when they are leveraged to create pathways to progress up the corporate ladder or increase opportunities for promotion or other incentives.

Finally, when companies, such as Humana, establish these goals, it would be useful to also state the expectations for or the status of those who do not participate in these initiatives. For example, what is happening with the other 78% of supervisors and executives at Humana who are not actively tracking their mentorships? In addition, it is vital to question the effectiveness of these programs. Does one even have an effective mentorship program if fewer than a third of senior-level employees are participating? Companies and organizations cannot assume that current and future employees will only value efforts and not expect well-conceptualized and substantiated results. Indications of progress are essential to improving employee morale, workplace environments, retention numbers, and/or recruitment potential.

Internal Employee Groups and Councils

Often employees require and pursue safe spaces in their working environments. As components of DEI initiatives, many companies are offering Employee Resource Groups or ERGs, which are also referred to as affinity groups and employee business networks, and Diversity and Inclusion Councils to satisfy this need. These groups provide employees with a sense of belonging and an escape from workplace frustrations and discomforts and are usually "organized around a shared identity, such as race, gender, age, or mental health" (Bethea, 2020, para. 1). Many ERGs and councils function as internal networks that can mobilize, advocate for workplace improvements, and develop action plans to achieve various DEI initiatives. Humana's 2019 Diversity and Inclusion Report outlines a system in which the company's executives form Diversity and Inclusion councils that interact "with leaders of the associate-led and driven Network Resource Groups, whose personal insight and expertise into diverse communities are heard and accounted for" (Humana, 2020, Executive Inclusion & Diversity Council section). In this report, the purpose of these interactions between Executive Inclusion & Diversity Council and the Network Resource are described as:

> The goal of the Executive Inclusion & Diversity Council is to help integrate I&D into the fabric of the organization from the top down. Its top priorities are: hiring, developing, and retaining a diverse workforce, creating an inclusive workforce, improving transparency and accountability to sustain outcomes. The council members aim to clearly link I&D strategy to the business strategy and position to help advance Humana's competitive advantage. This way, everyone understands that I&D is a critical component of our culture transformation and leader expectations.
>
> (Humana, 2020, Executive Inclusion & Diversity Council section)

The report also states that 30% of its employees belong to Network Resource Groups, which it describes as "inclusive" groups that are "open to absolutely everyone" (Humana, 2020, Network Resource Groups section). These groups meet to discuss projects and actions that could affect changes within their workplace and local communities. The report also mentions local, employee-led diversity councils that function as "change agents – leading celebrations of diversity, educating colleagues about the value of inclusion and diversity and planning innovative ways to foster greater inclusion, stronger engagement and a deeper sense of belonging" (Humana, 2020, Local I&D Councils Foster Community section). For substantial inclusive and equitable changes to occur in working environments, companies and organizations need to follow Humana's example and establish these lines of communication between executives and the employees they serve. In general, Humana appears to have dedicated a significant amount of effort cultivating their DEI initiatives, including their affinity groups and diversity councils, as well as communicating that this effort is a fundamental cause. These are essential preliminary steps.

However, to avoid claims of tokenism, performative allyship, and disingenuous virtue signaling, companies, and organizations, including

Humana, must establish clear goals and missions with regard to these DEI campaigns. These programs must also have consistent and recognizable support from members of leadership. Often, these campaigns are poorly funded and limited by underdeveloped promotional campaigns resulting in subpar employee participation. As noted in its 2019 report, only about 30% of Humana employees are currently participating in their Network Resource Groups. Many employees struggle to value the opportunity or understand the larger significance of participating in these and other DEI initiatives. Also, it is reasonable to assume that employees fear retaliation as a result of expressing any of their employment-related concerns and/or frustrations. Ultimately, it is paramount to involve employees in evaluating the success of DEI programs. Survey results and other forms of employee-communicated expectations with regard to these programs can help to determine their success. DEI initiatives that are developed with genuine intentions by members of leadership who are truly committed to allyship can create real progress, but they have to value metrics, reflection, honest dialogue, and accountability.

Supportive Employee Assistance Programs

Employee assistance programs (EAPs), which have existed for nearly a century in various forms, are designed to provide employees with short-term counseling for combatting the stressors associated with their jobs or lives. These programs are often voluntary programs designed to help participants with a range of issues, such as grief, substance abuse, anxiety, workplace issues, and relationship and family problems, among others (Macdonald et al., 2000). EAPs should be confidential, and either connect or refer employees to available counselors (Howard, 2016). Yet, one of the biggest barriers to employee use of EAPs is companies failing to alert employees to their availability (Bolden-Barrett, 2017). Many employees may also adhere to the outdated perception that EAPs are only for specialized matters, such as substance abuse. However, this can be ameliorated through efforts to share the availability with employees.

Frey (2020) challenges organizations to use EAPs to both reject passivity and encourage management to engage with the ongoing racial tension and political unrest. Ultimately, she says, EAPs have a great deal of power to cultivate an antiracist climate in the workplace. The expansion of EAPs to help employees cope with mental health issues should accompany training for HR employees to assess the level of cultural awareness of the affiliated therapists (Roberts et al., 2020). Some EAPs are directly addressing racism, microaggressions, and other forms of social disquiet in their offerings.

For instance, Best Buy states that it offers employees on-site services in locations afflicted by, "natural disasters, death, civil unrest or other critical incidents" (Vomhof, 2021, para. 7).

Humana appears to make EAPs readily available for its employees. Its website states that:

> Our Employee Assistance Program (EAP) and work-life services support employees in dealing with personal and work-related concerns that can increase their stress and lessen their productivity. EAPs help employees with issues of well-being, stress or productivity. The services and resources address challenges such as depression, anxiety, family matters, chemical dependency and financial difficulties.
>
> (Humana, 2022, Employee Assistance and
> Work-Life Services section)

It is difficult to assess the quality of these types of services, for employees and other staff may utilize them to deal with many challenging work and personal matters. However, it is important that companies publicize these programs and make them readily available as a best practice. Accessibility of these programs and the quality of care that they provide can have a tremendous impact on workplace culture.

Pay Equality

In the United States, pay equality is an injurious point of contention. Despite improvements in certain industries or organizations, in many cases, the gaps are worsening or failing to improve. According to a recent report from the National Partnership for Women & Families (NPWF, 2022), women in the United States earn 73 cents on the dollar of what white, non-Hispanic men earn. Specifically, when broken down by ethnic group (Latinas (49 cents), Black women (58 cents), Native American women (50 cents), Asian/Native Hawaiian/Pacific Islander (75 cents), and white women (73 cents)), it is clear that women of any race consistently under-earn white men.

Amending the persistent issue of pay equity requires ongoing scrutiny. McDonald's (2022) has pledged to annually evaluate any pay disparities based on gender or ethnicity. For the first time, they published their pay gap data from 2021 and have vowed to do so going forward. In 2021, they reported that women, "were paid on average $.9985 for every $1 paid to men for comparable work. Historically underrepresented groups in the US were paid on average $1.0063 for every $1 paid to other groups for comparable work" (p. 12). This is on par with other massive global companies. Nike

(2022) also reported that their 2021 gender-based and ethnically diverse employee pay levels are $1 to $1. However, wage-based discrimination is likely to occur and is difficult to remedy because of the secrecy surrounding wages (Moriarty, 2018). Many organizations instruct their employees not to discuss their wages with coworkers.

According to its 2019 Diversity and Inclusion Report, "in November of 2019 Humana joined the Catalyst CEO Champions For Change, a transformational diversity and inclusion initiative launched by Catalyst—a global thought leader and partner in accelerating the progress of women at work" (Humana, 2020, Catalyst CEO Champions For Change section). The company seems to be leading the charge in leveling the playing for women in the workplace. The report also states that "72% of its employee associates are women and 59% of management and 43% of senior leaders are women" (Humana, 2020, Diversity in Management, Women section). These numbers are clear indicators of progress.

Conclusion

Progress can be slow moving with regard to DEI campaigns, but employees and consumers tend to respect genuine effort. Small organizations, non-profits, or those without any existing DEI initiatives may have more difficulty in implementing these programs. DEI initiatives can be costly, and US companies were estimated to have spent $3.8 billion in 2021, while the global costs of DEI were $7.5 billion (Global Analysts Incorporated 2021). However, some actions are easier to implement and do not pose financial burdens. For instance, ensuring that the organizational mission statement includes a commitment to DEI, providing clear policy and language in employee handbooks, and updating website language are easy places to start. More inclusive organizational efforts must prioritize employee voices and focus on assessment through critical evaluation of organizational shortcomings.

For companies and organizations, authenticity and accountability should set the standard. When comparing Humana's 2019 report to its 2020 Diversity and Inclusion Report, it is clear that Humana understands the importance of accountability. The 2020 report includes more visible assessment data that more clearly demonstrates the company's goals and progress. Humana's 2020 D&I report details the following achievement measures that reflect major improvements: "(1) 5% increase in people of color in senior management positions, (2) 8% increase in females in executive leadership positions, (3)22% increase in leaders in mentoring, (4) 94% of Humana senior leaders participating in Disrupting Everyday Bias workshop training" (Humana, 2021, Diversity in Management & A Year Like No Other Section).

Most importantly, Humana's CEO, Bruce Broussard, acknowledges the most essential practice of DEI initiatives in its 2020 report and that is to be truly dedicated to the cause:

> Diversity is a strong suit for us—in fact, we were ranked by DiversityInc as the 13th most diverse company in the country (a 35-spot jump from 2018) ... while we've made progress, we must continue to evolve our efforts to advance positive change. Our associates demand it, our customers demand it, and we know we must continue to build on the efforts we have in place today in order to be the company we want to be tomorrow.
>
> (Humana, 2020, A Year Like No Other Section)

Discussion Questions

1 If you were designing a DEI program for your employer, what would you want to include?
2 What outcomes of a DEI campaign would one expect to see to indicate that it has been successful?
3 How can leaders avoid claims of performative allyship with regard to DEI initiatives?

Author Bios

Erin E. Gilles, Ph.D., is an Associate Professor of Advertising and Public Relations at the University of Southern Indiana, where she also directs their Master of Arts in Communication program. Her research focuses on social support, parasocial relationships, social justice, and gender, race, and sexuality in media representations.

Saleema Mustafa Campbell, Ph.D., is the current director of the Adolescent Literacy Project at Kentucky State University, an adjunct professor, and a special education interventionist with Fayette County schools. She also worked as an executive staff advisor in the Office of Diversity, Equality, and Training for Kentucky State government.

References

Berdahl, J. L., & Min, J.-A. (2012). Prescriptive stereotypes and workplace consequences for East Asians in North America. *Cultural Diversity and Ethnic Minority Psychology, 18*(2), 141–152. 10.1037/a0027692
Bethea, A. (2020, June 29). What Black employee resource groups need right now. *Harvard Business Review*, 5.

Bolden-Barrett, V. (2017, September 20). *Employees' health, productivity improve after EAP counseling, report says.* HR Dive. https://www.hrdive.com/news/employees-health-productivity-improve-after-eap-counseling-report-says/505288/

Buchanan, N. T., & Settles, I. H. (2019). Managing (in)visibility and hypervisibility in the workplace. *Journal of Vocational Behavior, 113,* 1–5. 10.1016/j.jvb.2018.11.001

CEO Action. (2022). About CEO Action. https://www.ceoaction.com/?utm_source=Humana&utm_medium=Internal%20comms&utm_campaign=Signatory_comms

DeCuir-Gunby, J. T., & Gunby, N. W. (2016). Racial microaggressions in the workplace: A critical race analysis of the experiences of African American educators. *Urban Education, 51*(4), 390–414. 10.1177/0042085916628610

Desimone, L. M. (2011). A primer on effective professional development. *Phi Delta Kappan, 92*(6), 68–71. 10.1177/003172171109200616

Doane, W. (2017). Beyond color-blindness: (Re) theorizing racial ideology. *Sociological Perspectives, 60*(5), 975–991. 10.1177/0731121417719697

Egetenmeyer, R., Breitschwerdt, L., & Lechner, R. (2019). From 'traditional professions' to 'new professionalism': A multi-level perspective for analysing professionalisation in adult and continuing education. *Journal of Adult and Continuing Education, 25*(1), 7–24. 10.1177/1477971418814009

Fortune. (2022). *Humana company profile.* Fortune 500. https://fortune.com/company/humana/fortune500/

Frey, J. J. (2020). Actively working to be more antiracist in the employee assistance field. *Journal of Workplace Behavioral Health, 35*(2), 69–79. 10.1080/15555240.2020.1785887

Galupo, M. P., & Resnick, C. A. (2016). Experiences of LGBT microaggressions in the workplace: Implications for policy. In T. Köllen (Ed.), *Sexual orientation and transgender issues in organizations* (pp. 271–287). Springer International Publishing. 10.1007/978-3-319-29623-4_16

Global Industry Analysts, Inc. (2021, November 3). *With global spending projected to reach $15.4 billion by 2026, Diversity, Equity & Inclusion takes the lead role in the creation of stronger businesses* [Press Release]. https://www.prnewswire.com/news-releases/with-global-spending-projected-to-reach-15-4-billion-by-2026--diversity-equity--inclusion-takes-the-lead-role-in-the-creation-of-stronger-businesses-301413808.html

Hassan, N. (2021, June). Black Lives Matter and the problem of performative activism. *Women's Republic.* https://www.womensrepublic.net/black-lives-matter-and-the-problem-of-performative-activism/

Howard, T. (2016). *Civil unrest and employees: When community concerns become workplace challenges* (pp. 1–8). FEI Behavioral Health. https://www.feinet.com/assets/uploads/2019/01/Whitepaper-Q4_Civil-Unrest_0.pdf

Humana. (2021). *Humana 2020 Diversity and Inclusion Report.* https://wellbeing.humana.com/inclusion/associate-experience.html

Humana. (2022). *Employee assistance and work-life services.* https://www.humana.com/employer/products-services/wellness-programs/employee-assistance-work-life

Kanter, R. M. (1977). Some effects of proportions on group life: Skewed sex ratios and responses to token women. *American Journal of Sociology, 82*(5), 965–990. 10.1086/226425

Kim, J. Y.-J., Block, C. J., & Nguyen, D. (2019). What's visible is my race, what's invisible is my contribution: Understanding the effects of race and color-blind racial attitudes on the perceived impact of microaggressions toward Asians in the workplace. *Journal of Vocational Behavior, 113*, 75–87. 10.1016/j.jvb. 2018.08.011

King, E. B., Hebl, M. R., George, J. M., & Matusik, S. F. (2010). Understanding tokenism: Antecedents and consequences of a psychological climate of gender inequity. *Journal of Management, 36*(2), 482–510. 10.1177/0149206308328508

Liu, H., & Baker, C. (2016). White Knights: Leadership as the heroicisation of whiteness. *Leadership, 12*(4), 420–448. 10.1177/1742715014565127

Macdonald, S., Wells, S., Lothian, S., & Shain, M. (2000). Absenteeism and other workplace indicators of employee assistance program clients and matched controls. *Employee Assistance Quarterly, 15*(3), 41–57. 10.1300/J022v15n03_04

McDonald's. (2022). *Diversity, equity &inclusion.* Diversity, Equity & Inclusion. https://corporate.mcdonalds.com/corpmcd/our-purpose-and-impact/jobs-inclusion-and-empowerment/diversity-and-inclusion.html

McKenna, B. G., Mekawi, Y., Katrinli, S., Carter, S., Stevens, J. S., Powers, A., Smith, A. K., & Michopoulos, V. (2021). When anger remains unspoken: Anger and accelerated epigenetic aging among stress-exposed black Americans. *Psychosomatic Medicine, 83*(9), 949–958. 10.1097/PSY.0000000000001007

Moriarty, J. (2018). Against pay secrecy. *Journal of Applied Philosophy, 35*(4), 689–704. 10.1111/japp.12273

Nielsen, V. L., & Madsen, M. B. (2019). Token status and management aspirations among male and female employees in public sector workplaces. *Public Personnel Management, 48*(2), 226–251. 10.1177/0091026018808822

Niemann, Y. F. (2016). Tokenism. In N. Naples (Ed.). *The Wiley Blackwell encyclopedia of gender and sexuality studies* (pp. 1–2). Wiley Blackwell.

Nike. (2022). *FY21 representation & Pay _ Nike purpose 2022.pdf.* FY21 Representation & Pay. https://purpose.nike.com/fy21-representation-pay

NPWF. (2022). *Quantifying America's gender wage gap by race/ethnicity* (pp. 1–4). National Partnership for Women & Families. https://www.nationalpartnership. org/our-work/resources/economic-justice/fair-pay/quantifying-americas-gender-wage-gap.pdf

Roberts, L. M., McCluney, C. L., Thomas, E. L., & Kim, M. (2020, May 22). How U.S. companies can support employees of color through the pandemic. *Harvard Business Review.* https://hbr.org/2020/05/how-u-s-companies-can-support-employees-of-color-through-the-pandemic

Simons, R. L., Lei, M.-K., Klopack, E., Zhang, Y., Gibbons, F. X., & Beach, S. R. H. (2021). Racial discrimination, inflammation, and chronic illness among African American women at midlife: Support for the weathering perspective. *Journal of Racial and Ethnic Health Disparities, 8*(2), 339–349. 10.1007/s40615-02 0-00786-8

Sue, D. W., Capodilupo, C. M., Torino, G. C., Bucceri, J. M., Holder, A. M. B., Nadal, K. L., & Esquilin, M. (2007). Racial microaggressions in everyday life: Implications for clinical practice. *American Psychologist, 62*(4), 271–286. 10.1037/0003-066X.62.4.271

Tosi, J., & Warmke, B. (2016). Moral grandstanding. *Philosophy & Public Affairs,* *44*(3), 197–217. 10.1111/papa.12075

Vomhof, J. (2021, May 28). *How Best Buy is investing in our employees' mental health* [Press Room]. https://corporate.bestbuy.com/how-best-buy-is-investing-in-our-employees-mental-health/

Wang, J., Leu, J., & Shoda, Y. (2011). When the seemingly innocuous "stings": Racial microaggressions and their emotional consequences. *Personality and Social Psychology Bulletin, 37*(12), 1666–1678. 10.1177/0146167211416130

Wellman, M. L. (2022). Black squares for Black lives? Performative allyship as credibility maintenance for social media influencers on Instagram. *Social Media + Society, 8*(1), 205630512210804. 10.1177/20563051221080473

Yuan, K. (2020, June 19). *Black employees say 'performative allyship' is an unchecked problem in the office.* Fortune. https://fortune.com/2020/06/19/performative-allyship-working-while-black-white-allies-corporate-diversity-racism/

PART 2

Challenging Dominant Discourses and Fostering Dialogue

9

"WORK-LIFE BALANCE? THAT'S JUST FOR MANAGERS"

Time Policies and Practices in Blue-Collar and White-Collar Work

Sunshine Webster[1] and Dawna I. Ballard[2]
[1]*Talent Development, Q2;* [2]*The University of Texas*

Learning Objectives

After reading this chapter, you will:

1 Understand the uneven impact of work-life balance policies across different types of work and workers.
2 Learn how the concept of "work-life" is designed to extract additional labor out of individuals through the creation of the ideal worker.
3 Identify actions to redress the problematic use of work-life policies across various types of work.

Introduction

The assumptions about workplace wellness afforded to particular people and denied to others are prominently featured in social constructions of time and work (Ballard & Aguilar, 2020). These assumptions circulate in a broader historical context ranging from state-sanctioned violence in the United States against enslaved bodies who did not perform fast enough (Berry, 2017) to a Jim Crow era mythical legend John Henry who gladly sacrificed his life in a race against a steam drill, symbolizing the countless non-mythical African Americans who died building and maintaining American railways (James, 1994). Despite the creation of contemporary labor unions (including the United Farm Workers of America owed to the work of Cesar Chavez) and the end of Jim Crow, norms about time and work continued to intersect around race in the late 20th and early 21st century.

DOI: 10.4324/9781003333746-11

James (1994) first accounted for this intersection in his *active coping hypothesis* (measured through items about personal agency realized through hard work and unrelenting commitment to achieving difficult goals), ultimately naming the construct *John Henryism* in honor of an African American sharecropper he met with the same name as the steel-driving legend. The increased risk of hypertension among African American men engaged in *blue*-collar work (who score highly on John Henryism) exemplifies the quality-of-life costs that certain bodies bear in the workplace in exchange for gainful employment and upward mobility. Notably, James found no relationship between John Henryism and hypertension among those engaged in *white*-collar work. Equally telling, it was not the work alone but the individual's *relationship to their work* that was associated with hypertension. Thus, there is evidence to suggest a complex interrelationship between class, race, access to wellbeing, and the structure of work (i.e., blue or white collar).

The COVID-19 pandemic helped bear witness to the high costs of effortful coping for some bodies, as a disproportionate number of essential workers were BIPOC (Black, Indigenous, People of Color) individuals engaged in blue-collar work, and suffered greater exposure and death associated with the virus as a result (Rogers et al., 2020). Accordingly, our focus in this case study is how early industrial and pre-industrial era assumptions about wellbeing at work are reproduced in the structure of contemporary work—and this is readily seen in everyday popular discussions of work-life balance and the related policies to achieve it. Ultimately, we make several claims guided initially by the literature and, later, by findings in the present case:

- The history of work-life as a concept was intended to professionalize workers by creating and nurturing a professional identity as the "ideal worker" separate from their personal identity.
- Contemporary work-life policies help to accentuate the ideal worker identity by affording unique privileges while simultaneously being problematic for personal autonomy.
- Organizations tend to reserve work-life policies for individuals in white-collar jobs, despite the time-based concerns shared by all organizational members.
- If organizations want to improve access to wellbeing for all members, a shift to focusing on time-based policies rather than work-life balance policies can create a more inclusive and resilient organization.

We elaborate on these issues below, first by clarifying the key problems with work-life balance as a policy and then move to elaborate on its origins in early industrial work. Next, we more closely consider the exclusionary and implicit time-based issues in work-life policies and practices. Finally, we describe the methods used for this case study, report our findings, and conclude with a discussion and implications for future research.

The Problem with Work-Life Balance

As a construct, work-life balance can be defined as a worker's attempt to attend to personal and professional responsibilities with the same level of engagement and satisfaction (McMillian et al., 2011; Greenhaus et al., 2003). Despite research identifying the practical, ethical, and discursive problems associated with work-life research (Lewis et al., 2007; Shockley et al., 2018), this area of scholarship continues to enjoy considerable interest among scholars as well as in popular parlance (Hjálmsdóttir & Bjarnadóttir, 2021; Powell et al., 2019; Wood et al., 2020). This interest is not surprising given the compelling focus on everyday quality-of-life issues and the emancipatory aims associated with work-life research (Leslie et al., 2019). Nonetheless, not only is it a problematic approach to wellness as scholars have argued for decades, but work-life policies are simultaneously characterized by: 1) the exclusion of (disproportionately BIPOC) individuals in blue-collar work, and 2) the demand for additional labor from those in white-collar professions. Thus, we argue that work-life balance policies reproduce—rather than overcome—the constraints of capitalism. As such, traditional work-life policies are without merit as a tool to support DEI (diversity, equity, and inclusion) issues.

Rather than being based on DEI principles, the work-life balance literature and related policies are remarkably limited with regard to *whose* autonomy, agency, and wellbeing the research addresses and the interrelated question of *how* these emancipatory ideals can be achieved across varied types of working arrangements. Notwithstanding the laudable aims driving work-life research, this body of scholarship conspicuously overlooks two central, constitutive issues tied to work: (1) the exclusionary nature of structures that organize labor (i.e., *whose* work matters); and (2) time (i.e., *how* work-life ideals can be achieved given the different types of working arrangements held by a range of organizational members). Given the dangers of these costs, highlighted during the pandemic and the ensuing Great Resignation (Shaban, 2022), they demand our attention.

Concerning the first failure—i.e., *whose* work life is the focus of research—scholars have critiqued the overwhelming use of white individuals (mostly women) working in white-collar roles upon which the scholarship has been built, advocating that research expand to consider how the discourse applies across BIPOC groups and in blue-collar roles (Kelliher et al., 2019; Kossek & Lautsch, 2017). Concerning the second omission, time is an important site of privilege across different types of work. Bochantin and Cowan (2016) point to the lack of time-based accommodations (including time off and flexible working arrangements) that characterize blue-collar work. Ballard and Aguilar (2020) also elaborate on the ways in which pacing norms (which include work-life policies that permit time for recovery and wellbeing) are a privilege afforded to some bodies and denied to others.

Therefore, any policies designed to improve the quality of life for all organizational members must necessarily pay special attention to time if it is to be inclusive. Accordingly, the current case takes on the issue of time in extant work-life research. Our objective is to consider the power chronography of work-life balance (Sharma, 2014). As Sharma describes, "Power chronography is based on a conception of time as lived experience, always political, produced at the intersection of a range of social differences and institutions, and of which the clock is only one chronometer" (p. 15). That is, time must be understood subjectively, including its relationship to power based upon a variety of social intersections and structural inequities rather than only an objective unit of measurement. A brief historical perspective illuminates these various intersections.

The origin of "work-life" balance as a concept is based on a fundamental dualism between work and life that originated in Western cultural attitudes toward work (Cheney et al., 2009). Particularly, during the Industrial Revolution, factory owners relied on this dualistic language to manufacture a strategic time-based boundary around the workplace that taught factory workers to separate their "work" time from some other time in their "lives." Of course, members' personal lives do not exclude their work activities as the research on spillover illustrates (Kelliher et al., 2019). Nonetheless, this language afforded factory owners a valuable tool to build the ideal worker *and* effectively excluded women of color and women in blue-collar roles (Davies & Frink, 2014):

> The ideal worker is one who is devoted single-mindedly to the good of the employer, and is not subject to personal distractions from family or other responsibilities. This ideal is most readily approximated by White, middle-class men because this group is the most likely to have a stay-at-home spouse who provides backstage support. (p. 20)

Historian E.P. Thompson (1967) observed that this separation between work and life was a defining characteristic of *time orientation* (also referred to as *time discipline* and *work discipline*) and contrasted it with the earlier *task orientation* that preceded the Industrial Revolution. Time orientation was driven by a preoccupation with the clock as a measure of worth and of work. More time (on the clock) invested in work was prized as an outcome in and of itself. Whereas task orientation was focused on high-quality task completion as the measure of work, time orientation made the clock the measure of a worthy employee. Thus, time use became bound up with identity, as it remains today (Feldman et al., 2020). This orientation toward the clock perpetuates exclusions based upon gender, race, and socio-economic status, as some people are able to commit more time to work while they receive domestic support from their partners.

One way to expand beyond the class- and race-based limitations of the identity work that is bound up with the ideal worker conception is simply to look at time in work. In the "work-life" literature, scholars implicitly reference time but do not address the underlying time-based issues. Instead, researchers often discuss topics such as boundaries, roles, identities, policy implementation, and social responsibilities. Explicitly considering the role of time in member wellbeing, work-life policies are designed to support unifying underlying aspects of the literature and point to practices with relevance for all organizational members.

Common time-based issues discussed in work-life literature center on: the *pace* of work itself—reflected in concerns about regular time off as well as vacation and family leave policies (Kirby & Krone, 2002); *flexibility*—exemplified by policies and norms that permit flexible work arrangements (Meyers et al., 2012); *scheduling*—control over when work happens (Schwartz et al., 2015); and *separation*—centered on the boundaries organizations and their members erect between work and home (Feldman et al., 2020). Notably, many of these practices are not available to those who perform blue-collar work (Bochantin & Cowan, 2016). For instance, policies that permit self-pacing—such as vacation time, sick leave, and family leave—are often not included in their benefits packages. Flexible working arrangements are also not logistically feasible for many roles. Schedules are typically precarious and change from week to week outside of the employee's control. In contrast, reduced separation is more commonly an experience in white-collar work because of the prevalence of remote work as well as the identity issues tied to the ideal worker (Golden, 2013; Rahmouni Elidrissi & Courpasson, 2021).

Therefore, we are interested in learning more about the implications of work-life balance across organizational members, with a focus on those in low-wage jobs. As such, the following research question guided this investigation: *How do organizational members—across racial and class-based groups—describe the role of time in their work and personal lives?*

Method

Interviews using a semi-structured protocol were used to elicit personal narratives about participants' experiences of time as related to their professional and personal life. A scheduled but flexible (Lindlof & Taylor, 2011) eight-question, multi-tiered interview guide structured the interviews. Interview participants were informed of the work-life aspects of the study.

Participants

While in the overall project, 67 working individuals were interviewed, for this case study, we report and analyze the data from 47 participants that represented mid-career and late-career professionals. Classification of participants was based upon national and regional economic statistics indicating the low-income line and hourly wages (< $10.00/hour). In total, 20 participants engaged in blue-collar, low-wage occupations, 18 of whom identified as people of color (16 Latinx and 2 African American). We did not observe notably different responses from the two white participants in this group, although we use quotes below exclusively from Latinx and African American interviewees. In total, 27 participants (all white) engaged in white-collar, mid-to-high-wage occupations. Participants lived in three geographic areas: Central Texas, Eastern Tennessee, and South Louisiana. While interviews were scheduled for 60 minutes, not all interviews lasted for that amount of time. One interview lasted 3½ hours, and a shorter interview only covered 33 minutes. All interviews summed to a total of 72 hours, but the average length of time was 64 minutes. Interviews were recorded (when organizations allowed) and transcribed into manuscript form resulting in 268, single-spaced typed pages. Notably, this data was collected before the COVID-19 global health pandemic, during the early rise in the mainstream popularity of "work-life balance" as a solution to employee woes. It forecast the fundamental problems that would intensify for both blue-collar and white-collar workers, especially during the pandemic.

Data Analysis

Based on the work of Glaser and Strauss (1967), we employed grounded theory to analyze and interpret interview data. Consistent content themes emerged within the interview transcripts offering useful insight into answering our research question. After combining and condensing themes, seven categories emerged. Of these seven categories, three categories provided the most fruitful answers to the current research question. Specifically, the following themes emerged as class-based and racial time constructions: discourse around "work-life balance," the control of time related to work, and the use of technology to achieve work-life balance.

Findings and Interpretations

The Experience of Time Scarcity Across Participants

Interviewees in both blue-collar and white-collar roles experienced time as a scarce commodity to be taken, protected, controlled, and used before it is taken away. When asked to describe their work and personal time, many participants claim to just "take time" for their personal life. In this regard, "taking time" refers to the perceived possessive nature of time. These workers view time as an entity to exercise agency and control over before someone else exerts control over their time. For instance, in their white-collar roles, Emily "just take[s] time for my family. If I don't take it, I won't have it" and Michael "generally schedule[s] my day so that I can take the time I need with my family in the afternoons and evenings." Similarly, in her blue-collar role, Meagan also "take[s] the time when I need it; if I need it for a sick child or a doctor visit ... I just do the things I need to do. Work comes second. When I need personal time, I take it." For all of these participants, nonwork time is scarce and needs to be taken (and often protected) before it is lost or taken by someone else.

Access to Work-Life Policies Denied in Blue-Collar Roles

The similarities ended with this basic idea of time as a scarce commodity. When participants were asked to, "Tell me your work-life story" reactions fell along lines of class and race. In terms of class, while the idea of work-life balance permeated and consumed the conversations and identities of participants in white-collar roles, it was not a concept with any purchase for participants in blue-collar roles. Among this group, the only interviewees who had heard of the phrase work-life balance worked for larger corporations. James cited hearing his previous employer using the concept, stating: "I remember [Organization] would post signs and talk about work-life balance, but they didn't mean it. At least, they didn't mean it for us on the line." Similarly, Julie recalled how "people began talking about it 9 or 10 years ago, but nobody meant it." Claudia works for a large, corporate chain organization, and she literally laughed when asked to define work-life balance, noting: "Oh yeah, that's just for managers [laughter]." These interviewees have heard of the concept "work-life balance," but they did not find a connection to it. Due to the discourse surrounding it within their organizations, the term did not resonate as something available or relevant to them.

Some struggled with defining the term "work-life balance," even admitting to never hearing of the concept at all. For example, Christy asked, "What do you mean by work-life balance?" and Jeremy questioned the concept: "What do you mean? I've never heard that word." When Jeremy was probed for his experiences of work and personal time, he asked: "Why wouldn't I spend enough time here? I work here ... and then I go home. At home, I spend time with [son], I watch TV, we eat; I have a nice life. I love my job and my family." Once the definition was clarified, all but two interview participants recognized the desire for something resembling balance. Thus, at a conceptual level, the idea of attending to work and life with the same level of engagement and satisfaction appeared somewhat absurd on its face, even though all participants were actively engaged in working toward the same. They were simply viewing it from different vantage points based on the tools available to them.

Ideal Worker Identity as Constraint on Personal Agency

Participants in blue-collar work viewed their personal time as *their time*. For instance, James clearly stated, "People are in control of work-life balance. If they want more time with their families and less time at work, they can change that." As a former employee of a large organization offering work-life balance initiatives, James recalled hearing about work-life balance at work: "I remember hearing all those managers and executives talking about work-life balance, 'be sure to have work-life balance.' YOU make your work-life balance." Similarly, Julie stated that she "would love to do everything, but I can't. So I prioritize and do what I can. Instead of choosing to stay up until 2 in the morning, I have learned to say, 'No.'" A newly divorced mother of two, Julie focuses on decreasing her pace in order to achieve work-life balance. While a power chronography perspective calls attention to structures of power at play—such as the likely need to work more than one job—in this case study we simply want to call attention to the weaknesses of the ideal worker identity and related preoccupation with work-life balance. In contrast to what we describe in the next section on white-collar work, none of the BIPOC participants in blue-collar roles had expectations of the organization extending support to them outside of a paycheck. We argue that this is due to a historical context in which BIPOC and blue-collar workers were not afforded the same consideration as white or white-collar workers. It reflects structural inequity and it suggests the need for greater formal protection and consideration for their wellbeing at work.

While participants in blue-collar roles viewed their time as a personal responsibility—for better or worse—those in white-collar roles viewed their personal time as a commodity given to and extracted from them by the organization. Thus, the ideal worker identity deprived them of agency through a self-imposed (as opposed to structurally or formally imposed) set of demands. George recalled stories of an organization unwilling to allow for personal time: "Ten years ago, I remember thinking, 'How much more do I have to give here?' [Organization] demanded so much of me and my time. Now I know I just have to take it; otherwise, they'll take it from me." George's experience was shared by a number of other interviewees in white-collar roles. Jeanne explained how "It has gotten better here. Before, you would feel guilty asking for personal time. Now, I just take time. [Organization] provides me with enough tools that if I need to finish working at home, I can." Likewise, Connie added, "I have balance 60–70% of the time, but sometimes I think that work wants more out of me than I ought to be giving." These accounts suggest the ideal worker identity constrains their sense of personal agency. Instead, the organization controls, even owns, employees' time.

Time Discipline by Any Other Name

While the policies did not actually help participants in white-collar roles solve the fundamental problem of time scarcity, the ability to work from home or away from the office was described as balanced. Gina "work[s] more than 40 hours a week, but I have balance because my work and home are connected!. ... I truly only 'disconnect' a few times a year, maybe a vacation or if I am out of the country." Through the conversation, Gina continued, "I love that I can work from home; I can be on a conference call and still fold laundry." For Connie, "Technology allows me to always connect to work. Even if I am sick or traveling, I can check-in every hour or so ... instead of having 650 e-mails when I return." Similarly, when Beatty "feel[s] overwhelmed in my work-life balance, I take a 'work from home day.' I can work while I catch up on things like laundry, making beds, watering the plants. It feels like 'me' time." For Jeanne, "before technology, I was in work by 5 AM and would work until 7 or 8 PM each night. That is no work-life balance. Now, I can work from home early or late [and] help my family too."

Mothers described working at home as personal time, despite the fact that they simultaneously engaged in both paid and unpaid labor. Thus, the policies available to them simply allow them to work more hours, from home. While fathers did not mention household chores, they also described being available around the clock as work-life balance. Tim explains: "Good work-life balance is you and your laptop on the couch. You use tools to never let work interfere with what I need to do at home. I would have to work 18 hours at work otherwise. People may look at me and say I don't have balance because I am texting or emailing work from my daughter's volleyball game. At least I get to go. Without the tools, I can't go."

Summary

In summary, participants shared three interrelated experiences with both practical and theoretical relevance for the study of work-life balance. First, consistent with the structure of post-industrial capitalism, all participants experienced time as a commodity. However, work-life balance stemmed from a privileged class position. Individuals in white collar positions had the opportunity—both from a policy perspective and a logistic one—to re-arrange their schedules both in terms of when and where they work. Despite the promise of such policies and their desirability, such "flexibility" also led to more time spent working for the organization. This additional time spent engaged in paid labor also occurred alongside unpaid work (creating a world where women worked all the time), forecasting what would unfold during the pandemic (Schaeffer, 2022). Additionally, while this came to serve as a form of time discipline for those in white-collar positions and most heavily benefited the organization, none of the individuals in our study who occupied blue-collar positions were afforded a means to address this tension through organizational policies. Instead, work-life balance policies were not available to lower-wage earners.

These findings predicted both the structurally uneven and the generally problematic nature of work during the pandemic. That is, individuals in blue-collar positions had to go to a workplace where they faced immediate threats to their safety (and died at greater numbers as a result). Meanwhile, as the physical safety of individuals in white-collar positions was protected, they were likely to work around the clock—especially if they were mothers—doing paid and unpaid labor simultaneously. Taken together, below we use the findings in this case study to describe the inherently flawed premise of work-life balance as a policy to enact greater organizational DEI.

Practical Applications

The contemporary allure of work-life balance inheres in the idea that organizations are protecting, even enabling, the wellbeing of their members through policies that support flexible work hours and work-from-home options (Beckman & Mazmanian, 2020). In this chapter, however, we report data from a project that considered the power chronography of work-life balance. This case study focused on participants' lived experience of time in relationship to their work and sought to illuminate the political dimensions of these policies as a function of class, race, and post-industrial capitalism.

Based on these findings, it becomes clearer that simply extending common work-life policies to organizational members in blue-collar roles who are disproportionately BIPOC will not support the underlying aim of DEI policies. Instead, this study suggests that we need to consider how well work-life balance policies actually align with the best interests of organizational members more generally and work from there. Accordingly, we suggest that looking more closely at issues of time helps identify a better path to support DEI efforts. For instance, participants who held white-collar positions placed a great deal of value on flexible working arrangements. They enjoyed working from home as it appeared to offer them a great deal of autonomy. However, it tipped the scales of "balance," offering the greatest benefit to organizations because they described being available for work at virtually all hours of the day. This served to reinforce the ideal worker identity whose time is owned by the organization. So, while the policies were associated with privilege, they were still associated with overwork.

Recognize Time as a Site of Privilege

Therefore, taking a power chronography perspective calls into question the political dimension of work-life balance policies. While the policies certainly privilege some bodies and disproportionately deny these privileges to BIPOC individuals who occupy blue-collar roles, the story is more complex. Additionally, even if flexible working arrangements were a fix-all solution to burnout and overwork (which they are not), the logistics associated with blue-collar work often mean that flexible working arrangements are not possible. As such, in multiple ways, work-life policies fail to offer access to wellbeing. Instead, we recommend refocusing attention on the ways that time is a site of privilege that can be extended across types of work and workers. It provides a far more reaching solution to DEI concerns as well as overall employee wellbeing.

At a formal organizational policy level, paid vacation time, paid sick leave, and paid family and medical leave are all time-based policies that would support individuals in blue-collar roles. These policies would be a more fruitful path to support greater DEI than remote work policies that cannot be accommodated by the logistics of certain work. They are time-based policies that can be applied to and benefit all organizational members.

Reconsider Traditional Time-Based Policies

Additionally, we recommend the inclusion of specific time-based policies that address the unique challenges associated with blue-collar positions. For example, hourly work is often organized in an ad-hoc based that results in irregular schedules that change from week to week (Bochantin & Cowan, 2016; Schwartz et al., 2015). This is a common problem that can be addressed through innovations in scheduling. Solutions might be a nine-day fortnight, where individuals work the same number of hours condensed from ten to only nine days. Recently, an owner-operator at one food service chain has experimented with the three-day workweek "to reduce burnout, increase employee retention, and demonstrate more generous leadership" (Murphy, 2022). The owner-operator behind the innovation reflects, "Obviously that's pay, but beyond pay, it's *time*. So, I thought, how can I get them more time? ... How can I get them an opportunity to know their schedule in perpetuity ... and they could build their lives, and their vacations, and their plans, and their child care and their school and all of those things around that? And then on a business side of it, it was really I was searching for consistency." His implementation of this policy—which is much more fluid and locally driven than traditional organizational policies—has been associated with reduced turnover and absenteeism.

Co-Construct Work Schedules and Practices

More informally, team leaders can also work collaboratively and cooperatively with team members to define and build practices that serve each of them. The important issue is to refocus solutions on time. For instance, allow team members to participate in the construction of the specific hours they work. Instead of feeling like time has to be guarded, encourage team members to help to co-create the schedules that fit their life goals. Additionally, help team members find areas to grow and offer them protected time to learn. Set aside specific time at regular intervals for your team members to learn. This investment of time will help team members feel supported toward learning and growing in the ways they want to grow. Even more, stay connected with team members to remain aware of the times they feel stress from the time and timing of work. Coach them through stressful conflicts to enable more agency in meeting the demands of life. All of these suggestions require open and transparent communication with our team members—working *together* to address the time and timing of work instead of working against one another.

Conclusion

In summary, our findings suggest that for practitioners and organizations committed to effective DEI policy, attention to the underlying *time-based issues* of interest in work-life balance discussions is critical. While work-life balance policies were applied unevenly across white-collar and blue-collar positions, all of our participants were equally attentive to the critical role of time in their work lives. These policy omissions reflect the classed, racialized nature of work-life balance discourse, consistent with previous research. We also showed how this discourse has had unintended consequences—both for those seeking greater wellness in their personal and professional lives and for those promoting it as a path toward the same. It further reproduces structural inequalities based on class and race while extracting additional labor out of workers who enjoy more privileged positions.

Discussion Questions

1 How is the ideal worker identity tied to work-life balance policies?
2 How does a power chronography perspective offer a new lens on work-life balance?
3 What are some other time-based policies that would support DEI efforts?

Author Bios

Sunshine Webster (Ph.D., University of Texas Austin) leads talent development learning for a software company in Austin, Texas. She sees learning as the answer to many questions posed by team members. When managers want to lead better, team members want to perform better, and executives want to deliver greater impact to the business, learning offers the avenue toward these achievements.

Dawna I. Ballard (Ph.D., University of California, Santa Barbara) is an Associate Professor of organizational communication and technology at the University of Texas at Austin and an expert in chronemics—the study of time as it is bound to human communication. She researches what drives our pace of life and its impact on the communication practices and long-term vitality of organizations, communities, and individuals. She is currently completing a book, *Time by Design* (under contract at MIT Press), about how effective organizations routinely communicate slow to go fast.

Author Note

Correspondence concerning this chapter should be addressed to Sunshine Webster, Q2, 10355 Pecan Park Boulevard, Austin, TX 78729, United States. Email: sonealwebster@gmail.com.

References

Ballard, D. I., & Aguilar, A. (2020). When pacing is a privilege: The time scale of exclusion. In M. L. Doerfyl & J. L. Gibbs (Eds.), *Building inclusiveness in organizations, institutions, and communities: Communication theory perspectives*. New York, NY: Routledge.

Beckman, C. M., & Mazmanian, M. (2020). *Dreams of the overworked*. Stanford University Press.

Berry, D. (2017). *The price for their pound of flesh: The value of the enslaved from womb to grave in the building of a nation*. Beacon Press.

Bochantin, J. E., & Cowan, R. L. (2016). Acting and reacting: Work/life accommodation and blue-collar Workers. *International Journal of Business Communication, 53*(3), 306–325. 10.1177/2329488414525457

Cheney, G., Lair, D. J., Ritz, D., & Kendall, B. E. (2009). *Just a job?: Communication, ethics, and professional life*. Oxford University Press.

Davies, A. R., & Frink, B. D. (2014). The origins of the ideal worker: The separation of work and home in the United States from the market revolution to 1950. *Work and Occupations, 41*(1), 18–39. 10.1177/0730888413515893

Feldman, E., Reid, E. M., & Mazmanian, M. (2020). Signs of our time: Time-use as dedication, performance, identity, and power in contemporary workplaces. *Academy of Management Annals, 14*(2), 598–626. 10.5465/annals.2018.0148

Glaser, B., & Strauss, A. (1967). *The discovery of grounded theory*. Chicago, IL: Aldine.

Golden, A. G. (2013). The structuration of information and communication technologies and work–life interrelationships: Shared organizational and family rules and resources and implications for work in a high-technology organization. *Communication Monographs, 80*, 101–123.

Greenhaus, J. H., Collins, K. M., & Shaw, J. D. (2003). The relation between work-family balance and quality of life. *Journal of Vocational Behavior, 63*(3), 510–531.

Hjálmsdóttir, A., & Bjarnadóttir, V. S. (2021). "I have turned into a foreman here at home": Families and work–life balance in times of COVID-19 in a gender equality paradise. *Gender, Work & Organization, 28*(1), 268–283. 10.1111/gwao.12552

James, S. A. (1994). John Henryism and the health of African-Americans. *Culture, Medicine and Psychiatry, 18*(2), 163–182.

Kelliher, C., Richardson, J., & Boiarintseva, G. (2019). All of work? All of life? Reconceptualising work-life balance for the 21st century. *Human Resource Management Journal, 29*(2), 97–112. 10.1111/1748-8583.12215

Kirby, E. L., & Krone, K. J. (2002). "The policy exists but you can't really use it": Communication and the structuration of work-family policies. *Journal of Applied Communication Research, 30*, 50–77.

Kossek, E., & Lautsch, B. (2017). Work-life flexibility for whom? Occupational status and work-life inequality in upper, middle, and lower level jobs. *Academy of Management Annals, 12*, annals.2016.0059. 10.5465/annals.2016.0059

Leslie, L. M., King, E. B., & Clair, J. A. (2019). Work-life ideologies: The contextual basis and consequences of beliefs about work and life. *Academy of Management Review, 44*(1), 72–98. 10.5465/amr.2016.0410

Lewis, S., Gambles, R., & Rapoport, R. (2007). The constraints of "work-life balance" approach: An international perspective. *The International Journal of Human Resource Management, 18*, 360–378.

Lindlof, T. R., & Taylor, B. C. (2011). *Qualitative research methods*. Thousand Oaks, CA: Sage.

McMillan, H. S., Morris, M. L., & Atchley, E. K. (2011). Constructs of the work/life interface: A synthesis of the literature and introduction of the concept of work/life harmony. *Human Resource Development Review, 10*(1), 6–25. 10.1177/1534484310384958

Murphy, Jr., B. (2022, October 29). Price, D. (2018, March 23). *Chick-fil-A just introduced a 3-day workweek, and people think it's the best idea ever: Yes, that's right: Chick-fil-A*. Inc. https://www.inc.com/bill-murphy-jr/chick-fil-a-just-introduced-a-3-day-work-week-people-think-its-best-idea-ever.html

Myers, K. K., Gailliard, B. M., & Putnam, L. L. (2012). Reconsidering the concept of workplace flexibility: Is adaptability a better solution? In C. T. Salmon (Ed.), *Communication Yearbook 36* (pp. 195–230). New York, NY: Routledge/Taylor Frances.

Powell, G. N., Greenhaus, J. H., Allen, T. D., & Johnson, R. E. (2019). Introduction to special topic forum: Advancing and expanding work-life theory from multiple perspectives. *Academy of Management Review, 44*(1), 54–71. 10.5465/amr.2018.0310

Rahmouni Elidrissi, Y., & Courpasson, D. (2021). Body breakdowns as politics: Identity regulation in a high-commitment activist organization. *Organization Studies, 42*(1), 35–59.

Rogers, T. N., Rogers, C. R., VanSant-Webb, E., Gu, L. Y., Yan, B., & Qeadan, F. (2020). Racial disparities in COVID-19: Mortality among essential workers in the United States. *World Medical & Health Policy*, 10.1002/wmh3.358. 10.1002/wmh3.358

Schwartz, A., Wasser, M., Gillard, M., & Paarlberg, M. (2015). *Unpredictable, unsustainable: The impact of employers' scheduling practices in DC*. Washington, DC: DC Jobs with Justice.

Shaban, H. (2022, November 1). *They quit their jobs. Here's what they are doing now*. The Washington Post. https://www.washingtonpost.com/business/2022/11/01/workers-great-resignation-now/

Schaeffer, K. (2022, May 6). *Working moms in the U.S. have faced challenges on multiple fronts during the pandemic*. Pew Research Center. https://www.pewresearch.org/fact-tank/2022/05/06/working-moms-in-the-u-s-have-faced-challenges-on-multiple-fronts-during-the-pandemic/

Sharma, S. (2014). *In the meantime*. New York, NY: Duke University Press. 10.1515/9780822378334

Shockley, K. M., Johnson, R. C., & Shen, W. (2018). The meanings of worklife balance: a cultural perspective. In K. Shockley, & W. Shen and R. Johnson (Eds.), *The Cambridge handbook of the global work-family interface* (pp. 720–732). Cambridge Handbooks in Psychology. Cambridge: Cambridge University Press.

Thompson, E. P. (1967). Time, work-discipline and industrial capitalism. *Past and Present, 38*, 56–97.

Wood, J., Oh, J., Park, J., & Kim, W. (2020). The relationship between work engagement and work–life balance in organizations: A review of the empirical research. *Human Resource Development Review, 19*(3), 240–262. 10.1177/15344 84320917560

10

CHALLENGING INSTITUTIONAL WHITENESS

The Lived Experiences of Structural Tensions in Diversity Work

Heewon Kim[1] and Ashton Mouton[2]

[1]*Arizona State University;* [2]*Sam Houston State University*

Learning Objectives

After reading this chapter, you will:

1 Demonstrate your understanding of the nature of hierarchical organizational structures and the challenges associated with transforming such structures.
2 Examine the experiences of *diversity work* drawing on a case study and explore how to plan, perform, and integrate diversity work.
3 Develop alternative methods of decision making that can be participatory, less hierarchical, inclusive, and built on members' consensus.

Challenging Institutional Whiteness through Diversity Work

This chapter provides (a) a brief reflective account of our experiences of *diversity work* (Ahmed, 2017), particularly focusing on structural whiteness that can be manifested through organizational hierarchies, policies and procedures, and interpersonal communication, (b) our takeaways and practical recommendations that can be useful to other organizational changemakers committed to diversity work, and (c) invitational discussion questions to connect with future students, professionals, and comrades and thereby continue our diversity work. According to Ahmed (2017), diversity work has double-layered meanings. First, it is the work that we do to transform an institution. For example, we (as members of a committee) ideated and executed a range

DOI: 10.4324/9781003333746-12

of tasks to make our community more just and inclusive. Second, it is the work we do when we do not inhabit the norms of the institution. As minoritized individuals in varied senses, we tend to perform additional labor (e.g., emotional labor) when we navigate the academia built on whiteness (e.g., norms, cultures, and practices). We deeply understand, agree, and feel these meanings after our common experiences of diversity work, which has been filled with tensions, frustrations, and pains. As Ahmed (2021) stated, "Trying to address an institutional problem often means inhabiting the institution all the more" (p. 275). This chapter is one of many stories that we can document and share. Through writing this chapter, we seek to collectively analyze our histories, make our voices heard, and renew our commitment to sustainable diversity work.

Introductory Background

Like other disciplines, the field of communication accounts for various injustices that have created experiences of marginalization. This chapter is not only formed by our own experiences, but against the backdrop of institutional whiteness that has pervaded the communication discipline. For example, Chakravarty et al. (2018), focusing on #CommunicationSoWhite, exposed the normalization of whiteness through the underrepresentation of Black, Indigenous, and People of Color scholars in publishing and citational practices. In 2019, National Communication Association (NCA) received national attention because all but one of its 70 Distinguished Scholars were white, which led to heated debates among NCA members.

The co-authors of this chapter served on the *ad hoc* committee for diversity and inclusion in the Organizational Communication Division of the NCA (hereafter the Division). The *ad hoc* committee was later formally named the Committee for Inclusion, Diversity, Equity, and Access (IDEA). It has been simply referred to as "the IDEA Committee" since then. Although the membership of the IDEA Committee has changed over time, we both completed a full two-year term and still continue to collaborate for various IDEA-related projects. The IDEA Committee was formed immediately after a racist incident that occurred during the Division's top paper panel at the 105th Convention of the NCA. The first author stood up to respond to the call for constituting "a diversity committee" while she felt hesitant and frustrated in the aftermath of the traumatic event. Several individuals approached her to join the endeavor, without knowing what would happen to them down the road despite their resolution and commitment. As anticipated, our diversity work involved facing more traumatic events that have shaped our collective memories, emotions, and histories. The first author served as an *ad hoc* committee chair for two years. The second author served on the *ad hoc* committee for the first year and then served on the official IDEA Committee for the second year after the Committee was legitimized through member voting.

It is important to note our positionality, namely, how we were situated under intersectional discrimination and oppression (Crenshaw, 1991) within and beyond the Division. First, we identify ourselves as minoritized individuals in terms of gender, sexuality, race, ethnicity, nationality, and language. Second, we were both early career scholars during our term, such as non-tenured assistant professors (some people use "junior" scholars). Third, we were "*ad hoc*" members that consisted of volunteers, which indicated that neither of us were elected officials at the time of committee formation. Finally, we were embedded in a rigid system of bureaucracy that had us play an "advisory" role constrained by hierarchies. These interlocked systems of oppression (The Combahee River Collective, 1977) are intimately linked to the structural tensions that complicated and challenged our diversity work. It is thus important to be mindful of the influences of intersectionality (Crenshaw, 1991) when reading our stories. The next section discusses two core examples of the structural tensions in diversity work, followed by our reflections and analyses on those examples.

Structural Tensions in Diversity Work

Structure refers to the communicative and spatio-temporal (re)production of rules and resources that make up organizational practice (McPhee et al., 2014). Although organizational structures are communicative in nature, they can also constrain future individual and organizational behaviors as rules are established and reified at varying levels of the organization. Tensions represent embodied states of feeling (such as discomfort or anxiety) that can emerge from dilemmas, frustration, and the inability to make decisions (Putnam et al., 2016). We utilize the term "structural tension" to highlight (a) how the Division's reliance on rules and resources constrained decision making and (re)produced whiteness and (b) how whiteness embedded in organizations and social networks sidelined minoritized members' involvement.

Hierarchies vs. Voice

This section describes the emerging tensions between relying on structural hierarchies and embracing marginalized voices, which may undermine equitable decision making in groups and organizations. In centralized organizations, decision-making power is concentrated at the top levels of the organization, allowing high-status members to dominate influential decisions (Kim & Leach, 2020). As NCA resembles a hierarchical bureaucracy, decision-making power was often centralized within the Executive Committee (EC) of the Division. This indicates that the EC had a final say on all decisions, including those surrounding IDEA-related issues. This left the IDEA Committee with little decision-making power and with an undefined role per the extant bureaucratic structure or policies.

The IDEA Committee was originally an "*ad hoc*" committee, meaning "as necessary" or "for a particular purpose." This is central to understanding how we were viewed. It also placed us hierarchically within the Division in a way that did not make us part of the decision-making processes. While our informal purpose was to address IDEA-related issues, the committee lacked a defined role within the bylaws; the IDEA chair was not an elected position with a specified tenure; members did not serve predetermined terms (e.g., two years); and our role as a committee was never adequately discussed and determined by the EC. In part because of the institutional whiteness ingrained in the Division, the role and participation of the IDEA committee were constrained by the request to remain "advisory to the EC." Given our charge to "advise," we were often expected to conform to the existing hierarchy. The belief that the IDEA Committee was an "advisory group" would go on to shape several important organizational moments.

One representative example was the Division's Edited Book Award decision process where the IDEA Committee had been initially sidelined despite the fact that the central issues around that decision were directly related to racism as well as concomitant conflicts and trauma. The book chosen for the 2021 Award was co-edited by a scholar who played a key role in the aforementioned racist incident at the 105th NCA convention. Awarding this book would retraumatize the division members who were harmed during previous racist incidents that prompted the formation of the IDEA Committee. Owing to the persistence of institutional whiteness, minoritized members still continued to experience exclusion and hurt; little healing occurred. The award decision could recenter whiteness and indeed uphold systemic racism in the Division.

When the EC informed the IDEA Committee of their decision to award the book, one IDEA Committee member, a graduate student, was the quickest to denounce this decision. In what followed, all IDEA Committee members and several EC members responded to either offer new perspectives on the situation or suggest ways to change the awards process. After several tension- and hurt-filled email exchanges, an IDEA Committee member sent a resignation letter that highlighted the physical and emotional toll of the past two years, as well as the very limiting hierarchical relationship between the IDEA Committee and the EC. Prompted by the IDEA committee, the EC decided to re-evaluate their decision to award the book and challenge NCA headquarters. After submitting resignations of all leadership positions, which would dissolve the Division, NCA only then switched their stance and allowed the EC to change the awards process. After intense and painful discussions, a new decision was made to award the contributors of the book (i.e., all chapter authors) rather than the co-editors. This is an exemplar case of whiteness embedded in institutions, hierarchies, and bureaucratic rules.

Voice means consistent and ongoing participation that warrants influence. To make it meaningful and impactful, organizational changemaking should interrogate discriminatory and inequitable practices. Traditionally, the EC, as well as the voting processes that elect EC members, have been the primary decision-making mechanisms within the Division. The IDEA Committee's formation was necessary but disrupted many established practices and assumptions. At first glance, the EC involved in this incident was arguably diverse—it included non-white members and both tenured and tenure-track members. However, as preexisting practices were at the crux of their decision making, the Division struggled to make sense of the role of the IDEA Committee, a group with no previous role in their structure.

For participatory decision making, the IDEA Committee should have been included in the decision-making processes sooner, with more voice, and with less hierarchical separation. Nonetheless, after we vocalized our disapproval, we were able to recognize noticeable changes in our working relationships. The EC made efforts not only to revisit their decision but also to protect the IDEA Committee from any backlash, retaliation, and other negative consequences. The EC also strived to explicate the rationale and processes of the award decision so that other division members could have a better understanding of what happened behind the scene. That way, the EC took responsibility and prevented any unfair blame that could target the IDEA Committee. Although most division members were unaware of backstories, all IDEA Committee members had experienced emerging tensions around dominant norms and expectations, rigid hierarchies and centralized power dynamics, and the dismissal of marginalized, bottom-up voices. As most groups and organizations tend to rely on structural hierarchies for decision making, which may silence different opinions and block organizational learning, all organizational members (particularly those in leadership positions) should be mindful of the potential negative consequences of hierarchical decision making.

Structural Whiteness vs. Agency of Marginalized Members

This section describes the emerging tensions between whiteness embedded in organizational structures and social networks and centering the agencies of members in minoritized groups. Although the IDEA Committee should have been able to engage in participatory planning with the EC, the planning was mostly hierarchical and bureaucratic, with specific moments and meetings framed as "joint endeavors" between the EC and the IDEA Committee. In the fall of 2020 and 2021, the IDEA Committee and the EC jointly hosted a Division's Town Hall meeting, as part of the NCA convention. Our hope was that the annual Town Hall could be a space for healing from past racist moments, voice and belonging for the marginalized in the Division, and growth for the Division. The 2021 Town Hall meeting followed a very contentious business meeting about the awards decision-making processes discussed above. As such, the IDEA Committee met separately to consider potential harm caused by the business meeting and what our marginalized members who were retraumatized would need from us. Instead of sharing results from the second climate survey and mimicking the structure of the 2020 Town Hall, we decided to re-vision the Town Hall.

Our re-visioning included three main sections for the Town Hall: an opening focused on checking in, a main portion focused on dialogue and connection, and a wrap-up focused on reflection (grounded by invitational rhetoric, which communicatively creates the external conditions of safety, value, and freedom; Foss & Griffin, 1995). We opened by checking in on the members, asking about how they were feeling—related to the pandemic and otherwise—and also asked about what kind of support was needed for members to really feel like the Division was their academic "home." The main part of the Town Hall focused on three dialogues that would build on the opening. The goal of the first dialogue was self- and other-care: "Given recent incidents and tensions within our division, how have you navigated your emotional, intellectual, and physical challenges?" The second dialogue aimed to generate connection and belonging: "How can we connect and work with people from different backgrounds, training, and perspectives?" Finally, the third dialogue was meant to generate meaningful allyship between dominant and marginalized groups: "What does allyship look like to you? If we want to reach that level of allyship, what do we need to do to learn and do?" The final portion of the Town Hall was a reflection where we asked members to think about the most important discussions for the day and to start creating bridges between members with different backgrounds. During the Town Hall, our view of the discussion, chat, and even private messages demonstrated that the participants felt positively about the direction of the Town Hall and welcomed the safe space for dialogue, connection, and catharsis.

After the Town Hall, we had a short meeting to debrief. As organizing the Town Hall was emotionally and physically loaded work, we needed room to (virtually) hug, thank, and support each other. We also wanted to celebrate the safe space we created at the two-year anniversary of the IDEA Committee's formation, inclusion of marginalized members, and the healing that took place. Instead, a member of the EC used the space to question our methods for planning the Town Hall. Immediately after wrapping the Town Hall, we were warned that the Town Hall might have created more harm in the long run. The pejorative tone of the reprimand nullified our success and delegitimized our emotional/physical labor in the planning processes. And yet, in the days that followed the 2021 Town Hall, the IDEA Committee received countless messages from both colleagues and other division members in both dominant and marginalized groups extending support and solidarity with the IDEA mission, praising that we created a safe and intentional space to navigate difficult conversations. Although the EC member later reached out to apologize for their in-the-moment reaction, the IDEA Committee tried to determine why our "joint endeavors" to create safe and inclusionary spaces within the Division were perceived as exclusionary to a section of dominant group members.

When joint endeavors are bureaucratic and hierarchical, rather than truly participatory, they are routed in a structure built from whiteness rather than our new focus on inclusion and change. In our experiences with Town Hall planning, the term "joint endeavor" was used rhetorically, a bureaucratic move to both control the IDEA committee's planning/actions and then highlight accomplishments for the EC members (Ariss et al., 2014). For organizational changemaking, we must call attention not only to bureaucracy and structure but also to interpersonal relationships with dominant groups. We realized that members from dominant groups have louder voices because of direct access to the EC. Although the Chair of the IDEA Committee sits on the EC, the dominant members of the Division still have more embedded bureaucratic power because of their access to the top of the hierarchy (the EC) than even the IDEA committee. Privileging and prioritizing these voices in response to IDEA work negates efforts for inclusion, as it amplifies whiteness as a knee-jerk response to changemaking (Shome, 2000). When organizational members use their bureaucratic roles to diminish IDEA work or to distance themselves from IDEA work, they unwittingly create a line between "us" and "them," increasing resistance and reducing possibilities for change (Shome, 2000).

Practical Applications

Based on our shared experiences, we suggest two practical recommendations focusing primarily on (a) the alternative approaches to decision making in diversity work and (b) the individual and collective agency needed for meaningful diversity work.

Consensus Decision Making

According to Poole and Hirokawa (1996), communication constitutes group decisions in two aspects. First, the form and content of decisions are worked out through communication. We can trace group members' communication processes of accumulation, deletion, elaboration, and alteration of premises. In this respect, decisions can be viewed as emerging texts. Second, decisions are social products embedded in social realities. Group members' experiences of social realities are created through communication and therefore become the prerequisites for decision making. Our communicative interactions while performing diversity work with various members in the Division also affected the outcomes, quality, and processes of decision making.

Decision making is intimately linked to our experiences of organizational justice. In any groups and organizations, decision making is a central activity that shapes members' perceptions and enactments of distributive justice (e.g., outcomes of decisions, tasks, and collaboration), procedural justice (e.g., rules and steps to determine outcomes), and interactional justice (e.g., experiences of interpersonal communication during decision-making processes). A good (or bad) decision can have cascading effects on members' task performance, interpersonal relationships, and coordination activities. As organizational and group members increasingly call for democratic, just, and inclusive work environments, scholars and practitioners alike have developed ideas around participatory decision making, shared governance, or workplace democracy (Deetz, 1992). Despite such efforts, it is true that most of us experience the opposite. We are often simply being told (i.e., top-down decision making) or allowed to cast a vote (i.e., the majority rule).

However, in small groups, particularly in groups, committees, or coalitions committed to missions like IDEA, it is increasingly feasible to experiment or normalize more participatory, shared modes of decision making. As illustrated in our example above, centralized decision-making procedures may constrain voice and participation, especially from marginalized members, create a divisional line between different parties, and curtail the possibility to seek out a more innovative, just, and inclusive solution. Furthermore, centralized or hierarchical decision making could hamper achieving the very missions of IDEA. Contrary to large for-profit organizations or bureaucratic government agencies, it was possible for us to experiment with different interactional principles for decision making, especially among members who had high readiness and demands for equality and justice. Unfortunately, many groups performing diversity work also tend to operate within bureaucratic structures, reducing individuals' motivation and effort to challenge dominant norms. Oftentimes, even people engaging in diversity work do not question the processes of top-down decision making, as they are afraid of potential retribution or they have accepted top-down processes as common (and normal) practice across a range of sectors such as families, schools, universities, churches, and corporations.

We propose some principles and tactics of consensus decision making especially for groups or collectives performing diversity work, drawing on the lessons from mutual aid groups (Spade, 2020). In consensus decision making, group members operate based on the following philosophies: (a) everyone has a say in decisions that affect them; (b) everyone cares about all members' consent; and (c) everyone directly participates in decisions without relying on representatives, supervisors, or "powerful" members (in terms of age, race, gender, hierarchical ranks, and others).

Small groups or collectives can create their own protocols for consensus decision making, taking into account various factors such as their size, prior histories, interpersonal closeness or conflicts, and timeframe, just to name a few. As one possible guideline, Spade (2020) proposed the following steps for consensus decision making: (1) have a discussion on an agenda item; (2) create a proposal based on the discussion; (3) identify any unsatisfied concerns; (4) collaboratively modify the proposal; (5) assess the degree of support; and (6) either finalize the decision or circle back to Step (1) or Step (3).

Depending on members' commitment, prior experiences of collaboration or training, the nature of agenda, and other contextual factors such as communication modalities, the process and duration of consensus decision making may vary. However, one of the most important procedures that require members' attention is carefully investigating the levels of (dis)agreements among group members (Step 3). For example, there could be members who want to express disagreements but do not want to block the proposal. By contrast, there could be members who feel that the proposal cannot be passed without modification. Based on listening, candid sharing of concerns, and comparing different ideas, a group can continue to discuss the proposed idea until everyone approves the proposal. In consensus decision making, no one has a final say or exclusive decision-making authority. Group members communicate with one another until everyone is satisfied enough to implement the proposed idea. Such consensus could be especially crucial for groups that pursue missions related to justice, equity, and inclusion so that the procedures do not betray their purposes. For instance, in many cases of decision making within the Division, the concerns and suggestions from the IDEA Committee were often dismissed by the EC without any rationales or explanations. Instead, those concerns and proposals could be discussed until all committee members understand and collectively find a solution.

Consensus decision making yields a variety of benefits for group members and their group as a whole. Although no decision-making method can prevent all conflicts, consensus decision making can help us address power dynamics and avoid the potential negative outcomes of centralization, hierarchies, and the majority rule (Spade, 2020), such as abuse of power, demobilization of members, lack of member engagement, and suppression of marginalized voices. In fact, low-status members' voices are likely to be suppressed in organizations, although such negative effects of hierarchies can be ameliorated when organizations have a more just climate (Kim & Kiura, 2020).

When consensus decision-making practices are embraced by a group, decisions are likely to be based on the best interest and wisdom of all participants, followed by their willingness to implement their decision. Especially in diverse groups in which people have different expertise, backgrounds, and social status, it is critical for us to learn how to create a climate and structure to enable everyone to speak up about their concerns and ideas without fear, hesitancy, or cynicism. Any groups that seek to conduct diversity work can practice consensus decision making to improve their collaborative relationships, decision outcomes, and decision implementation.

Individual and Collective Agency

Giddens (1984) claims that workers are actors that have agency and the organizational structure is brought into being by the communicative actions of those workers. Structural inequity is inherent given the history of academic intuitions as spaces for only white men. It is telling, though, that Giddens leads with agency, as there is no structure at all without the actions of people who seek to both maintain and change the structure. When organizational members exert their agency in opposition to diversity work, they seek—whether intentionally or not—to maintain the privilege they receive from the structure. Yet, from our own IDEA work and the tensions discussed in this chapter, it is evident that organizational change is possible through agency. This process demonstrates the duality of structure; structure is built from communication and interaction between actors in the organization, and then the structure guides future interactions while it is also simultaneously transformed by those interactions (Giddens, 1984). McPhee et al. (2014) explain that careful attention to the interactions between rules/resources and actors provides insight into how organizations and the actors within them can change and adapt through communication and agency. As such, it is through individual and collective agency that organizational changemaking is possible.

Our committee was formed through the agency of an individual followed by a small collective. Over the last couple of years, we have at times had to act within the confines of the rules (e.g., going through the process of becoming a standing committee) and the preexisting bureaucracy of the Division and NCA. We have also found ourselves at times without decision-making power and with no options for action. In those instances, our individual and collective resistance was required. Our actions at every turn have been to make tangible the structures that exclude and marginalize our members so that we might change them. The lived outcomes of our work have been incremental, slow, and at times hard-won. However, we collectively continue this work, exerting our individual and collective agency one moment at a time, one decision at a time, to change the structure. Grounded in structuration theory and based on our own experiences of collective agency, we provide four guidelines below for organizational changemakers.

First, individuals and collectives can exert their agency for change. Poole and McPhee (2005) discuss how actions of organizational members can lead to transformations in the structure and these actions can take the form of individual or group agency. Individuals exert their agency by breaking the rules, pushing against the rules, and even working within the rules to advocate for change. No matter how one exerts their agency, organizational transformation often requires mindful and intentional aspects of agency. Structuration theory replaces an essentialist view of identity as a stable or core set of characteristics with a "view of identity as a structure of resources (our beliefs, attitudes, and knowledge; our work experience; our knowledge about ourselves) and rules (norms, routines, and habits that characterize us) that people can draw on when they interact in social situations" (Poole & McPhee, 2005, p. 181). This means that individuals looking to exert their agency for diversity work should think of their own identities and behaviors as mini-structures to avoid simply reproducing the privilege and marginalization that already exists in the organizational structure. We must constantly question our own positions and privileges within the organization, remaining mindful of the structures we (re)produce through our actions. In addition to individual agency, collectives can exert their agency in similar ways, but with larger impacts. At this group level, collectives utilize and understand rules and resources through interaction, but also can reject structures more openly through collective action and dialogue (Poole & McPhee, 2005). For our committee, diversity work was a collective agentic action necessary to change the structure of the Division.

Second, individuals and collectives should make structure tangible through agency and action. Structure is often intangible as it guides our behavior (e.g., following an awards process dictated by Division bylaws); diversity work should make structure *tangible* by highlighting how the structure marginalizes, diminishes, and constrains non-dominant members. Giddens (1984) specifically names division of labor, hierarchical organizing, bureaucracy, procedures in text, and organizational culture as places where structure becomes invisible, especially to dominant organizational members. Consequently, these are the same spaces dominant organizational members are able to exert their power over others. Individuals and collectives seeking to change their organizations and/or engage in diversity work should look for opportunities to make structure tangible by highlighting how the structure marginalizes, diminishes, and constrains non-dominant members and non-dominant ways of thinking, acting, and feeling. Unfortunately for us, the awards process was made tangible after its implosion. We could have anticipated challenges by examining who had been most and least represented in the awards process, discussing possible enactments of the structure, and identifying barriers to inclusion/success. Structure can be made visible by individual questioning (e.g., a resignation email issued in opposition) as well as collective organizing (e.g., awards sub-committees are now guided through inclusive reviewing practices and are encouraged to share individual decision making based on the criteria).

Third, resistance is a powerful option. Poole and McPhee (2005) argue that structures are bound by a paradox where the structure creates efficiency and coordination through rules and resources while also becoming limiting and oppressive. Through adherence or resistance to the rules, practitioners working within organizations both produce and reproduce the structure, while also creating space for transformation. When even the semblance of adherence is not an option, when individually or collectively there is no decision-making power, open resistance to the rules or the actions of others is an option. For the IDEA Committee, a member's resignation and the Committee's explicit resistance exerted a significant influence on the EC's change in their decision. Furthermore, when the Division's leadership informed the NCA headquarters of their decision to collectively resign, the NCA allowed for revising the processes. Collective, rather than individual, resistance can indeed challenge oppressive systems.

Finally, recognize that change is not immediate. While organizational change can be instant and drastic, it is more often gradual and subtle (McPhee et al., 2014). To take a term from geology, our recommendation is to engage in ice wedging. Think of the organizational structure as a rock and agency as water and ice. As changemakers exert agency, those actions seep into the cracks of the structure. Over time, agency solidifies into tangible changes, however small, and can eventually crack the structure for large-scale organizational change. During the two years, we served together on the IDEA Committee, we made incremental movements in rethinking awards, encouraging the Division to recognize mentorship, teaching, and service as important, and questioning bylaws and "traditions." Our small committee started as "*ad hoc*" and is now a permanent committee with 15 members and an elected position. After three years of seeing this committee in action, even though we are no longer serving, the changes have been evident and impactful.

Conclusion

In this chapter, we focus on the moments of tension that emerged in our Division at NCA. These are also key moments that led to organizational change. Hoping to further engage in decolonizing organizational communication (Pal et al., 2022), we present our cases as examples that reveal various forms of structural whiteness, struggles in diversity work, and possibilities for alternative organizing. First, we examined how structural whiteness produced and reproduced hierarchy and bureaucracy in the Division as well as the tensional difficulties that changemakers experienced. Second, drawing on our experiences of diversity work, we specifically identified two structural tensions that permeated the IDEA Committee and the EC's relationship and how each tension affected the processes of decision making. Third, we offer practical recommendations that envision participatory, just, and inclusive futures. We propose that consensus decision making cultivates participatory practices of interactions in which all members can exert influence. Additionally, practitioners should pay attention to the role of agency and resistance, however incremental, in crafting change. Finally, we suggest that changemakers be mindful of their positionality and daily interactions. Collaboratively both the IDEA Committee and the EC acknowledged their own limitations and adapted to new ways of organizing. We hope that our recommendations and discussion questions challenge how scholars and practitioners approach change efforts and diversity work in their organizations, groups/teams, and communities.

Discussion Questions

1 Think about a recent case in which your group, team, or organization made a critical decision that would exert a significant impact on its members (e.g., change of the working-from-home policy, revision of merit review criteria). Then, answer the following questions on that particular decision-making experience.

   a What are the taken-for-granted practices of decision making in your group or organization?
   b To what extent was the decision-making process hierarchical or participatory? Was your group able to assess the degree of consensus among its members? If so, how?
   c To what degree were you able to express your concerns or thoughts? Did you feel safe to speak up when you disagree with leaders or other members?
   d Reflecting on your answers to the questions above, what would you do differently? What would you do the same? Explain why.

2 Let's think about how we can transform organizational structure to address institutional whiteness and related power dynamics (e.g., power abuse, discrimination, bullying).

   a To what extent do you think that your organization is diverse, inclusive, and just? What aspect can be improved or changed? Provide one or two examples that support your suggestions for change.
   b What are the dominant practices, procedures, policies, or relationships that limit such organizational change?
   c What can be done to challenge the existing barriers that stem from the dominant norms of whiteness? What types of support or resources would you need?

3 Think about a group or collective that is designed to conduct diversity work in your organization. If there are no such groups or committees at the moment, imagine that your organization plans to create a group of changemakers.

   a Do you know the roles and work of the diversity committee in your organization? Are you aware of which task the committee recently accomplished? Do you believe that their labor is (in)visible? If so, please explain. If it is difficult to learn about the committee's work, what are the obstacles?
   b Within the organizational hierarchy or decision-making structures, where is the diversity committee located? What kinds of influences can the committee make?

c If you would like to join or collaborate with the committee, how could you express your intention? Does your organization have an established procedure?

d How can your organizational leadership better advocate such a committee's work?

Author Bios

Dr. Heewon Kim (she/her) is an Associate Professor in the Hugh Downs School of Human Communication at Arizona State University. Her research interests include organizational justice and inclusion, workers' voice and resistance, and institutional violence, with particular attention to marginalized groups and individuals.

Dr. Ashton Mouton (she/her) is an Assistant Professor of Business Administration at Sam Houston State University. She teaches classes in business communication and project design. Her service efforts are dedicated to diversity, equity, and inclusion. Her research examines project and message design as well as organizational structure, intersectionality, and career success.

References

Ahmed, S. (2017). *Living a feminist life*. Duke University Press.

Ahmed, S. (2021). *Complaint!* Duke University Press.

Ariss, A., Özbilgin, M., Tatli, A., & April, K. (2014). Tackling whiteness in organizations and management. *Journal of Managerial Psychology*, *29*(4), 362–369. 10.1108/JMP-10-2013-0331

Crenshaw, K. (1991). Mapping the margins: Intersectionality, identity politics, and violence against women of color. *Stanford Law Review*, *43*(6), 1241–1299.

Chakravartty, P., Kuo, R., Grubbs, V., & McIlwain, C. (2018). #Communicationsowhite. *Journal of Communication, 68*(2), 254–266. 10.1093/joc/jqy003

Deetz, S. (1992). *Democracy in an age of corporate colonization: Developments in communication and the politics of everyday life*. The State University of New York Press.

Foss, S. K., & Griffin, C. L. (1995). Beyond persuasion: A proposal for an invitational rhetoric. *Communication Monographs*, *62*(1), 2–18.

Giddens, A. (1984). *The constitution of society: Introduction of the theory of structuration*. University of California Press.

Kim, H., & Kiura, M. (2020). The influences of social status and organizational justice on employee voice: A case of customer care workers. *International Journal of Business Communication*. Online advance publication. 10.1177/2329488420969776

Kim, H., & Leach, R. (2020). The role of digitally-enabled voice in fostering positive change and affective commitment in centralized organizations. *Communication Monographs*, *87*(4), 425–444. 10.1080/03637751.2020.1745859

McPhee, R. D., Poole, M. S., & Iverson, J. (2014). Structuration theory. In L. L. Putnam, & D. K. Mumby (Eds.), *The Sage handbook of organizational communication: Advances in theory, research, and methods* (pp. 75–99). Sage.

Pal, M., Kim, H., Harris, K. L., Long, Z., Linabary, J., Wilhoit Larson, E., Jensen, P. R., Gist-Mackey, A. N., McDonald, J., Nieto-Fernandez, B., Jiang, J., Misra, S., & Dempsey, S. E. (2022). Decolonizing organizational communication. *Management Communication Quarterly, 36*(3), 547–577. 10.1177/089331 8922109025

Poole, M. S., & Hirokawa, R. Y. (1996). Introduction: Communication and group decision-making. In R. Y. Hirokawa, & M. S. Poole (Eds.), *Communication and group decision-making* (pp. 3–18). SAGE.

Poole, M. S., & McPhee, R. D. (2005). Structuration theory. In S. May, & D. K. Mumby (Eds.), *Engaging organizational communication theory and research: Multiple perspectives* (pp. 171–195). Sage.

Putnam, L. L., Fairhurst, G. T., & Banghart, S. (2016). Contradictions, dialectics, and paradoxes in organizations: A constitutive approach. *Academy of Management Annals, 10*(1), 65–171. 10.5465/19416520.2016.1162421

Shome, R. (2000). Outing whiteness. *Critical Studies in Media Communication, 17*(3), 366–371.

Spade, D. (2020). *Mutual aid: Building solidarity during this crisis.* Verso.

The Combahee River Collective. (1977). The Combahee River Collective: A Black feminist statement. In Z. R. Eisenstein (Ed.), *Capitalist patriarchy and the case for socialist feminism* (pp. 362–372). Monthly Review Press.

11

"#BEINGBLACKANDMUSLIM"

Addressing Intersectional Invisibility in Muslim American Communities

Marwa Abdalla

University of California, San Diego

Learning Objectives

After reading this chapter, you will:

1 Understand the concept of intersectional invisibility.
2 Be able to analyze organizational initiatives aimed at representing and addressing the needs of multi-racial and multi-ethnic group identities.
3 Explore tensions inherent in discourses of "unity" and "oneness" as they relate to organizational contexts.

Introduction

Diversity, equity, and inclusion (DEI) work has become increasingly salient against the backdrop of racial injustice, police brutality, and the disproportionate effects of the COVID-19 pandemic among communities of color. Within organizational contexts, such work is often framed by an emphasis on unity. Yet, as this chapter explores, discourses of unity regularly privilege prototypical group members—those who typically come to mind when group identity is invoked—at the expense of non-prototypical ones (Chawansky, 2016). The term *intersectional invisibility* describes the seeming erasure experienced by individuals who are not viewed as typical or representative members of an already marginalized group (Purdie-Vaughns & Eibach, 2008). For example, intersectional invisibility has been used to describe the experiences of Black and Asian women professionals (Coles & Pasek, 2020; Wong et al., 2022) as well as those of sexual and ethnic minorities (Chawansky, 2016; Smith et al., 2019). Recently, it has

DOI: 10.4324/9781003333746-13

been used to describe Black Muslims' experiences in the United States (Muslim Wellness Foundation, 2020). Although researchers have focused on the factors contributing to intersectional invisibility, less attention has been paid to how individuals and organizations address this challenge.

Drawing on theories of intersectionality, this chapter considers historical and theoretical factors contributing to Black Muslim intersectional invisibility in the United States (hereafter U.S.). It then presents exemplars related to #BeingBlackandMuslim, a social media campaign aimed at centering the experiences of Black Muslims, along with organizational discourses responding to such concerns from the Islamic Society of North America (ISNA), a national, historically non-Black Muslim-led institution. It concludes with practical insights on addressing intersectional invisibility and questions to encourage further exploration of these issues in organizational contexts.

Before commencing, a few notes on terminology are in order. Although the terms "Black" and "African-American" are often used interchangeably in the U.S., I use "Black Muslim" in this chapter to inclusively connote both Muslim-identifying American-born descendants of enslaved Africans as well as diasporic groups from various parts of Africa and the Caribbean. I do so while recognizing the immense cultural diversity inherent in this identity label. Though not avowed by all Muslims living in the U.S., I use the term "Muslim American" throughout this chapter to refer to individuals who identify as Muslim within a U.S. American context, regardless of their citizenship status, national background of origin, or self-described ethnic/racial identity.

Historical and Theoretical Considerations

Between 25 and 30% of Muslims in the U.S. identify as Black or African American (Mogahed & Chouhoud, 2017). Despite representing the single largest demographic segment of the Muslim American population, Black Muslims have historically been marginalized in dominant discourses and media representations, with Arab and South Asian ethnicities viewed as the norm (Abdul Khabeer, 2016). The #BlackLivesMatter movement reignited conversations about the marginality of Black Muslims in many Muslim American communities, prompting an international social media campaign, #BeingBlackandMuslim, along with responses from numerous non-Black Muslim-led institutions (Chouhoud & Abdullah, 2020; MuslimARC, 2021). Although research on Black Muslim experiences is increasing (Abdalla, 2022; Abdul Khabeer, 2016; Jackson, 2005; Latif, 2018), scholars focused on DEI initiatives have paid little attention to the implications discourses on Blackness and Muslimness have for understanding multi-ethnic and multi-racial groups. To better understand the historical context in which #BeingBlackandMuslim emerged, it is helpful first to chart how Muslim identities have been racialized in the U.S.

The Racialization of Muslims in the U.S.

Muslim American narratives are often told through the lens of immigration; however, enslaved Africans, not immigrants, comprised the first critical mass of Muslims in North America (Jackson, 2005). Early legal prohibitions on the practice of non-Christian religions made the intergenerational transfer of Muslim identity among enslaved populations nearly impossible (Beydoun, 2018; Jackson, 2005). Yet, Muslim identities persisted in the U.S. in different forms. Early non-Black Muslim immigrants from the Middle East, Europe, and Asia were racialized as "Turks," "Arabs," and "Asians" and considered outside the statutory definition of whiteness required for citizenship (Bayoumi, 2006). Dominant racial hierarchies within the U.S. incentivized the adoption of white norms as a means of social mobility, causing many non-Black Muslims to distance themselves from Black racial groups (Abdul Khabeer, 2016). Meanwhile, the early 20th century saw the advent and growth of national organizations bridging African American heritage with Islamic philosophies, such as the Moorish Science Temple of America (MSTA) and the Nation of Islam (NOI) (Gibson, 2012). Even after the alignment of some of these organizations with Sunni Islam in the 1970s, there remained divisions between predominantly Black or African American mosques and mosques of different racial, ethnic, or sectarian backgrounds (Bagby, 2021; Marsh, 1984).

The reform of naturalization laws in 1965 and the resulting uptick in immigration from Muslim-majority countries shifted the representational face of Islam in the U.S. from Black Muslims to Muslims of Arab or South Asian descent, a shift reinforced by many popular media representations (Alsultany, 2012, 2022; Latif, 2018). The erasure of Black Muslims was complicated by what Sherman Jackson (2011) has described as "racial agnosia," the disavowal of race and dismissal of its centrality to life in the U.S. by non-Black Muslims. In a country where enduring legacies of slavery, segregation, and systemic racism have translated into less income, less education, poorer health, and decreased lifespans for Black individuals, the unique challenges faced by Black Muslims were often obscured by ideals of unity and oneness espoused in many Muslim American communities (Farole, 2011; Jackson, 2011).

Unity and Intersectional Invisibility After 9/11

Although the unity of all Muslims—often described as an "ummah" or nation—represents a central component of Islamic theology (Afsaruddin, 2020), legacies of colorism and anti-Black racism in many Muslim-majority countries have long impacted Muslim American communities (Grewal, 2009). Despite accounts of racism within their institutions, non-Black Muslim leaders and laypersons alike have characteristically adopted a colorblind ideology to race, further obscuring the felt realities of many Black Muslims (Bonilla-Silva, 2010; Farole, 2011). "Muslims cannot be racist," such thinking goes, not only because Islam prohibits it but also because Muslims are "Muslim first," united in their faith above all other identity markers (Guhin, 2018). Non-Black Muslims' historical insistence on disavowing race has resulted in the disregard for its centrality in U.S. American life, especially for Black Americans (Jackson, 2011). Additionally, such disavowals functioned to obscure Black Muslims' experiences with marginalization, micro-aggressions, and discrimination at the hands of their co-religionists (Chouhoud & Abdullah, 2020; Farole, 2011).

After the attacks of 9/11, the U.S. witnessed an alarming normalization of anti-Muslim animus often directed at individuals who "looked Muslim" by virtue of phenotypic features such as skin tone, perceived Arab ethnicity, or stereotypical cultural features such as a beard, head covering, prayer beads, or style of dress (Cainkar, 2011; Considine, 2017). In the face of undue detainment, hostility, racial profiling, and the explicit compromising of their civil liberties, many Muslim leaders advocated for the shedding of ethnic and racial differences and unity under the cultural banner of Islam (Osman, 2006). As Muslims of different backgrounds cohered to challenge anti-Muslim hostility, Muslim leadership writ large failed to recognize how Black Muslims' experiences with such hostility intersected with deep-seated anti-Black racism. As a result, the intersecting oppressions and unique challenges faced by many Black Muslims' including disparities in wealth, health, education, police brutality, employment, housing, and political representation often went ignored (Walid, 2016). Perceived neither as prototypical members of the Muslim American community, where Arab and South Asian Muslims were viewed as the norm, nor as prototypical members of the non-Muslim Black American society, in which Christianity was viewed as dominant, Black Muslims—both native-born and immigrant—experienced intersectional invisibility within and outside their faith communities (Muslim Wellness Foundation, 2020). As this chapter suggests, such challenges continue today. Given this history, I now turn to theorizations of intersectionality as a framework for analyzing the examples which follow.

Intersectionality as a Theoretical Framework

The term *intersectionality* captures the complex relationship between analytic categories such as race, gender, sexuality, and class, helping to name what decades of Black feminists and scholars including Sojourner

Truth, the Combahee River Collective, and Audre Lorde, had described as the "interlocking" workings of oppression (Collins, 2019; Taylor, 2017). Theoretically, intersectionality opened up space for analyzing intra-group differences in relation to power. For example, in her initial description of the term, Kimberlé Crenshaw (1991) described "internal exclusions and marginalizations" *within* groups and identified how collective group identities are often "centered on the intersectional identities of a few" (p. 1299). While acknowledging its utility, scholars have argued for intersectionality's further development as a critical social theory (Collins, 2019), including an emphasis on the "intra-categorical complexity" inherent in multiply marginalized subjects' experiences (Nash, 2008, p. 6).

Building on intersectional scholarship and social identity theory, psychologists Valerie Purdie-Vaughns and Richard Eibach (2008) coined the term *intersectional invisibility* to describe the experiences of multiply marginalized individuals who fall outside the prototypical identity for their ascribed social groups. The term has been used to describe the failure to recognize non-prototypical individuals as members of their constituent groups and distort individuals' characteristics to fit them into prototypical frameworks (Chawansky, 2016; Wong et al., 2022). For example, because of their non-white race and non-male gender, Black women have faced intersectional invisibility in the context of women's liberation and Black liberation movements, respectively, and have been asked to "choose" between advocating on behalf of their gender or their race (Crenshaw, 1991; King, 1988). Similarly, non-White transgender individuals specific needs may be overlooked because their intersectional identities fall outside the dominant norms in White trans communities and cis-gender communities of color (Hennekam & Dumazert, 2023). While scholarship has focused on how such invisibility informs individual experiences (Coles & Pasek, 2020; Simpson & Taylor, 2021; Smith et al., 2019), less attention has been paid to how it is addressed in interpersonal and institutional settings (i.e., Chawansky, 2016; Muslim Wellness Foundation, 2020; Wong et al., 2022). Taken together, these theories of intersectionality help frame the examples discussed in this chapter as lessons on addressing intersectional invisibility.

Recognizing the importance of self-reflexivity in research, I consider my positionality concerning the texts I am analyzing before turning to these examples. I identify as the second-generation daughter of non-Black Muslim parents who immigrated to the U.S. in the 1980s to pursue professional degrees. My heritage is Middle Eastern and North African, and I speak Arabic fluently, which places me squarely within what Suad Abdul Khabeer (2016) describes as the Arab and South Asian "ethnoreligious hegemony" among Muslim Americans (p. 3). I draw on Abdul Khabeer's (2016) notion of ethnoreligious hegemony to describe how Muslim immigrants from North Africa, the Middle East, and South Asia and their descendants are afforded—or have afforded themselves—various degrees of power based on claims of proximity to the Islamic tradition in *defining* and *policing* the boundaries of Islamic identity in the U.S. (pp. 84–85). I also use this term because it connotes how these perceived ethnic identities have been taken for granted, unquestioned, and assumed natural in relation to Muslimness. Despite years of working as a community educator, I recognize that to the extent I was not challenging anti-Black racism, I was complicit in its persistence. I see my research on Muslim American communities as one means of addressing intersectional invisibility and anti-Black racism within and outside those communities.

Challenging Intersectional Invisibility

I begin this analysis with exemplars related to #BeingBlackandMuslim, a social media campaign aimed at centering the experiences of Black Muslims, before transitioning to organizational discourses from the ISNA addressing racial justice.

#BeingBlackandMuslim

In 2014, the Muslim Anti-Racism Collaborative (MuslimARC) launched with the hashtag #BeingBlackandMuslim. Executive Director Margari Aziza Hill (2016) describes the impetus for the organization's formation as follows: "In late 2013, a group of activists, scholars, and concerned netizens coalesced around the issue of anti-Blackness perpetrated by Muslim youth on social media ... Out of that group, Muslim Anti-Racism Collaborative formed to give voice to Black Muslims and celebrate their contributions."

#BeingBlackandMuslim has generated numerous online conversations through annual "relaunches" to help foster Black Muslim pride (Blay, 2017). The hashtag's popularity was amplified in 2017 when Bobby Rogers, a self-identified Black Muslim visual historian, photographer, and art director from Minneapolis, Minnesota, created a portrait series to accompany it (Rogers, 2017a, 2017b, 2021). Soon after its release on April 19, 2017, the #BeingBlackandMuslim portrait series achieved "viral" status and praise in the popular press as "raw," "powerful," "awesome," and "needed" (Alami, 2019; Dahir, 2017). In this chapter, I focus on the image texts themselves and not the re-Tweets in which they were

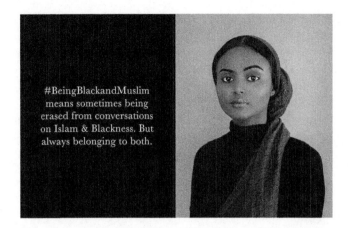

FIGURE 11.1   #BeingBlackandMuslim Sample Image.

featured; however, I consider each against the broader backdrop of the #BeingBlackandMuslim campaign.

As represented in Figure 11.1, the nine image texts from the #BeingBlackandMuslim series share a compositional structure: each is divided in half, with the right side featuring a portrait of an individual set against a light green background and the left side containing a quote set in white text against a black background. The portraits and captions represent powerful visual arguments: in words, they name the erasure and invisibility of Black Muslims; in pictures, they belie that invisibility with individuals identifying as such. Three overlapping themes emerged from the analysis of this series against the backdrop of the broader social media campaign: invisibility, double marginalization, and centering Black Muslim identities.

Invisibility

One portrait featuring a young man in a grey t-shirt and olive green and fatigue-print hoodie highlighted the non-prototypical status and resulting invisibility of Black Muslims with the statement: "#BeingBlackand Muslim means having to recite a verse from the Quran to non-Black Muslims to prove that you're Muslim" (Rogers, 2017a). The image and the caption echoed sentiments from the #BeingBlackandMuslim campaign indicting non-Black Muslims for doubting Black Muslims' religious identities. Other portraits explicitly named the invisibility of Black Muslims in Muslim-American communities. For example, one featuring a young woman with a beige-colored hijab draped over her right and left shoulders stated: "#BeingBlackandMuslim means you are the largest group of American-Muslims but you are the last to be asked to speak on Islam" (Rogers, 2017a). Another (Figure 11.1), featuring a woman with a dark brown printed hijab wrapped behind her head and draped over her left shoulder, stated: "#BeingBlackandMuslim means sometimes being erased from conversations on Islam and Blackness. But always belonging to both" (Rogers, 2017a). These examples highlight Black and African American Muslims' experiences with invisibility, despite comprising the largest single segment of the U.S. Muslim population (Mogahed & Chouhoud, 2017). By reinforcing Black Muslims' belonging to conversations "on Islam and Blackness," they also challenge that invisibility.

Double Marginalization

In addition to naming and challenging invisibility, the #BeingBlackandMuslim portrait series testified to the double marginalization experienced by Black Muslims through discourses of anti-Blackness and Islamophobia. For example, two image texts contained the following: "#BeingBlackandMuslim means dealing with Anti-Blackness, Arab supremacy, and Islamophobia within and outside of the Ummah;" and "#BeingBlackandMuslim means if you're not being called a nigger, you're being called a terrorist," accompanied by images of men, one wearing a light stone-colored shirt and the other, a grey sweater with a beige outer jacket, respectively (Rogers, 2017a). Another featuring a young woman with curls framing her crown references the Arabic word *abeed*, defined as "slave" but "used by many Arabs to describe black people" (Walid, 2013). These double epithets and multiple forms of marginalization point to the challenges experienced by Black Muslims on double fronts. They also underscore the effects flattened representations of "Black" and "Muslim" identities have on effacing them from the struggles in which they were active stakeholders.

Centering Black Muslim Identities

Lastly, some of the image texts from the series encouraged the centering of Black Muslim identity and reclamation of Black heritage in the history of Muslim Americans: "#BeingBlackandMuslim means understanding there's no American Muslim identity without exploring Black religious thought and political identity;" and "#BeingBlackandMuslim means celebrating the legacy of Black Muhaddithin [narrators of Prophetic tradition] and Fuqaha [Muslim theologians versed in *fiqh* or law] and passing on their legacy to the next generation." These image texts center Black Muslims in narratives on Muslims in the U.S. and globally, challenging both invisibility and marginalization. They echo other texts from the campaign affirming the coexistence of Black and Muslim identities and making visible previously ignored Black Muslim narratives.

Considered together, the texts from the #BeingBlackandMuslim portrait series exhibit the rhetorical power of speaking as "a marginalized group within a marginalized group" (Rogers as cited in Dahir, 2017). They also exemplify strategies of addressing intra and inter-group experiences of invisibility and its attendant oppression while calling for collective action by naming experiences previously unacknowledged. As the following subsection discusses, historically non-Black Muslim-led institutions found themselves positioned to respond to such accounts of intersectional invisibility within their organizations.

Reckoning with Intersectional Invisibility in Institutional Discourses

Discourses surrounding the campaign #BeingBlackandMuslim drew attention to the "unconscious omission" and "deliberate white-washing" of Black identities in contemporary Muslim American discourses (Walid, 2016). The death of George Floyd at the hands of police and the ensuing national protests prompted several historically non-Black Muslim-led organizations, including the ISNA, to host or join protests, panels, and webinars to challenge racial injustice. As an offshoot of a rapidly growing, largely immigrant Muslim population, ISNA was established in the 1980s to foster understanding of "emerging" Muslim communities in society and became one of the most prominent Muslim organizations in North America. One of the goals of this study was to explore how formal and informal communication patterns utilized by ISNA enabled and constrained certain subject positions as the intended audience of its discourses. Examination of specific texts addressing anti-Black racism in the wake of #BlackLivesMatter and #BeingBlackandMuslim revealed shifts in these subject positions. Although my analysis of ISNA texts covered a span of eight years, for this chapter, I focus on two moments in ISNA discourses from 2020 which exemplify these shifts and the tensions therein: a panel on racial justice entitled, "Islam Against Racism," published on the ISNA Facebook page in June 2020 (2020a) and texts from the 57th Annual ISNA Conference held in September 2020 entitled, "The Struggle for Social and Racial Justice: A Moral Imperative" (ISNA, 2020b). These texts included marketing materials for the panel and conference, the conference program, video recordings, and transcriptions of the panel and conference proceedings. In total, these texts produced 63 pages of single-spaced transcript.

"Islam Against Racism"

The first moment I focus on occurred in June 2020 when ISNA co-hosted a five-speaker panel on its Facebook page, "Islam Against Racism." Historically non-Black Muslim-led organizations such as ISNA had hosted highly publicized events, conferences, and panel discussions characterized by a lack of Black Muslim representation (Chouhoud & Abdullah, 2020; Walid, 2016). Upon first impression, the poster advertising the panel appeared to follow this trend, and numerous posts and comments on social media called out the absence of Black Muslims on the panel. For example, in response to the "Islam Against Racism" poster, one Facebook user commented: "Confront your issue internally first, you are in no position to preach to the world" (ISNA, 2020a). Such concerns were echoed in other posts and comments.

In order to contextualize reactions to the "Islam Against Racism" panel, I fast forward to a short article written just days after the panel by professors Youssef Chouhoud and Quaiser Abdullah. This article entitled, "Non-Black Muslims Will Need to Do More Than Post Hashtags and Attend Rallies to Combat Anti-Black Racism," highlighted how non-Black Muslims had a "long history" of ignoring Black suffering and excluding Black Muslims from "discourse on the American Muslim experience." In specific reference to Black Muslim representation, they described how "organizations have hosted or publicized events that do not have Black Muslims on their panels." They then referenced "one example from less than a month ago" in which "two national organizations were prominently featured as co-hosts ... and approved the final list of speakers while choosing not to correct or be more just in their representation of Islam in America." The authors concluded this "points to this issue of anti-Black racism as not merely being interpersonal but systemic" (Chouhoud & Abdullah, 2020). Although unclear whether the authors were referencing the "Islam Against Racism" panel, Chouhoud and Abdullah's commentary helps contextualize the panel discourse and reactions to it.

The "Islam Against Racism" panel aired on Facebook Live on June 13, 2020, and lasted for 1 hour and 37 minutes. Dr. Zulfiqar Ali Shah, a prolific scholar of Islamic theology and author of numerous books, served as moderator. Shah, originally from Pakistan, introduced the discussion by describing "a great awakening taking place in the American society" related to recognizing "systematic discrimination against the African American community" (ISNA, 2020a). Shah acknowledged a "gap in theory and practice" in the global Muslim community with regard to racism and identified the panel's goal as providing "practical steps that can be taken to bridge that gap" (ISNA, 2020a). Yet, the remainder of the panel took a defensive tone, highlighting ISNA's commitment to promoting unity over acknowledging the marginality and invisibility experienced by many Black Muslims.

For example, one panelist expressed her surprise to reactions on social media about the lack of Black representation. She recounted her experiences growing up in a mixed-race household and stated the terms "interracial or multiracial" were never used by her Black and Lebanese parents, who taught their children there was "one race, and that is the human race" (ISNA, 2020a). Another panelist emphasized negative stereotypes from both sides of the community—namely, Black or African American Muslims and non-Black immigrant Muslims—and the need to "come together" to "know one another" and challenge injustice through unity (ISNA, 2020a). One exception came from Dr. Ihsan Bagby, whom Shah called upon "to address something that has been coming to us via social media: that the panel does not have the proper representation of the African American community." Shah asked Dr. Bagby to "tell us something about your African American heritage, legacy, your activism, to satisfy some of the agitations ... on Facebook and a number of other platforms." Bagby described the concerns and criticism of the lack of representation on the panel as "understandable" and "legitimate", especially in light of how "marginalized" and "invisible" many African-American Muslims have felt in Muslim spaces dominated by non-Black immigrants. Despite this acknowledgment, the panel's emphasis on unity overshadowed the realities of racism in Muslim communities and exemplified how colorblindness came at the cost of acknowledging the erasure and invisibility many Black Muslims experienced in institutional spaces.

"A Moral Imperative"

The 2020 ISNA annual convention entitled "The Struggle for Social and Racial Justice: A Moral Imperative" represented another pivotal moment in these discourses. Occurring three months after the "Islam Against Racism" panel, the convention represented a shift from themes of colorblindness and unity to addressing intersectional invisibility and anti-Black racism. For example, rather than identify ISNA's roots in the 1980s, the Opening Session detailed how ISNA "stood on the shoulders of those Muslims who were brought to this country hundreds of years ago and struggled under unspeakable conditions of slavery," emphasizing the long history of Black Muslim presence in the U.S. (ISNA, 2020c). In another moment in the program, speakers highlighted how the 1965 march from "Selma to Montgomery" to "protest the killing of a 26-year-old man, Jimmy Lee Jackson," was not far removed from the moment in 2020, when "we are mourning the death of George Floydd" (ISNA, 2020c). Although contemporary racial justice struggles are often tied to the Civil Rights movement of the 1960s, such references represent a shift in dominant discourses from historically non-Black Muslim institutions (Farole, 2011).

Conference sessions further exemplified this shift, with three of the six main sessions focused on racial justice. One of these, "20/20 Vision on Racism," referenced the need for the "broader Muslim community" to "overcome blind spots" in racial justice work (ISNA, 2020b). It advised individuals and organizations to "turn to one another, listen to the knowledge and experiences of our brothers and sisters, especially from among the African American community, so a recognition of adjustments can be made" (ISNA, 2020b, p. 7). Similarly, several parallel sessions over the two-day program described the ways "we may be complicit in racism, may have internalized white supremacy" and called upon "time, resources, energy" to help challenge the "systemic oppression" (ISNA, 2020b, p. 7), "systemic racism," and "racial injustice" (ISNA, 2020b, p. 9).

These examples point to a shift from disavowing race through colorblind ideologies to acknowledging its centrality to contemporary social justice efforts. They also recognize the epistemological salience of Black and African American subject positions and the importance of rendering the perspectives of those previously marginalized positions visible and heard. As discussed in the next section, these examples have several implications for organizational contexts.

Addressing Intersectional Invisibility in Organizational Contexts

This chapter has explored how anti-black racism, Islamophobia, and dominant discourses conflating Arab and South Asian ethnicities with Muslim identity have contributed to the marginalization and invisibility of Black Muslims in the U.S. The #BeingBlackandMuslim portrait series exemplifies how naming invisibility, recounting experiences with margin-alization, and centering intersectional identities function to challenge such intersectional invisibility. The institutional discourses from the ISNA ex-emplify how organizations navigate historical "blind spots" in relation to DEI work. Together, the history and examples presented in this chapter provide several important practical insights for DEI work.

Practical Applications

One practical insight gleaned from this chapter relates to the tension inherent in discourses of unity that contribute to the acute social invisibility of some group members. As the exemplars from #BeingBlackandMuslim and ISNA suggest, one means of addressing this tension involves reframing unity as a common goal rather than as a common identity. I draw on a personal example to help elucidate this point. In 2021, one of the institutions with which I am affiliated hosted a week-long symposium entitled, "Enhancing the Black Student Experience" that emphasized institutional responsibility for DEI initiatives. I attended much of the symposium but was bothered by the repetition of the phrase "the Black student experience" because it suggested a singular, unified experience shared by all students who identify as Black. I communicated to the organizers my appreciation for the program but suggested the title be changed to "Enhancing Black Student Experiences" to recognize the plurality of experiences *within* the demographic of students identifying as Black. The symposium is now in its third year and the title remains unchanged; however, in continuing to raise this issue, I hope to support the goal of enhancing minoritized students' experiences while challenging the presumption that all members of a marginalized group members' experiences are the same. Organizations can avoid this "blind spot" by predicating unity upon the recognition, rather than the disavowal, of difference *within* groups. By creating space for a plurality of intersectional experiences within a single identity category, such recognition allows individuals to feel seen and heard while moving organizations toward their overarching DEI goals.

A second insight relates to the importance of expanding identity-based activism to represent the challenges faced by non-prototypical group members. Within Muslim American communities, anti-Islamophobia work has historically drawn attention to the challenges faced by first and second-generation immigrant Muslims in ways that erased the challenges faced by Black American Muslims. As the examples in this chapter highlight, organizational work aimed at racial justice must be proactive about understanding the challenges faced by individuals who do not immediately come to mind when a marginalized group identity is invoked. Proactive measures include seeking out non-prototypical group members to include them in both the planning of DEI events and in the representation of panelists and speakers. Such measures also include recognizing the experiential knowledge attained by individuals who face multiple forms of marginalization and compensating them when they share their time, insights, and expertise.

A third insight relates to the importance of consistency in DEI work. In her 2022 book, *Broken: The Failed Promise of Muslim Inclusion*, Evelyn Alsultany describes the term "crisis diversity" as follows: a crisis event or series of events leads the general public to become aware of a long-standing problem affecting a particular identity group; this results in urgent calls upon people of that group to educate the public and embark on new diversity initiatives; after the crisis abates, little attention is paid to the issue until another crisis emerges, which starts the cycle all over again (pp. 14–15). The article by Professors Youssef Chouhoud and Quaiser Abdullah cited earlier in this chapter describes frustration with the "long history" of national Muslim organizations such as ISNA ignoring Black suffering and excluding Black Muslims from discourses on Muslim Americans. In one section of the article, the authors critique the "sporadic" attention non-Black Muslim-led institutions have paid to racial injustice, often in response to crises such as the brutal murder of George Floyd (Chouhoud & Abdullah, 2020). Crises, whether in the form of horrific incidents of police brutality or racist administrative policies such as the "Muslim Ban," often create the conditions to initiate or amplify existing DEI efforts. However, as the analysis in this chapter underscores, only sustained effort will result in actual organizational-level change. While responding to crises remains important, consistent and inclusive programming will move organizations toward their DEI goals more effectively than sporadic crisis diversity work alone.

Conclusion

DEI work has the potential to bring about transformative change but involves addressing multi-layered systemic and interpersonal workings of injustice and oppression that may otherwise go unnoticed. The results of such work can be amplified if, in working for unity and solidarity, organizational leaders acknowledge the valuable insights of previously marginalized sub-groups and counter their intersectional invisibility through representation and inclusion. Although this chapter has explored some of the tensions inherent in marginalized communities and how intersectional invisibility can be challenged, it has done so only in part. I hope that communication scholarship will continue exploring how attending to intersectional invisibility can help cultivate justice and inclusion efforts in organizational contexts.

Discussion Questions

1 How do institutional discourses inform group identities? How can practitioners better account for intersectional invisibility in their organizations?
2 To what extent do discourses of unity and oneness stifle discussions about the diverse, intersectional experiences inherent in most groups?
3 Consider three intersecting identity categories: for example, race, gender, and sexuality. Do some intersectional identities take precedence over others? In what contexts? How does this contribute to intersectional invisibility?

Author Bio

Marwa Abdalla is a Ph.D. student and Jacobs Fellow in the Department of Communication at UC San Diego. Her research focuses on Islamophobia and anti-Muslim racism in the context of U.S. media and political discourse. Her work has been recognized with several top paper awards at national and regional conferences, as well as with the President's Award for Research, the Young Scholar Award for Outstanding Research on American Muslims, and the National Communication Association's John T. Warren Award.

References

Abdalla, M. I. (2022). "My Islam be Black": Resisting erasure, silence, and marginality at the intersection of race and religion. *Communication, Culture and Critique*, tcac042. 10.1093/ccc/tcac042

Abdul Khabeer, S. (2016). *Muslim cool: Race, religion and hip hop in the United States*. New York University Press.

Afsaruddin, A. (2020, July 6). Islam's anti-racist message from the seventh century still resonates today. *The Salt Lake Tribune*. https://www.sltrib.com/religion/2020/07/06/conversation-islams-anti/

Alami, A. (2019, August 21). A Black Minneapolis artist brings hidden communities to light. *Bloomberg City Lab*. Retrieved from: https://www.bloomberg.com/news/articles/2019-08-21/a-minneapolis-artist-documents-unseen-communities

Alsultany, E. (2012). *Arabs and Muslims in the media: Race and representation after 9/11*. New York University Press.

Alsultany, E. (2022). *Broken: The failed promise of Muslim inclusion*. New York University Press.

Aziza Hill, M. (2016). The N-Word. Reflections on the Intersection of Religion, Race, and Gender. [blog]. https://margariaziza.com/2016/02/26/the-n-word/

Bagby, I. (2021). The American mosque 2020: Growing and evolving, report 2: Perspectives and attitudes. *Institute for Social Policy and Understanding*. https://www.ispu.org/report-2-mosque-survey-2020/

Bayoumi, M. (2006). Racing religion. *CR: The New Centennial Review*, 6(2), 267–293. 10.1353/ncr.2007.0000

Beydoun, K. A. (2018). *American Islamophobia: Understanding the roots and rise of fear*. University of California Press.

Blay, Z. (2017, February 14). #BeingBlackAndMuslim is the hashtag bringing light to an ignored identity. *Huffington Post*. https://www.huffpost.com/entry/beingblackandmuslim-is-the-hashtag-bringing-light-to-an-ignored-identity_n_58a3728ae4b094a129efca0f

Bonilla-Silva, E. (2010). *Racism without racists: Color-blind racism and the persistence of racial inequality in the United States* (3rd ed). Rowman & Littlefield.

Cainkar, L. A. (2011). *Homeland insecurity: The Arab American and Muslim American experience after 9/11*. Russell Sage Foundation.

Chawansky, M. (2016). Be who you are and be proud: Brittney Griner, intersectional invisibility and digital possibilities for lesbian sporting celebrity. *Leisure Studies*, *35*(6), 771–782. 10.1080/02614367.2015.1128476

Chouhoud, Y. & Abdullah, Q. (2020, June 15). *Non-Black Muslims will need to do more than post hashtags and attend rallies to combat anti-black racism.* Institute for Social Policy and Understanding. https://www.ispu.org/non-black-muslims-will-need-to-do-more-than-post-hashtags-and-attend-rallies-to-combat-anti-black-racism/

Collins, P. H. (2019). *Intersectionality as critical social theory.* Duke University Press. 10.2307/j.ctv11hpkdj

Coles, S. M., & Pasek, J. (2020). Intersectional invisibility revisited: How group prototypes lead to the erasure and exclusion of Black women. *Translational Issues in Psychological Science*, *6*(4), 314–324. 10.1037/tps0000256

Considine, C. (2017). The racialization of Islam in the United States: Islamophobia, hate crimes, and "flying while brown". *Religions*, *8*(9), 165.

Crenshaw, K. (1991). Mapping the margins: Intersectionality, identity politics, and violence against women of color. *Stanford Law Review*, *43*(6), 1241–1300.

Dahir, I. (2017, April 25). This powerful photo series is showing what it is like to be Black and Muslim in the US. *Buzz Feed News*. https://www.buzzfeed.com/ikrd/this-powerful-photoseries-is-showing-what-it-is-like-to-be

Farole, S. (2011, February 21). *Race matters: Colorblind racism in the Ummah.* Muslim Matters. https://muslimmatters.org/2011/02/21/race-matters-colorblind-racism-in-the-ummah/

Gibson, D. (2012). *A history of the nation of Islam: Race, Islam, and the quest for freedom.* Praeger.

Grewal, Z. A. (2009). Marriage in color: Race, religion and spouse selection in four American mosques. *Ethnic and Racial Studies*, *32*(2), 323–345. 10.1080/0141 9870801961490

Guhin, J. (2018). Colorblind Islam: The racial hinges of immigrant Muslims in the United States. *Social Inclusion*, *6*(2), 87–97. 10.17645/si.v6i2.1422

Hennekam, S., & Dumazert, J.-P. (2023). Intersectional (in)visibility of transgender individuals with an ethnic minority background throughout a gender transition: Four longitudinal case studies. *Gender, Work & Organization*, gwao.12992, https://doi.or g/10.1111/gwao.12992

Islamic Society of North America. (2020a, July 13). *Islam against racism.* [Video attached][Status update]. Facebook. https://www.facebook.com/isnahq/videos/264141601475422/

Islamic Society of North America. (2020b). The struggle for social and racial justice: A moral imperative. https://isna.net/wp-content/uploads/2020/04/ISNA-2020-Program-8.pdf

Islamic Society of North America. (2020c, September 8). *Opening Session* [Address]. ISNA 2020 Annual Convention. https://www.youtube.com/watch?v=2C16-4GxSHY

Islamic Society of North America. (2021). *Mission and Vision.* https://isna.net/mission-and-vision/

Jackson, S. (2005). *Islam and the Black American: Looking toward the third resurrection.* Oxford University Press.

Jackson, S. A. (2011). Islam, Muslims and the wages of racial agnosia in America. *Journal of Islamic Law and Culture, 13*(1), 1–17. 10.1080/1528817X.2012.693386

King, D. K. (1988). Multiple jeopardy, multiple Consciousness: The context of a Black feminist ideology. *Signs: Journal of Women in Culture and Society, 14*(1), 42–72. 10.1086/494491

Latif, J. (2018). Muslim American cyber contestations between scholars and activists debating racism, Islamophobia and Black Lives Matter. *Journal of Religion, Media and Digital Culture, 7*(1), 67–89. 10.1163/25888099-00701005

Marsh, C. E. (1984). *From Black Muslims to Muslims.* Scarecrow Press.

Mogahed, D., & Chouhoud, Y. (2017). *American Muslim poll 2017: Muslims at the crossroads.* Institute for Social Policy and Understanding. https://www.ispu.org/wp-content/uploads/2017/03/American-Muslim-Poll-2017-Report.pdf

MuslimARC. (2021). *Resources.* http://www.muslimarc.org/resources

Muslim Wellness Foundation. (2020). *Black Muslim intersectional invisibility: Between anti-Blackness, racism & Islamophobia.* Black Muslim Psychology Conference. https://www.blackmuslimpsychology.org/invisibility

Nash, J. C. (2008). Rethinking intersectionality, *Feminist Review,* 89(1), 1–15. 10.1057/fr.2008.4

Osman, G. (2006). Identity and community in a new generation: The Muslim community in the early seventh century and today. In J. L. Heft (Ed.), *Passing on the faith: Transforming traditions for the next generation of Jews, Christians, and Muslims* (pp. 187–203). Fordham University Press.

Purdie-Vaughns, V., & Eibach, R. P. (2008). Intersectional invisibility: The distinctive advantages and disadvantages of multiple subordinate-group identities. *Sex Roles, 59*(5–6), 377–391. 10.1007/s11199-008-9424-4

Rogers, B. [@bobbyrogers_]. (2017a, April 19). For the past few months I've been creating a portrait series inspired by the #BeingBlackandMuslim hashtag. I'm ready to share [Tweet; images attached]. Twitter. https://twitter.com/Bobbyrogers_/status/854843683727912961

Rogers, B. (2017b). *2017: The year according to Bobby Rogers.* Walker Art. https://walkerart.org/magazine/2017-the-year-according-to-bobby-rogers

Rogers, B. (2021). *Info.* Bobby Rogers. https://bobby-rogers.com/INFO

Simpson, A., & Taylor, P. C. (2021). Marital Shade. *Philosophical Topics, 49*(1), 45–60.

Smith, A. N., Watkins, M. B., Ladge, J. J., & Carlton, P. (2019). Making the Invisible Visible: Paradoxical Effects of Intersectional Invisibility on the Career Experiences of Executive Black Women. *Academy of Management Journal, 62*(6), 1705–1734. 10.5465/amj.2017.1513

Taylor, K. Y. (2017). *How we get free: Black feminism and the Combahee River Collective.* Haymarket.

Walid, D. (2013, November 24). *Responses to my calling out the term 'abeed'.* Weblog of Dawud Walid. https://dawudwalid.wordpress.com/2013/11/24/responses-to-my-calling-out-the-term-abeed/

Walid, D. (2016, February 10). *Why centering Muslims who were Black in early Islamic history matters.* Al Madina Institute. https://almadinainstitute.org/blog/why-centering-muslims-who-were-black-in-early-islamic-history-matters/

Wong, C. Y. E., Kirby, T. A., Rink, F., & Ryan, M. K. (2022). Intersectional invisibility in women's diversity interventions. *Frontiers in Psychology, 13,* Article 791572. 10.3389/fpsyg.2022.791572

12

PEDAGOGY AND MENTORSHIP AS ORGANIZATIONAL CHANGEMAKING

An Autoethnographic Vignette Approach

Stevie M. Munz[1], Leandra H. Hernández[2], and Elizabeht Hernandez[3]

[1]*Utah Valley University;* [2]*University of Utah;* [3]*Independent Scholar*

Learning Objectives

After reading this chapter, you will:

1 Identify the role of organizational changemaking in higher education.
2 Summarize the effects of DEI efforts in higher education.
3 Understand the relationship of autoethnography and organizational changemaking.

Introduction

In this chapter, we as two cisgender women professors of communication at Utah Valley University (UVU) and a cisgender woman—a recent graduate and mentee—explore the possibilities of pedagogy or teaching practices and mentorship as organizational changemaking through an autoethnographic (self-reflections) vignette (mini-stories) approach. As Stevie identifies as white and Leandra and Elizabeht as Latina, we also understand our positionalities and lived experiences as different. In past research, we have developed a case for autoethnography as assessment through an analysis of our social justice pedagogies at a public institution in a conservative state where over 70% of the student body identifies as white, and as part of the local dominant faith, identities that the three authors we do not ascribe to (Hernández & Munz, 2021). In earlier research, we have discussed our embodied positionalities—our approach to teaching from the flesh (Gutierrez-Perez, 2018; Moraga & Anzaldúa, 1981)—and the ways in which our social justice pedagogies impact our

DOI: 10.4324/9781003333746-14

pedagogical, mentorship, and assessment strategies (Hernández & Munz, 2021; Hernández et al., in press). In this chapter, we extend our earlier argument by exploring how pedagogy and mentorship can serve as mechanisms of organizational changemaking at our institution. Over the past several years, we have explored how, at pedagogical and institutional levels, collective mentorship of women, BIPOC students, and queer students has engendered new student organizations, faculty-staff-student social support, and student well-being, all to support larger goals of student retention, student access to research and teaching opportunities to prepare them for graduate school, and overall student success.

We assert that our mentorship efforts and our argument are less than progressive per se in our field, but they *are* progressive in our conservative state because of the delicately and intimately intertwined relationship at our public institution of the dominant faith and the dominant culture. Given our social justice pedagogies and mentorship philosophies, in this chapter, we trace how we both subversively and explicitly leverage social justice principles and practices to inspire organizational change through mentorship teams, mentorship reading circles, and our own teaching practices. We also discuss the barriers we face, such as the multiple layers of power in the institution (at the mid-term tenure review process, the tenure review process, and at higher levels of administration). The barriers we face encompass not only those created by machinated whiteness and microaggressions, but also the pervasive and dominant religious and cultural impacts that permeate *all* of our institutional systems and structures. Moreover, by engaging in worldmaking and conversation with Elizabeht, a recently graduated student, we explore how organizational changemaking related to DEI principles and efforts are viewed by students and, by extension, how Latina/o/x/e students view belonging in a predominantly white, religious institution.

In this chapter, our conversations are guided by the following question: *If autoethnography can serve as an important form of assessment* (Hernández & Munz, 2021), *can mentorship and pedagogy serve as mechanisms of organizational changemaking?* Through a re-remembering of memories, we seek to develop our argument, as a way "to give voice to experience" to "expand our knowledges of self-other/context by continually (re)activating our methods of representation" (Spry, 2006, p. 339). We utilize three vignettes to illustrate experiences related to engaged learning, service learning, and mentorship contexts as well as narrativize the betwixt and in-betweenness of Latina and The Church of Jesus Christ of Latter-day Saints (LDS) membership identities (Turner, 1969). As a layered representation, we offer the vignettes as a weaving together of our memories, ethnographic observations, and composite characters (Denzin, 1996). The following stories are each a fragment of knowledge that we have directly experienced, while layered into other interactions, moments, and ways of living—*we* invite the reader to enter the stories and to consider, alongside us, whether and to what extent we can expect academic institutions to be accountable with their DEI promises. As we know, organizational public statements about DEI support often complicate long-term commitments for diversity and inclusion with little follow-through (Tarin et al., 2021), and it is through this lens that we complicate organizational changemaking and inclusion in academic spaces.

Ultimately, through our autoethnographic vignettes, we consider the ways in which mentorship and pedagogy can potentially serve as mechanisms of organizational changemaking. Our approach explores the extent we can hold academic institutions accountable regarding their DEI promises and efforts. Thus, following each vignette, we present three recommendations: 1) the need for educators, practitioners, and administrators to do more than support DEI principles and practices; 2) for teachers and practitioners to utilize critical service learning as a tool in educational spaces; and 3) for institutions to provide tangible forms of support to true initiators of organizational changemaking.

*****

Race: "[T]he Lord God did cause a skin of blackness to come upon them" —no longer fair, white, or worthy of salvation (Nephi 5:21).

I read the words: The professor said, "I don't think you belong in this class ... people like you aren't in my classes." My eyes stare at the screen. Many would think I sat in disbelief, but after some years there's mundaneness to racialized comments like these around me. I take a deep breath and exhale, trying to re-attune my mind and body. I re-read the journal entry again and confirmed somewhere on my campus a white male professor told a Latino student to leave a biology class. Sitting back in my office chair, I scan the remainder of Frederico's journal entry. He describes how he has heard these words before but is dedicated to becoming a doctor to improve the healthcare his community receives. As a pre-med, biology major with a 4.0 GPA I read on as he details, "I struggle with being a member of the Church ... my mom is a lesbian and I'm not like anyone else in my ward (church meeting house) ... I've thought about quitting UVU many times ... ."

Ding.

I watch as my email vanishes from my outlook box on its way to Frederico. A few days later,

Frederico responds and we set up our first of *many* meetings to chat.

*

Having been raised by a strong, independent, immigrant, single mother taught me a lot. Her example allowed me to see beyond limitations and work hard for what I wanted in life. Even after a marathon of obstacles, her example was a constant reminder of perseverance. My mother's philosophy is, "No es fácil, pero no es imposible, (It's not easy, but it's not impossible)."

Brown and Black spaces matter—a lot. I never felt like I belonged at UVU even though I identified with the larger religious culture. As a historically white institution, I searched for brown and Black spaces (Tichavakunda, 2020) to feel heard. When I came to the university, I anticipated fitting in and finding a sense of belonging. After all, Utah is one of the few spaces heavily dominated by members of the LDS church. However, I soon realized my experiences as a Latina were "too diverse" and I lacked the religious cultural cache to be perceived as righteous of a member as my white classmates. After all, my mother was a single mom to three daughters, who escaped an abusive husband, and worked two jobs when we were growing up. In the eyes of my classmates, my mom was "less than" because she wasn't a stay-at-home mom. As a dutiful member of the church, my mom never asked the government for assistance, but she was quickly reminded by religious leadership "if you can't do it here (United States), you should probably go back to your country."

Many professors ignored or failed to recognize passive-aggressive comments like these made to brown and Black students (especially LDS members). As a Latina who is/was LDS, I was continually met with skepticism about my understanding of religious doctrine. After all, any translation of religious texts is understood as having less meaning once translated. I was more visibly (publicly) disciplined by professors when I engaged in similar communication to my white counterparts. Once even being told, "Elizabeht, sit down" during my presentation when I refused to allow a white female student to talk over me. While the professor apologized after class, the punishment stung and the humiliation lingered. Where was the equity?

In an educational space like ours, Leandra and I often "know" all of the brown, Black, and queer students. "They find you both," a colleague comments with a chuckle. Their words are a reminder of how the work we do is "seen" by our colleagues, but often fails to receive understanding of its importance. As hooks (1994) details, caring teachers who engage in critical and political work, often fail to receive the "normal rewards" associated with forwarding the status quo (p. 90). Through the years, I've witnessed as whiteness, purity, superiority, and perfectionism are seamlessly bonded through everyday talk and in quotes, students casually mention from religious leaders—gospel, as they are the mouthpiece of God. Our students explain how the family structure, headed by a man is essential and pre-ordained and how motherhood and childbearing are a woman's primary role in life; stories about white leaders who narrate savior and colorblind stories permeate our classroom. And so, each church leader is believed to be divinely chosen and stands above infallibility. When Leandra joined the department, I had no way of knowing how we would become intertwined in our efforts to create spaces of liberation (hooks, 2014). After all, what would a health communication scholar and an oral historian have in common?

As our identities became more enmeshed, we increasingly reflected on the erasure of brown student experiences at our institution. As a white faculty member, I witnessed as faculty and staff engaged in negotiations over the intersections of identities. Brown or immigrant; female or Chicana; Mexican, but not Latinx (because of the politics)—the layering of identities was part of the "institutional silencing" in the university (Cruz, 2018, p. 363). To counter this silencing, we teach through social justice pedagogical practices that embrace *vivencias* or an understanding of lived experiences. Rooted in Chicana feminist epistemologies, the concept of vivencias challenges objectivist, Western systems of knowledge in favor of "border/transformative pedagogies" through its honoring of students' lived experiences (Elenes, 2010; Hernández & De Los Santos Upton, 2020; Trinidad Galván, 2015). Moreover, such a pedagogical approach honors seemingly mundane, ordinary, everyday lived experiences as important sites of teaching and learning. Galván (2001) explains how everyday experiences like "the kitchen table and church steps must also be analyzed as real pedagogical spaces for many underprivileged groups" (p. 606). By honoring students' lived experiences and bringing them together in the educational spaces as valid contributions, a form of community or togetherness is created wherein convivencia is created, a version of meaningful, impactful co-existence (Trinidad Galván, 2001, 2015). It is this space that we seek to honor as creators, a similar togetherness and approach to understanding.

Recommendation #1

Our *first* recommendation for educators, practitioners, and administrators is first and foremost, academic institutions must do more than support DEI principles and practices at face value or, in other words, on the surface. Such support is fundamentally necessary to aid in the tensions between "the cultural sustainability of privilege and cultural transformation for social justice," particularly when queer and BIPOC faculty members become, as Alexander (2022) notes, the "reified spectacle in and target of DEI-A [accessibility] reform" (pp. 605–606). As Alexander (2022) asserts, university administrators must articulate and strengthen their support of DEI efforts to support faculty members in our unending quest for representation and social justice, lest they continue to engage in silencing invisibility tactics and the maintenance of racist, exclusionary structures: "In which case, the study of spectacle of in/visibility in DEI-A work is not the JEDI warrior-of-color or those important others doing the work, but the socio-cultural structures that maintain the relational dynamic of racism and bias coming to the defense of the (presumed to be) newly aggrieved" (p. 2). Thus, in order for DEI-based organizational changemaking to occur meaningfully, organizations must engage in several steps from DEI planning to implementation, including 1) issuing a public, formal acknowledgment of DEI practices on campus, 2) creating and releasing a DEI plan, with metrics and an implementation timeline, and 3) ensuring that there are forums and spaces in place to continuously engage in dialogue about DEI efforts and their efficacy. University administrators must also engage in continuous communication about portfolio implementation and feedback, such as is the case with Leandra's service-learning course where students wanted (and expected) communication with administrators about their work and contributions, even after the course ended. We offer these suggestions based on our vignettes and our past experience serving on DEI committees and hiring committees for DEI professionals at our institution and at local organizations with which we are affiliated. History has shown us time and time again that the organizational release of statements in support of DEI efforts and racial justice is less meaningful when concrete action is not specified, especially when organizations engage in conciliatory discourses that obfuscate commitments to action and a reinforcement of previous actions and processes (Tarin et al., 2021).

Faculty, staff, students, and community members must be empowered to hold academic institutions and legislators accountable, particularly in DEI contexts. DEI work requires collaboration and teamwork in order to build a more fair, equitable, and just institutional environment. The work must always focus on the most vulnerable and unheard and requires white folks on campus to reflect, engage, and understand their privilege and power. Leadership must be held accountable for promises and called on to explain *how* DEI initiatives will be actionable; and they should be informed of the harm that is possible if they fail to structurally and financially support the labor. For example, recently at our university a general education, conversation emerged suggesting the inclusion of a diversity course without any conversation about the importance of teacher training to teach such courses.

*****

Ethnicity, Critical Perspectives, and Engaged Learning: "And Once Again, We Give and Receive Nothing in Return"

As the newly minted Associate Academic Director of Service-Learning, I reflected upon how I could transform two of my upper-level courses into service-learning and engaged-learning courses to connect students with valuable applied research projects on campus. As an educator, if I may be so honest, service- and engaged-learning courses for me are about much more than *just* applied research and "real-world" experience; they also help students explore what meaningful organizational changemaking could look like on university campuses, especially as students are working within their homespaces to envision transformative possibilities for diversity, inclusion, and equity.

Fast forward to the first day of class. I tell my students how overjoyed I am that this is the *first time* in the history of our department that this particular ethnic studies course is being offered. I beam, explaining how this course is my dream come true at our predominantly white institution, particularly because it represents my lived experiences and my labor of love as a queer Latina/o/x/e Communication Studies scholar who has worked diligently to bring this class to life. When I first mentioned I wanted to create this class, however, administrators across the campus reacted with expressions of doubt and shock, as if the class didn't represent an entire academic sub-field in its own right:

> *Oh, an ethnic studies class. Why do you want to teach that here? No one will enroll.*
> *Will students learn about anything valuable?*
>> *Don't you think it's racist to have a class that focuses on only one ethnicity?*
>> *Will it have any applied impacts?*
>>> *Come on, this is a great idea. She'll teach students how to conduct*
>>>> *better business transactions with brown people.*

On the first day of class, I breathe in students' exclamations of happiness seeing themselves represented in the course curriculum. However, the collective tone shifted as I explained that the course was an engaged-learning course where students would be working with our university's marketing and communication department to develop more inclusive marketing strategies and campaigns for Latinx populations. One student in particular—brilliant and wise beyond their years, one whom I have mentored closely over the past two years—looks critical of the course project (and, I suspect, of *me* for selecting such a course project as a critical scholar or a researcher concerned with systems of power and structures). Service learning has been explored as a means of sensemaking or assigning meaning to experiences in organizational change (Chadwick & Pawlowski, 2007), but what about sensemaking and change for students? Critical service-learning approaches that center social justice aims (Mitchell, 2008) result in more complex critical thinking abilities, more complex reasoning skills, and require faculty members to focus on social responsibility and critical community issues (Mitchell 2008; Wang & Rodgers, 2006); however, they do not always fulfill their goals of impacting the very people and communities educators purport to serve (Butin, 2015). Would that be possible at this moment? Would the university honor these goals?

Fast forward to the last day of class. Students are delivering their final presentations, which are mind-blowingly interdisciplinary and intersectional. Powerful. My critical scholar student, a student of color, delivers a dynamite presentation where they and their group members explicate the power of interdisciplinary research in critical goal-setting and change-making contexts. However, they mention a cautionary tale (and incisive critique) of engaged research in their conclusion:

And once again, we give and receive nothing in return.

My heart sank to my most inner physical depths. At that point in time, I was of the mindset that we have to leverage our powers to make change, even if the impacts of institutional change take months, even years, to observe. However, how could I explain to them that I understood how they felt, too? The self-doubt and impostor syndrome suffocated me, paralyzing my response at that moment. It haunts me even *now*.

Do I have the power to ensure that the institution will follow through with its promises of inclusion for Latinx students? Does the class even matter at all?

Recommendation #2

Our *second* recommendation for teachers and practitioners contends critical service learning can be utilized as a tool in educational spaces to include the students who are most marginalized and oppressed (Hart, 2006), but the university must follow through on its implementation policies for changemaking to occur ... to matter. As a proposed strategy for DEI-minded faculty members, we call upon white faculty at historically white institutions like ours who identify as DEI allies to commit to the work. Our Latinx students are engulfed in deeply entrenched white spaces, built through a supremacy of whiteness. Their existence in the classroom is vulnerable as their bodies are marked as *different* and frequently conditional on their adherence to white rules and ideologies. We must also remain attuned to the cultural, political, and historical hi/stories layered into our institutions for changemaking to occur.

As outsiders to the LDS faith, we are continually navigating learning with our students about their identity experiences and reconciling ruptures to notions of identity, space, politics, religion, race, and ethnicity. For example, many queer and BIPOC students at our institution with varying proximities to the LDS faith have shared with us their feelings of otherness and exclusion in other engaged-learning and service-learning courses where faculty members construct and teach the course through a white savior lens. Faculty members can advocate for more service-learning and social-impact training courses to inform their service-learning course teaching philosophies. At our institution, the Center for Social Impact has sponsored a Service-Learning Faculty Fellowship certification course for several years, and the Center is now in the process of creating a Social-Impact Faculty Fellowship certification course to educate faculty members on how to develop and implement service-learning courses rooted in principles of social impact and social change. It is our hope that such courses—in conjunction with service-learning faculty meetings and communities of practice—will assist faculty members in developing DEI-based service-learning courses that will do no harm to all involved.

*****

Gender & Heterosexuality: "Gender to be an "essential characteristic" of sons and daughters of God, and an "eternal identity (see "The Family: A Proclamation to the World", 1995).

Twice a year it happens. In the spring when the flowers are blooming and in the fall just as the leaves turn to fire red and burnt orange and the air becomes crisp. As an outsider, even I have become attuned to the times when The Church of Jesus Christ of Latter-day Saints (LDS) General Conference happens. It was on one of those quietly windy mornings in the valley, where summer is still lingering but fall is ever present. I watch as my classroom fills with students, who one by one take a seat for our 9:00 AM class. "Yes," I say and nod in the direction of a raised hand. "So, I don't want to start anything … but I'm having a difficult time today." "Oh?" I respond and move in her direction. She responds,

> Last week when we were talking about gender, I felt really good about it. This weekend though, well … now I'm having a hard time.

As I lean on the table, I watch as eyes gaze in the student's direction. It's quiet and each student is focused.

Me: Tell me what you're thinking …

Student: You said gender is socially constructed … and not essential … but this weekend at the General Conference the prophet said "gender is essential," so what am I supposed to believe?

Rupture. My mind is like a rolodex, shuffle, shuffle, shuffle; I sieve through thoughts and ideas. I stand before my students as *different* because of how I live my life, how I love, my absence of worship, the fuel for my ethics and convictions, and commitment to social justice are all *mysterious* to them …

In many ways, to the outside eye, the content of our courses falls short of being as complex, maybe even not as critical or questioning of norms, biases, and assumptions about identity experiences in society. As a professor, I have realized through the years that my mentorship in the classroom walks a line of pushing and pulling my students to understand their lived experiences and the experiences of others in ways that meet them where they are—not in ways that *always* make me feel good about my identity or beliefs. Thinking through the beliefs and ways of living that many of my students fervently adhere to, I realized I had to open myself up to *valuing* everyone in the classroom (hooks, 1994). Frequently, falling short is what I have come to understand as my pedagogical blueprint and the way I teach from the flesh as a mentor and guide in the classroom (hooks, 1994). As bell hooks (1994) notes, when teaching and learning are liberatory, we are then truly "committed to education as the practice of freedom" (p. 6). The challenge, however, becomes even more fraught with complexity when the ways our students see and understand the world directly harm and create violent spaces for folks (in our classroom) and beyond.

For example, in the course reflected through the vignette there was a queer, gender fluid, post-Mormon identifying student. Their verbal presence in the classroom was quiet, but their written reflections, essays, and quizzes were powerful and evidenced careful self-reflexive thinking. Their body in my classroom, a space laced with strict gender norms consecrated on a bed of patriarchy is a disruption for the majority of LDS-identifying students. A Queer body in my classroom reflects a transgression to God's law. Bending the perceived essentialness of identity is not without challenges, but as I continue to become more attuned to the needs of BIPOC and LGBTQ+ students, my teaching seeks to create spaces of critical love through collaborative projects with students (hooks, 2014). To create a singular counter-hegemonic classroom without scaffolding of similar spaces would abandon students and likely leave them navigating back to the status quo.

P.S. Thank you for saying, Queer. You made me feel proud of myself.

The words sting. "Thank you for seeing you," I think, as I read the note on the back of the quiz. The words leave me feeling urgency. "We gotta do more," I think …

Recommendation #3

Our *third* recommendation inspired by this vignette contends that students, staff, and faculty members serve as the true initiators of organizational changemaking in DEI contexts and should be supported by the institution with tangible forms of support, whether that entails stipends for DEI work, grants, and awards for DEI pedagogy and mentorship, and adjustments to tenure criteria that value DEI work, not penalize faculty members for serving as organizational changemakers. For example, at our institution, we (Stevie and Leandra) have received grants and stipends to develop DEI-based training for both faculty members and students. First, we received a $10,000 Diversity Dialogues grant to lead faculty members in our department on a DEI journey over the 2020–2021 academic year wherein we read several books (Ibram Kendi's *How to Be An Anti-Racist,* as an example) and discussed how we could incorporate anti-racist and gender-inclusive principles in our pedagogy. We have found our work is well-received by internal grant funds focusing on pedagogy, learning, and teaching. Second, we have developed a Gender & Sexuality workshop for faculty members as part of our Global/ Intercultural Faculty Initiative, and Leandra has worked with four other faculty and staff members to develop a semester-long Anti-Racist Pedagogy Faculty Certification Course. For the certification, topics taught include: the history of racisim in the United States, ways in which minoritized communities organized in anti-racist spaces, and best practices to incorporoate anti-racisit principles in the classroom. The course originated as one two-hour workshop in our university's Global Intercultural Distinction Program and as result of faculty interest and demand evolved into a semester-long faculty certification course. Third, alongside two other faculty members, we applied for a $24,000 grant from the UVU Center for the Study of Ethics (funded by the state legislature) to mentor 13 undergraduate students for our inaugural Media Ethics and Media Literacy Fair. Our student teams focused on news coverage of race and activism and news coverage of missing and murdered indigenous women (MMIW). We are both compensated for our efforts through grants and stipends, and we have built meaningful relationships with students, faculty, and staff along the way. Moreover, we have worked to advocate on campus for the recognition of such certification courses and grants as valuable components of faculty members' tenure portfolios. Without institutional and financial support, we would have encountered several barriers to engaging in DEI world-making at our institution.

For faculty claiming DEI identities, *we* must dedicate our classrooms to spaces of changemaking for our BIPOC students in order to foster organizational changemaking—our minoritized students' lives depend on it. We have to move beyond the politics of citationality or the belief that including non-white authors in our classroom is enough. Instead, we must include Black and Brown voices through a lens of intersectionality to present the complexity of identity and the story of politics and the situatedness of history. Our classrooms should include assignments that honor different ways of knowing and understanding (e.g., poetry and Podcast assignments). We also suggest evaluating the ways we, the teacher, engage students day-to-day in the classroom. Rather than expecting oral participation and dialogue, we can create "participation logs" to allow students to self-assess their participation in class and shift the white western expectations of orality as the only form of engagement.

Conclusion

Through our autoethnographic vignettes, as two professors and one former student and research assistant, we consider the ways in which mentorship and pedagogy can potentially serve as mechanisms of organizational changemaking. We also analyze the ways in which we have overcome certain institutional barriers to organizational changemaking in diversity and inclusion contexts (such as lack of access to research and programmatic structures [see Haeger et al., 2021]) and the ways in which undergraduate students and research assistants play fundamentally transformative roles in organizational changemaking in both religious and academic contexts. Our approach has explored to what extent we can hold academic institutions accountable regarding their DEI promises and efforts, as well.

Ultimately, we provide the vignettes and our recommendations as a call to action to educators, practitioners, and IDEA changemakers and leave the reader with incisive words from Alexander 2022) about organizational changemaking and DEI efforts in academic spaces:

> The hope is that we can stay strong (enough) in the process to protect our vision/sight, strength, spirit, and souls in a battle over the very nature of our humanity. This as we fight for and embody *cura personalis*, the concern and care for the personal development and reality of the whole person; of every person, globally and those perpetual others who are both particular/plural in the places we live, work, and circulate (Traub, 2008). We do the work that is also committed to reaffirming the values of democracy *with liberty and justice for all*; even as we encounter the vernacular resistance that signifies the tensiveness (and defensiveness) in any form of cultural change. (p. 607)

We invite—nay, call upon—academic administrators to join us in the continued fight for social justice on university campuses.

Discussion Questions

1 What sorts of barriers and facilitators for DEI-based changemaking exist in your institution?
2 What role can you play in facilitating DEI-based changemaking in your institution?
3 How can we create Black and brown spaces for narrativizing to facilitate organizational changemaking?

Author Bios

Dr. Stevie M. Munz, (she/her) (Ph.D., Ohio University), is an Associate Professor in the Department of Communication at Utah Valley University in Orem, Utah. As a scholar, she is invested in a line of inquiry that engages questions about how human beings understand and communicate their relational, political, and social identity experiences. Through critical ethnographic and narrative methods, her published research reflects a commitment to understanding and archiving the stories from women, LGBTQ+ students, teachers, and historically minoritized voices. Her research can be found in *Communication Education, Communication Teacher, Departures, and Women & Language* among others.

Dr. Leandra H. Hernández (she/her) (Ph.D., Texas A&M University) is an Assistant Professor in the Department of Communication at the University of Utah. She enjoys teaching journalism and health communication courses. She utilizes Chicana feminist and qualitative approaches to explore 1) Latina/o/x cultural health experiences, 2) Latina/o/x journalism and media representations, 3) reproductive justice and gendered violence contexts, and 4) critical communication pedagogical approaches. Her research has been published in journals such as *Women & Language, Health Communication, Frontiers in Communication,* and *Women's Studies in Communication,* among others.

Elizabeht Hernandez is an independent scholar and graduate of the Department of Communication from Utah Valley University.

References

Alexander, B. K. (2022). A warning/a call: The spectacle of (In) visibility in the vernacular response to DEI-A work. *Cultural Studies↔ Critical Methodologies, 22*(6), 605–607. 10.1177/15327086221090660

Butin, D. (2015). Dreaming of justice: Critical service-learning and the need to wake up. *Theory Into Practice, 54*(1), 5–10. 10.1080/00405841.2015.977646

Chadwick, S. A., & Pawlowski, D. R. (2007). Assessing institutional support for service-learning: A case study of organizational sensemaking. *Michigan Journal of Community Service Learning, 13*(2), 31–39.

Cruz, J. M. (2018). Brown body of knowledge: A tale of erasure. *Cultural Studies ↔ Critical Methodologies, 18*(5), 363–365. 10.1177/1532708617735131

Denzin, N. K. 1996. *Interpretive Ethnography*. Thousand Oaks, CA: Sage.

Elenes, A. C. (2010). *Transforming Borders: Chicana/o Popular Culture and Pedagogy*. Lanham, MD: Lexington Books.

Gutierrez-Perez, R. (2018). Theories in the flesh and flights of the imagination: Embracing the soul and spirit of critical performative writing in communication research. *Women's Studies in Communication, 41*(4), 404–415. 10.1080/07491409.2018.1551695

Haeger, H., White, C., Martinez, S., & Velasquez, S. (2021). Creating more inclusive research environments for undergraduates. *Journal of the Scholarship of Teaching and Learning, 21*(1), 320–260. 10.14434/josotl.v21i1.30101

Hart, S. (2006). Breaking literacy boundaries through critical service-learning: Education for the silenced and marginalized. *Mentoring & Tutoring, 14*(1), 17–32. 10.1080/13611260500432236

Hernández, L. H., & De Los Santos Upton, S. (2020). Honoring vivencias: A Borderlands Approach to Higher Education Pedagogy Justice. In K. Blinne (Ed.), *Grading Justice: Teacher-Activist Approaches to Assessment* (pp. 91–108). Lanham: Lexington Books.

Hernández, L. H., & Munz, S. M. (2021). Autoethnography as assessment: Communication pedagogies as social justice activism. *Communication Teacher*, 1–18. 10.1080/17404622.2021.1923769

Hernández, L. H., Munz, S. M. Diaz, A., Hernandez, E., & Ruiz, D. (In press.) A Multigenre and Multivocal Faculty-Student Exploration of bell hooks, Teaching, and Mentorship. In K. Comeforo & M. Matacin (Eds.), *Honoring the Immeasurable: bell hooks' Feminist Pedagogy in Teaching*. Lexington Books.

hooks, bell. (1994). *Teaching to Transgress: Education as the Practice of Freedom*. Taylor & Francis Group.

hooks, bell. (2014). *Ain't I a Woman: Black Women and Feminism* (2nd edition). Routledge.

Mitchell, T. D. (2008). Traditional vs. critical service-learning: Engaging the literature to differentiate two models. *Michigan Journal of Community Service Learning*, *14*(2), 50–65.

Moraga, C., & Anzaldúa, G. (1981). Theory in the flesh. In C. Moraga & G. Anzaldúa (Eds.), *This bridge called my back: Writings by radical women of color* (p. 23). Kitchen Table: Women of Color Press.

Spry, T. (2006). A 'performative-I' copresence: Embodying the ethnographic turn in performance and the performative turn in ethnography. *Text and Performance Quarterly*, *26*(4): 339–346.

Tarin, C. A., Upton, S. D. L. S., & Hernández, L. H. (2021). "We Need to be Better": Race, Outdoor Recreation, and Corporate Social Advocacy. *Frontiers in Communication*, *6*, 1–10. 10.3389/fcomm.2021.726417

Tichavakunda, A. A. (2020). Studying Black student life on campus: Toward a theory of Black placemaking in higher education. *Urban Education*, *0*(0) 10.1177/0042085920971354

Trinidad Galván, R. (2001). "Portraits of mujeres desjuiciadas: Womanist pedagogies of the everyday, the mundane and the ordinary." *International Journal of Qualitative Studies in Education*, *14*(5): 603–621.

Trinidad Galván, R. (2015). *Women Who Stay Behind: Pedagogies of Survival in Rural Transmigrant Mexico*. Tucson: University of Arizona Press.

Turner, V. (1969). Liminality and Communitas. In *The Ritual Process: Structure and Anti-Structure* (pp. 359–374). Adline Publishing.

Wang, Y. & Rodgers, R. (2006). Impact of service-learning and social justice education on college students' cognitive development. *NASPA Journal*, *43*(2), 316–337. 10.2202/1949-6605.1642

13

COMPASSION AT THE MARGINS

Increasing Compassion for Employees from Traditionally Marginalized Groups

Cris J. Tietsort[1] *and Rebecca B. Leach*[2]

[1]*University of Denver;* [2]*University of Arkansas*

Learning Objectives

After reading this chapter, you will:

1 Understand how the compassion process unfolds within organizational contexts.
2 Identify unique challenges for employees with marginalized identities and how these challenges limit their experience of compassion.
3 Reflect on practical steps one can take to help cultivate compassion at work for employees with marginalized identities.

Introduction

The need for compassion at work has never been greater. In the United States and globally, employee's levels of burnout, stress, and anxiety are at historic highs (Deloitte, 2015; Gallup, 2022). The COVID-19 pandemic has exacerbated these challenges, as high unemployment (Schwartz et al., 2020), work-from-home stressors (Hall et al., 2020), and historic levels of anxiety (Center for Disease Control, 2022) have created a special type of "mental-health disaster" (Stern, 2020) that is likely to impact people for years.

Suffering has been even greater for those holding traditionally marginalized identities. Black Americans have endured continued police violence and the ongoing politicization of policing. Asian Americans have faced increasing violence due to anti-Asian stereotyping related to the COVID-19 pandemic. Members of the LGBTQIA+ communities continue to fight for equitable rights in the United States—according to the Human Rights

DOI: 10.4324/9781003333746-15

Campaign, over 250 bills were introduced in 2020 that would limit LGBTQIA+ rights (Human Rights Campaign, 2020). And Hispanic, Black, and American Indians have experienced disparate levels of hospitalization and death from COVID-19 (Center for Disease Control, 2020), furthering the physical, emotional, and mental toll on marginalized groups.

In the face of such suffering, compassion can make a real difference. At an individual level, compassion helps suffering employees cope with anxiety (Lilius et al., 2008) and helps alleviate the physical, emotional, and psychological challenges associated with suffering (Dutton et al., 2014). Compassion can also help strengthen relationships with coworkers (Lilius et al., 2011; Powley, 2009) and even heighten an employee's sense of commitment to their organization (Grant et al., 2008). Taken collectively, compassion can help alleviate the challenges of suffering at the individual, relational, and organizational levels.

Unfortunately, not all employees experience compassion equitably, and those holding traditionally marginalized identities face challenges that are likely to limit the compassion they experience at work (Tietsort, 2021). As we will outline throughout this chapter, marginalized groups can't express suffering as openly as others and, when they do, their experiences are often minimized or discounted. These challenges become even more acute when their suffering stems from aspects of their marginalized identity.

Against this backdrop, the goal of this chapter is to equip practitioners and scholars with tools to cultivate compassion within their organizations, specifically focusing on employees holding traditionally marginalized identities. To do so, we have divided this chapter into two primary sections. First, we discuss how compassion functions at work and highlight the specific challenges for those holding traditionally marginalized identities. Next, we offer practical suggestions on how to navigate these challenges and increase compassion for marginalized groups. Collectively, we hope that this equips readers with both a theoretical and practical understanding of how they can cultivate compassion for marginalized employees at work.

Compassion Theory: A Brief Introduction

Compassion theory has a relatively short history in organizational studies. At the most basic level, compassion unfolds when someone (1) *recognizes* another person is suffering, (2) *relates* empathically to that person, and (3) *(re)acts* to alleviate their suffering (Way & Tracy, 2012). Compassion is distinct from similar concepts like empathy. Empathy implies a sense of connection as one feels for another person and tries to put themselves "in their shoes" (Zaki, 2014). However, one can feel empathy and still choose not to act on behalf of another. Compassion, then, is defined by *action*—when one is moved to alleviate another's suffering through action (Way & Tracy, 2012).

In addition to these core processes of *recognizing* suffering, *relating* empathically, and *reacting* to alleviate suffering, two additional elements heavily influence how compassion unfolds. First, while compassion theory emphasizes *recognition* as the first step of the compassion process, the real key is that *suffering becomes known.* While suffering may be recognized, most often sufferers *express suffering.* This may seem like a simple distinction. However, work contexts have historically excluded personal sharing and emotions (Fineman, 2000), leading many to feel it is unsafe to share suffering at work (Kanov et al., 2017; Tietsort, 2021). So, although intertwined, it is critical to distinguish the unique challenges to each aspect of how suffering becomes known. Second, research suggests not all suffering triggers empathy; rather, *how* one perceives another's suffering is most important (Atkins & Parker, 2012). For example, someone is unlikely to feel empathy for another if they feel like the situation is their fault. People may also lack empathy when they can't understand another's experience, such as someone in a majority group trying to empathize with the pain another feels due to repeated microaggressions at work. Research suggests that greater similarity among individuals supports compassion (Valdesolo & DeSteno, 2011), whereas power dynamics between individuals may constrain compassion (Dutton et al., 2014). These appraisals are critical, as someone could share their suffering and still not receive compassion.

So, in summary (and depicted below in Figure 13.1), compassion is a relational process by which a compassion provider (1) recognizes another's suffering, either proactively by noticing small cues or when the sufferer expresses their suffering, (2) appraises their suffering in a way that engenders empathy, (3) relates empathically to that person, and (4) reacts in a way that works to alleviate their suffering (see Figure 13.1). This process most often unfolds in a linear manner, but it doesn't have to. As depicted in Figure 13.1 by the bi-directional arrows, each step can overlap or double-back to inform each other. For example, one might work to alleviate

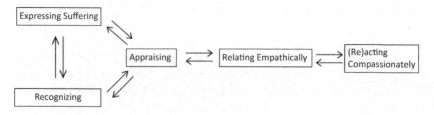

FIGURE 13.1 Compassion Processes.

another's suffering even when they don't feel empathy or recognize the depth of another's suffering while relating to them.

Constrained Compassion: Challenges for Employees with Marginalized Identities

We are making the case that employees with traditionally marginalized identities experience their workplaces differently and, consequently, are less likely to receive compassion when they are suffering. These challenges are especially acute when their suffering stems from aspects of their marginalized or minoritized identity. In what follows, we briefly outline the specific challenges that are present across each aspect of the compassion process discussed above.

Expressed Suffering

A critical yet often overlooked aspect of the compassion process is that suffering must be *expressed*. Theoretically, all employees should be able to openly share when they are suffering. However, historical discourses have privileged rational approaches to business and decision making, where emotions were often seen as untrustworthy (Fineman, 2000). Consequently, individuals' expressions of suffering are shaped by how they perceive their organizations' "feeling rules," or the implicit expectations of what is appropriate to feel and display at work (Fineman, 2000; Hochschild, 1983). In the United States, these "feeling rules" have typically privileged positive emotions while restricting negative, intense displays of emotion (i.e., suffering) (Riforgiate & Komarova, 2017).

Unfortunately, feeling rules are not applied to all individuals equitably, with additional feeling rules for many minoritized employees. Stereotype threat (Spencer et al., 2016)—when an employee fears that their behavior may be perceived as validating a negative stereotype—often creates additional hesitancy for certain groups. For example, if a Black employee is in pain and frustrated with a situation, they may hesitate to share this for fear of validating stereotypes of the "angry Black employee" (see Wingfield, 2007 for more on racial stereotypes at work). Even when stereotypes do not exist, others may carry a burden of representation where they worry that their behavior will be extrapolated to their broader identity group. So, a trans employee who is consistently misgendered may choose to suffer in silence if they worry bringing the issue up will make them seem difficult. In this case, the worry isn't that they as an individual will be seen as difficult but that coworkers may extrapolate that *all trans people* are difficult. In both situations, those holding marginalized identities are forced to consider broader implications of how their expressed suffering will be perceived, which often results in them deciding it is too risky to share pain and suffering at work.

Recognizing Suffering

Compassion typically unfolds when one employee simply recognizes that another is not doing well. In many instances, suffering is so overwhelming that it would be impossible not to notice it, such as the intense grief of losing a loved one or receiving news of a terrible health complication. Much of the time, however, recognizing is more subtle, where one may simply notice someone has missed a few days of work and inquire as to how they are doing. These small everyday acts of recognizing are simple but can often prove challenging amidst the time pressures of everyday organizational life.

Given these challenges, research suggests personal similarities and context for employee's personal lives are key enablers for recognizing suffering (Dutton et al., 2014; Miller, 2007). However, what about employees who share little similarity with their coworkers? Or, what happens when an employee experiences suffering related to an aspect of their personal life they haven't felt comfortable sharing at work? These factors may be commonplace for minoritized employees.

When an employee identifies as a minority in their organization, their experiences are more likely to be missed or minimized. Many people tend to recognize suffering around them when they themselves are suffering. For example, an employee struggling with work-from-home challenges due to the pandemic may be quick to ask if others are struggling with this. Similarly, team leaders often create space for recognizing through simple check-ins at a team meeting and may even reference shared challenges people may be experiencing. However, if the leader is in a majority group, it is likely these check-ins will focus primarily on experiences related to majority groups. So, a team leader may ask about work-from-home situations, which they experience, but fail to ask about discrimination against Asian Americans. In sum, organizations that primarily have majority group leaders may fail to proactively recognize the suffering of their minoritized employees.

Appraisals of Suffering

Even when suffering is recognized, this recognition does not always lead to compassion. A central factor becomes *how* one perceives another suffering—if they view the suffering as legitimate (i.e., they don't deserve this), then they are likely to be empathic, whereas if they think it is illegitimate (i.e., it's their own fault), then they are unlikely to be empathic (Atkins & Parker, 2012). Many types of suffering are seen broadly as genuine, such as the loss of a loved one or experiencing serious medical issues. By contrast, some may not feel empathy for someone who loses their job after consistent feedback on how to improve, as this pain the other person is experiencing is in a way their own fault. Many types of suffering are more difficult to assess, though. In these cases, most people draw on their own experiences to appraise others' situations.

If experience is a primary influence on appraisals, then those with minority experiences are at greater likelihood to have their suffering viewed as illegitimate. Take microaggressions, for example. Microaggressions are the small everyday messages which reinforce negative stereotypes around traditionally marginalized groups (Sue et al., 2007) and have been found to be both common (Douds & Hout, 2020) and associated with negative outcomes (Nadal et al., 2015, 2017). Majority employees, who likely have never experienced microaggressions, may find it very difficult to emotionally connect with the feelings of minoritized employees. So, if a coworker opens up about the difficulty of everyday microaggressions, one can see how another employee may wonder if it is really *that bad*. And, if they don't feel it is that bad, they are unlikely to be moved toward compassion.

The disconnect in understanding and appraising the experiences of marginalized groups extends beyond microaggressions. Those in majority groups may struggle to empathize with a wide range of suffering stemming from minority experiences because they lack the experiential context to connect with it. Additionally, majority group identities are rarely tied to politics in the way minoritized identities are. For example, a workplace may say that they can't discuss issues surrounding Black Lives Matter if they see it as a political issue, a move that would disproportionately affect Black employees' ability to speak up if they are struggling with issues related to police violence. Not only may labeling certain issues as political makes it difficult to speak up about that issue, but it might allow someone to discredit another's experience more readily if they differ in political viewpoints.

Relating to Others' Suffering

Compassion requires the ability to relate to another person's pain and suffering. Relating to someone's suffering involves cognitive, affective, and communicative skills in perspective-taking, empathy, and listening, respectively (Miller, 2007; Way & Tracy, 2012). Some individuals may be biologically inclined to feel compassion for others (i.e., have a genetic predisposition toward empathy) (Hou et al., 2017), but most employees need to demonstrate effort when relating to a coworker's suffering, especially if that coworker's identity is significantly different from their own.

Perspective-taking is commonly described as putting yourself in someone else's shoes. More precisely, perspective-taking is a cognitive effort to understand another person's life, motives, and needs (Miller, 2007). Although such efforts may increase feelings of empathy between two people, it does not necessarily increase interpersonal understanding (i.e., the ability to accurately predict a person's thoughts and feelings) (Eyal et al., 2018). In other words, perspective-taking may increase a sense of connection, but we cannot assume that trying on another person's perspective yields accurate knowledge about that person's unique struggles. This logic is consistent with standpoint theory, which posits that an individual can attempt to understand another person's perspective and social location by recognizing that cultural values and power often lead to the systemic oppression of certain groups (Wood, 2009). Some standpoint theorists claim that members of dominant groups are less likely to have accurate or complete knowledge of the world because they may be unmotivated or even unable to understand the perspectives of a subordinate group. Members of the majority are privileged in many ways, and that privilege may act as a cognitive barrier for perspective-taking. Those in privileged positions often do not readily see the benefit of taking on other perspectives, whereas marginalized groups enact perspective-taking to survive. As such, relating to the suffering of marginalized and minoritized groups requires consistent and intentional efforts to understand not only their experiences, but also the ways in which our knowledge can be limited.

To effectively relate to someone else, perspective-taking must be combined with empathy. Together, perspective-taking and empathy create a foundation for a consubstantial relationship where two people can cooperate and identify with one another (Way & Tracy, 2012). Just as cultivating a standpoint requires regular reflection, building a mutually beneficial relationship should be an ongoing effort. A relationship built on feelings of connection and identification is sustained by communication skills such as listening and creating space for others to share their emotions and decisions (Way & Tracy, 2012). Creating safe spaces for emotional expression is especially important for employees with marginalized identities, who may feel that their emotions cannot be safely expressed in the workplace.

(Re)acting to Suffering

Reacting to the pain of others has been called the "heart of compassion" (Way & Tracy, 2012, p. 308). Importantly, responding to suffering can either be reactive or proactive. Given that pain is inevitable in organizational life (Frost, 1999), acting compassionately sometimes takes the form of anticipating pain and creating measures to alleviate it. Many organizations claim to proactively address pain through the implementation of "compassionate" policies, but these policies are often focused on legal compliance and liability rather than actionable change for suffering employees (Simpson et al., 2014). In some organizations, managers may strategically use compassion as a mode of power by creating routines and procedures that only benefit some people and excluding certain groups from conversation (e.g., inaccessible PTO and scheduling policies, competitive rewards for certain groups, etc.) (Simpson et al., 2014).

By offering solutions without fully understanding a person or group's unique suffering, managers and organizational leaders take control of the narrative of the problem. Compassion at the organizational level can be a form of systemic domination, where those in power determine what problems deserve attention and how people should react to those problems (Simpson et al., 2020). Dominating the narrative in an organization can easily exclude those in lower authority and marginalized positions. To create more inclusive workplaces, organizational leaders must engage in reflexivity and create space for dialogues where employees and managers can jointly define problems and solutions (Bouten-Pinto, 2016).

(Re)acting to suffering can be an interpersonal effort, but it can also be a structural goal as well. By instilling compassion into an organization's values, routines, and stories, compassion can be actualized at the organizational level (Dutton et al., 2006). In principle, infusing compassion into an organization may appear relatively simple, but it is crucial to recognize that compassion can take on different meanings and forms. An act that may be compassionate to someone in a dominant group may not feel compassionate to someone in a marginalized group. For example, many organizations may choose to appoint an employee as a chief wellness officer—a living emblem of compassion and work–life balance. However, if that person largely identifies with majority markers (e.g., white, male, etc.) and operates from a privileged standpoint, those with marginalized identities may be skeptical that their concerns would be fully heard or understood. Effectively (re)acting to suffering first requires a deep understanding of employees' issues and concerns.

Practical Recommendations for Cultivating Compassion

The issues discussed above are complicated and reflect the intersection of individual, relational, and organizational factors compounded by historical discourses which privilege and oppress different groups. As such, there is no "easy fix" that will transform a workplace, and we would not want the reader to have the assumption that they can easily disrupt these deeply seated issues. However, we believe small, practical steps can have a tangible impact on how marginalized groups experience their workplace. With that in mind, we offer individual, relational, and organizational strategies to cultivate compassion at work. We intentionally start with *individual* strategies, as we believe anyone seeking to cultivate compassion for marginalized groups must start with themselves.

Individual Strategies

Compassion often evokes a sense of urgency and action. In our haste to (re)act to the suffering of coworkers, we can overestimate our ability to understand both the situation causing distress and possible solutions. As previously discussed, practicing perspective-taking does not necessarily lead to a holistic understanding of someone else's standpoint. However, individual efforts to recognize and broaden the limits of our viewpoints are a critical first step toward a more compassionate workplace.

It can be daunting to evaluate oneself. Although it may be tempting to immediately apply a skeptical eye toward yourself and your actions, we recommend first approaching yourself with a healthy sense of curiosity. Self-reflexivity begins with a self-examination of core beliefs and values, followed by a thoughtful consideration of where those values may come from (Cunliffe, 2009). The values and truths we hold close to the heart are borne from our social experiences, many of which begin in childhood. It may be helpful to imagine analyzing yourself from a bird's eye view—can you identify the key people and situations in your life that have influenced and molded your belief system? The next step in this process is to recognize that many of us have different life experiences, challenges, and values that continue to shape us today. Compassion will not have the same face for everyone.

After engaging in self-reflexivity, you can further push yourself by engaging in critical reflexivity. Although these practices are similar because both involve self-examination, critical reflexivity is focused on actively unsettling our taken-for-granted assumptions and interrogating how our actions may include or exclude certain groups (Cunliffe, 2009).

In other words, critical reflexivity extends beyond examining the self and encourages us to consider the impact of our actions on others. Engaging in critical reflexivity requires a commitment to inclusion and dialogue, which would create spaces where compassion is possible for a variety of groups. Together, self-reflexivity and critical reflexivity challenge the concept of what is "normal." Through these lenses, there are no "normal" problems and solutions. Instead, there are unique lived experiences represented all throughout an organization, and those unique experiences can only be approached through perspective-taking and empathy.

Relational Strategies

Compassion is, at its core, a form of interpersonal work. As discussed above, however, things like stereotype threat may make it difficult to relate to other's suffering. So, what can be improve how we relate compassionately to others? First, research suggests it is critical to get to know others at a more personal level beyond traditional work-life boundaries (Lilius et al., 2011). By getting to know others personally, people tend to see similarities that minimize the potential for their view of another to be influenced by stereotypes or faulty assumptions. Additionally, getting to know others at this level may create opportunities to hear about experiences that diverge from their own, such as the experience of microaggressions or the politicization of another's identity. These deeper personal connections expand awareness around diverse experiences, which may minimize faulty appraisals and increase motivation to react compassionately to others.

To cultivate these types of interactions, one could consider creating space for authentic connections among employees at work. This could take on several forms. Informal check-ins before or after meetings, where participants are encouraged to share how they are doing, can be useful. Additionally, given that some individuals may feel uncomfortable sharing personally at work, organizations could consider events outside of formal work contexts, such as happy hour or going to a sporting event together. It is important, of course, for these moments of sharing to be genuine, as opposed to performative. Put another way, if employees come to see check-ins as something to get done before the real work starts, they are unlikely to cultivate a sense of closeness. However, when these events are framed appropriately and honored by leaders through their own participation, they are simple tools that can help shape culture over time.

Before moving to our second recommendation, we do want to provide a few comments on creating space for personal sharing at work, as this tends to raise some anxieties when we discuss it with practitioners. First, it is critical people are not *pressured* to share personal information. Individuals vary on their work-related disclosure preferences and pushing them beyond their comfort is likely to undermine the culture of safety these practices aim to cultivate. Second, we are *not* suggesting that work should become a space where employees just share anything and everything. Indeed, work contexts need to balance personal relationships with task orientations and finding the right balance can be difficult. However, what we *are* suggesting is that historical discourses have often privileged task orientations, which has minimized personal relationships and employees' perceptions that they can share personal struggles at work.

Second, we believe that people can help minimize barriers to compassion for marginalized identities through a move we call *anticipatory compassion* (Tietsort, 2021). Anticipatory compassion involves proactively reaching out to someone who you think might be experiencing suffering or may experience some form of suffering in the future, with hopes of communicating a sense of care while simultaneously signaling that it is okay for them to share or discuss that kind of suffering at work. For example, consider issues in the United States around policing and the killing of unarmed Black people. Given that this has become a highly politicized issue, Black employees may feel uncertain about discussing pain they are feeling related to a recent police shooting. However, if a leader proactively reaches out to them, acknowledges that this could be a difficult time for them, and encourages them to take time to take care of themselves, this *may* normalize the pain they are feeling and create space for them to share more about how they are doing. Of course, authenticity while engaging *anticipatory compassion* is critical, as this move *could* be used with no real intent to follow-up or honor requests from suffering employees. Still, we believe this move can work to cultivate greater openness around specific issues that marginalized employees may not feel comfortable discussing. When those in majority groups have done enough personal work to recognize these moments, *anticipatory compassion* can help convey care and shift communication climates in ways that generate compassion for marginalized groups.

Organizational Strategies

Acting compassionately at the group and organizational levels can happen in a multitude of ways. Formal and informal, structured and unstructured, and tangible and discursive efforts can all be theoretically helpful in the pursuit of compassion. There is not a one-size-fits-all strategy that applies to all organizations, but we offer an initial starting point that any organization can take to understand the needs of its members and develop strategies accordingly.

Just as individuals have unique life experiences that continually shape them, organizations have unique histories, cultures, and practices that influence employees' experiences in the workplace. Organizational scholars (e.g., Dutton et al., 2006) have previously theorized that organizational culture is particularly important in the activation and mobilization of compassion at work. Dutton et al. (2006) argued that organizations that treat employees as humans (i.e., recognizing employees beyond their professional identities) and frame workers as family are more likely to effectively notice and respond to pain. An organization's values, routines, and stories can potentially foster emotional expression and collaborative action in the face of suffering. As such, organizations interested in cultivating compassion may first want to perform a culture audit of the workplace, focusing on gathering the thoughts and opinions of employees across the organization. What is valued in the organization? What is not valued—or even taboo—in the organization? What voices and stories are privileged in the organization? By gathering answers to these questions, an organization can start to determine whether its existing culture is conducive to compassion.

Organizations may also be interested in creating formal structures that support compassion. For example, a flexible leave policy could be an attractive option, particularly if this policy is paired with communication emphasizing that personal and mental health days are sometimes necessary for employee wellbeing. A compassionate policy is one that not only provides a roadmap for acting compassionately, but also normalizes pain and suffering as experiences that inevitably occur in the workplace. That said, organizations and leaders should be wary of believing that a "compassionate" policy will lead to positive outcomes for all employees. Policies are often crafted to serve the interests of the majority, which means that the needs of marginalized groups may only be partially addressed or perhaps neglected entirely. To minimize the potential for such situations, one approach is to create a policy-audit committee of members representing diverse groups in the organization. The goal of such a committee would be to thoroughly vet policies for strengths, weaknesses, and disproportionate consequences. Inviting diverse voices throughout the development of any organizational policy or program can help organizations be mindful of various groups and their needs (Table 13.1).

TABLE 13.1 Practical Recommendations to Cultivate Compassion at Work

Level of Intervention	Core Challenge to Address	Practices
Individual	Unearth and challenge problematic beliefs and assumptions one may hold that limit their ability to relate to and act compassionately toward others	Self-reflexivity—reflect on one's core values, beliefs, and assumption Critical Self-Reflexivity— assess one's values, beliefs, and assumptions with a willingness to disrupt ones that negatively impact others
Relational	Understand a greater diversity of experiences to avoid minimizing or inaccurately appraising others suffering	Create space at work to connect with others about personal elements of their life Create opportunities outside of work for personal connections Engage in *anticipatory compassion* when appropriate
Organizational	Create policies and culture that enable *all* employees to express suffering and receive compassion equitably	Perform a (1) cultural audit, and (2) policy audit Implement flexible leave policies

Conclusion

In closing, we hope you feel a renewed sense of conviction in cultivating compassion at work for *all* employees. We believe compassion is a crucial ingredient in healthy organizations, acknowledging that all individuals struggle and that we cannot simply leave our personal lives at work. And, as we have argued, employees holding marginalized and minoritized identities face additional challenges in experiencing compassion at work. These issues are challenging and complex, and there is no quick fix in resolving these issues. However, we believe that taking steps at the individual, interpersonal, and organizational levels can have an impact to create greater compassion in your organizations and, over time, help structure a new way of relating to each other at work.

Discussion Questions

1 How have you experienced compassion at work, if at all? How do these experiences shape the ways you think about emotional expression and compassion at work?

2 How might your intersecting identities influence the way you make sense of other employees' pain and struggles?

3 Given the discussion on practical steps to cultivate compassion at work, which could you most readily adopt within the next month? Which of these might have the most value in your organizational context?

Author Bios

Cris J. Tietsort (Ph.D., Arizona State University) is an Assistant Professor of organizational communication at University of Denver. His research examines positive organizational relationships, with a focus on leadership, compassion, and voice, and appears in the *Journal of Applied Communication Research, Health Communication*, and *Communication Stu*dies.

Rebecca B. Leach (Ph.D., Arizona State University) is an Assistant Professor of organizational communication at the University of Arkansas. Her research examines the factors that foster flourishing in organizations, including compassion, resilience, and justice. Her research appears in journals such as *Management Communication Quarterly, Communication Monographs*, and*Communication Teacher*.

References

Atkins, P. W., & Parker, S. K. (2012). Understanding individual compassion in organizations: The role of appraisals and psychological flexibility. *Academy of Management Review, 37*(4), 524–546. 10.5465/amr.2010.0490

Bouten-Pinto, C. (2016). Reflexivity in managing diversity: A pracademic perspective. *Equality, Diversity and Inclusion, 35*(2), 136–153. 10.1108/EDI-10-2013-0087

Center for Disease Control and Prevention. (2020, December 10). *Disparities in Deaths from COVID-19: Racial and Ethnic Health Disparities*. COVID 19. https://www.cdc.gov/coronavirus/2019-ncov/community/health-equity/racial-ethnic-disparities/disparities-deaths.html

Center for Disease Control and Prevention. (2022, June 22). *Anxiety and depression*. Health care access, telemedicine, and mental health. https://www.cdc.gov/nchs/covid19/pulse/mental-health.htm

Cunliffe, A. L. (2009). The philosopher leader: On relationalism, ethics and reflexivity. a critical perspective to teaching leadership. *Management Learning, 40*(1), 87–101. 10.1177/1350507608099315

Deloitte. (2015). *Work-life balance and wellbeing report*. https://www2.deloitte.com/us/en/pages/about-deloitte/articles/well-being-survey.html.

Douds, K. W., & Hout, M. (2020). Microaggressions in the United States. *Sociological Science, 7*, 528–543. 10.15195/v7.a22

Dutton, J. E., Worline, M. C., Frost, P. J., & Lilius, J. (2006). Explaining compassion organizing. *Administrative Science Quarterly, 51*(1), 59–96. 10.2189/asqu.51.1.59

Dutton, J. E., Workman, K. M., & Hardin, A. E. (2014). Compassion at work. *Annual Review of Organizational Psychology and Organizational Behavior, 1*(1), 277–304.

Eyal, T., Steffel, M., & Epley, N. (2018). Perspective mistaking: Accurately understanding the mind of another requires getting perspective, not taking perspective. *Journal of Personality and Social Psychology, 114*(4), 547–571. 10.1037/pspa0000115

Fineman, S. (Ed.). (2000). *Emotion in organizations.* Sage. 10.4135/9781446219850

Frost, P. J. (1999). Why compassion counts. *Journal of Management Inquiry, 8*(2), 127–133. 10.1177/105649269982004

Gallup. (2022). *State of the global workplace report.* Retried from https://www.gallup.com/workplace/349484/state-of-the-global-workplace-2022-report.aspx.

Grant, A. M., Dutton, J. E., & Rosso, B. D. (2008). Giving commitment: Employee support programs and the prosocial sensemaking process. *Academy of Management Journal, 51*(5), 898–918. 10.5465/amj.2008.34789652

Hall, M., Nagasawa, K., & Tucker, D. (2020, May 13). *Why work from home causes stress in more than just zoom calls - and how to overcome it.* NPR. https://www.npr.org/local/309/2020/05/13/855225370/why-work-from-home-causes-stress-in-more-than-just-zoom-calls-and-how-to-overcome-it

Hochschild A. R. (1983). *The managed heart: Commercialization of human feeling.* University of California Press. 10.1525/9780520930414

Hou, X., Allen, T. A., Wei, D., Huang, H., Wang, K., DeYoung, C. G., & Qiu, J. (2017). Trait compassion is associated with the neural substrate of empathy. *Cognitive, Affective, & Behavioral Neuroscience, 17*(5), 1018–1027. 10.3758/s13415-017-0529-5

Human Rights Campaign. (2020). *We are suing.* Our Work. https://www.hrc.org/campaigns/we-are-suing

Kanov, J., Powley, E. H., & Walshe, N. D. (2017). Is it ok to care? How compassion falters and is courageously accomplished in the midst of uncertainty. *Human Relations, 70*(6), 751–777. 10.1177/0018726716673144

Lilius, J. M., Worline, M. C., Dutton, J. E., Kanov, J. M., & Maitlis, S. (2011). Understanding compassion capability. *Human Relations, 64*(7), 873–899. 10.1177/0018726710396250

Lilius, J. M., Worline, M. C., Maitlis, S., Kanov, J., Dutton, J. E., & Frost, P. (2008). The contours and consequences of compassion at work. *Journal of Organizational Behavior: The International Journal of Industrial, Occupational and Organizational Psychology and Behavior, 29*(2), 193–218. 10.1002/job.508

Miller, K. I. (2007). Compassionate communication in the workplace: Exploring processes of noticing, connecting, and responding. *Journal of Applied Communication Research, 35*(3), 223–245. 10.1080/00909880701434208

Nadal, K. L., Wong, Y., Sriken, J., Griffin, K., & Fujii-Doe, W. (2015). Racial microaggressions and Asian Americans: An exploratory study on within-group differences and mental health. *Asian American Journal of Psychology, 6*(2), 136–144. 10.1037/a0038058

Nadal, K. L., Griffin, K. E., Wong, Y., Davidoff, K. C., & Davis, L. S. (2017). The injurious relationship between racial microaggressions and physical health:

Implications for social work. *Journal of Ethnic & Cultural Diversity in Social Work*, *26*(1-2), 6–17. 10.1080/15313204.2016.1263813

Powley, E. H. (2009). Reclaiming resilience and safety: Resilience activation in the critical period of crisis. *Human Relations*, *62*(9), 1289–1326. 10.1177/001872 6709334881

Riforgiate, S. E., & Komarova, M. (2017). Emotion and work. In C. Scott & L. Lewis (Eds.), *The International Encyclopedia of Organizational Communication* (pp. 1–17). Wiley-Blackwell. 10.1002/9781118955567.wbieoc068

Schwartz, N. D., Casselman, B., & Koeze, E. (2020, May 8). *How bad is unemployment? 'Literally off the charts.'* The New York Times. https://www.nytimes.com/interactive/2020/05/08/business/economy/april-jobs-report.html

Simpson, A. V., & Berti, M. (2020). Transcending organizational compassion paradoxes by enacting wise compassion courageously. *Journal of Management Inquiry*, *29*(4), 433–449. 10.1177/1056492618821188

Simpson, A. V., Clegg, S., & Pitsis, T. (2014). "I used to care but things have changed": A genealogy of compassion in organizational theory. *Journal of Management Inquiry*, *23*(4), 347–359. 10.1177/1056492614521895

Spencer, S. J., Logel, C., & Davies, P. G. (2016). Stereotype threat. *Annual Review of Psychology*, *67*(1), 415–437. 10.1146/annurev-psych-073115-103235

Stern, J. (2020, July 7). *This is not a normal mental-health disaster*. The Atlantic. https://www.theatlantic.com/health/archive/2020/07/coronavirus-special-mental-health-disaster/613510

Sue, D. W., Capodilupo, C. M., Torino, G. C., Bucceri, J. M., Holder, A., Nadal, K. L., & Esquilin, M. (2007). Racial microaggressions in everyday life: implications for clinical practice. *American Psychologist*, *62*(4), 271–286. 10.1037/0003-066X.62.4.271

Tietsort, C. J. (2021). *Compassionate leadership at work: Cultivating compassion by reducing uncertainty, emphasizing personal well-being, and aligning compassionate actions*. [Doctoral dissertation, Arizona State University]. Proquest.

Valdesolo, P., & DeSteno, D. (2011). Synchrony and the social tuning of compassion. *Emotion*, *11*(2), 262–266. 10.1037/a0021302

Way, D., & Tracy, S. J. (2012). Conceptualizing compassion as recognizing, relating and (re)acting: A qualitative study of compassionate communication at hospice. *Communication Monographs*, *79*(3), 292–315. 10.1080/03637751.2012.697630

Wingfield, A. H. (2007). The modern mammy and the angry Black man: African American professionals' experiences with gendered racism in the workplace. *Race, Gender & Class*, *14*(1-2), 196–212.

Wood, J. (2009). Feminist standpoint theory. In S. Littlejohn & K. Foss (Eds.), *Encyclopedia of communication theory* (pp. 396–398). SAGE Publications, Inc. 10.4135/9781412959384.n147

Zaki, J. (2014). Empathy: a motivated account. *Psychological Bulletin*, *140*(6), 1608–1647. 10.1037/a0037679

14

ACTION-ORIENTED DIALOGUES FOR SYSTEMIC CHANGE

A Trauma-Informed Approach

Srividya Ramasubramanian[1] and Anna Wolfe[2]
[1]*Syracuse University;* [2]*Texas A&M University*

Learning Objectives

After reading this chapter, you will:

1 Appreciate the role of storytelling and dialogues in bringing about organizational change.
2 Apply the principles of trauma-informed systems approach to your own organizational context by designing dialogues to bring about organizational change.
3 Understand the 5 A's of the trauma-informed systems approach to designing antiracism dialogues: (1) Acknowledgment, (2) Active Listening, (3) Accepting Responsibility, (4) Action Orientation, and (5) Accountability.

Introduction

Antiracism work within organizational contexts can come in many formats such as mandatory diversity training sessions, lecture series, and online learning modules. In our work within the context of higher education, we have used "facilitated dialogues" as an effective format to discuss and address organizational changemaking as compared to some more passive formats such as lectures or online learning modules. Well-designed dialogues hold great potential for building shared understandings across differences, encouraging empathy and perspective-taking, and moving toward action-oriented steps to create more inclusive work environments (Gayles

DOI: 10.4324/9781003333746-16

et al., 2015; Ramasubramanian & Wolfe, 2020; Sue & Constantine, 2007). They allow participants to ask clarifying questions, share one's personal experiences, and take the time to understand alternative viewpoints. They are especially helpful to those who have experienced systemic biases, discrimination, and marginalization within the organization to feel validated in their experiences. Active listening, validation, and affirmations from co-workers and colleagues within an inclusive work environment can bring about healing.

This chapter outlines the nuts and bolts of how a trauma-informed racially conscious approach can be used to design antiracism dialogues to create opportunities for greater connection, support, healing, and actionable change. Such an approach can help avoid unintentionally perpetuating misunderstandings, silences, and tensions instead of promoting shared understanding and organizational change. Stemming from the Difficult Dialogues Project founded by the first author in 2016, our insights are based on numerous dialogues that we have hosted at a Southern, historically white university during the Trump presidency from 2016 to 2020. We draw on our experiences hosting such dialogues about difficult topics such as race relations, COVID-19, and political differences. By facilitated dialogues, we mean focused conversations on a particular topic that are moderated by trained facilitators. We share these design elements and approaches in this chapter for practitioners working on antiracism initiatives with the purpose of organizational changemaking. We train students and faculty to serve as facilitators to lead dialogues in small groups of 6–8 people as part of a larger dialogue session of 30–50 people. We create space for honest conversations by using shared agreements and ground rules to share their thoughts and feelings as well as ideas for individual and collective action (Ramasubramanian et al., 2017). Although our experience is largely within higher education and university campuses, we believe that our experience and insights would translate to other complex organizational contexts that are embedded within white structures.

Organizational Changemaking: A Trauma-Informed and Systems Approach

Organizations can be conceptualized as dynamic interconnected systems. Social systems theory approaches encourage reflection on the complex relationships between individuals, organizations, and their environments (Poole, 2014). People, relationships, groups, and organizations are always embedded in multiple social hierarchies with permeable boundaries, influenced by interactions with their environments, and affected by feedback from other elements of the system. A systems approach, then, must account for the interdependent relations between individuals, organizations, and society that structure possibilities for stability and change.

To bring about systemic change, it is necessary to address factors that affect organizational well-being for all members of the organization. Injustices, microaggressions, and inequalities in the organization affect all members of the organization, not just those who are targets of violence. In human body systems, for example, trauma experiences in one part of the body can affect the functioning of multiple systems, such as the muscular, circulatory, and nervous systems. And in organizations, when trauma is experienced repeatedly over long periods of time, it becomes chronic, generational, and cultural trauma experienced by the entire organizational system.

Trauma is defined as "an event, series of events, or set of circumstances that is experienced by an individual as physically or emotionally harmful or life-threatening and that has lasting adverse effects on the individual's functioning and mental, physical, social, emotional, or spiritual well-being" (The Substance Abuse and Mental Health Services Administration, 2014, p. 7). Racial microaggressions and racism are complex forms of trauma that often involve multiple layers of oppression, compounding adverse life situations, and intergenerational trauma. Chronic and systemic experiences of racial microaggressions can lead to long-term negative effects on physical, psychological, emotional, and spiritual well-being, which can contribute to stress, anxiety, depression, Post-traumatic stress disorder (PTSD), and mind-body illnesses (Carter, 2007; Clark et al., 1999; Harrell et al., 2003; McIntosh, 2019).

A trauma-informed systems approach starts by recognizing that organizations and systems can perpetuate trauma, thus reducing the ability of the organization to function at its best. Although racial trauma might be experienced at the individual level, it is embedded within the policies, practices, values, systems, and cultures within organizations. An important part of addressing long-term and chronic systemic trauma, including racism, within organizations is to build rapport and trust with those who are most impacted due to past negative experiences. This starts by creating an environment where employees and other organizational members can feel comfortable disclosing their experiences of microaggressions, exclusions, and invalidations without fear of retaliation. Within a trauma-informed approach to organizational changemaking, principles and values such as trust, safety, collaboration, agency, transparency, and cultural beliefs must be prioritized. In other words, organizations must create space and time for honest sharing where their experiences are acknowledged and addressed in safe ways that assure confidentiality.

The Role of Storytelling and Dialogues in Organizational Changemaking

Dialogue and deliberation have been celebrated as forms of communication that are oriented toward values of inclusivity and participation; but, in practice, designs often reinforce existing social hierarchies (Beauvais & Baechtiger, 2016; Fraser, 1990). For example, if the dialogue design takes a color-blind approach in selecting facilitators, they could end up with an all-white team of facilitators or notetakers. Under such circumstances, when the flow, topic, and duration of the dialogues are facilitated by members of largely or exclusively part of the dominant group, then members of marginalized groups will likely not feel comfortable expressing their views. In this example, the design was not racially conscious, which could lead to reinforcing existing racial hierarchies within the dialogue setting. Another example of a well-intentioned but not trauma-informed approach is one where a member of the dominant group might invalidate, shut down, or be aggressive toward members of marginalized groups within the dialogue.

In these situations, the ground rules have to be adhered to carefully so that marginalized group members' perspectives are not silenced, interrupted, or negated consistently. With reflective engagement, we can "make forms of communication possible that were once difficult, impossible, or unimagined" (Aakhus, 2007, p. 116). This is why we enter our design of antiracism dialogues with critical caution, centering an ethic of care. We draw on critical insights of race scholarship within applied communication (Orbe & Allen, 2008) to reject notions of "neutrality" in dialogue and deliberation and to center the lived experiences of racially marginalized groups. Fernandes (2017) challenges us to consider:

Under what conditions do stories reproduce dominant relations of power, and when can they be subversive? What are the stakes, and for whom, in the crafting and mobilization of storytelling? Rather than being the magical elixir we imagine, might … stories actually inhibit social change? (p. 3)

Therefore, in engaging stories and narratives for social change, we must pay particular attention to power relations such that they can help mobilize organizations toward positive action.

Storytelling plays a central role in the accomplishment of dialogic moments by making present people's experiences in powerful ways that promote perspective-taking and facilitate the negotiation between individual and collective identities (Black, 2008). In dialogic moments, participants experience spontaneous, profound awareness of self and others. To the extent that storytelling can materialize invisible social identities and create empathy for minoritized members of an organization through talk; this communicative practice can heighten perceptions of intimacy between dialogue participants and present opportunities for connection and the provision of social support. We focus on storytelling practices in dialogue events, therefore, because they provide opportunities for dissolving rigid group boundaries through narrative testifying and witnessing (Wolfe, 2018).

Narrative research is often accused of sentimental romanticism (e.g., Atkinson, 1997), whereby enthusiasm for the potential power of stories might come in the way of understanding how power may contribute to traumatization and healing. Stories may help with perspective-taking to understand others' experiences better but could also potentially contribute to voyeurism. They might build empathy but could also lead to paternalism. In this way, stories do not serve a monolithic purpose in intergroup dialogue—dialogue across groups of difference—and may facilitate retraumatization as well as healing. We take as a starting point this assumption that stories are power-*full* and that power can be mobilized in various ways to reproduce and subvert existing relations across differences. We also assume that storytelling and story-witnessing interactions are personal and temporally based, in that they affect different people differently at different times.

Case Study: The Difficult Dialogues Project

As racial and political tensions have boiled over into violence, universities have faced increasing public pressure to enact symbolic changes, such as removing monuments and changing building names that memorialize white supremacists. However, this focus on *histories* of exclusion can, at times, obscure the living legacies of inequity and racism that pulse throughout our campus communities. Racist incidents within universities are often framed by campus administrators as isolated events enacted by "bad actors" rather than as an essential part of the fabric of the educational system. Although engaging with campus stakeholders about histories of chronic and generational racial trauma can be empowering, designing dialogues on topics such as racism should be conducted with care to avoid retraumatization, alienation, and miscommunication.

Below, we recognize these legacies of trauma, and we offer our own experiences in designing antiracism dialogues in higher educational contexts as a case study to demonstrate how trauma-informed designs of antiracism dialogues produce fundamentally different priorities than color-evasive designs. Since 2016, we have been running the "Difficult Dialogues

Project," to host conversations about difficult topics such as race relations, COVID-19, and political differences. We center ethics of care and safety by developing clear shared agreements, recruiting facilitators with relevant lived experiences, providing participants the agency over how and when to tell their stories, and offering resources and support for the participants.

Should We Host Action-Oriented Dialogue Sessions?

Facilitated conversations in a structured format can promote a greater appreciation for diverse perspectives. Through facilitated dialogue sessions, we can help participants listen to multiple perspectives and lay the foundation for working collectively to address organizational inequities and microaggressions. Dialogues can help encourage participants to challenge their preconceived notions, create shared meaning with one another, and work collaboratively toward shared actions. However, they will only work if there is a willingness among participants to engage honestly, suspend their own beliefs, and seek to understand different perspectives. They will work only if leadership and change agents within the organization are committed to such change. While constructive conversations on oppression, power, and privilege can build empathy and perspective-taking and motivate participants to bring about changes within the organization, they can also be challenging. If not designed well, they can even end up perpetuating misunderstandings, producing anger and silence, and creating tension, anxiety, and awkwardness in open conversations on issues such as racism (Gayles et al., 2015; Sue & Constantine, 2007). In the paragraphs below, we provide recommendations for what to do and what not to do to avoid such unintended outcomes.

Whom to Invite to the Action-Oriented Dialogue Sessions?

We typically host dialogue sessions with about 30–50 participants and 8–10 trained co-facilitators, with one or two of them seated at each table. We find that an ideal group consists of five to seven participants whose conversation is guided by an active facilitator and/or two-person facilitation team. Our dialogue sessions are open to people from all backgrounds, races, positions, and units. We do not make them mandatory, but voluntary. That way, the hope is that the people who attend are committed to organizational changemaking. We also host dialogues for smaller, intact groups by invitation. These are typically student or staff groups within a larger organization composed of members of minoritized groups or units that are at the forefront of changemaking.

It is important to consider power differences, amount of structure, and group composition when deciding who to invite to the dialogues. If there are huge power differences within groups, this can lead to chilling effects, where those from minoritized groups may not feel comfortable sharing their experiences of trauma openly with those in positions of power, especially when there are direct supervisor–supervisee relationships involved. Depending on the context of the organization, this could mean hosting separate dialogue sessions for more powerful groups such as managers, administrators, and leadership. If this is not possible, then, within the same dialogue session, we have requested participants to move to another table.

All the dialogue sessions are facilitated by co-facilitators from within or outside the organization. They are selected based on their commitment to organizational changemaking, their facilitation skills, and their lived experiences as members of minoritized groups. They are provided training in facilitation skills to create well-rounded, honest discussions and to document critical conversations. It is best to host a separate facilitator training session ahead of time—say, a week or so before the dialogues.

When and Where to Host the Action-Oriented Dialogue Sessions?

Dialogues should ideally be offered at multiple times so that participants have the option to pick the times and days that work for them. We typically send out open invitations a week or two in advance to those who are invited to the session. We include a registration link that gives us an idea of the profile of those who are attending and how many small groups we will be hosting. We recommend sending out a couple of reminders a day or two before the dialogue session to all registered participants about what to expect and some guidelines for engagement. We let them know that they are expected to stay for the entire duration, follow the ground rules, and let us know if they need any additional accommodations. Pre-registration with waitlist options allows us to make room for waitlisted guests to take the spots of those who cancel last minute due to other commitments.

We reserve the space for three to four hours, giving us time to set up in the beginning and debrief plus clean up at the end. However, we have also worked with student and staff organizations where we met with the facilitators an hour or so before the start of the dialogue session to go over ground rules, their roles and responsibilities, and some tips and tricks. A typical workshop program lasts for approximately two hours and looks like this:

- Settling in and welcome: 10–15 minutes
- Ground rules and shared agreements: 10 minutes

- Read localized journal entries: 10 minutes
- Facilitated discussion in small groups with discussion prompts (30–45 minutes):

  - What were your thoughts and feelings as you read the journal entries? Which entries stood out to you and why?
  - What can we do individually and collectively to make our organization more welcoming and inclusive to all?

- Sharing of key points in the large group: 10–15 minutes
- Wrap-up and call to action: 10–15 minutes
- Feedback forms (can be shared during and/or after the session): 10 minutes

Meeting in-person in a fairly large space with a round table seating format is the preferred set-up for dialogue sessions. We encourage participants to sit at tables where they do not know others and to create heterogeneous groups with multiple races, genders, and job types, among other variables, at each table. During the evolving COVID-19 global pandemic, our project hosted several Zoom-based online dialogues. Using virtual spaces comes with the advantage of making breakout rooms, easily recording sessions, and being able to take notes without disrupting conversations. However, there are issues such as confidentiality (e.g., creating pseudonyms in virtual settings), safety (e.g., Zoom-bombing incidents), and access (e.g., unstable Wi-Fi) that need to be addressed.

What Topics to Include in the Action-Oriented Dialogue Sessions?

We start the session with some ground rules and shared agreements. Doing so sets the stage for co-facilitators to be able to serve in their roles, ensuring that the ground rules are being followed. We invite participants to raise their hand or otherwise indicate that they agree with them and also request that they ask questions or add their own additional ground rules for the dialogues. Here are the ground rules that we share:

- *Active listening*: Listen to understand, not only to respond.
- *Balanced air time*: If you tend to talk too much, let other voices be heard. If you do not tend to participate, step out of your comfort zone. Your opinion is a gift.
- *Confidentiality:* Speakers and their contributions should stay in the room; opinions offered here should not have consequences for participants outside of this safe space. Discussing issues is OK; discussing names is not.

- *Assume good intentions:* Give others the benefit of the doubt; we are all here because we want to learn from one another and understand, though we may have different levels of understanding.
- *Make I statements*: Use sentences such as "I feel that .... my experience is ..." instead of "those people are ...."
- *Avoid vulgar language:* No racial slurs or epithets or vulgar language. Even if the journal entries include racial slurs, do not repeat them during the dialogues.

The first half of the dialogue sessions are meant to produce honest discussions about their experiences, thoughts, and feelings regarding racial microaggressions within organizations. The centerpiece of our dialogue sessions is journal entries. We use 20–30 brief narrative vignettes of racial microaggressions shared with us by student groups and faculty members, collected via anonymous online feedback forms or class journals. These vignettes can be collected in multiple ways, such as through feedback forms, journaling exercises, and through social media or newspaper articles. In our work, we requested our colleague who taught courses on race and ethnicity to get the permission of their students to use their journals of everyday racial microaggressions for our project. Additionally, we also worked with a student organization within our campus to include vignettes that they have collected as part of a larger survey that they conducted to document racial biases and discrimination. We find that using real-world stories from the local context is much more powerful in eliciting deep and honest conversations than discussing racism using hypothetical case studies or without any narratives at all.

The second half of the dialogue session is focused on action steps. In this half of the dialogue session, we discuss resources (such as websites and support groups) and strategies (such as discursive responses to microaggressions) at the individual and collective levels. We do not simply create a space to recognize racism that exists within the organization, but also provide specific ways to take personal and collective responsibility to create a welcoming community for all members.

Below, we put forth the 5 A's of trauma-informed approaches to organizational changemaking in addressing the topics to include in the dialogue sessions: (1) Acknowledgment, (2) Active Listening, (3) Accepting Responsibility, (4) Action Orientation, and (5) Accountability. While we present them below as a step-by-step process, in the real world, they are not necessarily sequential as much as they are like back-and-forth dance steps.

1 **Acknowledgment:** The first step is to become aware that racism and other intersecting axes of oppression are woven into the fabric of our social

institutions and within how most organizations operate and are founded. Color-evasive racism,[1] for instance, is a contemporary form of prejudice that involves the belief that race is not a factor for success (or lack thereof) within organizations. It often shows up within organizations in statements such as "Our institution has race-neutral policies" or "I don't see color."

2 **Active Listening:** We cannot emphasize enough the role of active listening in organizational changemaking. Indeed, this is the most important step, especially for us as intercultural communication and dialogue researchers. Often, organizational leadership jumps into action without first listening deeply, actively, and with humility to the ways in which the organization might be complicit with oppressive social systems. This form of listening requires a sustained effort that prioritizes listening to *understand* over listening to *respond*. When we listen to respond, the judging mind interferes with comprehension and curiosity. As Buddhist monk and mindfulness teacher, Thich Nhat Hanh (1974) claimed, "With each judgment the experience of pure hearing becomes fainter and fainter until one no longer hears the sound but hears only his thoughts about it" (p. 10). Listening to respond is characterized by strategic focus on lines of argumentation, interruptions, or defensive posturing, and attempts to redirect the flow of interaction to one's own experience, knowledge, position, or agenda. In contrast, listening to understand functions "by inspiring (or frustrating) us to listen more closely to others, to inquire more deeply into their differences, and to question our own already well-formed understandings of the world" (Lipari, 2014, p. 8). We are listening, then, neither for affirmation of our already-established worldview nor for an opportunity to turn the conversation back to ourselves. Rather, listening to understand demands that we listen for differences, ask questions of genuine curiosity and care, and struggle for mutual, yet always imperfect, meaning-making in the spaces between language and experience. Allowing for safe and brave spaces for the honest sharing of experiences goes a long way in building trust among members of the organization.

3 **Accepting Responsibility:** The next step is to accept organizational responsibility for inequities and injustices. Often, the burden of addressing social inequalities is placed on minoritized groups rather than within organizational systems (Bonilla-Silva, 2015). Given that organizations are interconnected systems, *everyone* in the organization has shared responsibility for making the organization inclusive and welcoming for all of its members. Oftentimes, the responsibility of "fixing racism" is placed on racially minoritized groups. However, it is important for everyone in the organization, from both the majority and minoritized groups, to discuss how they all play a part in taking action to bring about systemic change.

4 **Action Orientation:** Action orientation means being willing to challenge the status quo, disrupting notions of what is "normal," and finding ways to address racism and other forms of intersecting oppressions. This means setting short-term and long-term goals for action steps within the organization. In our dialogue sessions, in both small and large groups, we spend significant amounts of time discussing what such action orientation should look like. For example, our dialogue participants spend considerable time discussing what they can do at the individual and organizational levels to change their practices and policies in order to move toward addressing systemic racism. We share information about ten practical ways to address racism within communities as well as provide strategies for countering racial microaggressions at the interpersonal level.

5 **Accountability:** Many times, goals and action steps are mentioned at a surface level, say, at an annual retreat. However, there are no discussions or concrete plans for following up or finding ways to support the action plan. Within our model, we often follow up our antiracism dialogues with meetings with the leadership team to facilitate action and accountability planning. Through this step, we provide the leadership team with solutions, ideas, and action steps generated from the dialogues. We often request a meeting or leadership dialogue session where these strategies are further discussed as part of action planning. We recommend that leaders start with "low-hanging fruits" to work toward small wins such as by recognizing and rewarding positive actions publicly to keep members of the organization motivated to stay accountable to their commitments. Changes cannot be brought about without also allocating resources and providing ample support for continued adherence to action commitments. Therefore, it is important to allocate time, money, and labor resources toward antiracism initiatives that are proposed for bringing about accountability through long-term changes.

How to Measure the Effectiveness of Action-Oriented Dialogue Sessions?

All of our dialogues end with opportunities for participants to provide feedback on their experiences. Inputs from these anonymous feedback forms have helped us continuously improve our design, delivery, and dialogue content. Participants routinely report how they cherish the opportunity to share honestly, listen actively, and have meaningful conversations with others who also care about the topic. Students of color report they feel validated, listened to, and affirmed through these antiracism dialogues. Some examples from our anonymous feedback form asking participants if they would recommend these antiracism dialogues to other participants follow:

"I would recommend this to everyone because it is nice to feel connected with other [members of the university community] who have experienced similar things."

"PLEASE, open this discussion up to the campus. It was very productive."

"Yes because you are able to really understand different outlooks in a safe space."

"Safe space to share feelings."

"Because it gives people ways to express their viewpoints and to hear others while learning ways to positively express themselves."

Practical Applications

Throughout this chapter, we offered practical details and recommendations based on our experiences within higher education about whether to host dialogue sessions, whom to invite, when and where to host them, what topics to include, and how to assess the effectiveness of dialogues. In particular, we share our ground rules for dialogue sessions as well as the 5 A's of (1) Acknowledgment, (2) Active Listening, (3) Accepting Responsibility, (4) Action Orientation, and (5) Accountability to move toward long-term systemic change within organizations. These guidelines can be applied across a variety of organizational contexts.

Conclusion

In conclusion, dialogues, storytelling, and narratives play a central role in building rapport, a sense of safety, confidentiality, trust, and agency. These principles are crucial to move toward collaborative action planning and organizational changemaking. They guide decisions about whether to host dialogues, whom to include, where and when to host them, what topics to include in them, and how to measure their effectiveness. Taking a trauma-informed and racially conscious approach means that we need to be flexible and context specific in our dialogue designs. These communication design decisions are guided by our focus on providing emotional support for coping with chronic trauma and systemic inequalities. It is from this space that one can then build trust and rapport to facilitate coalition-building, solidarity, and systemic changes.

Discussion Questions

1 How does systemic racism function within your organizational system in implicit and explicit ways?

2 What are the different types of racial microaggressions that you have witnessed or experienced in your organizational context? What are some strategies you have used (including avoidance) to address them?

3 How can you adapt the model provided in this chapter to design trauma-informed training and dialogues within your organizational context? Please use personal lived experiences, insights about your organizational structures and culture, as well as the resources you have in mind as you design these sessions.

Author Bios

Srividya "Srivi" Ramasubramanian is Newhouse Professor & Endowed Chair at the S.I. Newhouse School of Public Comm at Syracuse University. She is a diversity educator and consultant focusing on data justice, media literacy, and inclusive communication. She is the Co-Director of the Difficult Dialogues Project. You can learn more about her at www.drsrivi.com.

Anna Wiederhold Wolfe is an Associate Professor in the Department of Communication & Journalism at Texas A&M University and Co-Director of the Difficult Dialogues Project. Her work examines processes of constituting and contesting collective and stigmatized identities, with particular interest in how organizational and community structures enable and constrain engagement and coordinated social action with different others.

Acknowledgments

We are grateful to Raiana de Carvalho, Emilee Baker, and Ashley Hay for proofreading earlier versions of this chapter.

Note

1 We are avoiding the term colorblindness since it is ableist. Instead, we prefer the term "color-evasive racism."

References

Aakhus, M. (2007). Communication as design. *Communication Monographs, 74*(1), 112–117. 10.1080/03637750701196383

Atkinson, P. (1997). Narrative turn or blind alley. *Qualitative Health Research*, *7*(3), 325–344.

Beauvais, E., & Baechtiger, A. (2016). Taking the goals of deliberation seriously: A differentiated view on equality and equity in deliberative designs and processes. *Journal of Public Deliberation, 12*(2). Retrieved from https://www.publicdeliberation. net/jpd/vol12/iss2/art2

Black, L. W. (2008). Deliberation, storytelling, and dialogic moments. *Communication Theory, 18*(1), 93–116.

Bonilla-Silva, E. (2015). The structure of racism in color-blind, "Post-Racial" America. *American Behavioral Scientist, 59*(11), 1358–1376.

Carter, R. T. (2007). Racism and psychological and emotional injury: Recognizing and assessing race-based traumatic stress. *The Counseling Psychologist, 35*(1), 13–105. 10.1177/0011000006292033

Clark, R., Anderson, N., Clark, V. R., & Williams, D. R. (1999). Racism as a stressor for African Americans: A biopsychosocial model. *American Psychologist, 54*, 805–816.

Fernandes, S. (2017). *Curated stories: The uses and misuses of storytelling.* Oxford University Press.

Fraser, N. (1990). Rethinking the public sphere: A contribution to the critique of actually existing democracy. *Social Text, 25/26*, 56–80.

Gayles, J. G., Kelly, B. T., Grays, S., Zhang, J. J., & Porter, K. P. (2015). Faculty teaching diversity through difficult dialogues: Stories of challenges and success. *Journal of Student Affairs Research and Practice, 52*(3), 300–312. 10.1080/19496591.2015.1067223

Hanh, T. N. (1974). *Zen keys.* Doubleday.

Harrell, J. P., Hall, S., & Taliaferro, J. (2003). Physiological responses to racism and discrimination: An assessment of the evidence. *American Journal of Public Health, 93*(2), 243–248. 10.2105/ajph.93.2.243

Lipari, L. (2014). *Listening, thinking, being: Toward an ethics of attunement.* The Pennsylvania State University Press.

McIntosh, M. L. (2019). Compound fractures: Healing the intersectionality of racism, classism and trauma in schools with a trauma-informed approach as part of a social justice framework. *Journal of Educational Leadership and Policy Studies, 3*(1), 1–14.

Orbe, M. P., & Allen, B. J. (2008). "Race matters" in the journal of applied communication research. *Howard Journal of Communications, 19*(3), 201–220. 10.1080/10646170802218115

Poole, M. S. (2014). Systems theory. In L. L. Putnam & D. K. Mumby (Eds.), *The SAGE handbook of organizational communication: Advances in theory, research, and methods* (pp. 49–74). SAGE.

Ramasubramanian, S., Sousa, A. N., & Gonlin, V. (2017). Facilitated difficult dialogues on racism: A goal-based approach. *Journal of Applied Communication Research, 45*(5), 537–556. 10.1080/00909882.2017.1382706

Ramasubramanian, S. & Wolfe, A. (July 9, 2020). The promise and perils of interracial dialogue. *Communication Currents.* https://www.natcom.org/communication-currents/promise-and-perils-interracial-dialogue

Substance Abuse and Mental Health Services Administration, Trauma and Justice Strategic Initiative (2014). SAMHSA's working definition of trauma and guidance for trauma-informed approach. Rockville, MD.

Sue, D. W., & Constantine, M. G. (2007). Racial microaggressions as instigators of difficult dialogues on race: Implications for student affairs educators and students. *College Student Affairs Journal, 26*(2), 136–143.

Wolfe, A. W. (2018). Dialogue and deliberation as agonistic resistance: Designing interactional processes to reconstitute collective identities. *Journal of Deliberative Democracy, 14*(2).

15

FACILITATING STRUCTURES AND PROCESSES FOR ETHICAL DIALOGUE ACROSS DIFFERENCE

A Case Study of an Interorganizational Collaboration for Social Change

Laura Irwin and Kirsten Foot

University of Washington

Learning Objectives

After reading this chapter, you will:

1 Learn how to enact the value of egalitarianism through the communicative structures and processes of interorganizational collaboration.
2 Learn to facilitate productive conflict through gracious contestation and voice.
3 Appreciate the importance of centering voices of disproportionately impacted stakeholders and developing a racial consciousness with radical listening for the sake of ethicality, accountability, and long-term efficacy of collaborative outcomes through radical listening.

Introduction

This chapter examines communicative structures and practices within interorganizational collaboration for meaningful and sustainable changemaking through a case study. Although the practices recommended in this chapter could also apply in intraorganizational contexts, the unique challenges of interorganizational collaboration merit attention, because attempts at collaboration between organizations are often complicated by historically patterned differences between the organizations and the sectors in which they are embedded (Foot, 2016). The analysis we provide in this chapter includes recommendations for organizers to expand how and when diversity, equity, and inclusion (DEI) practices are implemented.

DOI: 10.4324/9781003333746-17

For these reasons, we focus on the case of a court-ordered and professionally facilitated mediation between four organizations which expanded to include the elicitation of input from many other stakeholders. In this case, disproportionately impacted stakeholders were marginalized through communication structures and processes that perpetuated power imbalances, despite efforts to the contrary. Through this analysis, we aim to provide facilitators of interorganizational and/or multi-stakeholder collaboration with insights and strategies for guiding diverse participants through difficult decision making by creating structures for—and modeling the processes of—egalitarianism, gracious contestation, and radical listening.

The case centers on an interorganizational effort undertaken in Cincinnati, Ohio, known as the Collaborative Agreement (referred to hereafter as the Agreement). The Agreement, a 33-page document, detailed a plan for fostering a community-engaged approach to policing in Cincinnati—a mid-sized, racially diverse U.S. city. The Agreement was co-generated and signed in 2002 by the Cincinnati Black United Front, the American Civil Liberties Union of Ohio, the City of Cincinnati, and the Fraternal Order of Police. According to the Agreement, it was intended to reduce friction between the police and community by fostering mutual trust, respect, equity, and accountability through interaction, communication, and the implementation of reforms such as Community Problem-Oriented Policing and federal mandates to reduce use-of-force and misdemeanor arrests.

Although the creation of the Agreement was viewed as a successful output, it did not address any of the race-related concerns that had precipitated the mediation between the organizations. This was because during the process of creating the Agreement, city attorneys and law enforcement representatives threatened to leave the negotiations if there was any discussion of racism, racial bias, or racial discrimination in policing (Hinton, 2021). This decision had multiple and long-lasting impacts on the collaboration itself and the people of Cincinnati, ultimately resulting in the collaborative effort falling short of ethicality.

According to interorganizational collaboration experts and communication scholars Renee Guariello Heath and Matthew Isbell (2017), communicative structures and processes are ethical when stakeholders balance power. Ethical collaborators craft their structures and processes in view of the potential impacts their decisions will have on the increase or decrease of trust, both within the collaboration and the community that will live with the consequences of the outcomes of the collaboration. (Heath & Isbell, 2017). According to Heath and Isbell (2017), "attending to the ethical impact of [collaborators'] interactions and [striving] to create ethical practices and processes are the best means of cultivating trust" (p. 73). In view of this understanding of ethical collaboration, the actions of precluding discussion of systemic racism were unethical, for three reasons. First, they perpetuated uneven power dynamics. Second, they suppressed productive conflict that could have led to more thorough accountability. Third, they distorted subsequent communication processes by silencing some stakeholders and forcing them to self-censure in the moment and in further interactions.

This chapter examines the implications of avoiding dialogue and straightforward discussions of race and racism when attempting to generate social change. Based on our observations and analysis, we make recommendations about ways to create ethical communication structures and processes using strategies to help participants engage in dialogue about race, racism, and racial bias between stakeholders. This chapter is an effort to learn from the past and recognize the advantages of the present in which conversations about systemic racism and racial bias might occur more readily. We argue that instantiating the value of egalitarianism, inviting and facilitating conflict productively, and ensuring radical listening among stakeholders are three strategies to encourage and advance communication processes founded on trust and respect, which in turn can increase participants' commitment to sustaining relationships and efforts toward lasting, equitable social change. Following a brief summary of the context in which the Agreement was created, we present our analysis and recommendations.

Context of Agreement's Creation

The origin of the Agreement dates back to March 2001, when the Cincinnati Black United Front (CBUF) and the Ohio American Civil Liberties Union (ACLU) jointly filed a federal class action lawsuit "charging that the police department had systematically targeted and illegally harassed Black residents for more than thirty years" (Hinton, 2021, p. 274). The suit charged city and law enforcement officials with complicity in the decades-long racial discrimination that occurred through the police force. The CBUF was founded in 2000 to grapple "with the deaths of more than a dozen Black men while in police custody over five years" (Calfano, 2020). Since its inception, the organization has prioritized and voiced the concerns and needs of Black residents in Cincinnati, focusing especially on policing and how to create a sense of belonging and safety for the Black community (Calfano, 2020). The American Civil Liberties Union of Ohio (2022) is the state chapter of the national ACLU, founded in the 1920s to fight for and protect the civil liberties of Ohio citizens through "education, litigation, and lobbying" (ACLU Ohio, 2022). Together CBUF and the ACLU leveraged their knowledge of the legal system and strong support from the Black community of Cincinnati to file a lawsuit against the city and police department in 2001.

When Judge Susan Dlott, U.S. District of Southern Ohio, received this case, she referred the plaintiffs and defendants (the City of Cincinnati (CC) and the Fraternal Order of Police (FOP)) to court-mandated mediation, rather than litigate what Dlott termed "the problem of racial profiling" (Smith, 2021, n.p.). In a retrospective interview, Dlott said that she encouraged mediation because "litigation would be long and expensive, and it would only probably make matters worse because nobody would end up being a winner" (Smith, 2021, n.p.). Dlott, along with Jay Rothman, president of the ARIA group, a conflict resolution and consulting firm (Hinton, 2021, p. 275), worked with the plaintiffs and defendants to mediate and create the Agreement.

Elizabeth Hinton (2021), a scholar of African American history, demonstrated contemporaneous evidence that the CC and FOP responded to the mediation referral with an ultimatum that if systemic racism in policing was on the mediation agenda, they would withdraw from the mediation process and let the case revert to litigation, as they could simply deny accusations during litigation proceedings. The defendants argued that racial profiling did not exist and, as a result, was unnecessary to discuss let alone remedy. In a phone interview with Rothman, he mentioned that keeping race, systemic racism, and racial bias out of the discussion was a recurring "theme" throughout the mediation process (J. Rothman, personal communication, July 25, 2022). According to Rothman, in order to keep the police involved in the mediation, he had to shift his focus from past experiences to future action, from systemic racism to police-community relationships (J. Rothman, personal communication, July 25, 2022). This was partially due to the fact that stakeholders didn't have a shared definition of racial profiling; therefore, Rothman (2017) encouraged them to recognize that "even if we cannot agree with each other about the problem coming to us from the past, we can get on the same page about a future that we would like to create together" (p. 86).

Soon after Dlott initiated mediation, 19-year-old Timothy Thomas was murdered by the police in April of 2021. Thomas became the fifteenth Black man to be killed by police in Cincinnati since 1995 and the sixth Black man to be killed in "as many months" (Akinnibi, 2021 n.p.) where "no other Cincinnati residents were killed by police during this period" (Hinton, 2021, p. 260). His death and the resulting riots catalyzed the parties involved in the lawsuit to intensify the mediation process to address obvious and harmful tensions between police and the community.

While the mediation began before Thomas's death, his murder and resulting riots propelled the conversations to be taken more seriously by all parties, and they became less adversarial (Hinton, 2021). It wasn't until after Thomas's murder and the crisis that followed that the four organizations agreed to Rothman's proposed, large-scale participatory process to elicit community input rather than expedite the process to a negotiated settlement (Rothman, 2017). Thus, the mediation between four organizations broadened to include the views of many more stakeholders.

Rothman and his consulting team gathered input from 3,500 citizens through focus groups, feedback sessions, and goal-setting meetings (Rothman, 2006). Dlott described this "collaborative process" as including input "from every race, economic group and political perspective" (Smith, 2021, n.p.). The original plaintiffs and defendants used citizens' ideals and goals for the future to guide the crafting of the Agreement (Rothman, 2006).

However, during forums for Black community members, many participants voiced frustration that systemic racism and racial bias in policing weren't being discussed and argued that it would be impossible to reform without discussing race (J. Rothman, personal communication, July 25, 2022; Hinton, 2021). Rothman told them that a focus on the future of police-community relations rather than the past of racism would be most beneficial. He foresaw that temporary federal oversight of the Cincinnati police department was likely, and encouraged stakeholders concerned about racism that such oversight would guarantee implementation of the Agreement (J. Rothman, personal communication, July 25, 2022).

A 2001 study of traffic stops in the city determined that African Americans "were stopped in excess of their proportion to either their numbers in these communities or the amount of driving they do in these communities" (ACLU Ohio, 2003, p. 4; Eck et al., 2003). The ACLU argued that the traffic stop study findings indicated racial bias in policing. However, the study authors were "unwilling" to definitively conclude that racial bias was involved because they attempted a race-neutral approach to the study and didn't record the race of the officers collecting the data during the stops (ACLU Ohio, 2003, p. 6; Eck et al., 2003). Despite the overwhelming evidence of both racial bias and racism in the criminal justice system, the CC and the FOP continued to prohibit discussion of either during the mediation process.

After a year of contentious deliberation, the Agreement was completed and ratified by all parties in April 2002. At the time, this Agreement "looked as though it established the most comprehensive and ambitious police-community relations initiative in the nation. It called for the entire city to 'work together' … instead of relying on arrests, the goal was to encourage officers to seek other options during encounters with residents ... they would need to get to know residents and listen to their concerns" (Hinton, 2021, p. 278). The overarching aim of the Agreement was to reduce friction between the police and community by fostering mutual trust, respect, equity, and accountability (*Front and ACLU* v.*City and FOP,* 2001). Within the Agreement, the parties established five interrelated goals: 1) make police and community members more active partners in community problem solving, 2) build trust, cooperation, and respect between the police and community, 3) improve the education, monitoring, and accountability of the police department, 4) fair, equitable, and courteous treatment for all, and 5) establish the public's understanding of police procedures and recognition of exceptional service in an effort to foster support for the police (*Front and ACLU* v.*City and FOP,* 2001).

During the decade following the establishment of the Agreement, some significant, positive changes in police-community relations in Cincinnati were observed. From "2008 to 2014, felony arrests declined 41.9%, according to a University of Cincinnati study. From 2000 to 2014, the department's use of force fell 70%, according to city data" (Akinnibi, 2021, n.p.). Cincinnati was lauded as the model for police reform and the Collaborative Agreement was its proof. However, despite its clear and impactful improvements to police and community relations in Cincinnati, neither the original Agreement nor an update in 2017 indicates that the agreed-upon changes were fully implemented. A 2021 article on the current state of the Agreement observed that "in recent years, however, city officials seem to have become complacent, and the police department, according to critics, has fallen into old habits. A 2017 report commissioned by the city found that the [Cincinnati Police Department] had essentially walked away from the Collaborative Agreement" (Akinnibi, n.p.). A recent "refresh" of the Agreement in 2017 which included surveys by the police revealed that many officers still believed policing was free of bias and that there was no discrimination in the department. There was still resistance on behalf of the police to discuss and consider the impact of systemic racism and racial bias whether they perceive themselves as involved in its perpetuation or not, which ultimately means there was still an obstacle to building trusting relationships between the police and community because there remained a limited understanding of racialized experiences.

Instances of racial profiling and discrimination had slowly crept back into the department. Akinnibi observed that the behavioral tracking of police has decreased along with a decrease in recording statistics of crime stops and the defunding of the Citizens Complaint Authority (CCA). The scathing 2017 report by Saul Green, the court-appointed monitor for the original Agreement about the current state of the

Agreement, noted "old signs of resistance" from police, stating they had "abandoned the principles of" and "unilaterally withdrawn from the Collaborative Agreement" (Akinnibi, 2021).

Other analysts have argued that the resurgent resistance to and de-implementation of the Agreement was due to multiple factors, including it becoming a victim of its own early success, increasing complacency, and the defunding of the CCA (Akinnibi, 2021; Hinton, 2021). While we acknowledge those factors, we argue that the unethical structures and processes of communication that occurred during the development of the Agreement—when police threatened to walk away from negotiations if racism and racial bias in policing were discussed—were also factors in its failure. Collaboration failure is produced through communication structures and practices, just as collaboration success can be (Koschmann, 2016). In the analysis that follows, we explain how not enacting the value of egalitarianism between the parties in the mediation, the avoidance of conflict over the history of systemic racism in policing, the refusal to grant voice to the CBUF, and a lack of listening to disproportionately impacted stakeholders all contributed to the eventual disintegration of efforts to implement the Agreement.

Enacting Egalitarianism

Equality between parties in an interorganizational collaboration may be impossible to achieve due to cultural-historical, economic, and/or sector-based differences between them (Foot, 2016; Heath and Isbell, 2017). However, a shared prioritization of the value of egalitarianism is essential for authentic and sustainable collaboration (Heath and Sias, 1999). According to Heath and Isbell (2017), "power in collaboration will never be uniformly equal, thus egalitarianism must be constructed via group behavior and attitudes, guided by a collaborative spirit" (p. 134). The enactment of egalitarianism takes place in both the structure and processes of a collaboration's communication and decision making, most fundamentally through power-sharing and mutual respect. In contrast, hegemony manifests in interorganizational relations when one group's leadership dominates another group, whether the subjugated group submits actively or acquiesces unwillingly (Clair, 1993).

It is not knowable retrospectively whether the parties in this case felt, at the time, that they had co-created equitable conditions for interaction and influence at the beginning of their work on what became the Agreement. However, the fact that the City of Cincinnati (CC) and the Fraternal Order of Police (FOP) refused from the outset to engage in discussions about racism—and furthermore threatened to withdraw from the collaboration if the topic of racism was pressed—indicates that egalitarianism was not valued by those parties. The defendants argued that racial profiling did not exist and, as a result, was unnecessary to discuss, let alone remedy. Their ultimatum was a stunning instance of hegemony by the CC and the FOB, acquiesced to not only by the ACLU and the CBUF but also Dlott and Rothman. The ultimatum precluded dialogue about race with the other parties, silencing those who viewed race as inextricable from police-community relations by denying them the opportunity for potential influence. It also created a condition of interactional precarity for the ACLU and the CBUF, requiring them to self-censor the topics they might otherwise have contributed to the collective agenda as well as their own speech throughout the process of developing the Agreement—due to the threat of the CC and FOB's withdrawal. It also created significant challenges for Rothman as a facilitator tasked with inviting and distilling input from a wide variety of stakeholders including those who viewed racism as the fundamental problem.

We suggest that the Agreement itself and its implementation would have been different if egalitarianism had been enacted in the communicative structures and processes of the mediation. For instance, Rothman could have established ground rules for collaboration at the outset through which all parties could add any topic to a collective agenda alongside an explicit process for facilitated articulation of divergent views. Although it is not humanly possible for any person to make another person listen, facilitators can structure interactions in ways that invite each party to speak (or write) their input and provide both explicit guidelines for—and embodied modeling of—responsive listening to each participant (Parks and Foot, 2019). Going further, we suggest that had they co-constructed a process for joint decision making that aimed toward brokering consensus among all four organizations prior to beginning work on the Agreement could have helped engender deeper and more constructive engagement between them— which in turn might have precipitated mind shifts and built stronger intrinsic motivation within the CC and the FOB for implementing the Agreement. These are just a few examples of ways that the value of egalitarianism could have been embodied in the structures and processes employed in this case, each of which could be employed by facilitators in other collaborations as well. A foundation of egalitarianism would have also made space for the stakeholders to engage in productive conflict because they would recognize and prioritize stakeholder disagreements and differing perspectives as part of the collaborative, power-sharing process.

Productive Conflict through Gracious Contestation

At its most basic conceptualization, "conflict entails an expressed struggle between two or more interdependent [parties] who perceive they have incompatible goals" (Guerrero & LaValley, 2006, p. 69). In the case between the police and the Black community in Cincinnati, incompatible definitions of racial profiling created by incompatible perceptions of the existence of systemic racism in policing catalyzed the conflict between the stakeholders. Productive conflict would have allowed stakeholders to unpack perceived incompatibility by making space to address diverse definitions and perspectives in a way that facilitated understanding rather than competition, domination, or rupturing between community members. Instead, conflict was suppressed when the FOP explicitly negotiated that any discussion of systemic racism or racial bias in policing was avoided and they created a space where disproportionately impacted stakeholders weren't able to fully contest or introduce divergent perspectives that could have helped to create productive conflict. By establishing communicative structures that ensured all voices could meaningfully contribute, productive conflict might have enabled participants to discuss their differing definitions and experiences, and possibly overcome their perceived incompatibility.

Rothman recalled that during the process of gathering input from citizens, systemic racism and racial bias in policing were frequently brought up by community members. Rothman could welcome the perspectives shared by community members but had to consistently guide them back to the goal of the Agreement: to look toward the future rather than the past (J. Rothman, personal communication, July 25, 2022). This kind of censoring placed constraints on the capacity for productive conflict to emerge because stakeholder goals of addressing a necessary yet challenging topic were suppressed. Although disproportionately impacted stakeholders were allowed to share their frustrations and experiences, those frustrations and experiences could not contribute to the effort given the unethical and un-egalitarian constraints of the collaboration.

We suggest that the Agreement and its implementation would have been more sustainable if this conflict had not been suppressed but rather embraced through the process of gracious contestation. One of the most important aspects of productive conflict is generating trust and orienting oneself toward the other. The Agreement attempted to do this by improving police-community relations centered around building trust and cooperation between the police and community. However, when some participants in a collaboration silence others by avoiding discussion of racial bias a stakeholder has experienced from another, that stakeholder is censored and their perspective is not considered nor allowed the chance to influence the collaboration, which renders trust difficult if not impossible to achieve.

Heath and Isbell (2017) explain that gracious contestation is useful for establishing trust not despite but through disagreement. They write, "Gracious contestation is our language for engaging in communicative behaviors that challenge, argue, and invite dissent from others ... An emphasis on graciousness asks us to be mindful of how we challenge one another ... Contestation serves a very different purpose than being adversarial ... gracious contestation facilitates respectful and openly transparent disagreement" (pp. 238–39). Essentially, gracious contestation is a process of creating productive conflict because it creates safety for stakeholders to share their voices with the guarantee that they will be heard, valued, and mindfully challenged.

Mindful challenging entails recognizing that the person contesting is bringing a valuable perspective that does not directly negate one's own but can expand new possibilities. Furthermore, gracious contestation allows for meaningful accountability because, by allowing stakeholders to respectfully disagree, they are able to challenge one another in ways that do not perpetuate hatred or violence but in ways that are purposeful for building a better collective future which sometimes consists of calling out those who intentionally or unintentionally perpetuate systemic oppression. Facilitators such as Rothman are mindful of how conflicts such as the one in Cincinnati can quickly devolve into personal attacks because of how complex and traumatic the relationship between stakeholders is. Therefore, to facilitate a space for gracious contestation, there needs to be a foundation of voice and vulnerability where stakeholders feel that their full perspectives are consequential to the process rather than silenced.

Ethical structures and processes for collaboration enable all participants to have "voice" in the collaboration, i.e., ways to share their perspectives with the expectation that they will be heard, valued, and have influence in the decision-making process (Heath & Isbell, 2017). Heath and Isbell (2017) establish a distinction between voice and expression because while the goal of expression is simply to "have a say" (p. 240), giving voice is making sure contributions are thoroughly considered, allowing room to deeply digest what is being shared, and ensuring what is shared has influence over the decisions being made. In these ways, voice asks us to be inclusive with who shares, is held accountable to what is shared, and creates a space where those who share are safe and heard (Heath & Isbell, 2017, p. 241).

Consequently, voice involves vulnerability for the person sharing and the person listening which is why gracious contestation requires the facilitation of a safe space, especially when engaging in identity-based conflict. Speaking truth during conversations about race, systemic racism, and racial bias involves risk because those who experience racism are vulnerable to retaliation while those who enact racism (intentionally or unintentionally) are vulnerable to being held accountable; both are scary and uncomfortable positions to be in because they require momentarily disrupting external peace in order to achieve understanding and trust. According to Glenn E. Singleton (2021), a strategist of sustained dialogue about race in institutions, white Americans have been trained to not talk about race and, therefore, assume a deflecting, colorblind approach to conversations about race; Black Americans, on the other hand, spend their whole lives understanding and being implicated by race and racism and, therefore, not only cannot afford to take a colorblind approach but also mistrust white Americans who do.

A similar dynamic appears between police and the Black community where the police assume a colorblind approach and only see crime rather than color in order to ensure neutrality, objectivity, and equality under the law. However, living in a country where the police originated as an institution to hunt escaped enslaved Black people and are now used to over-patrol Black communities, race cannot be separated from policing because policing is heavily implicated in racial history as the arm of the law that maintains racist practices.

Facilitators can work to establish gracious contestation by encouraging and modeling vulnerability for their participants and by creating scaling dialogue activities in which participants practice voice and vulnerability to the point where they can embrace being challenged without feeling attacked. Of course, it is impossible to create safe spaces for everyone or to ensure all participants enact vulnerability and not defensiveness, but facilitators can help lay the foundation for this space by ensuring conflict is not suppressed but reframed productively to ensure stakeholders are not silenced.

Radical Listening

At the same time that collaborators are primed to share voice, they must also be oriented to listen to one another. Creating space for disproportionately impacted stakeholders to speak up and out to graciously contest and share their experiences and perspectives must also include creating a space where those voices will be heard and meaningfully contribute to the collaboration. Listening in the context of interorganizational collaboration with disproportionately impacted stakeholders is a practice that makes room for voices to be received because it requires individual and collective reflection and awareness to understand the meaning behind what is being shared and recognizing how what is being shared fits into larger systems of inequality and power. Such reflexivity allows room for the contestation that generates accountability and the development of a "racial consciousness," which is particularly important for racialized conflict because a racial consciousness enables participants to admit, acknowledge, or recognize explicit or implicit assumptions they carry about themselves and one another to confront "myopic and distorted [views] of self and of others" (Singleton, 2021, p. 77). A racial consciousness helps everyone "live more authentically within our own racial experience and deal more honestly with the racialized existence of others" (Singleton, 2021, p. 78). Developing a racial consciousness is a crucial component to being able to meaningfully listen to racialized experiences that challenge or expand your own perceptions and understand different experiences.

Developing a racial consciousness can be exhausting and difficult because of the pain it involves in not only recognizing the extent of racialization, but also acknowledging one's participation in and internalization of it. Singleton (2021) suggests that participants engaging in courageous conversations about race must commit to staying engaged, meaning "remaining morally, emotionally, intellectually, and relationally involved in the dialogue. To stay engaged is to not let your heart and mind check out of the conversation" (Singleton, 2021, p. 82). Many times, our tendency is to gloss over discomfort with these conversations or avoid them entirely—as evidenced by the CC and FOB in this case. However, avoiding discomfort or accountability is one of the many barriers that prevents changemaking.

In the development of the Agreement, there was no orientation toward a racial consciousness, meaning that there was an inability to honestly deal with or recognize the racialized experiences of stakeholders, specifically the stakeholders who had hegemonic power (i.e., the police). The unwillingness of the CC and FOB to discuss the implications of police racism suggests that not only did they lack racial consciousness but also that a racial consciousness would have allowed this conversation to occur in a way that made space for voice while also priming participants to listen. A racial consciousness is explicitly tied to the listening component of gracious contestation because it means participants are able to hear about other racialized experiences and critically reflect on how those experiences are part of larger patterns of histories. Simultaneously, they are able to make room for the racialized experiences they hear about and adapt their own understanding to this new information. In Singleton's (2021) view, "we cannot discover a solution to a challenge if we have not been able to talk, specifically and intentionally, about that challenge" (p. 86). It requires active, intentional, and *radical* listening.

Radical listening is an intervention and practice. It is utilized by the Center for Communication, Difference, and Equity (CCDE) at the University of Washington under the leadership of Ralina Joseph in a number of projects focused on centering marginalized voices. The practice involves cultivating curious and nonjudgmental listening to the speaker's words and meanings while also recognizing the overarching scripts of power and inequity at play, being aware of and confronting one's own assumptions, and acting to interrupt the inequities shared by collaborating between the listener and the speaker (Joseph & Briscoe-Smith, 2021). What is "radical" about this kind of listening is the attention placed on power and how it shapes racialized difference in order to hear "not just discrete experiences, but oppressive histories, unequal structures, and repressive institutions" (Joseph & Briscoe-Smith, 2021, p. 4). This practice ensures that those who traditionally hold positions of power, such as white people (or, in this case, the police), engage in critical reflection about their own assumptions, identities, and actions while listening to marginalized voices. In an interview, Ralina Joseph suggests those engaging in radical listening work on quieting their minds and the impulse to judge or respond with their own thoughts (Suderman, n.d.). Instead, listeners focus on repeating back what is heard and checking for understanding, which is a radical form of communication that can ensure traditionally excluded and silenced individuals are given the opportunity to speak and be heard fully. Joseph adds, "It's not about giving everyone the mic and all speaking equally ... It's giving the mic to those who are often silenced and taking it away from people who jealously guard it" (Suderman, n.d.). Radical listening prioritizes perspective sharing of disempowered groups. In perspective sharing, disempowered groups exercise their voices by sharing their stories and perspectives while dominant groups practice listening to understand rather than respond (Bruneau & Saxe, 2012). Perspective sharing is a mechanism that recognizes the labor required of nondominant groups to raise the racial consciousness of dominant groups, and how often perspective-taking activities only benefit dominant groups while nondominant groups are left feeling used and unheard (Bruneau & Saxe, 2012). Instead, through perspective sharing, intentional attention is given to the needs of nondominant groups to ensure their voices are heard and encourage radical listening from dominant groups that disrupt impulses to judge or react defensively, which are impulses that contribute to silencing or censoring. Radical listening allows for marginalized and discriminated experiences to take center stage and establish equity as the precedent for communication.

Ultimately, radical listening facilitates racial consciousness because it asks stakeholders to be reflexive, accountable, and honest about their power, identities, and relationships. Facilitators looking to encourage and guide stakeholders through radical listening must first grapple with their own power in the space and use it to center marginalized voices. As facilitators develop their own racial consciousness, they engage their own discomfort and gaps in knowledge which makes them aware of gaps between stakeholders. Being intimately familiar with one's own discomfort helps facilitators guide stakeholders through similar discomfort and open dialogue about racial bias and systemic racism using radical listening as a practice. It is a cyclical process whereby stakeholders become progressively more honest and open by learning the difference between speaking and listening for collective understanding in contrast to speaking and listening for control and avoidance of discomfort. Radical listening also disrupts historic silencing of disempowered groups by prioritizing their voices in a deliberate and intentional practice.

Concluding Thoughts: Practical Implications

This case analysis indicates that the experiences of those disproportionately affected by a problem must be centered in discussions within an interorganizational collaboration for it to be ethical. There are both structural design decisions and procedural and decision-making practices that contribute or undermine ethicality. Ethicality is enhanced by structuring interorganizational collaborations around the value of egalitarianism in the inclusion of disproportionately impacted stakeholders—not just in the collaboration, but also in the design of leadership mechanisms. Correspondingly, the value of egalitarianism can be supported through the implementation of procedural and decision-making practices that enable voice rather than simply expression.

Finally, it is important to acknowledge how complex and challenging these processes are and how much patience and grace are required by all parties entering into collaborative efforts on all issues related to systemic racism, including police reform. It can be incredibly discouraging. Being able to remain open, honest, vulnerable, and accountable to one another strengthens collaborators' commitment to enact change. Allowing all voices to be heard and experiences to be included and welcomed in dialogue is foundational.

Discussion Questions

1 When have you observed either the enactment or absence of egalitarianism in the structure and processes of a collaboration's communication and decision making?

2 In what ways do you see conflict being suppressed or avoided in communication processes within collaborative efforts for social change? How can you reframe conflict through gracious contestation by scaffolding voice and vulnerability in difficult discussions?

3 In what spaces can you begin practicing radical listening as an individual? As a facilitator? As a facilitator, you have power in organizational spaces to disrupt power dynamics between stakeholders and ensure you can center marginalized voices. How might you encourage your stakeholders to quiet their impulse to respond rather than listen?

Author Bios

Laura Irwin is a Ph.D. student in Communication at the University of Washington, where she received her Master's. Her BA is in Writing and Rhetoric from St. Edward's University. Her research interests include dialogue-based processes of peacemaking and justice; Chicana, Indigenous, and mixed-race embodiment and representation; and participatory critical rhetoric and community-based methodologies.

Kirsten Foot is the Dart Endowed Professor of Trauma, Journalism, and Communication at the University of Washington. Her expertise areas include practice-based theories of collaboration and organizing processes. Her current research focuses on multisector collaboration in efforts to counter human trafficking, and re-thinking the power dynamics of partnering.

References

Akinnibi, F. (2021, Sept 2). *Cincinnati was a model for police reform. What happened?* Bloomberg Business. https://www.bloomberg.com/news/features/2021-09-02/police-reform-behind-the-rise-and-fall-of-community-policing-in-cincinnati

American Civil Liberties Union Ohio. (2003). *Racial bias and policing: A study guide prepared by the ACLU and plaintiffs' as part of their advocacy for reform.* https://www.acluohio.org/sites/default/files/acluofohio_cincinnaticollaborativeagreement_racialbiasandpolicing.pdf

American Civil Liberties Union Ohio. (2022). *About us.* https://www.acluohio.org/en/about/about-us

Bruneau, E. G., & Saxe, R. (2012). The power of being heard: The benefits of 'perspective-giving' in the context of intergroup conflict. *Journal of Experimental Social Psychology, 48,* 855–866. 10.1016/j.jesp.2012.02.017

Calfano, B. (2020, June 8). *Cincinnati Black United Front Turns 20.* Spectrum News. https://spectrumnews1.com/oh/columbus/news/2020/06/08/cincinnati-black-united-front-turns-20

Clair, R. P. (1993). The use of framing devices to sequester organizational narratives: Hegemony and harassment. *Communication Monographs, 60*(2), 113–136. 10.1080/03637759309376304

Eck, J., Liu, L., & Bostaph, L. (2003). *Police stops in Cincinnati: July 1- December 31, 2001.* City of Cincinnati. https://www.cincinnati-oh.gov/police/department-references/collaborative-agreement/eck-report-on-police-vehicle-stops/

Foot, K. (2016). *Collaborating against human trafficking: Cross-sector challenges and practices.* Rowman.

Front and ACLU v. City and FOP. United States District Court Southern District of Ohio Western Division. (2001). https://www.cincinnati-oh.gov/police/department-references/collaborative-agreement/collaborative-agreement1/

Guerrero, L. K., & LaValley, A. G. (2006). Conflict, emotion, and communication. In J. G. Oetzel & S. Ting-Toomey. (Eds.), *The SAGE handbook of conflict communication: Integrating theory, research, and practice.* (pp. 159–183). SAGE publications.

Heath, R. G., & Isbell, M. G. (2017). *Interorganizational collaboration: Complexity, ethics, and communication.* Waveland Press Inc.

Heath, R. G., & Sias, P. M. (1999). Communicating spirit in a collaborative alliance. *Journal of Applied Communication Research, 27*(4), 356–376. 10.1080/00909889909365545

Hinton, E. (2021). *America on fire: The untold history of police violence and Black rebellion since the 1960s.* Liveright Publishing Corporation.

Joseph, R. L., & Briscoe-Smith, A. (2021). *Generation mixed goes to school: radically listening to multiracial kids.* Teachers College Press.

Koschmann, M. A. (2016). The communicative accomplishment of collaboration failure. *Journal of Communication, 66*(3), 409–432.

Parks, E., & Foot, K. (2019). Conceptualizing listening as voice and its affordances for collaboration scholarship. In P. Moy & D. Matheson (eds.), *Voices: ICA International Communication Association Annual Conference Theme Book Series, Vol. 6.* (pp. 13–34). Peter Lang.

Rothman, J. (2006). Identity and conflict: Collaboratively addressing police-community conflict in Cincinnati, Ohio. *Ohio State Journal on Dispute Resolution, 22*(1), 105–132.

Rothman, J. (2017). *Re-envisioning conflict resolution: Vision, action, and evaluation in creative conflict management.* Routledge.

Singleton, G. E. (2021). *Courageous conversations about race: A field guide for achieving equity in schools and beyond.* Corwin Press.

Smith, L. (2021, Apr 8). *Voices of the collaborative: Participants offer perspective on agreement that changed the city.* ABC 9 WCPO Cincinnati. https://www.wcpo.com/news/local-news/voices-of-the-collaborative-participants-offer-perspectives-on-agreement-that-changed-the-city

Sudermann, H. (n.d.). *Radical listening.* University of Washington Magazine. https://magazine.washington.edu/feature/radical-listening/

16

IT'S THE HOPE THAT KILLS YOU

Belonging and Organizational Change in *Ted Lasso*

Raymond Blanton
University of the Incarnate Word

Learning Objectives

After reading this chapter, you will:

1 Connect the value of belonging to organizational changemaking.
2 Improve habits related to conversation, civility, and commitment to enhance diversity, equity, and inclusion practices and promote organizational change.

Introduction

On many fronts, our culture is teeming with a desire for change, full of emotive energy to mobilize for justice-oriented causes. Among these, many organizations have condemned identity-based hate and committed to advance initiatives for diversity, equity, and inclusion (DEI). It is important to remember that the need for change presupposes something essential: hope. We want to believe the world we inhabit is capable of change, even as we harbor entrenched cynicism about that potential. Is meaningful and sustainable change actually possible? As arduously difficult and elusive as purposeful change may be, this project is an effort to embody that hope and exact organizational change.

Broadly, I take three progressive critical steps to enact this hope for change. First, I provide a framework that situates DEI values in the context of the critical theories and practices of bell hooks. Second, I provide an inductive case study of the Apple+ workplace sitcom *Ted Lasso* to examine these dynamics collectively. Third, I delineate and promote four purposeful

DOI: 10.4324/9781003333746-18

practices from the series that I argue can help us enhance belonging and promote organizational changemaking.

Critically, using a communication and rhetorical lens, I want to provide practitioners both perspective and possibility. I do this by imagining *Ted Lasso* in a similar way to how the workplace sitcom series *The Office* plays on a range of tropes in an organizational context, i.e., classifying types of people, composites of situational crises and humor, management styles, and the like. I argue *Ted Lasso* functions as both mirror and window. As a mirror, the series helps us see ourselves more clearly by simulating real experiences in the workplace that foreground dynamics pertinent to DEI, belonging, and organizational change. In this, it is important to remember that while the show is syndicated, it is also actually an embodiment of organizational dynamics—a diverse production team comprised of actors, producers, writers, editors, and the like, in a cross-cultural (i.e., America and Britain) environment. In other words, the series both depicts and represents DEI dynamics and values. As a window, the series can help us project enhanced clarity into our own organizational cultures, inspire practices that promote organizational change, and enhance DEI values and belonging.

Ted Lasso is the story of an American college football coach hired to manage a struggling English Premier League football club in London, AFC Richmond. The series premiered on Apple+ on August 14, 2020, and broke records as the most-nominated freshman comedy in Emmy Award history with 20 nominations. It garnered four wins including Outstanding Comedy Series, Outstanding Actor in a Comedy Series (Jason Sudeikis), Outstanding Supporting Actor in a Comedy Series (Brett Goldstein), and Outstanding Supporting Actress in a Comedy Series (Hannah Waddingham). With season two, the series collected an additional 20 Emmy Award nominations, again winning four, including Outstanding Lead Actor in a Comedy Series (Jason Sudeikis), Outstanding Supporting Actor in a Comedy Series (Brett Goldstein), Outstanding Directing for a Comedy Series (MJ Delaney), and Outstanding Comedy Series, becoming only the eighth series in the genre in the 74-year history of the Emmys to win back-to-back awards.

Ted Lasso is unique in two particular ways. First, the series is a depiction of organizational change and personal transformation centering on belonging in the context of cross-cultural experiences. Second, the progression of the plot and characters aesthetically and narratively animates a variety of DEI values related to race, gender, sexuality, class, and mental health while also confronting hateful culprits such as narrow-mindedness, racism, bigotry, misogyny, sexism, and inequality. As such, I use the series as an inductive case study to explore DEI as it relates to belonging in order to animate practices related to organizational change.

In sum, I argue *Ted Lasso* is centered on the notion of belonging and provides a unique narrative space to examine DEI values and dynamics. Moreover, I contend this case study provides a framework for practitioners to ponder and propagate the ideals of hope and kindness in a world that is rife with all manner of political disputes related to identity and belonging. Simply put, *Ted Lasso* provides a place for us to consider how the issues inherent to our identities in organizational life—most especially with DEI—extend to the global community.

Diversity, Equity, and Inclusion (DEI)

Broadly, diversity is defined as the presence of difference that can include race, religion, sexual orientation, ethnicity, gender, nationality, class, age, language, or disability, among others ("What Is Diversity, Equity, and Inclusions," n.d.); equity as an effort to promote justice programs, procedures, and processes that are fair and impartial ("What Is Diversity, Equity, and Inclusions," n.d.); and inclusion as an outcome that ensures diversity and equity and ultimately belonging, in decision making and development within an organization ("What Is Diversity, Equity, and Inclusions," n.d.). Altogether, these definitions are intended to provide a foundation for understanding DEI values. But more is needed. In this regard, I draw from the life and work of bell hooks to provide a framework for promoting justice-oriented causes. hooks is an ardent defender of not only DEI values and initiatives, but perhaps more substantively and importantly, belonging.

bell Hooks' Belonging

When we allude to DEI values and initiatives, we are essentially reaching for the ideal of belonging. In my estimation, hooks (2019) has identified the true aim of this project, that is, "to revise and renew our commitment to the present, to making a world where all people can live fully and well, where everyone can belong" (p. 5). In other words, hooks offers a simple and eloquent articulation of our true cause: belonging. And in so doing, hooks provides a foundation upon which we can stand together to envision purposeful practices. Specifically, I focus on hooks's notion of habits of the heart and denote three specific practices: healing talk, civility, and care and commitment—a community of care. Then, I coalesce these ideals with critical observations of the *Ted Lasso* series to demonstrate what effective leadership pertaining to DEI values and initiatives can look like and provide some examples for promoting practices and organizational changemaking.

Habits of the Heart

When actions prove hurtful or offensive, we are essentially confronting behavior animated by attitudes, values, and beliefs. Such conduct is inherently conditioned by our culture. But more specifically, these actions are a byproduct of our habits. Our choices. In my research on habits, I believe hooks's call, inspired in part by Carol Lee Flinders's *Rebalancing the World,* is vital: "It is useful to think of the values of belonging as habits of the heart" (hooks, 2019, p. 217). This is the heart of our framework and essential to my analysis. hooks has given us a portrait of our cause in her chapter phrase, "Take Back the Night—Remake the Present." Put differently, hooks indicates that our essential concern as humans is to belong, that this is predicated on habits, and to actualize this we must remake the present—take back the night. For hooks, "a true home is the place—any place—where growth is nurtured, where there is constancy. As much as change is always happening whether we want it to or not, there is still a need we have for constancy" (hooks, 2019, p. 203). Our function, then, in organizational culture should be to create spaces that nurture growth with constancy. It is in the heart where this spirit of constancy must coalesce with habits and practices to enact the belonging we long for to remake the present.

In attempting to remake the present, we are reaching for something far more profound than simply effective DEI initiatives and organizational change. More explicitly, as hooks contends, "I contemplate what our lives would be like if we knew how to cultivate awareness, to live mindfully, peacefully; if we learned habits of being that would bring us closer together, that would help us build beloved community" (hooks, 2019, p. 223). Beloved community. Here, I consider three particular habits of the heart—healing talk, civility, and a community of care, each capable of confronting DEI values and experiences, from the politics of race, class, and gender to any realm of difference and discrimination in which we can often become trapped in our "sadness steady and constant" (hooks, 2019, p. 218).

Healing Talk

The first habit of the heart is denoted in hooks's *Belonging,* "Healing Talk." In actuality, it is a conversation between hooks and Wendell Berry and it provides us not only with our first habit of the heart, but also a vision—a framework for breaking silences and creating spaces for conversation that can help us transgress boundaries that keep us from talking together and knowing one another. In essence, hooks is identifying the value of conversation as healing talk. In context, hooks notes that while their conversation could have veered toward poetry, writing, farming, or beauty, hooks chose to talk about race and racism. Quite eloquently and incisively, hooks notes, "It was my hope that our words would break through the profound racial silence that is present in public discourse on the subject, a silence that must be broken if we are to truly find ways to end racism" (hooks, 2019, p. 185).

So, how do we do this? Specifically, hooks alludes to their talk and laughter, their conversation, as a precursor to transgressing the boundaries of race, class, and experience. "Talking together, we listen and hear beneath our own words the possibility of making beloved community" (hooks, 2019, p. 185). Perhaps this should be applied merely to their conversation. But I do not think that is hooks's intention. Rather, in the spirit of M.I.T. professor Sherry Turkle's *Reclaiming Conversation,* healing talk is a practice we must claim and reclaim to break silences and transgress the boundaries of our differences to promote organizational change and belonging. Healing talk and conversation, casual as it may seem, is actually a practice of transformative potential that attempts to remake the present, a possibility for making beloved community.

Civility

When we engage in the practice of healing talk, it seems inevitable that we will face dissent and discord. This brings us to the second habit of the heart—the practice of civility. In M. Scott Peck's *A World Waiting to be Born,* hooks notes this about civility:

By practicing civility, we remind ourselves, that, 'each and every human being—you, every friend, every stranger, every foreigner is precious'. The etiquette of civility then is far more than the performance of manners: it includes an understanding of the deeper psychoanalytic relationship to recognition as that which makes us subject to one another rather than objects.

(hooks, 2019, p. 148)

For hooks, civility means accounting for a deeper understanding of human dignity and our interconnectedness as humans. Civility, then, implies being able to embody this more profound understanding even in the presence of incivility. Indeed, a call for such a practice presumes a grievous reality: incivility. As a habit of the heart, civility means being subject to one another rather than object. It means recognizing and responding to practices such as love and forgiveness. In *All About Love,* hooks, addressing the idea of loving community, offers a vision for how to engage in these practices:

True forgiveness requires that we understand the negative actions of another [...] Realistically, being part of a loving community does not mean we will not face conflicts, betrayals, negative outcomes from positive actions, or bad things happening to good people. Love allows us to confront these negative realities in a manner that is life-affirming and life-enhancing.

(hooks, 2018, p. 139)

Moreover, referencing Robin Casarjian's *Forgiveness: A Bold Choice for a Peaceful Heart,* hooks notes: "Forgiveness is a way of life that gradually transforms us from being helpless victims of our circumstances to being powerful and loving 'co-creators' of our reality [...] It is the fading away of the perceptions that cloud our ability to love" (hooks, 2018, pp. 139–140).

Put differently, through the practice of compassion and forgiveness, we can learn to cope with the grief and disappointment that comes from incivility. And in so doing, we can enact the practice of civility and self-love.

Intriguingly, hooks's framework for civility is positioned in a chapter entitled, "A Place Where the Soul Can Rest," with a particular focus on public spaces like street corners and the porch, which hooks describes as, "a democratic meeting place, capable of containing folks from various walks of life, with diverse perspectives" (hooks, 2019, p. 147). In a sense, hooks is calling us to find, if not create, figurative porches; democratic meeting places that welcome diverse perspectives. Perhaps our organizational contexts can become such a place? Regardless, the practice of civility must be "consciously motivated," an "ethical practice" (hooks, 2019, p. 148).

Care and Commitment

In "A Community of Care," hooks reflects on the life and marriage of her parents, noting her admiration for their capacity for disciplined commitment, "their engagement in making and sustaining a life in community" (hooks, 2019, pp. 227–228). For hooks, their love was sown by two particular seeds: care and commitment. This, the third habit of the heart, results in a "community of care." Moreover, in reference to Norman Wirzba's "An Economy of Gratitude," hooks notes how a sustained commitment to community includes the marks of "affection, attention, delight, kindness, praise, conviviality, and repentance" (p. 228). These authenticating hallmarks of a community of care likewise involve relationships that are "governed by conviviality rather than suspicion, by praise rather than blame" (hooks, 2019, p. 228). In a similar manner to civility, that is, being subject to one another rather than object, the practice of care and commitment means relationships are "turned toward one another" (hooks, 2019, p. 228).

Altogether, these habits of the heart—healing talk, civility, and a community of care—are the means by and through which we can attempt to remake the present. These habits and practices are the particular ways we can embody DEI values and implement meaningful initiatives to exact organizational change and promote belonging.

Case Study: Ted Lasso

Having delineated a framework for belonging and habits of the heart dedicated to healing talk, civility, and care and commitment, I now turn my critical attention to demonstrating how these ideals manifest in *Ted Lasso*. Specifically, I argue that the central character, Ted Lasso (Jason Sudeikis), is an embodiment of these ideals. In essence, the series is an anthem for belonging and community. Specifically, I focus briefly on two aspects of *Ted Lasso* to enhance the credibility of its relevance and usefulness in assessing DEI values and organizational change: context and story. To be clear, the purpose of this analysis is to narrow our focus on the relationship between the framework I have outlined and the creative and critical aspects of the series as primers for actional recommendations to utilize for organizational change. In this, more specifically, I focus on organizational change within the series and exclusively on leadership and mental health with angles on gender, ethnicity, and class.

Organizational Change

To begin, the series hinges on organizational change. It functions as a resource, both a mirror and a window. In season one, episode five, "Tan Lines," for instance, Ted addresses the team in the locker room. It is a pivotal moment of change for the club and the series. Ted has just benched his best player, the lively but self-consumed star, Jamie Tartt. Ted is likewise attempting to make sense of his own change, moving from America to England and managing the difficulties of a divorce he does not want. This is the moment:

> We are broken. We need to change. And look, I know change can be scary [...] Most of the time, change is a good thing. Now, I think that's what it's all about. Embracing change. Being brave. Doing whatever you have to, so that everyone in your life can move forward with theirs.
>
> (Goldstein & Hegarty, 2020)

In other words, the series, and all of its central players, are each enduring some sort of personal and professional change. For instance, Keeley Jones (Juno Temple) changes from being the trophy girlfriend of the star player to an independent public relations executive. Sam Obisanya (Toheeb Jimoh) changes from being a homesick and timid player to one of the team's undeniable leaders and stars. Nathan Shelley (Nick Mohammed) changes from a timorous kit man to an assistant coach. Isaac McAdoo (Kola Bokinni) changes from being a role player bully of Nate to the team captain. And on and on. *Lasso* characters are predicated on change, moving through their insecurities and identity crises to become something new.

Leadership

Within the theme of organizational change, I focus first on leadership. By this, I mean to imply the role of teachers, coaches, mentors, counselors, and the like—those who attempt to help us to see ourselves more clearly and multidimensionally than we dare imagine. These people are essential to our sense of belonging. In this way, leadership becomes the basis of the story. For example, in season one, episode two, "Biscuits," Ted teaches Jamie through positive reinforcement: "If you just figure out some way to turn that 'me', into 'us' [...] The sky's the limit for you" (Kelly & Braff, 2020). Additionally, in season one, episode three, "Trent Crimm: The Independent," Ted reiterates this to the media, "It's about helping these people become the best versions of themselves on and off the field. And that ain't always easy. And neither is growing up without someone believing in you" (Becker & Marshall, 2020).

But perhaps journalist Trent Crimm (James Lance) articulates it best when he sums up Ted in what was supposed to be a seething article set up by Rebecca to embarrass Ted:

> In a business that celebrates ego, Ted reins his in. His coaching style is subtle. It never hits you over the head. Slowly growing until you can no longer ignore its presence.
>
> (Becker & Marshall, 2020)

Moreover, providing a more explicit point of connection and relevance to DEI, I argue the series inverts traditional gender norms, particularly as it pertains to leadership. For instance, the most ardent leaders in the series are women: A.F.C. Richmond's owner, Rebecca (Hannah Waddingham); Keeley Jones (Juno Temple), who becomes a marketing executive; team therapist Dr. Sharon Fieldstone (Sarah Niles) [in season two], who helps players and coaches manage mental health issues; the local pub owner Mae (Annette Badland); Rebecca's best mate, Flo "Sassy" Collins (Ellie Taylor), a respected child psychologist and mother; Julie Higgins (Mary Roscoe), the wife of the Director of Football Operations; and even a local teenager, Shannon (Shannon Hayes) who serves as a confidant to Ted throughout the series.

But perhaps the best summation of this inversion comes in season two, episode six, "The Signal." Jaime Tartt is seeking advice for how to reconcile his tense working relationship with club legend turned coach, Roy Kent (Brett Goldstein). Ted's response is: "Jaime, you and Roy have your own history. Ya'll got to get together and woman up." Jaime bemusedly retorts, "I think you mean man up, mate." Ted makes the inversion distinct, "No. Ya'll been manning up for a while now. Look where that's got you" (Goldstein & Dunton, 2021). Then, as if to reemphasize the point, Ted turns to Keeley for advice. Each of these examples is evidence to a prevalent trend related to gender roles and leadership, promoting a nuanced perspective on DEI values and organizational changemaking.

Mental Health

The second area to consider is mental health. This issue is prevalent but subtle, manifested in character development throughout the series. In season one, mental health is explored progressively through escalating panic attacks experienced by Ted. In season two, mental health issues intensify substantially and include issues of identity and confidence amongst various players, and ultimately, Ted himself. Moreover, these mental health concerns are revealed in the life of the therapist, Dr. Sharon Fieldstone as well. Altogether, I want to embolden these issues as an integral part of DEI values and organizational change. While traditional dynamics related to race, ethnicity, gender, and class are important, this series gives us reason to explore and expand our practices.

An ideal example comes in season two, episode eight, "Man City." Dr. Fieldstone is on the phone with her therapist, processing her annoyance with Ted refusing to be vulnerable. Her therapist responds with this insight: "Sounds like someone I know [...] Sharon you do the same thing. He uses humor to deflect. You use your intelligence." Dr. Fieldstone's response reveals this truth, "Please, I do not harness my savantish nature to alienate people and isolate myself." After a brief revelatory pause, Dr. Fieldstone realizes the irony of her response, "Okay, I hear that." But then the therapist of the therapist offers this insight: "I doubt you'll make any headway with Coach Lasso until you let your guard down yourself and meet him halfway." Dr. Fieldstone acknowledges, "You're right." And the therapist's response is a call to us, "Of course, I'm right. So, what are you going to do about it?" (Lee & Lipsey, 2021).

Actionable Recommendations

As I noted at the forefront of this chapter, my aim is to consider a case study approach that models DEI dynamics in order to outline actionable recommendations. As bell hooks has reminded us, "all contributions that document and give voice to diverse experiences are needed" (hooks, 2019, p. 178). In this way, I argue *Ted Lasso* gives voice to such experiences and helps us address the question of what effective leadership in the realms of DEI looks like in practice. Specifically, I identify four practices, intended to be considered as a progression, though not necessarily limited to this. These are civil language, rituals of regard, a challenge network, and yearnings of expression. Moreover, I intend these to be understood in relationship to the foundational value of belonging and the development of habits of the heart and the practice of healing talk, civility, and care and commitment.

The aim of this section is to coalesce the foundation and framework of hooks' belonging, cultivated by habits of the heart with critical observations from the *Ted Lasso* series. In other words, I draw practices from specific situations and scenes that buttress the ideals delineated by hooks' work.

Civil Language

An invaluable practice featured in the series is the practice of civility in language. Language is our most essential resource for living in relationship with one another. The language we use is foundational to the quality of our communities. Words matter. At a basic level, I am arguing that the choices we make regarding civil language are the building blocks for effective practices. While I believe these are ultimately a result of our attitudes, values, and beliefs, I see civil language as a reconditioning tool for reshaping these dimensions of meaning and transforming our practices.

One of the preeminent violations of DEI values comes by way of our language. When offensive words are uttered, what role does apology play? Throughout the series, characters' everyday encounters feature the recognition of offense (i.e., I'm sorry), an attempted binding (i.e., I forgive you), and constant acts of gratitude (i.e., you are welcome). I want to argue that this civil language is so common and casual that we may miss its prevalence and constancy.

Collectively, civil language as a practice is fundamentally an effort to promote belonging and community. It can be a mode of healing talk. It is an embodiment of civility. It is an explicit means of care and commitment to people. These habits of the heart are buttressed by the practice of civil language and embodied in the characters throughout the series.

In sum, the practice of civil language is a means of agency. If we want to hold our organizations (and ourselves) more accountable to DEI standards and practices, we must commit to practicing civil language.

Rituals of Regard

Interestingly, hooks regards communities of care as being "sustained by rituals of regard," using the example of eating together around a table as ideal for creating the conditions for conviviality and praise (hook, 2019, p. 229). In other words, just as hooks believes we need new rituals of regard, I argue the series embodies this practice. For instance, one such encounter, "biscuits with the boss," debuts in season one, episode two, "Biscuits." It fosters the habits of the heart, particularly healing talk and civility. Broadly, the practice is intent on establishing belonging—an effort to get acquainted with persons and values. Beyond "biscuits with the boss," the practice of getting acquainted with colleagues over meals is prevalent in the series. Ted has lunches with Higgins in his office, pub dinners with Beard, impromptu lunches with Roy at his favorite kebob restaurant, and an informal advice session over street food with Keeley.

As an organizational practice, similar informal conversations could be useful and beneficial for building momentum and rapport in particular relational dynamics inside *and* outside of the office that could influence more formal interactions. Similar to the series, the practice could be useful in recruiting employee advocacy and agency and for promoting more remote healing talk and civility. Uniquely, this practice mirrors the research of Sherry Turkle's *Reclaiming Conversation: The Power of Talk in a Digital Age,* with a "pro-conversation" focus on developing empathy (Turkle, 2015, p. 25).

Altogether, Turkle's argument is that face-to-face conversation is one of the primary places we learn and develop empathy—and empathy is essential to cultivating human connection and negotiating conflict. This has great value for DEI issues and practices. Moreover, given that our socially mediated world is rapidly becoming less prone to conversation and more to digital connection, one additional practice could be the prioritization of talk by limiting digital technology in particular meetings and spaces. In essence, then, utilizing the necessity of nourishment as a basis for developing relational practices that promote healing talk could be quite practical.

Challenge Network

The third practice moves from civil language and rituals of regard to small group dynamics. Specifically, "Diamond Dogs" is one of the more humorous and intriguing practices within the series. It nurtures all of the aforementioned habits of the heart—healing talk, civility, and care and commitment. In essence, it is a small support group devoted to honesty, emotional support in times of crisis, and seeking advice to enhance perspective and decision making. The group debuts in season one, episode eight, "Diamond Dogs," in response to a relational crisis regarding Ted, and continues sporadically throughout the series with Ted, Beard, Nate, and Higgins (and at times, reluctantly, Roy).

As an organizational practice, Diamond Dogs offers a model for belonging in the workplace and can serve as a precursor to larger group practices that serve to assist in problem solving. The question is, can this practice be implemented in an actual organizational context? Or is this merely an ideal fit for an entertaining series but not a workplace? Interestingly, this practice mirrors Adam Grant's "challenge network" in organizational dynamics. For Grant, the ideal members of a challenge network are:

> disagreeable, because they're fearless about questioning the way things have always been done and holding us accountable or thinking again. There's evidence that disagreeable people speak up more frequently— especially when leaders aren't receptive—and foster more task conflict […] They give the critical feedback we might not want to hear but need to hear.
>
> (Grant, 2021, p. 83)

Broadly, this practice could be useful both formally and informally. Regardless, each is compatible with the habits of the heart related to healing talk, civility, and care and commitment.

Yearnings of Expression

Recalling a conversation with an artist "about the way public art can be a vehicle for the sharing of life-affirming thoughts," hooks contends, "There are not many public discussions of love in our culture right now. At best, popular culture is the one domain in which our longing for love is talked about" (hooks, 2018, p. xvii). In essence, hooks notes, "Movies, music, magazines, and books are the place where we turn to hear our yearnings for love expressed" (hooks, 2018, p. xvii). Yet hooks clarifies and decries the popularity of these longings as being centrally about the meaning-lessness and irrelevance of love. I argue, however, that *Ted Lasso* is an exception to this tendency and makes a unique contribution to our discourse on organizational change and belonging.

The fourth practice, playing on hooks's notion of books as "yearnings for love expressed," is another innocuous means of demonstrating leadership and promoting mental acuity. In season one, episode three, "Trent Crimm: The Independent," Ted gifts books to every player, seemingly correlating the themes of the books to an aspect of the players own development. Jaime Tartt is gifted F. Scott Fitzgerald's *The Beautiful and the Damned.* Sam Obisanya, Orson Scott Card's *Ender's Game.* And Roy Kent, Madeleine L'Engle's, *A Wrinkle in Time.*

Confused by the tactic, Roy Kent questions Ted's tactics, "Enough. I have had it with your mind games and your stupid gifts. I mean, what even is *A Wrinkle in Time?*" Before Ted answers, Trent Crimm interjects, "It's a lovely novel. It's the story of a young girl's struggle with the burden of leadership as she journeys through space." Perplexed, Kent exclaims, "Am I supposed to be the little girl?" And Ted responds, "I'd like you to be" (Becker & Marshall, 2020). A bit later in the episode, the tactic deepens its development as Kent sits beside his niece Phoebe and reads *A Wrinkle in Time* to her before bed. Reading aloud, Kent makes a connection between the book and his own role within the team: "Mrs. Which's voice was grave. What do you understand? That is has to be me. Can't be anyone else" (Becker & Marshall, 2020).

With immediacy, Kent realizes comparably that it has to be him. In context, keep in mind we are early in the series' development, a cultural crisis of belonging grips the team. The star player has coaxed other players into bullying the team kit man, Nate. Roy approached Ted with the issue but was rebuffed in part to stoke Roy's leadership. The scene that follows Roy's revelation features Kent confronting various players on the team, including its star, Jaimie Tartt, at a local club. And the scene concludes with a voiceover of Trent Crimm reading the article he has written about Ted, noting Lasso's subtle coaching style, "whether that means allowing followers to become leaders," as Kent concludes his confrontation (Becker & Marshall, 2020). It is an adept display of the practice of leadership and the practice of utilizing books, yearnings of expression, to draw out belonging and promote organizational change.

Collectively, identifying yearnings of love expressed, whether movies, television, books, or otherwise, is a viable practice for promoting conversation. They are a specific means for transgressing the boundaries that often keep us from talking together and from knowing one another. hooks provides an alternative perspective on books: "In a world where I did not belong, I struggled to find strategies for survival. In the world of dominator culture, both within our household and beyond, I found a place of refuge in books, ways of perceiving the world which expanded my consciousness and left me wanting more from life than I believed was possible" (hooks, 2019, p. 218).

Beyond these specific examples, reading and books feature prevalently throughout the series, particularly with Coach Beard. These serve two purposes. On one hand, the books Beard reads often correlate to prevalent themes in the series and advance the storyline and provide subtle insights on characters and their development. On the other hand, this constancy provides a model for the practice of assigning books or other yearnings of love expressed.

Conclusion

For hooks (2018), "there is no better place to learn the art of loving than in community" (p. 129). And for fans of *Ted Lasso,* the series provides an intriguing case study for exploring various aspects of what it means to learn the art of love in community. Broadly, I have sought to use the *Ted Lasso* series as both a mirror and a window to help us reflect on DEI values and initiatives as it relates to establishing belonging through the development of habits of the heart and practices such as healing talk, civility, and care and commitment. Specifically, I provided a framework, identifying the motivation for the project while providing an overview of my inductive case study and situating DEI values in the context of the critical theories and practices of bell hooks. Second, I provided an inductive case study of the Apple+ workplace sitcom *Ted Lasso,* assessing the significance of its depiction of leadership and inversion of gender roles as well as its representation of mental health issues to demonstrate its role in promoting belonging and organizational change. Third, I provided actionable recommendations that delineated four purposeful practices from the series that I argue can help us further enhance belonging and promote organizational changemaking in our own organizations.

In sum, I want to leave with a charge from hook's meditation on love, what she titled, "Commitment: Let Love Be Love in Me." In this, she contends, "One of the best guides to how to be self-loving is to give ourselves the love we are often dreaming about receiving from others" (hooks, 2018, p. 67). Put differently, in the struggle for DEI—in our quest for belonging—our habits of the heart and our practices are essential. In our organizations, while we may benefit from healing talk, civility, and care and commitment; or in practices that include civil language, rituals of regard, challenger networks, or yearnings of love expressed; as we grasp for love and belonging, perhaps our greatest resource is our commitment to let love be love in me.

Discussion Questions

1 What cultural forces most inhibit our sense of belonging? Why?
2 What cultural forces, examples, and/or practices have contributed/can contribute to the reclamation of conversation, empathy, and belonging to enhance organizational change?
3 When it comes to building belonging, what cultures have you been a part of that embody this example? What cultures have failed in this regard and why?
4 What practices could you tactically use to enrich your current organization and culture?

Author Bio

Raymond Blanton is an Associate Professor of Communication Arts in the School of Media and Design at the University of the Incarnate Word in San Antonio, TX. His research is concerned with the rhetorical and civic dimensions of communication, media, and culture in intellectual history and American culture.

References

Becker, J. (Writer), & Marshall, T. (Director). (2020, August 14). Episode 3 (Season 1, Episode 3) [TV series episode]. In Lawrence, B., & Sudeikis, J. (Executive Producers), *Ted Lasso*. Warner Bros. Television.

Casarjian, R. (1992). *Forgiveness: A bold choice for a peaceful heart*. New York: Bantam.

Goldstein, B. (Writer), & Dunton, E. (Director). (2021, August 27). Episode 6 (Season 2, Episode 6) [TV series episode]. In Lawrence, B., & Sudeikis, J. (Executive Producers), *Ted Lasso*. Warner Bros. Television.

Goldstein, B. (Writer), & Hegarty, E. (Director). (2020, August 28). Episode 5 (Season 1, Episode 5) [TV series episode]. In Lawrence, B., & Sudeikis, J. (Executive Producers), *Ted Lasso*. Warner Bros. Television.

Grant, A. (2021). *Think again: The power of knowing what you don't know*. New York: Viking.

hooks, b. (2018). *All about love: New visions*. New York: William Morrow.

hooks, b. (2019) *Belonging: A culture of place*. Taylor & Francis.

Kelly, J. (Writer), & Braff, Z. (Director). (2020, August 14). Episode 2 (Season 1, Episode 2) [TV series episode]. In Lawrence, B., & Sudeikis, J. (Executive Producers), *Ted Lasso*. Warner Bros. Television.

Lee, J. (Writer), & Lipsey, M. (Director). (2021, September 10). Episode 8 (Season 2, Episode 8) [TV series episode]. In Lawrence, B., & Sudeikis, J. (Executive Producers), *Ted Lasso*. Warner Bros. Television.

Turkle, S. (2015). *Reclaiming conversation: The power of talk in a digital age.* New York: Penguin.

"What is diversity, equity, and inclusion?" (n.d.) Retrieved from https://dei. extension.org/

PART 3

Promoting Meaningful and Impactful Organizational Leadership

17

"IT'S A SAFE SPACE, RIGHT?"

The Complexities of Communicating LGBTQ+ Inclusion Via Artifacts

Sidney Murray[1], Elizabeth Yanas[2], Jasmine T. Austin[2], and Elizabeth K. Eger[2]

[1]*University of South Florida;* [2]*Texas State University*

Learning Objectives

After reading this chapter, you will:

1 Visualize how certain inclusion strategies can unintentionally harm employees.
2 Justify and communicate dissatisfaction or dissent with organizational practices.
3 Create spaces for conversations with employees about displays of support.

Introduction

A certification or degree on a wall of a business displays credibility. An 'Established in 1950' sign on the outside of a building demonstrates how long-lasting a business is in a community. A pride flag, which is a flag with a rainbow on it that represents LGBTQ+ rights, symbolizes inclusion. Or does it? This case study presents a framework from which to examine communication practices where there are nuanced relationships with artifacts, especially for systemically marginalized workers. Artifacts are the "tangible and physical features of an organization [that] contribute to its culture" (Eisenberg et al., 2017, p. 127), like pictures and décor. Artifacts express to both employees and guests what to expect from the organization's ideals (Cheung et al., 2011). However, there can be unforeseen tensions employees face if they feel forced to disclose facets of their identities and experiences because of an organizational artifact. In order to give managers and employees guidance about how to communicate inclusion

DOI: 10.4324/9781003333746-20

with artifacts, they must consider how displays of support can have unintended consequences.

In this chapter, first, we provide a review of research discussing why LGBTQ+ inclusion matters, how it fits into the workplace, and negative effects of forced outing of employees. Then, we use a case study of a gym in Texas that displayed a large LGBTQ+ artifact with the goal of making employees and the gym community feel welcomed. Unfortunately, this display was followed by negative effects—that is, the forced outing of employees. We conclude with recommendations for both the managers and employees who might encounter negative effects due to displays of allyship in the workplace and leave them with actionable steps to take to communicate together.

Literature Review

In this section, we review research on LGBTQ+ people in the workplace and the potential consequences of management taking or not taking responsibility for the inclusion of employees from systemically marginalized groups. We elaborate on forced disclosure as a negative consequence and an affirming work environment as a positive outcome.

LGBTQ+ People in the Workplace

Despite current federal rules in place meant to protect LGBTQ+ people from discrimination at work and as customers in organizations, the "role of federal protections continues to be precarious and at the whim of politics and new rulings, elections, and administrators" (Eger et al., 2022, p. 5) and require legal support and financial access. More than 340 anti-LGBTQ+ state bills were proposed in 2022 (Human Rights Coalition, 2022). Furthermore, barriers remain in local organizational policies for LGBTQ+ people, and this "may reduce the potential for career advancement for LGBT[Q+] persons, reduce the effectiveness in sustaining diverse teams, and can post psychological risks" (Paisley & Tayar, 2016, p. 767). While building an inclusive organization, management must take into consideration the conceptualization of "heterosexism," which Herek (1990) defines as "an ideological system that denies, denigrates, and stigmatizes any non-heterosexual form of behavior, identity, relationship or community" (p. 316). Heterosexism shapes organizational decision making, opportunities, comfort, and even safety for LGBTQ+ workers. Additionally, heterosexism harms the organization, including leading to poor job commitment levels and high turnover rates (King & Cortina, 2010). Creating an organizational culture where LGBTQ+ members feel comfortable, safe, and open to sharing their identities can reap many benefits for both employees and the organization.

Management's Responsibility for Inclusion

In order to include LGBTQ+ people in organizations, managers must create and sustain organizational cultures where queer, trans, and intersex employees are welcomed. Creating such cultures is vital, especially when organizations reinforce cisheteronormativity—that is, the privileging of cisgender and heterosexual experiences, beliefs, and norms in both policies and practices that reinforce privilege and structures of exclusion and violence (Chevrette & Eguchi, 2020).

To be considered an ally, according to Pickett and Tucker (2020), one must be an individual who "supports, empowers, or stands for another person or a group of people" (p. 297). For a person to fully integrate and have a sense of comfort in the workplace, they must be confident that those they are surrounded by will be advocates. However, allyship is not halted at agreeing for support, but one must partake in activistic endeavors. As Bohonos and Sisco (2021) note, "LGBTQ[+] allies are encouraged to self-identify as individuals who recognize variations in gender expression and sexual preference" (p. 92). Management maintaining the ability to present themselves as an advocate for all workers, not only those within the LGBTQ+ community, aids in forming an inclusive workspace. Eger et al. (2022) highlight how "if coworkers and superiors disclose queer or trans identities, other LGBTQ+ may feel more inclined to be out as well" (p. 17). This can be a deciding factor to determine whether the workspace is inclusive or exclusive of LGBTQ+ workers.

For those without allies, showing up to scheduled work can become an unsafe scenario, and as described by Hill (2009), unsafe workplaces can have severe consequences such as "organizational exclusion, ridicule, verbal and physical threats, violence, marginalization, or hitting the lavender ceiling" (p. 41). The lavender ceiling is a barrier to professional advancement that queer people experience during their careers. Research also illustrates how transgender and nonbinary workers experience disproportionate violence at work, and how these experiences increase for trans people who are also people of color, living with disabilities, experiencing poverty, and/or immigrants (Eger, 2018). LGBTQ+ people of color and LGBTQ+ immigrants also face more discrimination and safety risks at work than white and citizen peers (Movement Advancement Project, 2013).

Social support is an important aspect for LGBTQ+ employees because it can alleviate stressors and support mental health. Managers and coworkers can communicate social support and intentionally create policies and best practices for an inclusive organization (see Eger et al.'s review, 2022). Such inclusive communicative processes allow an employee to feel like an asset to the organization. However, one must remain wary of inconsistent supportive efforts, as acts such as this can turn a well-intentioned form of allyship in the workplace into more of a performance than contributive to change in any effective capacity (Bohonos & Sisco, 2021).

Additionally, Duhigg et al. (2010) describe the privilege that comes from heterosexual and cisgender individuals since their identities are considered normative in society. They can create reform in the treatment of those in marginalized groups, and this emphasizes the pivotal role that allies play in contributing to the conversation by developing skills required by a *true*, rather than a *performative*, advocate. This is crucial to note considering that simply the appearance of managers being advocates can be detrimental to the inclusivity process since it can turn employees away from trusting managers' intentions. Allyship and advocacy should take place at all times, but it is especially important to form a sense of allyship for LGBTQ+ employees at work.

Forced Disclosure

Cunningham (2011) states within a "proactive workplace" the likelihood of employees who identify within the LGBTQ+ community feeling welcomed, reassured to self-disclose identifiers, and supported to share experiences is heightened (p. 455). Rose (2020) describes how members of the LGBTQ+ community have faced much discrimination, and though there have been significant advancements, individuals still "have their overall well-being impeded by systems which blatantly seek to oppress or marginalize them" (p. 363). Because employees want to portray themselves in a positive light, they may be conscious of conversations and nonverbal behaviors they are displaying more often than others. For LGBTQ+ employees, they must not only navigate how their peers and managers perceive them but also consider their safety and potential consequences of disclosing their gender identity and/or sexuality (see Eger et al., 2022).

LGBTQ+ employees must consider when they may want to communicate about their identities and can fear unwanted disclosure. There is a significant amount of risk when opting to disclose in the workplace considering that "LGBT[Q+] employees continue to be the recipients of hostility" (Madera, 2010, p. 86). LGBTQ+ employees may struggle with how, when, and with whom they reveal their experiences in organizations. This tension can cause them stress and anxiety in workplace social interactions. Eger et al. (2022) traced three interconnected "complexities of workplace disclosure of LGBTQ+ identities, including through closeting, passing, and outing communication" (p. 11). Closeting takes place when LGBTQ+ people conceal portions or all of their identities. As McDonald et al. (2020) explain, "Because heterosexuality is the presumed norm in most contexts, recognizing one's LGB[TQ+] identity automatically closets individuals, who must then negotiate when, whether, to whom, and how to disclose this information" (p. 86). Closeting is an ongoing communication process, not a one-time moment, as LGBTQ+ people navigate coming out across moments, relationships, and organizations in formal and informal settings. Furthermore, closeting involves not only sexuality and gender identity but also other marginalized identities and experiences (Eger, 2018; McDonald et al., 2020). Madera (2010) highlights that this comes at a great cost considering these individuals are forced to "regulate" behaviors while at work which can cause a stressed and hyper-fixated individual who is constantly in fear of their identity being revealed without consent or a feeling of being left optionless. Furthermore, employees may engage in passing as heterosexual or cisgender, such as through suppressing information about their lives or dodging questions (Spradlin, 1998). Others may experience forcible outing without their consent, when someone else discloses their sexuality or gender identity.

Contrastingly, Clair et al. (2005) discuss a revealing strategy known as "normalizing," when an individual opts to "reveal their invisible social identity to others and then attempting to make their differences seem commonplace or ordinary" (p. 90). However, one is forced to consider that if the owner or manager of an organization is attempting to normalize their own marginalized identification, then it could lead employees feeling forced to partake in disclosure when they would have chosen a different workplace strategy if provided an alternative. In this sense, supervisors are attempting to make "safe spaces," but without requesting employees' sentiments prior to implementation, it can become a counter-productive strategy. Crucially, cornered employees must now face the decision of disclosing to potentially feel connected to coworkers or to continue concealing to avoid a "coming out" scenario.

Affirming Spaces and Artifacts

Artifacts are items displayed that can signal or represent ideas, communities, or identities (Austin et al., 2020). Organizations can demonstrate their culture through artifacts that represent deeper sets of their ideals, like a skating rink having a "Wall of Fame" to encourage high achievement among their competitive skaters (Mills & Hoeber, 2013). Organizational members can use artifacts to demonstrate or promote certain ideals within the culture and set expectations for those involved (Cheung et al., 2011).

Organizational leaders and members create physical space, organizational design layouts, and artifacts to influence employee and customer responses about what the space communicates to them. Responses to physical space can vary by person and can even create organizational tensions around space and artifacts (Pepper, 2008).

In research about LGBTQ+ people's experiences, the use of organizational space and artifacts can increase experiences of inclusion. For example, for older LGBTQ+ adults, Croghan et al. (2015) found that physical artifacts such as flags, pins, and signs and using inclusive language on forms impacted how welcomed they felt accessing services. Eger (2021) traced how artifacts and spatial layouts (such as couches, bookshelves, and magazines) communicated experiences of being at "home" for transgender and nonbinary workers at a nonprofit organization. Managers can thus examine how artifacts communicate culture and encourage and/or discourage organizational members to communicate about their identities.

Case Study

To examine LGBTQ+ workspaces, responsibility for inclusion, forced disclosure, and affirming spaces and artifacts, we present a case that demonstrates how an organizational artifact selected to promote inclusion can create complicated impacts. This case study will give owners and managers insights into how to properly support their employees as well as provide employees with tools to address their feelings about the nuances of having their LGBTQ+ identities openly known.

This case study derives from our larger research project examining leadership in Texas small businesses owned by systematically marginalized groups and the impact of COVID-19. This case follows a gym in Texas where we completed two interviews with an owner and an employee. All names used in this case study are pseudonyms, and we have changed certain details to protect the participants' confidentiality. The owner, Emily, previously worked at the gym and then took over as the owner. An employee, Brody, worked at the gym for over a year.

Background/Scenario

When Emily took over as owner of the gym, she wanted to be sure to encourage a community of warmth and inclusion. To do this, she decided to hang a pride flag, and explained, "I want to attract the right community members. So, we hung up an LGBTQ+ flag. Since then, we have had a lot of members come into our space expressing how they feel welcome." As a queer woman, her goal was to make a clear statement about the people she wanted to welcome to the gym. She wanted to ensure that the gym was a welcoming environment where LGBTQ+ people felt comfortable and safe to be themselves. While there was some initial pushback, such as gym members asking for a straight pride flag to be hung up, she said,

> The people that pushed back are no longer a part of the community. And I think that ... it's kind of like creating space for more of likeminded people and kind of, not purging, but other people that aren't the best fit go elsewhere, right?

This mindset of wanting to create opportunities for those who shared similar ideals to feel comfortable in the space was a big part of Emily's vision, and it translated to employees.

Brody, a gay man who was previously a member of the gym, joined as a member of Emily's staff and became head coach. He felt supported by her leadership and credited part of it to the pride flag hung in the gym saying,

> Being able to see that we have a pride flag is where I know I'm in a safe space, right? I know that—especially as far as leadership—no one's gonna ever fire me or ever judge me for [being gay] because they're just here to support.

The symbol of the flag demonstrated the priority that Emily gave to attempting to make the gym a supportive space.

However, Brody simultaneously felt tensions in having parts of his identities be so open at work. While the flag hanging up instilled the ideal of inclusion, he struggled with feeling like it identified him as gay and forced him into disclosing his sexuality. While it made him feel supported, it also made him more cautious about openness. Clients, who might have never discussed sexuality beforehand, were having new conversations about it. Brody recounted a story of when he wore a pride shirt and a customer interacted positively with him, but later in the day made an anti-gay post on social media. There was emotional whiplash of having someone interact with him nicely but then seeing their actions quickly contrasted. This unintentional outcome of the pride flag created new conversations and added labor to discuss his gay identity without knowing if gym members were welcoming or not.

Brody discussed the duality of being proud but also not wanting to be *only* seen as his sexual identity. He felt tensions between being supported and being forced to engage in conversations about LGBTQ+ topics. He shared:

> I don't ever wear a pride shirt at the gym just because I just don't want it to even be the focal point of anybody's day. I don't want anyone to look at me and be like, "Oh okay, here's the 'gay coach'" or whatever.

Brody expressed the pressure to not use further artifacts of queerness in order to avoid the focus on his queer identity. He addressed the competing feelings of happiness about the pride flag as a symbol of inclusion, but also worry about how his clients would react to him being gay. He asked,

> Do they know I have a husband? Does it matter to them that I have a husband or are they gonna freak out? If I have to come over and speak to them one-on-one or if ... I'm able to give them a tactical cue, are they gonna be like, "Oh, don't touch me."

These questions arose as he was concerned about his identity impacting his relationship with clients. Through having the pride flag artifact, it cemented feelings of acceptance but also created opportunities for conversations that might scrutinize his sexuality. Being labeled as "the gay coach" could have a negative impact on his career.

The pride flag artifact in the gym to communicate inclusion can be interpreted in several different ways. Emily thought of the pride flag as a chance to reduce conversations on disclosure, stating,

> Having a signal flag like a pride flag on your wall is such a great sign marker of, I don't want to have this conversation every day, so I'm gonna put this here and hope it saves me half the conversations.

She felt that it added to people feeling safe, including her as a queer leader, and had no downsides. However, during the interview, Brody mentioned, "Obviously, it's great to have up there but since there was pushback, it was two steps forward, one step back ... We're in a great place. But then I'm also like, oh, but not everyone agrees." While the flag symbolized acceptance, it also serves as a reminder that not everyone is supportive or allies.

Artifacts can display a culture, but ultimately cultures are built by the people within the community. This case study shows how an artifact that is meant to signify and create acceptance can also serve to produce organizational tensions. When Emily made the decision to hang up the pride flag, she wanted to attract customers who shared the same ideals of inclusion and create a LGBTQ+ affirming and safe space. While it later brought complications to Brody's workday, he credited the pride flag and leadership as reasons why he felt comfortable transitioning from a customer to an employee. When Emily broke down the decision, she said,

I think it was one of the better decisions I ever made because you really figure out who are the people you want to serve and work with. And you really do create a space and a culture where everybody feels welcome, everybody feels encouraged. And they feel safe. It's a safe space, right?

Here, Emily encapsulated the idea of how the artifact could communicate the LGBTQ+ welcoming gym culture. However, the ambiguity of the artifact created areas of tension within the organization as manager's intentions can be misconstrued. We now examine recommendations for the tensions of communicating inclusion via artifacts for multiple audiences.

Recommendations

As seen in the case of Emily and Brody, the best intentions with displays of support can put undue emotional labor on employees. Emily wanted to signal to her employees that she supported LGBTQ+ people, especially being a queer woman herself. She intended it to be interpreted *entirely* as a positive experience; however, Brody's multilayered interpretation reveals that the artifact had unforeseen consequences. Displays of inclusion might have good intentions but can still have negative impacts when put into action. Managers need to be aware of how their visible allyship might force employees to have conversations surrounding a hidden part of their identities that makes them vulnerable, especially employees who experience systemic marginalization because of their identities. The following recommendations are designed to give readers practical and purposeful tools to address similar issues should they arise at their workplace. We offer possibilities for what managers and employees can do to address these concerns.

Manager Recommendations

Inclusive Decision Making

Based on Brody's experiences with gym clients, we can deduce that Emily did not include employees in her artifact decision-making process. This exclusion of employee perspective is a unifying theme in the failure of organizational decision-making groups. Research suggests that "a group's ability to arrive at a high-quality decision is dependent on the quality of interaction or discussion that precedes choice making in the group" (Hirokawa & Rost, 1992,

p. 268). In other words, generating multiple ideas from organizational members allows groups to create and select high-quality decisions. If Emily had discussed the flag with Brody and other employees beforehand, Brody might have had a chance to voice his concern with being outed to customers or being forced to entertain conversations with them about sexuality that he previously did not have to engage.

Depending on the organizational structure, here is a recommendation for encouraging voice in group decision making: during an employee meeting or in one-on-one conversations, foster a brainstorming (i.e., idea generation) session where for a set amount of time, everyone can pitch ideas toward an organizational initiative or problem. Following these ideas, instead of precariously narrowing them down, ask the question, "What could go wrong?" with each idea. This is a mindful and thoughtful way of ensuring support is provided, all voices can be heard, and multiple ideas are considered before decisions are made.

Communicating the Artifact and Feedback

The act of vigilantly and communally developing an artifact (e.g., hanging a pride flag) "among teammates or organizational members who have a shared stake in the success of their design efforts" (Austin et al., 2020, p. 296) is a process called collective communication design work (CCDW). For the long-term success of a design, organizational members may discuss ways to communicate their culture to stakeholders (e.g., gym members). Two strategies for communicating their culture via artifacts and ensuring all organizational members are heard and safe are through *backstage recounted piloting* and *frontstage personalized mimicry*. Backstage recounted piloting is a feedback loop where organizational members can discuss what is working, what is not working, and what is going wrong with the new artifact. Managers can engage in clear dialogue with employees to find alternative artifacts, like a rainbow version of the gym logo or a rainbow wrist band. Frontstage personalized mimicry is the opportunity to take what one learned backstage and implement those strategies in their own practice. In this way, "CCDW will be constituted by recursive cycles of crafting, testing, problematizing, and evaluating over time" (Austin, et al., 2020, p. 296). So, for effective CCDW, we recommend scheduling multiple meetings following the implementation of a new design, to gain feedback from employees to ensure everyone feels heard and valued, which would help employees like Brody.

Creating Space for Dissenting

Dissent is the opportunity for members to voice dissatisfaction and/or disagreement. In an organizational context, though dissent involves "feeling apart from one's organization" and "expressing disagreement or contradictory opinions about one's organization" (Kassing, 1997, p. 312), dissent has been positively linked to job satisfaction, procedural justice, increasing employee performance, and better problem solving and decision making (Garner, 2013). Though dissenting is focused on employee behavior (discussed below), what is missing is how managers and leaders can co-construct organizational dissent and dissent effectiveness with employees. Dissent effectiveness can be operationalized in three ways, as Garner (2013) describes:

1 *Instrumental change:* Giving employees opportunities to influence change in the organization, from collecting their ideas for how to foster inclusivity in the organization to policy change.
2 *Voice opportunities:* Giving employees opportunities to voice their opinions and desires within the organization. Their perspective can be valuable if the leader is willing to ask what those perspectives are. Asking for feedback openly and often is a strategy to generate communication about what is working or might work better.
3 *Collective action:* Co-creating plans, actions, policies, interventions, etc. allows employees to have a voice and to feel invested and bought into an organizational endeavor.

Stemming from our case study, creating a healthy dissenting environment can allow managers to better consider if an employee is forced to engage in a conversation about an identity that they might otherwise have not discussed. Because closeting, passing, and outing are ongoing communication processes across contexts (Eger, 2018; Spradlin, 1998), letting employees take the lead about their level of comfort in disclosure across contexts is important. For example, an LGBTQ+ employee may feel comfortable sharing about their gender identity or sexuality to a manager, but not to their peers; or to their peers, but not to their customers. Should an employee disclose their identities or experiences to a manager or HR, such as sharing about their romantic partner, their health needs, or their pronouns, this should be paired with a conversation about with whom the information can be shared.

Employee Recommendations for Dissenting

Here, we discuss recommendations for employees navigating conversations with managers surrounding their hidden and/or systematically marginalized identities. Revisiting the dissent literature from the employee standpoint can provide tools for expressing their dissatisfaction or disagreement with an issue (Garner, 2013; Kassing, 1997; Zoller & Fairhurst, 2007). Dissent is made up of three stages: *the precipitation stage* (where the employee recognizes the disconnect between the manager's goals and theirs), *the initial conversation stage* (where the dissenter expresses the concern while carefully choosing the context), and *the residual communication stage* (where the employee reminds the manager of the dissent after the original conversation) (Garner, 2013). When employees disagree with something, they need to pay specific attention to the initial conversation stage. There are three types of dissent that employees can utilize when approaching the initial communication stage. Employees can use *articulated dissent* to dissent to audiences that can influence the organization to change, *antagonistic dissent* using organizational leverage through certain relationships (familial, seniority, expertise, etc.) in order to avoid retaliation, and *displaced dissent* when employees think that their dissent will not be well-received by the organization so they dissent to those uninvolved (Kassing, 1997). These types can all be deployed in order to choose the audience within the organization.

In the instance of the gym case study, Brody can use dissenting strategies to discuss the issue with Emily about how the pride artifact has increased conversations about his queer identity as well as forces him and other future LGBTQ+ employees to out themselves. However, sharing concerns and critiques with a leader does entail a certain amount of risk that must be appropriately assessed, especially in unreceptive cultures. If this is the case, employees should choose *who* they dissent to and the words they choose in order to get the best results from dissenting.

Though an employee can dissent alone to their manager, another option is to dissent with coworkers. This is not to say create an uproar in front of a manager's door. Instead, selecting coworkers that identify with the goal to impact a change can help leaders see employee feedback and the group as positive instead of villainized (Garner, 2013) as well as motivate each other to continue dissenting (Zoller & Fairhurst, 2007). By choosing a receptive audience, whether that be through getting a coworker on their side or a manager who relates to them, employees increase their ability to dissent effectively (Garner, 2013; Kassing, 1997).

As seen in the example, Brody could have approached Emily and framed his dissent as appreciating the support, but also noting that it was causing him additional emotional strain to engage in discussions about hidden parts of his identity at work. Bringing up this concern would show the manager that their inclusion is appreciated, but that a different show of support could cause less strain. As noted above, a receptive audience plays a key role in dissenting. If Brody had dissented to Emily, since they both are members of LGBTQ+ communities, they could potentially connect over creating an LGBTQ+-affirming organizational culture.

However, this could have gone differently when dissenting about a problem to someone who has systematic power through job positions and structural inequality. In these cases, displaced dissent might be more beneficial in order to protect Brody from retaliation or the added stress of negative reception. Employees must weigh the benefits and risks of articulated or antagonistic dissent by considering the organization's culture (i.e., would it be receptive?) and the person who is receiving the dissent (i.e., is there a shared viewpoint?). Research shows that employees and managers can utilize open discussions, such as forum meetings, to address challenges to sustaining an LGBTQ+ inclusive organizational culture, and ongoing communication can help reaffirm shared values and articulate new needs (see Eger, 2021).

Conclusion

When managers think of demonstrating inclusion in the workplace, it is typically created to support employees and customers to create a cohesive community. However, an act of support without employee input can turn into an artifact that makes the workday harder for an employee. Managers might have the best intention when hanging up a pride flag or displaying another marker of support; however, this can force employees to engage in conversations surrounding topics they might have previously avoided at work. In which case, those who want to support systematically marginalized communities can sometimes put those communities at more risk through identifying them or forcing them into conversations about their identity. To this end, we encourage leaders to engage with employees in conversation before displaying artifacts of support in order to make sure they are being an ally in a way that makes everyone feel comfortable, valued, and safe.

Discussion Questions

1 In what ways can a manager be an advocate for their employees to assist in forming an inclusive workplace without forcing disclosure of their identities?
2 In the case of Emily and Brody, the leader was well-intentioned in attempting to help attract customers who were supportive of LGBTQ+ people, but ultimately employees could be potentially vulnerable to unsupportive customers, discrimination, or hate. What are alternative ways a leader could support representation and inclusion without forcing employees to engage unsupportive customers?

3 It is essential for employees to be able to express organizational dissent, but not every individual feels capable of having this conversation. What are some practices that could assist in forming a sense of comfort for employees to communicate their unsatisfactory feelings toward an organizational move, artifact, or policy?

Author Bios

Sidney Murray, M.A., is an organizational scholar with specific interests in identity and queerness. She earned a BFA in Performance and Production, an M.A. in Communication, and a Certificate of Corporate Communication at Texas State University. She is currently earning her Ph.D. at the University of South Florida.

Elizabeth Yanas, M.A. (Texas State University), research interests surround organizational communication in conjunction with leadership, identification, and work/life. She earned a BS in Public Relations, a master's in communication studies, and a certificate in Corporate Communication and Training. With this training, she assists organizations to better serve their employees.

Jasmine T. Austin, Ph.D., has two main areas of research that are socialization and marginalized identities. This includes theorizing about Black women and examining the impact of early racialized conversations between group members (e.g., supervisor/member and parent/child) on future interactions, experiences, and identity development. She is the lead editor of *Communication Theory: Racially Diverse and Inclusive Perspectives.* https://orcid.org/0000-0002-4131-1273

Elizabeth K. Eger (Ph.D., University of Colorado, Boulder) is an Assistant Professor in the Department of Communication Studies at Texas State University. She examines intersectional organizing and difference, LGBTQ+ workers, and how work shapes our identities and health. Her recent research appears in *Management Communication Quarterly*, *International Journal of Business Communication*, and *Feminist Media Studies.*

Acknowledgement

This research was supported by a Texas State University Research Enhancement Project grant.

References

Austin, J. T., Wallace, B. S., Gilmore, B. N., & Bisel, R. S. (2020). The micro-skills of collective communication design work: An academic team's development of sensebreaking messages. *Communication Studies, 71*(2), 295–314. 10.1080/10510974.2020.1722720

Bohonos, J. W., & Sisco, S. (2021). Advocating for social justice, equity, and inclusion in the workplace: An agenda for anti-racist learning organizations. *New Directions for Adult and Continuing Education, 2021*(170), 89–98. 10.1002/ ace.20428

Cheung, S. O., Wong, P. S. P., & Wu, A. W. Y. (2011). Towards an organizational culture framework in construction. *International Journal of Project Management, 29*(1), 33–44. 10.1016/j.ijproman.2010.01.014

Chevrette, R., & Eguchi, S. (2020). "We don't see LGBTQ differences": Cisheteronormativity and concealing phobias and irrational fears behind rhetorics of acceptance. *QED: A Journal in GLBTQ Worldmaking, 7*(1), 55–59. https://www.muse.jhu.edu/article/754453

Clair, J. A., Beatty, J. E., & Maclean, T. L. (2005). Out of sight but not out of mind: Managing invisible social identities in the workplace. *Academy of Management Review, 30*(1), 78–95. 10.5465/amr.2005.15281431

Croghan, C. F., Moone, R. P., & Olson, A. M. (2015). Working with LGBT baby boomers and older adults: Factors that signal a welcoming service environment. *Journal of Gerontological Social Work, 58*(6), 637–651. 10.1080/01634372. 2015.1072759

Cunningham, G. B. (2011). The LGBT advantage: Examining the relationship among sexual orientation diversity, diversity strategy, and performance. *Sport Management Review, 14*(4), 453–461. 10.1016/j.smr.2010.11.003

Duhigg, J. M., Rostosky, S. S., Gray, B. E., & Wimsatt, M. K. (2010). Development of heterosexuals into sexual-minority allies: A qualitative exploration. *Sexuality Research and Social Policy, 7*(1), 2–14. 10.1007/ s13178-010-0005-2

Eisenberg, E. M., Goodall, H. L., & Trethewey, A. (2017). *Organizational communication: Balancing creativity and constraint* (8th edition). Bedford/St.Martin's.

Eger, E. K. (2018). Transgender jobseekers navigating closeting communication. *Management Communication Quarterly, 32*(2), 276–281. 10.1177/089331891 7740226

Eger, E. K. (2021). Co-constructing organizational identity and culture with those we serve: An ethnography of a transgender nonprofit organization communicating family identity and identification. *International Journal of Business Communication, 58*(2), 254–281. 10.1177/2329488419893738

Eger, E. K., Litrenta, M. L., Kane, S. R., & Senegal, L. D. (2022). LGBTQ+ workers. In Isaac West (Ed.), *Encyclopedia of queer studies and communication* (pp. 1–38). Oxford University Press. 10.1093/acrefore/9780190228613. 013.1247

Garner, J. T. (2013). Dissenters, managers, and coworkers: The process of co-constructing organizational dissent and dissent effectiveness. *Management Communication Quarterly, 27*(3), 373–395. 10.1177/0893318913488946

Herek, G. M. (1990). The context of anti-gay violence: Notes on cultural and psychological heterosexism. *Journal of Interpersonal Violence, 5*, 316–333.

Hill, R. J. (2009). Incorporating queers: Blowback, backlash, and other forms of resistance to workplace diversity initiatives that support sexual minorities. *Advances in Developing Human Resources, 11*(1), 37–53. 10.1177/152342230832 8128

Hirokawa, R. Y., & Rost, K. M. (1992). Effective group decision making in organizations: Field test of the vigilant interaction theory. *Management Communication Quarterly*, *5*(3), 267–288.

Human Rights Coalition. (2022). United against hate: Fighting back on state legislative attacks on LGBTQ+ People. Retrieved from: https://www.hrc.org/campaigns/the-state-legislative-attack-on-lgbtq-people

Kassing, J. W. (1997) Articulating, antagonizing, and displacing: A model of employee dissent. *Communication Studies*, *48*(4), 311–332. 10.1080/10510979709368510

King, E. B., & Cortina, J. M. (2010). The social and economic imperative of lesbian, gay, bisexual, and transgendered supportive organizational policies. *Industrial and Organizational Psychology*, *3*(1), 69–78. 10.1111/j.1754-9434.2009.01201.x

Madera, J. M. (2010). The cognitive effects of hiding one's homosexuality in the workplace. *Industrial and Organizational Psychology*, *3*(1), 86–89.

McDonald, J., Harris, K. L., & Ramirez, J. (2020). Revealing and concealing difference: A critical approach to disclosure and an intersectional theory of "closeting." *Communication Theory*, *30*(1), 84–104. 10.1093/ct/qtz017 10.1080/1553118X.2016.1226172

Mills, C. & Hoeber, L. (2013). Exploring organizational culture through artifacts in a community figure skating club. *Journal of Sports Management*, *27*(1), 482–496. 10.1123/jsm.27.6.482

Movement Advancement Project, Center for American Progress, Human Rights Campaign, Freedom to Work, and National Black Justice Coalition. (2013, November). A broken bargain for LGBT workers of color. Retrieved from: https://www.lgbtmap.org/workers-of-color

Paisley, V., & Tayar, M. (2016). Lesbian, gay, bisexual and transgender (LGBT) expatriates: an intersectionality perspective. *International Journal of Human Resource Management*, *27*(7), 766–780. 10.1080/09585192.2015.1111249

Pepper, G. L. (2008). The physical organization as equivocal message. *Journal of Applied Communication Research*, *36*, 318–338. doi:10.1080/00909880802104882

Pickett, J., & Tucker, C. (2020). Allyship: Standing with Chicago's Bisexual + Community. *Journal of Bisexuality*, *20*(3), 296–300. 10.1080/15299716.2020.1764434

Rose, J. S. (2020). Advocacy and social justice within and on behalf of the LGBTGEQIAP+ community. *Journal of LGBT Issues in Counseling*, *14*(4), 362–373. 10.1080/15538605.2020.1827477

Spradlin, A. L. (1998). The price of "passing": A lesbian perspective on authenticity in organizations. *Management Communication Quarterly*, *11*(4), 598–605. 10.1177/0893318998114006

Zoller, H. M. & Fairhust, G. T. (2007). Resistance leadership: The overlooked potential in crisis organization and leadership studies. *Human Relations*, *60*(9), 1331–1360. 10.1177/0018726707082850

18

MEANDERING, MISTAKES, AND MOVEMENT

Stages of Organizational Culture Change for DEI

Richard D. Waters, Zifei Fay Chen, and
Lorena Gomez-Barris
University of San Francisco

Learning Objectives

After reading this chapter, you will:

1 Understand the complexity involved in changing organizational culture even when members outwardly support DEI change.
2 Be able to apply change management stages to overcome an organization's stalled intentions toward on-going DEI practices.
3 Be ready to advocate for practical behaviors and management practices that can be carried out in organizations for lasting DEI change.

Introduction

In the wake of racial justice protests and civil unrest following the murder of George Floyd, Ahmaud Arbery, and Breonna Taylor in 2020, organizations quickly released statements on their websites and on social media declaring their commitment to social justice and pledging to support diversity, equity, and inclusion (DEI) efforts. Corporate America acknowledged it could not stay silent and promised to confront systemic racism. The philanthropic sector saw foundations shift priorities to fund nonprofits in marginalized communities, specifically programs addressing social inequities. One year later, the *Washington Post* examined corporate and philanthropic organizations' commitments toward justice and discovered the limits of their power (Jan et al., 2021).

DOI: 10.4324/9781003333746-21

Case Study: Organizational Meandering on DEI Commitments

This chapter explores why organizations stall with organizational change efforts, focusing specifically on for-profit and nonprofit organizations in San Francisco as our case study. We also address what can be done to overcome institutional obstacles so that commitments to DEI come to fruition. Although we use San Francisco-based organizations as the primary focus of our case study, we advocate a step-by-step changemaking model that is applicable across all types of organizations.

Methods

To uncover the shortcomings of organizational changemaking following civil unrest in 2020, we recruited alumni from management graduate programs who took DEI coursework to participate in interviews about their organizations' DEI efforts. Interviews with 14 alumni, all of whom are communication professionals from San Francisco for-profit and non-profit organizations, were conducted during the first quarter of 2022 over Zoom.

Drawing on the conclusion of *The Washington Post*'s report that organizations have stalled on their DEI planning and commitment, this chapter examines how organizations can move forward using organizational change and development stages. Though several models of organizational change have been proposed, this chapter focuses on a streamlined four-stage model: (1) planning and preparatory work, (2) securing commitment to change, (3) implementing actions that produce change, and (4) evaluating programs to hold organizations accountable for maintaining cultural change (e.g., Jaros, 2010). This chapter focuses on practical applications of change management to help organizations to move beyond their DEI statements to create an environment where all employees are able to be themselves, unreservedly participate in organizational activities and decision making, and ultimately be and feel respected.

Stage 1: Preparatory Work and Planning

The planning stage lays the groundwork and sets the tone for organizational change. Particularly, this stage involves setting goals, measurement plans, understanding the scope of change, as well as identifying internal and external stakeholders involved in the change (Miller, 2020). This stage integrates the strategic planning process to manage organizational change. When it comes to organizational change for DEI, the planning stage includes: assessing an organization's DEI goals and its mission, vision, and values; setting up programs and actionable plans;

and anticipating challenges and opportunities. However, as organizations pledge to support DEI efforts, mistakes are often made by focusing on reactive (vs. proactive) efforts, thus failing to provide long-term, clear, actionable plans. In this section, we review some mistakes that organizations make during this stage and propose that organizations implement strategies to reduce fear of failure, and that they accept mistakes as they move forward with their DEI commitments.

Adopting Reactive DEI Statements but Inaction with Proactive Efforts

Following the summer of 2020, organizations were quick to adopt statements declaring their commitment to racial and social justice. While many companies' statements were followed up by donations and philanthropic activities, inaction soon followed. Facebook (now Meta), for instance, pledged $10 million to organizations working on racial justice, in addition to the substantial amount from Facebook co-founder Mark Zuckerberg's private philanthropy; yet the company's commitment to DEI was challenged due to its lack of diversity in its own workforce and leadership (Kerber et al., 2020). This lack of diversity is an example of an inaction, as proactive efforts might entail them diversifying the organization *before* civil unrest.

When organizations' DEI statements are not grounded in long-term organizational cultural change, these statements are simply performative. The DEI statements responding to racial injustice are merely strategies to get organizations out of scrutiny (Morris, 2020). Organizations often post supportive messages on their social media and make charitable donations to nonprofits to include in their corporate social responsibility reports to show outsiders they care, but little meaningful internal action is taken. Some organizations put DEI programs in place, but failed to make real changes because these programs focused on recruiting to meet quotas rather than providing inclusive, equitable cultures for employees. A Bay Area public affairs specialist who helped craft a DEI statement for her agency said, "I pushed to keep our statement internal rather than public until we had visible actions we were taking to demonstrate we were serious about DEI."

These sentiments echoed a member of a San Francisco special events firm's leadership team who commented that "our team wanted to do the right thing, but once our statement was written and posted to social media, we weren't sure what to do next." Performative efforts to secure public goodwill simply do not work. To foster real organizational change, the planning stage needs to take proactive efforts to create fair and equitable compensation, create evaluation and support structures, have long-range planning in place, have full commitment and accountability from the leadership and buy-in from the employees, and have diverse representation at the decision-making table (Johnson, 2021). Furthermore, the stage must extend beyond the implementation of short-term tactics and aim for long-term change to cultivate an inclusive and equitable culture. As the CEO of a Bay Area-based nonprofit foundation put it, "Thoughtful planning and then thoughtful implementation reinforce the understanding of DEI. As that continues, the work deepens and the shifts in culture are more impactful. This is how DEI becomes part of the fabric of an organization."

Resorting Back to HR-Focused Trainings/Workshops

To address DEI, many organizations resorted back to HR-focused training strategies for people to read materials or attend workshops and online trainings on diversity awareness and unconscious bias. Typically, these programs are run by human resources staff, or consultants hired outside of the company. Admittedly, some attendees complete these programs with increased awareness and new skills, but change often stalls. A tech recruiter felt that DEI trainings were necessary, even in culturally diverse San Francisco, but was concerned about them. "These sessions are mostly designed to be done solo when an employee can take them. While it's convenient for work schedules, it takes away all of the interactions needed to really talk through inclusion and equity." While confronting workplace DEI issues requires individuals to reflect on their own attitudes and actions, organizational change can only happen when employees are brought together to discuss issues in an open environment where they are exposed to others' thoughts and experiences. These exchanges are not facilitated in solo, online trainings, and this step to address DEI fails to make progress toward change.

The shortfall of HR-focused trainings and workshops lies in the gap and inconsistency between what was covered in the workshop and organizational culture, systems, policies, and behaviors. Furthermore, inequities could be reinforced when the responsibility for educating and training falls onto HR, or onto the shoulders of the Chief Diversity Officer (CDO) and/or people of color. As organizations meander through their DEI journey, a more comprehensive, reflective, and actionable set of plans is called for during the planning stage. Here, current organizational culture and mission statements are assessed, and clear steps are presented to meet goals that are inherent to the organization's values (Rinderle, 2020). As the CEO of a Bay Area-based foundation pointed out, DEI planning should not just fall under the scope of those departments with DEI in their title; leadership should provide resources throughout the organization—particularly for smaller organizations that may not have a DEI department—to spur their understanding of how everyone is connected to the DEI goals. "We tell them if the work is part of our theory of change and helps us meet our mission, then the resources must follow," says the Foundation CEO. They continued, "DEI should be part of our culture and part of our change."

The Fear of Failure and Difficult Conversations

Another obstacle organizations face in DEI changemaking is management's fear of failure. This fear makes it difficult for organizations to move beyond the planning stage. DEI work is not about checking the boxes. To foster real cultural change, difficult conversations are necessary. Facing pressure from various stakeholders (e.g., employees, communities, and investors), management may be reluctant to have difficult conversations, resulting in a lack of communication about organizations' status quo, systemic issues, and DEI progress (Austin & Bisel, 2022). However, authentic, transparent communication is essential in organizations' DEI efforts, and reducing the fear of failure is key to organizational innovation and change (Kuyatt, 2011). To reduce the fear of failure, leadership needs to view their mistakes in their DEI efforts as learning opportunities (Kucharska et al., 2020).

A social service nonprofit executive director said, "Some of the best work we have done around DEI has come when I have made mistakes and then shown up very authentically and vulnerably to talk about my mistakes." She continued, "Mistakes happen. We know they're coming. We just have to own up to them and then work to correct those mistakes." When failures are treated as learning opportunities, organizations can move on to securing commitments from leadership and throughout the organization for effective DEI implementation.

Stage 2: Securing Commitment to Change

Acknowledging that DEI statements are not enough for meaningful changemaking, organizations must secure dedication from leadership (Bligh et al., 2018). Recently, organizations rushed to hire employees specifically to tackle DEI issues. Hiring a CDO, or a comparable position, does not create lasting organizational change. Far too often the CDO or a specialized unit in the Human Resources Department is tasked with carrying out organizational DEI efforts while other employees continue their daily routines (Pewewardy, 2021). DEI leaders are often appointed to these positions as a result of tokenism so that organizations appear more diverse and accepting; however, these leaders are regularly challenged to implement DEI programming without being given appropriate resources.

Increased Communication about DEI

"Our company sent out emails asking for volunteers for a DEI committee, but then we never heard anything from the committee once it was formed," said one client manager at a consulting firm. Assigning a company's commitment to DEI as a task is a strong indicator that its work will remain performative. However, hiring staff to hold organizations accountable to DEI commitments is a step toward progress, but it will take more to create conditions for meaningful outcomes.

Research on successful DEI implementation found that the most important task management must address is the prioritization of DEI policies based on a rigorous assessment of their current DEI practices (Cooper & Gerlach, 2019). Communication of policies must be regularly communicated by all of an organization's management team. These messages must come regularly in different formats and in different voices so that DEI cannot be ignored within the organization or dismissed as an initiative by one member of the leadership team (Stanley et al., 2019). "Our executive director regularly spoke about diversity, equity, and inclusion, but it took the Board [of Directors] chair and development director talking about it to make it become real," said a library volunteer coordinator.

Furthermore, leaders cannot talk down to employees about workplace DEI issues and expect cultural change. Speaking down to employees reinforces the status quo; leadership must have genuine conversations to facilitate changemaking. DEI commitment requires active participation, support, and sponsorship of programs that increase inclusion and equity. Winters (2014) argues management should engage in as much active listening with employees as possible. Others agree that meaningful change cannot occur without steady communication throughout an organization in all directions. It cannot be top-down or bottom-up, only. Participation must be open to all members so that they feel connected to culture shift (Jonsdottir & Fridriksdottir, 2020). Much like crafted DEI statements, interaction with employees cannot be performative. Management must listen to concerns and address them by prioritizing activities, such as listening sessions with affinity groups and events that bring different employees together to get to know each other professionally and personally (Simmons & Yawson, 2022).

Moving Beyond Communication to Accountability Measures

When management begins speaking about their DEI commitments, people will hold them accountable for the organization's efforts. Corley (2020) argues that discussions of an individual's accountability are important, but not as important as measuring and demonstrating that accountability. Leaders have the responsibility to build an inclusive work environment and must lead by example. That commitment is demonstrated when there are behaviors employees can point to and determine whether the organization succeeded. When organizations fail to meet DEI targets, leadership must acknowledge the shortcomings publicly and create a corrective plan to get back on track (Fullan, 2018).

Management must promote equality and fairness of opportunities for all its employees. Leaders must create specific measures to ensure the representation of diverse talent across units. It must also enable equality of opportunity by using fair and transparent recruiting and evaluations. The Management Center encourages organizational leaders to conduct bias checks to help determine subtleties in how they treat regularly overlooked employees, such as people of color or differently abled peopled. In posing questions about how management interacts with employees differently, bias checks help managers look for behavior patterns that prevent equal opportunities for those they supervise (Management Center, 2021).

Incorporating these regular reviews with tools applying a critical eye will build increased accountability. A director at a healthcare nonprofit realized she unintentionally treated staff differently by focusing on areas they excelled in and not involving them in other tasks. She said, "My team has different strengths that I use them to maximize our results, but by focusing only on strengths they have, I'm preventing them from professional growth and other opportunities. I didn't see it that way until I sat down and tallied how often I asked certain people to participate in different tasks at work, or not to as the case may be." Tools like bias checks give managers the opportunity to reflect on how they lead their teams by asking how and when feedback is given, who is formally and informally mentored, and how professional growth opportunities are distributed.

Supporting and Sponsorship of DEI Initiatives

Holding leadership accountable for an organization's DEI commitment and their own work toward creating equal opportunities must be done. Adujumo (2021) agrees that leadership's accountability is necessary but argues the strongest indicator of DEI change is whether management transitions from voluntary DEI work to fully funding this work. Rather than seeking volunteers for DEI committees or encouraging employees to join affinity groups advocating for change on their own time, organizations should move to funding these initiatives.

DiversityInc began naming the top 50 corporations in the United States for diversity in 2021, and one of the strongest predictors of a strong DEI culture was whether the DEI work was supported financially (DiversityInc, 2022). A communication officer for a social media company joined a volunteer-based affinity group to talk about his experience in a safe environment and plan small events and learning opportunities for those in the company. He noted, "We did great work when we did it on our own, but the impact we had was limited because we didn't have resources to draw the attention of those who weren't already aware of us. Funding made a big difference at [our company], and we've grown considerably in number and power since."

Hon and Brunner (2000) found that communication practitioners excel at talking about diversity issues and their organizations' support of DEI; however, deeper reflection on what their organizations are doing found that funding these initiatives remains a significant problem. Progress toward DEI goals requires training, consultation, technical assistance, development of materials and resources, staff time, and employee engagement. Each piece of a meaningful DEI plan requires the allocation of resources. DiversityInc research shows that the average annual amount per resource group is between $7,000 and $15,000 (Johnson, n.d.). Making sure these groups are well-resourced is not a huge investment, and it enables the work to move forward.

Stage 3: Implementation Resulting in Change

Once commitments are secured (and resources are allocated), these commitments need to implemented. Organizations face mounting pressure from stakeholders to deliver on their DEI promises. It is not acceptable to have a plan without taking actionable steps toward full implementation and integration within an organization. DEI implementation is a slow and intentional journey that needs to be flexible, inclusive, and well-resourced. Thoughtful implementation will bring lasting organizational change that can evolve over time.

DEI is both an organizational responsibility and a personal journey for staff as they are also growing and learning. As aforementioned, successful DEI implementation requires a participatory approach by leaders to engage staff at every level of the implementation process. Allowing staff to have ownership of the process and making DEI resources available and accessible encourages participatory decision making and informed humility needed for this work (Villaluz & Hechanova, 2019). It also requires "patience, self-awareness, compassion, a humble heart and genuine curiosity," according to a senior foundation leader. Implementing DEI plans starts with open dialogue, participation, and engagement. None of this can happen without trust.

Creation of Safe Spaces for Discussions

Creating safe spaces for discussions on DEI issues is essential for building trust. One nonprofit leader exclaimed, "If you don't create a safe space then it is just performative. You have to build a space where staff can come together and really talk about the hard stuff." Often staff start from different places and have different experiences with DEI issues. Staff need to feel confident they will not be exposed to discrimination, criticism, or other emotional harm as they open up about their feelings and experiences (Cox & Lancefield, 2021).

For spaces to feel safe, they need to be intentionally crafted and co-designed *by* staff, and *for* staff. There are several ways of doing this. One Oakland nonprofit foundation co-created "Meeting Agreements" that incorporate language about how to foster inclusivity, mutual respect, full participation, active listening, appreciation, and grace. The meeting agreements provide a strong framework and common ground for the DEI work and give staff something tangible they can point to when conversations get tense.

Another way to create a safe space is to practice having difficult conversations. DEI work inevitably triggers people, and we all can make mistakes and inadvertently hurt someone. Practicing how to talk through an issue or an apology are invaluable tools when undertaking this work (Bramberger & Winter, 2021). A foundation CEO commented, "The important part is how we deal with the repair. The vulnerability in practicing and learning these skills side by side builds a powerful level of trust and connection."

Determining DEI baseline skills and a common DEI vocabulary can also reinforce a safe space. Terms, such as accessibility, discrimination, and inclusion, need to be clearly defined, as do more complex terms, such as empowerment, equity, and intersectionality. When employees start from common ground, they feel more empowered to discuss difficult topics and ask questions. As one leader points out, "As time passes, historically sensitive topics become less taboo, and the conversations become a foundation from which to build on." A shared understanding and information base around DEI enable staff to feel more comfortable discussing the work.

Securing Organizational Support for Affinity Groups

While employees need to have resources available to carry out DEI work, they should not be asked to take on these projects in addition to their existing workload. Organizations are better at talking about reducing the workload of individuals working on DEI programs than they are at reducing the workload (Lirio et al., 2008). Employees from marginalized communities often find that they're asked to take on these roles to ensure community representation but receive little for their work (Kluch et al., 2022).

Organizations should use work dashboards that track all of the tasks that an employee carries out for their employer so that product- or program-specific tasks are measured as well as those that serve greater organizational purposes, such as creation, implementation, and evaluation of DEI policies (Stoll et al., 2022). Another demonstration of organizational support is offering paid time off for employees who use time to support the work of affinity groups that go beyond regular organizational work (Bombaro, 2020).

The Employee Experience Advisory Group was founded two years ago at a Bay Area foundation, where leaders encourage participation in the group but maintain its voluntary status. Demonstrating commitment to the group, the foundation offers financial support for its work and gives paid time off to compensate employees who voluntarily work for the group. The group is coordinated by three senior leaders but decisions are determined by all staff who attend. The group has an ample budget to fund proposed activities. The result has been a combination of mandatory implicit bias trainings, the creation of a DEI onboarding training manual where new staff are given links to important readings and definitions, and access to a "buddy" who can help walk them through any questions they may have, and consultant facilitated discussions about how to have difficult conversations. A senior leader in a Bay Area nonprofit felt that "staff led decision making around DEI priorities means there is more active participation and learning at all levels."

Another benefit of staff-led resource groups is that staff work at their own pace. Implementation is not linear because everyone is adjusting and moving at their own pace; however, the group will move forward with activities and organizational shifts they are ready for given the pace of their learning. Over the long term, this approach speeds up quality and timeline of the implementation process, but it must be regularly evaluated to determine the organization's progress and where additional work must be done.

Stage 4: Measurement and Evaluation

Evaluation is an integral stage of organizational change; without it, the effectiveness of change cannot be measured. As in other stages, organizations also make mistakes in their evaluation of DEI efforts. One of the most common mistakes is the use of diversity frequency counts, where DEI evaluation focuses on the counts of the individuals hired that meet diversity quotas. This approach places DEI onto the responsibility of HR and dismisses the importance of cultivating an inclusive and equitable culture that could support employees from marginalized groups to succeed and thrive. It could even be more dangerous as organizations perceive themselves as diverse and thus do not spend efforts in changing the culture to allow marginalized communities to be their authentic selves (Reynolds & Tabron, 2022).

A human resource manager at an international nonprofit commented, "It's easy to show we're diverse if we just look at our local numbers. We're in one of the world's most diverse cities and have employees representing every neighborhood. We're diverse, but that simple metric doesn't begin to examine equity or inclusion." A Chief Operating Officer whose organization is going through its own DEI implementation struggles asked, "Is HR the best to measure DEI? They focus on legal requirements and quantitative measures of recruiting, hiring, and retention." While the human resources department maintains employment records and organization policies, DEI is an organizational phenomenon that requires support beyond a single department.

Another common DEI evaluation mistake is the focus on diverse representation in the leadership but ignoring the pipeline. While diverse representation in leadership is important, merely focusing on it when evaluating DEI could result in companies taking measures that only serve representation at face value. Some organizations provide bonus and incentives to seek greater diversity in leadership yet fail to build up diversity in their talent pipeline (Korn Ferry Institute, 2021).

Toward a More Comprehensive Evaluation of Organization Change for DEI

Recognizing and accepting the mistakes made in DEI evaluation, organizations could step forward with a more comprehensive evaluation plan. A comprehensive evaluation plan should involve departments and staff throughout the organization, rather than solely being an HR task. When DEI evaluation is performed throughout the organization, the emphasis shifts from "diversity frequency counts" to measures of culture, resources, and investment. Organizations' DEI evaluation plan needs to encompass various areas of organizational behavior. The DEI Maturity Index, for instance, measures five areas: compensation, recruitment, and retention; assessment; communication and education; organizational culture; and investment and infrastructure (CUPA-HR, 2020). A comprehensive evaluation plan with different areas helps shift organizations from the face-level of "diversity" to reflect and examine their DEI efforts throughout.

DEI evaluation should be conducted at least annually and at multiple points in time. Having a set time frame helps organizations benchmark their progress and flag improvement areas; thus, organizations can revisit and reflect on their efforts and adjust plans where necessary. An account coordinator, who serves on her public relations firm's DEI taskforce and helps carry out their review of DEI progress, noted that "we've made big steps improving our DEI policies because [we] measure what people care about and take those results seriously."

DEI Evaluation Starts from DEI Planning and the "SMART+IE" Mindset

Looking at the stages covered in the chapter, it is worth noting that DEI evaluation is not the end of the organizational change process, but really another beginning, where benchmarks are noted and areas of improvement are marked. As such, evaluation outcomes become starting points for the planning stage of continuing DEI efforts. Strategic communication literature has suggested the use of "SMART" principle in planning. The acronym represents specific, measurement, audience (stakeholder) focused, realistic, and timebound (e.g., Kelleher, 2020). While strategic and deliberate, the "SMART" principle does not take into consideration marginalized and under-resourced communities. An alternative, more inclusive "SMART+IE" mindset, is thus proposed, adding inclusivity and equity to the model (Waters et al., 2021).

The "SMART+IE" mindset helps organizations consider their DEI efforts during the planning stage, thereby making it clearer to evaluate the outcomes. The "SMART+IE" mindset also calls for reflection on their DEI commitments and for asking critical questions during DEI implementation and evaluation, including "How are communities elevated?" and "Are metrics in place to assess the inclusivity and equity components?." Incorporating the "SMART+IE" mindset emphasizes the circular process of organizational change needed for DEI, calling for continuous, long-term, and proactive efforts rather than one-shot, reactive programming.

Conclusion

This chapter has emphasized how DEI integration must occur at every level of an organization and requires a proactive effort to incorporate it into every stage of the change management process. Change management acknowledges that change can occur at the ground floor of an organization or with its leadership, and corporate America and our philanthropic sector have explored different avenues to creating DEI change in their institutions. Many stumbled after developing initial statements professing commitment to DEI; some were unsure what to do next while others were fearful of being embarrassed publicly. Organizations will stumble along the way, but those mistakes must not deter them from continuing to cultivate a strong DEI culture.

Missteps that happen provide opportunities to grow from these learning experiences. Acknowledging mistakes and having internal conversations about those incidents prepare current and future leaders to become better advocates for DEI initiatives. Whether these focus on including DEI in strategic plans, developing diversity-focused communications tools and campaigns, or incorporating DEI-focused events throughout organizations and conversations at regular staff meetings, there are opportunities to implement DEI at every level of an organization to shift DEI from being an HR function to being an integrated part of the organization culture.

For organizations exploring DEI and those still figuring out how to move from meandering to progressive movement, there are some simple actions they can take to demonstrate their support and commitment to DEI. First, organizations must include DEI as part of the strategic plan and add specific SMART+IE goals for departments to show their commitment to inclusion and equity. As part of the strategic planning process, organizations must review their existing policies to determine to what extent they align with DEI goals and how policies need to be updated to reflect their aspirational DEI values. At an educational level, organizations should also create a shared glossary of DEI terms that capture common vocabulary and provide examples of how it is used within the context of their operations. The glossary could be one part of a much larger DEI resource hub that can be accessed by everyone in the organization. This hub should include the organization's DEI plan, purpose statements, and a listing of all DEI activities and resource group contacts and meeting information.

Finally, organizations must document their DEI journey. Whether just beginning the process or strong supporters of DEI, organizations must be held accountable by their employees and the communities where they operate. Documenting DEI missteps, activities, and milestones and keeping that information available in a central location for anyone interested in reviewing it is a big step toward commitment. Assessment instruments should also be kept so that they can be reviewed and updated annually to ensure lasting change in how organizations support its diverse employees and stakeholders it serves.

Discussion Questions

1 If you were managing a department with diverse employees that often worked together in cliques rather than as a full team, how would you bring everyone together to discuss issues of inclusion?
2 As a manager of a team of employees, what actions would you take to make sure all employees were being evaluated fairly and given similar opportunities to work on rewarding and challenging projects?
3 After evaluating your organization's DEI practices, you found that the organization has not lived up to their DEI statement posted on the company website. What would you do to hold management accountable for their public-facing statement?

Author Bios

Richard D. Waters (Ph.D., U of Florida, 2007) is an Associate Professor in the School of Management at the University of San Francisco. His research focuses on how organizations cultivate relationships with their stakeholders, particularly donors, and volunteers in the nonprofit sector.

Zifei Fay Chen (Ph.D., University of Miami, 2017) is an Assistant Professor in the Communication Studies Department at the University of San Francisco. Her research interests involve corporate social responsibility and advocacy, startup and entrepreneurial communication, social media and digital communication, and prosocial communication.

Lorena Gomez-Barris (MNA, U of San Francisco, 2017) has more than 25 years of experience leading teams, setting and executing organizational strategy, and driving both external and internal communications efforts in the nonprofit sector. She is currently the Director of Administration at the Kenneth Rainin Foundation where she helps to realize the strategic direction of the organization by putting into motion efficient and effective administrative systems and co-leading the Foundation's DEI initiative. Lorena is passionate about storytelling, producing short films, and leading video production workshops internationally.

References

Adejumo, V. (2021). Beyond diversity, inclusion, and belonging. *Leadership, 17*(1), 62–73. 10.1177/2F1742715020976202

Austin, J. T., & Bisel, R. S. (2022). The influence of colorblind and race-acknowledged organizational socialization messages during offer consideration. *International Journal of Business Communication, 60*(3), 892–911. 10.1177/23294 88422111

Bligh, M. C., Kohles, J. C., & Yan, Q. (2018). Leading and learning to change: The role of leadership style and mindset in error learning and organizational change. *Journal of Change Management, 18*(2), 116–141. 10.1080/14697017.2018. 1446693

Bombaro, C. (Ed.). (2020). *Diversity, equity, and inclusion in action: Planning, leadership, and programming*. American Library Association.

Bramberger, A., & Winter, K. (2021). Ways of framing safe spaces. In K. Winter & A. Bramberger (Eds.), *Re-conceptualizing safe spaces* (pp. 33–50). Bingley, UK: Emerald Publishing Limited. 10.1108/978-1-83982-250-620211006

Cooper, C. A., & Gerlach, J. D. (2019). Diversity management in action: Chief diversity officer adoption in America's cities. *State and Local Government Review, 51*(2), 113–121. 10.1177%2F0160323X19879735

Corley, T. (2020). Creating accountability for inclusive, responsive leadership. *People & Strategy, 43*(1), 28–32. Retrieved online: https://www.ohiobar.org/globalassets/ advocacy/inclusion-and-diversity/todd-corley_shrm_peoplestrategy-journal_ winter2020.pdf

Cox, G., & Lancefield, D. (2021, May 19). 5 Strategies to Infuse D&I into Your Organization. Harvard Business Review. Retrieved online: https://hbr.org/2021/ 05/5-strategies-to-infuse-di-into-your-organization

CUPA-HR. (2020, May 5). *CUPA-HR's DEI Maturity Index – A tool to improve DEI among the higher ed workforce*. https://www.cupahr.org/blog/cupahr-dei-maturity-index-a-tool-to-improve-dei-among-the-higher-ed-workforce/

DiversityInc. (2022). *Overview of the DiversityInc top 50 companies for diversity*. Retrieved online July 13, 2022: https://www.diversityinc.com/about-the-diversityinc-top-50-process/

Fullan, M. (2018). *Nuance: Why some leaders succeed and others fail*. Corwin Press.

Hon, L. C., & Brunner, B. (2000). Diversity issues and public relations. *Journal of Public Relations Research, 12*(4), 309–340. 10.1207/S1532754XJPRR1204_2

Jan, T., McGregor, J., & Hoyer, M. (2021, August 23). *Corporate America's $50 billion promise*. The Washington Post. Retrieved online: https://www. washingtonpost.com/business/interactive/2021/george-floyd-corporate-america-racial-justice/.

Jaros, S. (2010). Commitment to organizational change: A critical review. *Journal of Change Management, 10*(1), 79–108. 10.1080/14697010903549457

Johnson, C. (no date). How do you fund resource groups? DiversityInc Best Practices. Retrieved online: https://www.diversityincbestpractices.com/how-do-you-fund-resource-groups/

Johnson, E. (2021, March 29). *Top 4 reasons diversity and inclusion programs fail*. Forbes. https://www.forbes.com/sites/forbeseq/2021/03/29/top-4-reasons-diversity-and-inclusion-programs-fail/?sh=7fd7094f7c84

Jonsdottir, I. J., & Fridriksdottir, K. (2020). Active listening: Is it the forgotten dimension in managerial communication? *International Journal of Listening, 34*(3), 178–188. 10.1080/10904018.2019.1613156

Kelleher, T. (2020). *Public relations* (2nd ed.). New York, NY: Oxford University Press.

Kerber, R., Coster, H., & McLymore, A. (2020, June 10). *INSIGHT-U.S. companies vow to fight racism but face critics on diversity.* Reuters. https://www. reuters.com/article/minneapolis-police-companies/insight-u-s-companies-vow-to-fight-racism-but-face-critics-on-diversity-idUSL1N2DM2MS

Kluch, Y., Wright-Mair, R., Swim, N., & Turick, R. (2022). "It's Like Being on an Island by Yourself": Diversity, Equity, and inclusion administrators' perceptions of barriers to diversity, equity, and inclusion work in intercollegiate athletics. *Journal of Sport Management, 37*(1), 1–14. 10.1123/jsm.2021-0250

Korn Ferry Institute. (2021). *Five classic (and overlooked) DE&I mistakes: What DE&I diagnostics have taught us.* https://focus.kornferry.com/wp-content/uploads/2021/04/KornFerry_The-Five-Classic-DEI-Mistakes.pdf

Kucharska, W., & Bedford, D. A. D. (2020). Love your mistakes!—they help you adapt to change. How do knowledge, collaboration and learning cultures foster organizational intelligence. *Journal of Organizational Change Management, 33*(7), 1329–1354. 10.1108/JOCM-02-2020-0052

Kuyatt, A. (2011). Managing for innovation: Reducing the fear of failure. *Journal of Strategic Leadership, 3*(2), 31–40.

Lirio, P., Lee, M. D., Williams, M. L., Haugen, L. K., & Kossek, E. E. (2008). The inclusion challenge with reduced-load professionals: The role of the manager. *Human Resource Management, 47*(3), 443–461. 10.1002/hrm.20226

The Management Center (2021, November 28). *Identifying choice points: The "bias check".* Retrieved online July 13, 2022: https://www.managementcenter.org/resources/tools-for-identifying-choice-points-the-bias-check/

Miller, K. (2020, March 19). *5 Critical steps in the change management process.* Harvard Business School Online. https://online.hbs.edu/blog/post/change-management-process

Morris, C. (2020, November 26). *Performative allyship: What are the signs and why leaders get exposed.* Forbes. https://www.forbes.com/sites/carmenmorris/2020/11/26/performative-allyship-what-are-the-signs-and-why-leaders-get-exposed/?sh=7e55940f22ec

Pewewardy, C. (2021). Why we can't ignore the "chief" in chief diversity officer. *Multicultural Education, 28*(3/4), 28–31.

Reynolds, A. L., & Tabron, L. A. (2022). Cultivating racial diversity or reproducing whiteness?: A quantcrit analysis of school districts' early principal hiring practices. *Leadership and Policy in Schools, 21*(1), 95–111. 10.1080/15700763.2021.2022710

Rinderle, S. (2020, July 22). *Want to end racism? Training doesn't Work. So what does?* Talent Management & HR. https://www.tlnt.com/want-to-end-racism-training-doesnt-work-so-what-does/

Simmons, S. V., & Yawson, R. M. (2022). Developing leaders for disruptive change: An inclusive leadership approach. *Advances in Developing Human Resources,* 10.1177/2F15234223221114359.

Stanley, C. A., Watson, K. L., Reyes, J. M., & Varela, K. S. (2019). Organizational change and the chief diversity officer: A case study of institutionalizing a diversity plan. *Journal of Diversity in Higher Education, 12*(3), 255–265. 10.1037/dhe0000099

Stoll, H., McLaughlin-Zamora, M., & Anderson, S. E. (2022). Concrete diversity initiatives in political science: A faculty workload intervention program. *PS: Political Science & Politics, 56*(1), 137–142. 10.1017/S1049096522000877

Villaluz, V. C., & Hechanova, M. R. M. (2019). Ownership and leadership in building an innovation culture. *Leadership & Organization Development Journal, 40*(2), 138–150. 10.1108/LODJ-05-2018-0184

Waters, R. D., Chen, Z. F., & Gomez-Barris, L. (2021). Rethinking campaign management to include "SMART+IE" objectives for inclusive and equitable efforts. In D. Pompper (Ed.), *Public relations for social responsibility: Affirming DEI commitment with action.* Emerald Publishing.

Winters, M. F. (2014). From diversity to inclusion: An inclusion equation. In Ferdman, B. F., & Deane, B. R. (Eds.), *Diversity at work: The practice of inclusion* (pp. 205–228). John Wiley & Sons.

19

COLLABORATIVE AND INCLUSIVE LEADERSHIP

Co-Cultural Calls for Dominant Group Action

Robert J. Razzante[1] and Al Waqqas Al Balushi[2]
[1]*Independent Scholar;* [2]*Arizona State University*

Learning Objectives

After reading this chapter, you will:

1 Classify different ways to respond to social injustice in the workplace.
2 Practice self-reflexivity in assessing your own toolkit for responding to social injustice in the workplace.
3 Modify how you listen to calls for action from those experiencing social injustice.

Introduction

In light of recent events, many organizations across the globe have taken action to improve diversity, equity, and inclusion (DEI). However, organizational leaders often fail to consult with their employees when advancing DEI initiatives, despite employees being able to provide first accounts about the inclusion/exclusion they experience. The present study examines one such organization, Valley Ridge Clinic, multi-national healthcare organization.

In an effort to promote DEI, Valley Ridge Clinic enlisted our help in conducting a study. For this study, we surveyed 67 employees who were members of employee resource groups and diversity councils within Valley Ridge Clinic. In what follows, we offer a review of relevant literature and explicate the theories guiding our case study. We then detail our research methods, followed by sharing our findings and implications for practice. Ultimately, we hope this chapter provides insight into how organizational

DOI: 10.4324/9781003333746-22

leaders can train employees in responding to social injustice when it occurs in the workplace to promote meaningful organizational change.

Literature Review

To situate this case study, we explore three areas of literature. First, we define co-cultural theory (Orbe, 1998) and dominant group theory (Razzante & Orbe, 2018) to understand intergroup group communication in the workplace. We then share a review of current research in the area of inclusion and the workplace at the macro-, meso-, and micro-level. We conclude by offering the research questions that guide our inquiry.

Co-Cultural Theory

Co-cultural theory seeks to understand how people with a relative disadvantage—a co-cultural group member—interact with those who experience power and privilege—a dominant group member (Orbe, 1998). Co-cultural theory has its roots in a) standpoint theory (Smith, 1987), which suggests that minorities have a different understanding of the world than dominant group members, and b) muted group theory (Kramarae, 1981), which suggests that minority cultures are silenced (or muted) in several ways by the dominant culture. Co-cultural theory expands on standpoint theory and muted group theory to examine the communicative behavior of those who experience marginalization. In essence, co-cultural theory places communication as the focal point for how people communicate culture—and how culture is communicated through people.

Dominant Group Theory

Dominant group theory is an extension of co-cultural theory. Rather than understanding how people communicate from standpoints of exclusion, dominant group theory seeks to understand dominant group members communicate in standpoints of power and privilege (Razzante & Orbe, 2018). Like co-cultural theory, influential factors inform how one communicates: abilities, situational context, field of experience, perceived costs and rewards, and communication approach. A main difference, however, is that whereas co-cultural theory takes into consideration one's *preferred outcome* (assimilation into, separation from, or accommodation with the dominant culture), dominant group theory, instead, focuses on the *interactional outcome* of a dominant group member's communication. More specifically, a dominant group member's communication may have the outcome of: a) reinforcing dominant oppressive structures, b) impeding dominant oppressive structures, and/or c) dismantling dominant oppressive structures.

Reinforcing oppressive structures involves (un)conscious actions that create, maintain, and/or sustain oppressive structures (i.e., -isms, phobias, discrimination). *Impeding oppressive structures* occurs when one (un)consciously disrupts oppression at the micro-level (e.g., recognizing one's privilege, practicing self-reflexivity, seeking further education). Finally, *dismantling oppressive structures* involves the conscious action of locating and re-working oppressive policies and cultural norms that passively sustain oppression.

A key consideration for interactional outcome is the role of (un)conscious actions—that is, one may communicate consciously in one moment yet unconsciously in another. Attending to the interactional outcome of a dominant group member's communication is significant because one's intention may be different than the impact of a communicative behavior. For example, although an organizational leader may want to create an inclusive workplace for their employees, their actions may have the opposite impact leading to employees feeling more excluded and distant from work.

In previous research, scholars have used dominant group theory to *describe* people's communicative behaviors in the workplace (Razzante et al., 2018; Razzante, 2018), in dialogic spaces (Razzante, 2020), in the news (Orbe & Bratten, 2017), in intimate relationships (Tang et al., 2020), and through intersectional identities (Razzante, 2018, Razzante 2021). This case study engages co-cultural and dominant group theory in a new way—particularly in a *prescriptive* manner—to understand how dominant group members *should* promote inclusion from the perspective of co-cultural group members. In what follows, we take a deeper dive into inclusion as a topical area for study.

Inclusion

Inclusion has been studied through the lens of diversity management (Mor Barak, 2015; Sabharwal, 2014), social psychology (Abrams et al., 2004; Van Prooijen et al., 2004), and sociology (Allman, 2013). Although inclusion research in the discipline of communication studies is fully articulated (Wilhoit Larson et al., 2022), scholars have researched and promoted inclusive curricula (Parker et al., 2020), financial inclusion (Vallée, 2020), and the benefits of including diverse stakeholders' input during decision-making processes (Mitra, 2020). In this case study, we contribute to the growing area of inclusion research by aiming to understand how dominant group members can communicatively constitute inclusion through macro-, meso-, and micro-actions (Ferdman, 2017).

Macro-level practices of inclusion are ones that express lofty rhetoric of inclusion with hopes of changing an organization's culture and, subsequently, people's behavior. For example, organizational leaders might promote "inclusive excellence" (Bauman et al., 2005) with hopes of changing employees' perceptions and practices of inclusion. Additionally, macro-level manifestations of inclusion occur when organizations advocate the need for diversity "to be embedded in the symbolic and cultural fabric of the institution" (Williams, 2007, p. 12). In offering such rhetoric, organizational leaders might hope that employees assume diversity as a value of their own, which would lead to changed behavior. However, without action, these macro-level messages become what Ahmed (2012) calls, "institutional speech acts" (p. 54)—empty messages from leadership that lack substantial action. Moving to the meso-level, one can see how organizations might follow through on institutional speech acts toward creating inclusion.

Meso-level practices are spaces where inclusion can manifest through educational literature (brochures, flyers, videos, etc.), trainings and classes, or a calling for councils and sub-committees. However, one concern that arises, especially in higher education, is the need for organizational rewards for taking part in such "extracurricular" service (see Fryberg & Martinez, 2014). Without organizational recognition, diversity and inclusion efforts may take on an "additive" function to the work employees already do. As such, organizational leaders either need to change hiring practices to make diversity and inclusion inherently valued or at least reward participation in diversity and inclusion meso-level practices.

To conclude, inclusion can also manifest at the micro-level through interactions and personal change. For example, organizational members can increase awareness about anti-Black racism through perspective-taking or strong and thoughtful leadership (Opie & Roberts, 2017). Additionally, in the context of creating an inclusive campus environment for dialogue, students, faculty, and staff can listen to others' experiences as a means to cultivate empathy and self-reflexivity (Broome et al., 2019). Finally, organizational members can create inclusion by actively disrupting exclusion when it occurs. Whether actively confronting bullying (Bowes-Sperry & O'Leary-Kelly, 2005) or oppressive ideologies in discourse (Razzante & Orbe, 2018), organizational members can create an awareness for why certain communicative behaviors breed exclusion.

Considering literature in co-cultural theory, dominant group theory, and inclusion, this current case study seeks to understand how dominant group members can create an inclusive workplace—yet from the perspective of co-cultural group members. In other words, this case study seeks to identify what communicative behaviors co-cultural group members call for from dominant group members when they create an inclusive workplace. As such, the research question we have for this case study is as follows: *What communication strategies do co-cultural group members suggest for creating an inclusive environment?* Furthermore, we also ask the following question: *Of these strategies, which do co-cultural group members suggest with the most frequency?* In the following section, we outline and detail the methods of data collection and data analysis for answering this research question.

Methodology

Engaged scholarship is an umbrella term that encapsulates five faces of action research: a) applied communication research, b) collaborative learning, c) activism and social justice, d) practical theory, and e) public scholarship (Putnam & Dempsey, 2015). This study is phase one of a three-phase applied communication research study that seeks to use collective intelligence (Hogan et al., 2020) for coordinating collective action. The goal of this phase was to generate as many responses as possible to the question: "In your experience, what are key characteristics of an inclusive workplace?" Although this was the first phase of data collection, the data participants generated was worthy of analysis in its own study.

Participants

Applied communication research seeks to conduct research with the goal of gathering data that key stakeholders can use for solving complex social issues (Cissna et al., 2009; Cissna & Frey, 2009). The key stakeholders of this study were employees of a multi-national healthcare system: Valley Ridge Clinic. More specifically, we sent out on open-ended qualitative survey to 256 employees who were members of Employee Resource Groups and/or Diversity Councils.

Out of the 256 employees from the listserv, 67 responded to the qualitative survey, generating 255 responses to the question, "In your experience, what are key characteristics of an inclusive workplace?" Sample responses were: "ability to pump at work," "advocacy for needs," and "policies that encourage teamwork." In addition to providing a response, participants also had the opportunity to offer a clarification for what they meant with their response. In all, participants generated 217 clarifications to their 255 responses.

Data Analysis

Considering the nature of the data, we used qualitative content analysis (Schreier, 2012) to discover the frequency of common characteristics of inclusion. Qualitative content analysis is characterized by three features:

"qualitative content analysis reduces data, it is systematic, and it is flexible" (Schreier, 2012, p. 170). The qualitative survey already generated reduced data to the key characteristics of an inclusive workplace. For our analysis, we used dominant group theory's (Razzante & Orbe, 2018) strategies as a heuristic for coding the responses and clarifications. Finally, qualitative content analysis offered us flexibility in identifying new strategies not listed in the original dominant group theory typology. Considering both authors' coded data, we first established inter-coder reliability after two rounds of coding on our own. After the second round of coding, we reached an inter-coder reliability of 93%. In what follows, we offer the findings from our analysis.

Findings

Here we divide our findings into two primary sections. First, we speak to the role of micro-level inclusion as demonstrated by dominant group members. We share examples and key takeaways when considering how micro-level inclusion contributes to workplace inclusion. We then speak to the shortage of Valley Ridge Clinic employees' calls for dominant group members to sacrifice themselves in order to promote workplace inclusion—meaning that inclusion does not have to lead to dominant group members' demise. These findings provide great insight into how organizational leaders can train employees in responding to social injustice when it occurs in the workplace.

Micro-Level Inclusion

When it comes to workplace inclusion, micro-level actions matter. According to the participants, the most frequently called for characteristics of inclusion tend to align with the following dominant group strategies: microaffirmations, awareness of relationality, and affirming co-cultural concerns. Microaffirmation was the most frequently called for communication strategy, where 27% of participants' responses were coded as such. Affirming co-cultural concerns was the second most frequent strategy, with 25% of coded responses. Finally, awareness of relationality was the fourth most frequent communication strategy, with 16% of coded responses. In total, these micro-level dominant group communication strategies constituted 37% of the total responses in this case study. Here we elaborate on each micro-level interaction and share their significance.

According to Razzante and Orbe (2018), microaffirmations are defined as everyday exchanges that feature affirming messages to others because of their disadvantaged co-cultural identities. Examples of microaffirmations from participants' comments were: "reaching out to a struggling colleague," "saying hello in your language," and "acknowledging one's presence." Microaffirmations matter because it materially relates to a workplace climate that promotes one's psychological wellbeing. Although the benefits of microaffirmations are great, dominant group members should take some caution prior to sharing microaffirmations without self-reflexivity. At their core, microaggressions and microaffirmations are ambiguous in nature (Jones, 2016). As such, people need to consider the situational context and their relationship with interlocutors before acting. For example, a dominant group member may wish to share a microaffirmation by placing their hand on the shoulder of a co-cultural group member experiencing a hard time. Yet, at the same time, this may be taken up as a patronizing gesture. One way to alleviate the ambiguity of microaffirmations is to ask people how they like to be affirmed and to act accordingly (Razzante et al., 2018).

An additional common micro-level dominant group strategy is awareness of relationality. We define awareness of relationality as the attention to our interrelatedness as human beings in a socially constructed web of power that creates material consequences. Participant responses that we coded as awareness of relationality include: "[a] leader connecting me to someone with similar interests," and "every hand is needed to make this [inclusion] work." Awareness of relationality is significant because it establishes an assumption that people are bound together within the same system that allows privilege—oppression to exist. Furthermore, it takes both dominant group members and co-cultural group members to collaboratively deconstruct and reconstruct norms of communicating about differences.

Finally, affirming co-cultural concerns is defined as "acknowledging the legitimacy and magnitude of co-cultural issues and the realities of societal oppression" (Razzante & Orbe, 2018, p. 363). An example of such affirmations from the responses of this case study was, "willingness to give paid time off." More specifically, the participant explained that fellow Jewish caregivers, for example, should be given paid time off for their holidays. Another example is, "embrace differences instead of trying to make everybody the same." This is significant because affirming one's concerns demonstrates mindful listening that shows an investment in co-cultural group members and their livelihood.

As noted in this finding, micro-level inclusion resonated with co-cultural participants the most. However, other participants also called for more meso- and macro-level inclusion strategies. While micro-level inclusion might be what is most called for in frequency, that does not mean that it is the *most important*. Rather, it means that micro-level inclusion is what is on the forefront of people's minds. This is important because interpersonal communication is a heavily experiential form of quotidian communication and should not be overlooked when creating an inclusive workplace.

Sacrificing Self?

A common dominant group member fear regarding inclusion is the idea that inclusion promotes the exclusion of dominant group members (Greer, 2017). The idea of promoting inclusion at the expense of one's own detriment is a fear supported by many dominant group members—especially white cis-men (Kimmel, 2017). However, according to our analysis of co-cultural group members' prescriptive calls for inclusion, only 1.96% of ideas spoke to inclusion that requires personal cost.

Within the framework of dominant group theory, there exists one non-assertive approach to dismantling oppressive structures: sacrificing self. According to Razzante and Orbe (2018), sacrificing self is defined as, "Efforts to challenge institutionalized oppression that come with significant personal cost" (p. 363). They later describe an action of self-sacrifice with the following, "Dominant group members who sacrifice themselves open themselves up to all kinds of costs (e.g., arrest, financial loss, social isolation, loss of employment) in order to demand change of oppressive societal structures" (p. 368). In the context of this case study, co-cultural group members very rarely called for dominant group members to sacrifice their personal success (~1.96% of ideas).

This finding is significant because it suggests that co-cultural group members are not demanding that dominant group members sacrifice themselves for the inclusion of marginalized groups. Although there are co-cultural calls that align with sacrificing self, it is not the majority of co-cultural group members. Rather than significant personal risk—such as financial loss, arrest, social isolation, and loss of employment—the personal risk at stake pertains to a challenged worldview—one that speaks to relationality over individualism.

People often experience cognitive dissonance when their worldview is challenged. As such, when pursuing research from the vantage point of promoting inclusion from a standpoint of power and privilege, researchers should examine the successes and failures dominant group members face when working through internal cognitive dissonance. Furthermore, research should seek to understand how narratives of ego-defensiveness circulate—along with counter-narratives that can promote working through cognitive dissonance toward committing to inclusion. In the context of existing research, inclusion can occur at the micro-, meso-, and macro-levels (Ferdman, 2017). When pursuing this line of research, scholars should seek to understand the interplay between inclusion and exclusion (Armstrong et al., 2011) as it occurs at the interpersonal level, organizational level, and cultural/political level. In other words, a research program rooted in inclusion should seek to cover various contexts—personal ego and cognitive dissonance, common circulated narratives, and policy to name a few.

Practical Applications

In this employee-driven case study, we asked participants the question, "In your experience, what are key characteristics of an inclusive workplace?." From this question, we generated data that offered insight into how dominant group members can and should use their standpoints of power and privilege to co-create inclusion. From our analysis, we identified the following strategies as the most called for by co-cultural employees: microaffirmations, awareness of relationality, and affirming co-cultural concerns. We conclude our chapter by returning to the original purpose for this case study—to identify key characteristics of an inclusive workplace for a specific organization. As such, we offer three practical implications.

First, at the meso-level, organizational leaders should take advantage of employee-driven research—especially when the results of the research directly impact employees. Oftentimes, organizations invite external consultants in to present on a topic, facilitate a workshop, or lead a BIG data organizational climate survey (i.e., meso-level, one-off injections of inclusion). External consultants are helpful for organizations that need outside help. However, organizational leaders should prioritize the infrastructure that allows for a climate where the organization's own employees can create organization-specific action plans that come from employees, for employees. For example, this study is part of a larger case study that Valley Ridge Clinic created to learn from their employees to drive organizational action to promote inclusion—all with Valley Ridge Clinic employees in mind as the beneficiaries.

Second, at the micro-level, dominant group members who wish to promote inclusion should first become reflexive beings who consciously choose their actions—and willingly accept the consequences of those actions. In order for dominant group members to change their habituated practices of being a dominant group member, they first need to develop an orientation to the world rooted in unlearning (Razzante, 2021). Unlearning occurs when someone empties their minds of old frameworks, changes old, habituated responses, and seeks to learn new frameworks and new habits. The unlearning process moves dominant group members to a state of learning and away from a state of defensiveness. The unlearning process can be challenging as, often, dominant group members have never been forced to do so. Yet, this foundational work is needed to unlearn actions that lead to reinforcing oppressive structures, as well as learning new actions that promote inclusion at the micro-, meso-, and macro-levels.

Although this may be a challenging task, there are several micro-level practices dominant group members can practice: a) develop an awareness of relationality, b) listen to co-cultural group members' concerns, and c) act in collaboration with others. As Dr. Brenda J. Allen (2017) noted, actions are response-able, yet not all actions are responsible. By developing an awareness of relationality, listening to co-cultural group members' concerns, and acting in collaboration with others promotes responsibility. Each of these three recommendations is rooted in being mindful of oneself and how their communication impacts others. This endeavor may have more success when the organizational culture promotes self-reflexivity in general and when people have peer accountability in place. For example, to unlearn habits on one's own is challenging, especially when accountability is low. However, creating a group-based (un)learning and development plan can be an effective strategy for creating accountability.

Finally, at the macro-level, researchers and organizational leaders promoting social justice need to get clear on what specifically their initiatives address. For example, rather than grouping DEI work together, scholars and practitioners would benefit from specificity on where DEI overlap yet also diverge. Such clarity can promote focused strategic planning and research without needing to account for all challenges faced from DEI research. A helpful heuristic is to conceptualize the three as interlocked facets of promoting social justice. Yet, one should take precedent in a given study or initiative with the other two being complimentary pieces. This framing and clarity can help in advancing DEI work as a complex social issue that requires time, space, and resources needed to do quality work.

Conclusion

Creating an inclusive workplace is challenging, especially when the concerns and input of marginalized employees are not considered. In this case study, Valley Ridge Clinic leaders sought input from their employees for how best to create an inclusive workplace. The findings suggested dominant group leaders and colleagues consider macro-, meso-, and micro-level communication practices for creating inclusion. Although micro-level communication cannot immediately change oppressive structures, they were most frequently called for by co-cultural employees. This finding suggests that micro-level actions (i.e., affirmations, recognizing concerns, and practicing self-reflexivity) can go a long way to create a sense of inclusion and should not be downplayed when compared to meso- and macro-level communicative actions. This finding also suggests that every member of an organization has the responsibility for using communication as a means for creating inclusion in daily interactions.

Discussion Questions

1 Describe a moment when you acted in response to a social injustice in the workplace? What did you do? What did you not do? And what was the consequence of your response?
2 Identify a dominant group member (i.e., in terms of race, class, gender, sex, ability, education level, etc.) who frequently responds to social injustice. What actions do they take? How might you model your own behavior based on theirs?
3 As a current or future leader, what actions can you take to facilitate collaborative learning and conflict among your colleagues?

Author Bios

Robert J. Razzante (Ph.D., Arizona State University) is an independent scholar and global learning and development professional. He works with communities and organizations to lead learning and research opportunities that promote impactful change in the areas of DEI, dialogue and deliberation, and training and development.

Al Waqqas Al Balushi (undergraduate student, Arizona State University) is a senior communication student pursuing research regarding queer POC identity and Middle Eastern tribal identity through autoethnography.

References

Abrams, D., Hogg, M. A., & Marques, J. M. (2004). A social psychological framework for understanding social inclusion and exclusion. In D. Abrams, M. Hogg, & J. Marques (Eds.), *Social psychology of inclusion and exclusion* (pp. 1–24). New York, NY: Taylor & Francis.

Ahmed, S. (2012). *On being included: Racism and diversity in institutional life.* Durham, NC: Duke University Press.

Allen, B. J. (2017). Keynote presentation at the 2017 Aspen Engaged Conference. Aspen, CO.

Allman, D. (2013). The sociology of social inclusion. *SAGE Open, 3*(1), 215824401247195. 10.1177/2158244012471957

Armstrong, D., Armstrong, A. C., & Spandagou, I. (2011). Inclusion: By choice or by chance? *International Journal of Inclusive Education, 15*(1), 29–39. doi: 10.1080/13603116.2010.496192

Bauman, G. L., Bustillos, L. T., Bensimon, E. M., Brown, C., & Bartee, R. D. (2005). Achieving equitable educational outcomes with all students: The institution's roles and responsibilities. *Association of American Colleges and Universities.* Retrieved from https://www.stetson.edu/other/alana-iacaucus/media/04%20%20Georgia%20Baumann,%20Equitable%20Educ%20Outcomes.pdf

Bowes-Sperry, L., & O'Leary-Kelly, A. M. (2005). To act or not to act: The dilemma faced by sexual harassment observers. *Academy of Management Review, 30*(2), 288–306. doi:10.5465/AMR.2005.16387886

Broome, B., Derk, I., Razzante, R., Steiner, E., Taylor, J., & Zamora, A. (2019). Building an inclusive climate for intercultural dialogue: A participant-generated framework. *Negotiation and Conflict Management Research, 12*(3), 234–255. doi:10.1111/ncmr.1215

Cissna, K. N., Eadie, W. F., & Hickson III, M. (2009). The development of applied communication research. In L. R. Frey & K. N. Cissna (Eds.), *Routledge handbook of applied communication research* (pp. 3–25). New York, NY: Routledge.

Cissna, K., & Frey, L. (2009). Introduction. In L. Frey & K. Cissna (Eds.), *Routledge handbook of applied communication research* (pp. xxix–xl). New York, NY: Routledge.

Ferdman, B. M. (2017). Paradoxes of inclusion: Understanding and managing the tensions of diversity and multiculturalism. *Journal of Applied Behavioral Science, 53*(2), 235–263. doi:10.1177/0021886317702608

Fryberg, S., & Martínez, E. (2014). *The truly diverse faculty: New dialogues in American higher education.* New York, NY: Springer.

Greer, S. (2017). *No campus for white men: The transformation of higher education into hateful indoctrination.* Chicago, IL: WND Books.

Hogan, M., Harney, O., Moroney, M., Hanlon, M., Khoo, S. M., Hall, T., ... & Broome, B. (2020). A group dynamics framework for 21st century collective intelligence facilitators. *Systems Research and Behavioral Science, 38,* 572–576. 10.1002/sres.2688

Jones, T. (2016). Refining "microaggression": A linguistic perspective. *Language Jones Blog.* https://www.languagejones.com/blog-1/2016/9/8/oi6379payz9mb4diadulndc244gq1s

Kimmel, M. (2017). *Angry white men: American masculinity at the end of an era.* Hachette, UK: Bold Type Books.

Kramarae, C. (1981). *Women and men speaking.* Rowley, MA: Newbury House.

Mitra, R. (2020). Organizing for sustainability: Including and engaging diverse stakeholders. In M. Doerfel & J. Gibbs (Eds.), *Organizing inclusion: Moving diversity from demographics to communication processes* (pp. 177–196). New York, NY: Routledge.

Mor Barak, M. E. (2015). Inclusion is the key to diversity management, but what is inclusion?. *Human Service Organizations: Management, Leadership & Governance, 39*(2), 83–88.

Opie, T., & Roberts, L. M. (2017). Do Black lives really matter in the workplace? Restorative justice as a means to reclaim humanity. *Equality, Diversity and Inclusion: An International Journal, 36*(8), 707–719. doi:10.1108/EDI-07-2017-0149

Orbe, M. P. (1998). *Constructing co-cultural theory: An explication of culture, power, and communication.* Sage Publications.

Orbe, M. P., & Batten, C. J. (2017). Diverse dominant group responses to contemporary co-cultural concerns: US intergroup dynamics in the Trump era. *Journal of Contemporary Rhetoric, 7*(1), 19–33. ISSN 2161-539X (online)

Parker, P., Holland, D., Dennison, J., Smith, S., & Jackson, M. (2020). Moving beyond inclusion: Lessons from the graduate certificate in participatory research at the University of North Carolina at Chapel Hill. In M. Doerfel & J. Gibbs (Eds.), *Organizing inclusion: Moving diversity from demographics to communication processes* (pp. 152–176). New York, NY: Routledge.

Putnam, L. L., & Dempsey, S. E. (2015). The five faces of engaged scholarship: Implications for feminist research. *Women & Language, 38*(1), 11–22.

Razzante, R. (2018). Intersectional agencies: Navigating predominantly White institutions as an administrator of color. *Journal of International and Intercultural Communication, 11*(4), 339–357. DOI: 10.1080/17513057.

Razzante, R. (2020). The fragility is real: Engaging white students' whiteness through dominant group theory. *Whiteness and Education, 5*(1), 17–36. DOI: 10.1080/23793406.2019.1682466.

Razzante, R. (2021). Challenging the hegemonic police within: A life-long process of unlearning. *Departures in Critical Qualitative Research, 10*(4), 54–76. DOI: 10.1525/dcqr.2021.10.4.54.

Razzante, R., Boylorn, R., Orbe, M. (2021). Embracing intersectionality in co-cultural and dominant group theorizing: Implications for theory, research, and pedagogy. *Communication Theory, 31*(2), 228–249. DOI: 10.1093/ct/qtab002

Razzante, R., & Orbe, M. (2018). Two sides of the same coin: Conceptualizing dominant group theory in the context of co-cultural theory. *Communication Theory, 28*(3), 354–375. doi:10.1093/ct/qtx008.

Razzante, R., Tracy, S. J., Orbe, M. (2018). How dominant group members can transform workplace bullying. In R. West & C. Beck (Eds.), *The Routledge handbook of communication and bullying* (pp. 46–56). New York, NY: Routledge.

Sabharwal, M. (2014). Is diversity management sufficient? Organizational inclusion to further performance. *Public Personnel Management, 43*(2), 197–217.

Schreier, M. (2012). *Qualitative content analysis in practice.* Thousand Oaks, CA: Sage publications.

Smith, D. E. (1987). *The everyday world as problematic: A feminist sociology of knowledge.* Boston, MA: Northeastern University Press.

Tang, L., Meadows, C., & Li, H. (2020). How gay men's wives in China practice co-cultural communication: Culture, identity, and sensemaking. *Journal of International and Intercultural Communication, 13*(1), 13–31.

Vallée, O. (2020). Toward financial inclusion: Pitfalls in illustrating and discussion financial inclusion. In M. Doerfel & J. Gibbs (Eds.), *Organizing inclusion: Moving diversity from demographics to communication processes* (pp. 197–214). New York, NY: Routledge.

Van Prooijen, J. W., Van den Bos, K., & Wilke, H. A. (2004). Group belongingness and procedural justice: Social inclusion and exclusion by peers affects the psychology of voice. *Journal of Personality and Social Psychology, 87*(1), 66–79. doi: 10.1037/0022-3514.87.1.66

Wilhoit Larson, E., Linabary, J. R., & Long, Z. (2022). Communicating inclusion: A review and research agenda on inclusion research in organizational communication. *Annals of the International Communication Association, 46*(2), 63–90. doi: 10.1080/23808985.2022.2069045

Williams, D. A. (2007). Achieving inclusive excellence: Strategies for creating real and sustainable change in quality and diversity. *About Campus, 12*(1), 8–14. doi: 10.1002/abc.198

20

BLACK WOMEN RELIGIOUS LEADERS DIVERSIFYING MENTAL HEALTH TRAINING

Tianna L. Cobb
Johns Hopkins University

Learning Objectives

After reading this chapter, you will:

1 Understand how mental health is essential to diversity, equity, and inclusion.
2 Identify educational barriers to inclusive leadership regarding mental health and illness and strategies for overcoming them.
3 Apply inclusive mental health and illness leadership strategies to various organizations and situations.

Introduction

"The daughter was holding a knife, almost ready to harm her family ... I walked into the kitchen to intervene. I told the daughter, 'Okay, I'm here. What's going on?' She was screaming and hollering ... I told her we had to do something different. I just kind of talked her down. It took a while, and I had all kinds of things going through my head, like, what do I say? How do I act? I was scared myself. She had this knife, and I just didn't know what to say to a person like this. That really stuck with me. It still does." (Reverend Delta, research participant)

It was a late evening when Reverend Delta received a call of panic from one of her congregational members. Their daughter was having a mental episode, and as a Black family, they were unsure who to trust other than their reverend. Black families have traditionally reached out to their church

DOI: 10.4324/9781003333746-23

leaders in times of need (Blank et al., 2002; Cooper & Mitra, 2018; King, 2009; Porter, 2018). Reverend Delta rushed over to intervene. Once she reached their front door, Reverend Delta heard screaming and yelling. The daughter's family tried to calm her down as the daughter had a knife and appeared ready to harm her family. Reverend Delta came over to talk to the daughter and eventually talked the daughter down from harming anyone. As a Black woman, Revered Delta served as a culturally trusted leader for the family. Still, Reverend Delta was unsure how to respond to such a crisis. She ultimately used her best judgment. However, had Reverend Delta received more extensive training in addressing mental health concerns through seminary school, she would have been better equipped to handle this mental health crisis. Though this example has a favorable ending, it also serves as a cautionary tale for Black women leaders in the church who are unequipped to handle situations of distress. As such, this case study focuses on Black women leaders' educational preparedness to address mental health disparities affecting their community in religious organizations.

Mental health disparities heavily impact Black communities. Compared to white communities, Black communities are less likely to be offered evidence-based medication or psychotherapy, more frequently misdiagnosed with a mental illness, and less likely to be included in mental health research (American Psychiatric Association, 2017). Research also shows that Black communities seek professional counseling and therapy at significantly lower rates than white communities due to healthcare barriers and social determinants (American Psychiatric Association, 2017). Many community members are left to deal with mental issues without professional help and often through unhealthy behaviors, suppression, or more informal forms of assistance (Jackson et al., 2010). As a result, Black communities often seek guidance from trusted sources within the community. One of the most trusted leadership positions within Black communities is the clergy of Black churches.

Black churches have historically served as a safe place for Black community members, especially during times of emotional turmoil (Blank et al., 2002; Cooper & Mitra, 2018; King, 2009; Porter, 2018). More specifically, Black churches have operated as public health organizations influencing the health behaviors of their congregation. While public health organizations are typically viewed as medical institutions, Zoller (2010) argues [other] organizations that influence political, social, and economic power and access should also be considered public health organizations. Thus, Black churches can also play an influential role, as public health organizations, in improving health concerns and eliminating mental health and illness inequities (Hays, 2015; King, 2009).

The Black Church and Mental Health

The leaders of Black churches play a prominent role in influencing mental health perceptions and informing decision making. Unfortunately, Black churches have historically further stigmatized mental health and illness in Black communities. Porter (2018) found that pastors of Black churches often reinforce silence as a response to mental health concerns. For instance, a participant in Cooper and Mitra's (2018) study shared they sought the support of their church pastor after being sexually abused, and the pastor advised them to remain silent regarding the traumatic event and to pray about it. Researchers have documented numerous amounts of such incidents as traditional practices in Black churches are not inclusive of members who voice mental health and illness concerns (Avent et al., 2015; Porter, 2018; Samuel, 2019). While the implications of studies often allude to inclusivity, mental health in organizations is rarely analyzed from the perspective of diversity, equity, and inclusion (DEI).

Addressing issues of DEI has been a growing practice within organizations as studies have largely assessed ways of improving DEI. Specific topics of concern include addressing issues of discrimination and prejudice in efforts to develop more equitable organizations (Austin & Bisel, 2022; Orbe et al., 2022; Parker, 2005, 2019). Similarly, mental health and illness have been a growing topic of concern in organizational research and practice. Researchers have assessed mental health in organizational settings, such as the impact of a profession, or organizational climate, on employee mental well-being (Bronkhorst et al., 2015; Stuijfzand et al., 2020). Other studies have examined organizational practices to promote employee mental well-being (Gray et al., 2019; Samuel, 2019). Both organizational DEI and mental health research have continued to build a robust research line.

Research intersecting the areas of DEI and mental health has mostly analyzed the effects of inadequate organizational DEI practices on workers' and/or members' mental health (Bronkhorst et al., 2015; Stuijfzand et al., 2020). Consequently, mental health and illness have been researched less extensively from a DEI lens. Organizational inclusivity also expands to organizational preparedness in addressing the vast amount of mental health issues and illnesses. This area of research has primarily been investigated in the fields of public health and health disparities, where scholars have highlighted the structural barriers in mental health and illness healthcare and ways of overcoming them (Beckley, 2021; Cobb, 2022; Jensen, 2020; Washington, 2006). As the idea of public health organizations begins to be inclusive of non-medical institutions, it is imperative to expand the intersection of DEI and mental health and illness work to non-medical institutions to promote mental health equity in all influential organizations, including Black churches.

Black Women Leaders of Mental Health within Black Churches

As mentioned, Black churches have historically reinforced mental health stigma and unhealthy coping behaviors, such as "just pray about it" or avoidance (Cooper & Mitra, 2018; Porter, 2018). Fortunately, evidence shows that Black women's religious leaders have shifted this practice (Cobb, 2021). Black women have not traditionally been appointed to leadership positions within Black churches, but they have begun to break the "glass ceiling" and obtain senior-level positions such as the pastor/ minister (Hardy, 2012; Parker-McCullough, 2020). This shift in leadership can be monumental for Black churches as Black women's identity has heightened their experience navigating various challenges and their ability to relate to multiple audiences (Eagly & Chin, 2010). Furthermore, research supports that Black women possess essential leadership traits, such as a collaborative and proactive style, to increase organizational inclusion (Parker, 2001, 2019). Black women's combination of experiences navigating a multitude of challenging situations and inclusive leadership traits can lead them to embody a progressive form of leadership needed to destigmatize perceptions of mental health within Black churches.

Similar to Reverend Delta's case, Pastor Danielle, A Black woman who serves as an Associate Pastor of a church, had various experiences with congregants seeking mental health counseling from her for various issues. Pastor Danielle became proactive in normalizing mental healthcare within her church by partnering with local organizations to offer professional counseling for her congregation members. Pastor Danielle is also intentional with her language use and actively connects her congregants to mental health resources outside the church. By using phrases such as "mental health," "medication," and "counseling," Pastor Danielle is working toward normalizing mental health within her church through her messages.

Unfortunately, Pastor Danielle learned to be overt in her communication on mental health and illness almost exclusively from her personal experience as a religious leader. Pastor Danielle felt she needed a separate degree specializing in mental healthcare to ensure she possessed the right tools and knowledge to assist her church and community members. As shown in Reverend Delta's and Pastor Danielle's case, Black women can draw from their experiences and use their best judgment to assist others. Yet, religious educational programs can improve the preparation of Black women religious leaders to address mental health and illness concerns adequately.

Black church leaders are often uneducated about handling mental health and illness concerns (Porter, 2018). Evidence supports that religious leaders may not adequately have the knowledge necessary to assist with mental health and illness concerns and are unaware of when to refer congregants to mental health professionals (Avent et al., 2015; Porter, 2018). It is further supported that religious organizations need additional mental health training as postsecondary and clinical mental health training increases clergy's mental health competency significantly compared to clergy who do not possess specialized training (Vermaas et al., 2017). Implementing extended mental health training in religious programs will proactively prepare Black women religious leaders to address mental health and illness concerns as they are often the first point of contact for their congregants. A crucial step to this addition in religious educational programs is first to understand the current role that religious educational programs play in preparing Black women religious leaders to address mental health and illness concerns, leading to the following research question: *In what ways are Black women religious leaders (un)prepared/(ill-)equipped to address mental health concerns in their communities?*

Interviewing Black Women Church Leaders

In response to the research question, 20 interviews were conducted with Black women religious leaders via the video conference program, Zoom. Question topics included inquiries about the participants' educational background and how their education affected their ability to respond to their congregants' mental health and illness concerns. Once the interviews were complete, each recording was transcribed and edited for accuracy. The data were then compared to identify themes relevant to the research question. These themes are shared below with each participant referenced throughout the paper by a pseudonym (i.e., false name) to maintain confidentiality.

It is important to note that all the participants received some formal higher education: 5% of the leaders received an associate's degree, 70% received a master's degree, and 25% received a Ph.D. All but two religious leaders were pastors/ministers of their church. Out of all the participants, 18 attended a seminary/theological or divinity program. Twelve participants attended seminary/theology school. Five participants attended a Master of Divinity program only. Four participants obtained additional degrees specializing in mental health and illness training (e.g., psychology). One participant did not have any religious educational background. The following paragraphs will explain the two themes that emerged from the findings to assess the participant's educational preparedness in addressing mental health and illness concerns.

Findings

Findings reveal that Black women religious leaders' educational preparedness to respond to mental health and illness concerns largely depends on specialized training outside of their specialized religious training.

Seminary/Theological and Divinity Programs Provided Minimal Mental Health Education

As mentioned, 18 participants received formal religious education from a seminary, theological, or divinity program. Each participant shared that the religious-specific programs provided a range of mental health and illness education. The educational preparedness provided ranged from none, to minimal side conversations in specific courses, to required psychology 101 courses.

No Mental Health Training

Participants whose only religious educational background was a Master of Divinity program received the least preparation. For example, Evangelist Vickie, a pastor of a northeastern church, shared her experience while obtaining her Master of Divinity,

> It came up, but I didn't have a class on it … If there was anything said, it was probably something that came up in class conversation amongst students, but I don't remember there being any formal in classes or from professors.

The extent of Evangelist Vickie's educational background on mental health and illness was conversations between herself and her classmates. Ultimately, she did not receive any training to address mental health and illness concerns. Instead, Evangelist Vickie learned to adopt her own practices in responding to congregants' mental health concerns through experience. She shared:

> When you are perceived as a strong person or a leader or someone people can come to, people always come to you, right? And so I spent many years being that counselor or having people come to me and me hearing them. And now I've adapted or adopted a new thing. And my thing is, you need to get counseling. So I refer people out. I'm not equipped to handle it.

In Evangelist Vickie's first few years as a religious leader, she over-extended herself. She had to identify changes to implement so she would not extend past her limitations as a religious leader.

Minimal Mental Health Training

While three of the five participants who only attended a Master of Divinity program said they did not receive any training, two other participants discussed minimal training. Pastor Danielle alluded to taking a basic psychology 101 course and enrolling in Clinical Pastoral Education (CPE) as the extent of her mental health training. She also expressed how she needed a separate degree for more education. She shared, "I probably needed to go ahead and get a separate degree. But part of [my] Master of Divinity involves pastoral work. So, part of getting yourself prepared is that you might have a year of very basic psychology." While some programs did not provide any training, other programs required basic courses to further understand the mind and behavior. Yet, those courses did not specifically cover ways to address mental health and illness concerns.

Another participant actively chose to supplement her Master of Divinity coursework with specialized mental health and illness courses to ensure her preparation to assist congregants. Minister Rae, a program coordinator for a collegial ministry foundation, expressed:

> Because I knew that I was interested in pastoral care and practical theology, I took additional courses that fortified those things because I knew I was going into what I'm doing now. So, I needed the resources and the information to have these types of conversations with people like, 'so I'm a Christian, but I don't think I should be going to therapy. What should I be doing?' And I'm like, you need to be going to therapy.

Minister Rae understood that as a minister, she would encounter conversations and congregant concerns around mental health and illness. She also knew she would not be adequately prepared to respond to such concerns solely with her Master of Divinity. Therefore, she was proactive in enrolling in those specialized mental health and illness courses to ensure she would be prepared to handle such instances.

The participants who attended a seminary/theological school received more mental health and illness training than those who only attended a Master of Divinity program. Nearly all participants had discussions in CPE regarding mental health and illness. However, findings still indicate that the extent of mental health and illness training depended on the school. Some schools only provided minimal education. While CPE was often mentioned, the program still did not guarantee mental health and illness education specifically. Pastor Pauletta, one of the founding co-lead pastors of a northeastern nondenominational church, shared how her program focused more on physical health, "I did a Clinical Pastoral Education placement at a hospital, so I did 400 hours of CPE as a pastoral intern ... but [mental health] certainly wasn't a focus at all anywhere. It was just like you shouldn't call folks crazy." In Pastor Pauletta's CPE program, she received guidance regarding ways not to address people experiencing mental health issues or illnesses. Still, the education was very surface level.

Extensive Mental Health Training

On the other hand, other seminary/theological schools provided more extensive training. Rev. Dr. Haddie Mae was required to take counseling in mental health courses in addition to CPE. Rev. Dr. Haddie Mae shared:

> In seminary, we had to take a counseling track. Our counseling track was new because they had just developed a counseling program. And so, before the counseling program was developed, that wasn't a part of your track. But as M. Div. students, I think we had to take about three or four mental health or pastoral counseling which was in counseling mental health classes. Those were some of my favorite classes.

Rev. Dr. Haddie Mae's program included multiple courses focused on responding to mental health and illness concerns as a pastor. She shared that these additional courses allowed her to develop skills in handling mental health concerns and led her to lead various religious youth and pastoral organizations to help others work through personal mental health concerns.

While some seminary/theological schools focused on the participant's preparation to address the mental health of others, other schools focused on providing the participants with tools to take care of their own mental health. Pastor Christine, a pastor of a midwestern church, stated:

> We were always reminded that pastoral care is not the same as clinical care for mental health care. You can provide spiritual care, but it is your job to refer to someone trained in mental health. We had lots of conversations about our own mental health care. My seminary had a fund where we could access free therapy and spiritual direction for like two sessions.

Certain seminary/theological programs focused on the mental health of the pastors themselves to ensure they protected their own well-being and understood their limits to care for congregants' mental health as pastors. Still, Pastor Christine's program did not specifically prepare her to respond to congregants' mental health and illness concerns.

Overall, the participants who went to seminary/theological schools or Master of Divinity programs received a spectrum of mental health and illness education. Those who only attended a Master of Divinity program were only trained in minimal psychology, if they were trained at all. At a minimum, participants who went to seminary/theological schools received some education through informal conversations, and others were required to enroll in various mental health courses. Ultimately, most participants alluded to a lack of educational preparation and desired more specialized training to better prepare them for handling mental health and illness concerns. This is consistent with Porter's (2018) findings that Black pastors are ill-equipped to address mental health and illness concerns.

A Specialized Mental Health Program Provided the Most Education

Five participants obtained specialized mental health and illness training in addition to their religious education. Three participants were licensed clinical social workers, the fourth was a licensed clinical psychologist, and the fifth received industry-specific training. It is important to note that the four participants who were trained as social workers and a psychologist received their specialized training prior to becoming religious leaders.

Specialized degrees, such as clinical psychology and social work, provided certain participants with extensive mental health and illness knowledge. Minister LaKeisha, an associate minister for a northeastern church, holds a master's in social work, a Master of Divinity, and is the owner of a business that provides counseling and communicative assistance on healing. Her educational route allowed her to focus specifically on mental health. Another participant, First Lady Sharlene of a southern church, is a school psychologist in an urban setting. Her educational background and work experiences have allowed her to understand mental health more thoroughly to assist her church members.

Another participant, Rev. Dr. Grace, who was previously a pastor of a southern church and currently runs a mentorship program for clergy, is also a clinical social worker by training. Having this formal training allowed her to merge the scientific with the spiritual. Rev. Dr. Grace stated:

I have an MSW [Master of Social Work]. So, I'm a clinical social worker by training licensed by the state. And I brought my clinical skills to the context of ministry and have worked on integrating spiritual health with mental health. Also, to help mental health shape ministry so that there is an intersection and interdependence of the two when we think about wholeness.

As noted above, some of the participants received their specialized training before becoming religious leaders. The preceding training allowed these participants to address mental health and illness more holistically as they had a different perspective entering their religious programs. Looking back at Rev. Dr. Grace, she shared:

I worked in a psychiatric setting … and created a community space for the mentally ill to feel like they could survive in a community and not live in a mental institution. I witnessed the internal struggles the mental health patients had with religion. Such as, Jesus or the Devil told me to do this. Understanding the protective resources that faith, religion, and spirituality can offer led me to pursue ministry.

Rev. Dr. Grace experiences in the community and clinical settings ultimately led her to explore religiosity as a form of assistance for her community. Her combination of clinical and religious knowledge allowed her to approach mental health and illness from an intersectional and inclusive perspective. She simultaneously understood the influence of religion and the importance of more tangible mental health and illness resources.

While the participants discussed in the previous paragraphs received specialized training in an educational setting, the fourth participant received more extensive training due to the industry her ministry is located. Rev. Dr. Amy, a military Chaplain, said:

I will say in pastoral care in theology, I did have a little introduction, but it wasn't extensive. When I got that to the military, we talked a lot more about it. And specifically, PTSD, moral injury, just general depression, and I guess you could say depression spectrum disorders like bipolar disorder management. So, I got more exposure in the military than civilian school training.

Ultimately, Rev. Dr. Amy's military experiences gave her a unique background exposing her to more mental health training. She received more extensive education and conversations around specific mental illnesses, such as post traumatic stress syndrome (PTSD) and bipolar disorder, and how to address them as a Chaplain. Rev. Dr. Amy shared how such training allowed her to understand how to address mental health and illness concerns and identify when to seek professional assistance.

The specified training these women received provided more training to understand how to handle mental health concerns from a practitioner's perspective. This finding is consistent with Vermaas et al. (2017)'s finding that postsecondary and clinical mental health training increases clergy's mental health competency in comparison to those who do not have specialized training. The participants in this current study were more knowledgeable about specific mental illnesses, how to identify cases of concern, and how to provide assistance. Their additional training also afforded them more hands-on experience in dealing with mental health issues before and during their pastoral roles within the church.

Practical Recommendations

Black communities are greatly affected by systematic mental health disparities and barriers that negatively impact their help-seeking behaviors (American Psychiatric Association, 2017). As a result, leaders of Black churches are often the go-to when community members are experiencing mental health hardships. However, studies support that clergy does not possess the proper training to address the mental health concerns of their congregants (Porter, 2018; Vermaas et al., 2017). Through the experiences of Black women religious leaders, the current study aimed to understand which educational paths most adequately prepared the participants to address congregant mental health concerns.

Findings indicate that Black women religious leaders' educational preparedness to respond to mental health and illness concerns depends on specialized mental health training obtained outside of their religious training. Black women religious leaders who only received specialized mental health training from a Master of Divinity program or a seminary/theological school were the least trained in mental health. Conversely, the Black women religious leaders who received specialized mental health training and degrees, such as clinical psychology or social work, received the most training in addressing mental health concerns. As such, this case study provides a justification for improving mental health and illness training in religious educational programs and recommendations for inclusive changemaking based on the lived experiences of Black women religious leaders. These findings lead us to three practical recommendations.

Provide Specialized Mental Health Courses in Religious Programs

Leaders who received more specialized mental health training felt more prepared, for instance, when members consulted them on such issues. However, during their regular training, many received no formal training on mental health issues. Instead, nearly all of these leaders received a specific degree in mental health or voluntarily took additional courses. Other leaders learned only through experience. Knowing religious leaders are often consulted regarding emotional hardships from members, at least one course providing training on handling such issues prior to referring congregates to an outside professional would benefit both the leaders and the congregants. Conversely, CPE could allot a certain amount of time to counseling training regarding mental health and illness issues specifically. Ideally, programs could include a mental course and hands-on training.

Provide Direct Mental Health Assistance in Religious Programs for Professionals

Three participants shared that their religious educational programs focused on clergy taking care of their mental health to ensure they do not overextend themselves. Other participants discussed how they felt unprepared to address mental health and illness concerns and often learned to reduce the assistance they provided through personal experiences. Clear direction regarding the limits of religious leaders as counselors should be implemented in educational programs to ensure leaders are not overextended their emotional capacity.

Connect with Black Women Religious Leaders

Evidence supports that Black women religious leaders are consulted on topics of mental health and illness by congregants. With this knowledge, religious leaders can be utilized to promote mental wellness. Practitioners, including therapists, psychologists, psychiatrists, social workers, medical professionals, medical researchers, and broader public health organizations such as governmental entities and non-profit organizations, should connect with Black women's religious leaders. First, practitioners should work to create educational programs with religious leaders. These programs could be in conjunction with spiritual guidance or be solely about mental health practices. Second, practitioners should build relationships with the religious leaders of organizations near their practices. This study found that all the participants referred members out. Findings also indicated that certain leaders wanted to ensure a good fit between the member and the practitioner prior to referring them. Building relationships with religious leaders can minimize this process and encourage referrals to ensure members receive adequate assistance. Furthermore, being intentional with organizations close in proximity can help bridge the gap in access regarding travel; especially if the practice is within a neighborhood that does not house many mental health organizations. Third, practitioners can also ensure that religious leaders handle mental health issues appropriately. While members are more likely to consult their religious leaders, many of the leaders need to be trained to address such issues. Therefore, programs can also be conducted specifically for the leaders as they will often act as a segue for the members receiving assistance.

Application to Other Organizational Contexts

While the practical implications section above focuses on Black women's religious leaders, these findings also apply in other organizational contexts. First, organizational leaders can benefit from receiving specialized mental health and illness training to address the concerns of organizational members adequately and inclusively. Second, at the very least, organizational leaders should be provided formal guidance on maintaining their own mental well-being and when to identify moments they have reached their emotional limits. This second implication is imperative for leaders from marginalized identities as they tend to do more emotional labor associated with their work. Such leaders must be provided support to ensure their work is equitable. Third, many non-medical organizations, including workplaces, act as public health organizations as they influence perceptions of inclusivity regarding mental health and illness through leadership, policy, and organizational culture. Thus, all organizations should critically analyze their practices and culture to identify changes to enact more inclusivity. Lastly, all organizations should actively partner with other practitioners and public health organizations to expand accurate mental health and illness knowledge as much as possible as organizations implement changes to promote mental health and illness inclusivity.

Conclusion

This chapter centers on the experiences of Black women religious leaders to identify organizational changemaking strategies to implement more inclusive mental health and illness leadership practices. These Black women religious leaders' educational experiences offer insight into understanding mental health and illness from a DEI perspective and the role of specialized leadership training in adequately preparing Black women religious leaders to respond to mental health and illness concerns. Ultimately, organizational leaders should receive specialized mental health and illness training to properly foster inclusivity.

Discussion Questions

1 In what ways do Black women religious leaders play a vital role in decreasing mental health disparities?
2 What educational barriers impede Black women religious leaders' preparation in addressing congregant mental health and illness concerns?
3 In what ways can mental health and illness training be improved to adequately prepare Black women religious leaders to address mental health and illness issues?

Author Bio

Tianna L. Cobb is a research postdoctoral fellow at Johns Hopkins University, Bloomberg School of Public Health. Tianna Cobb's program of research broadly aims to eliminate health inequities affecting Black communities through a critical and intersectional lens.

References

American Psychiatric Association (2017). *Mental health disparities: African Americans.* American Psychiatric Association. https://www.psychiatry.org/psychiatrists/cultural-competency/education/mental-health-facts

Austin, & Bisel, R. S. (2022). The influence of colorblind and race-acknowledged organizational socialization messages during offer consideration. *International Journal of Business Communication, 60*(3), 892–911. 10.1177/23294884221118909

Avent, J. R., Cashwell, C. S., & Brown-Jeffy, S. (2015). African American pastors on mental health, coping, and help seeking. *Counseling and Values, 60*, 32–47. 10.1002/j.2161-007X.2015.00059.x

Beckley, I. (Host). (2021, February 9). Thought (No. 3). [Audio podcast episode]. In *The bias diagnosis.* Audible. https://www.amazon.com/The-Bias-Diagnosis/dp/B08W4YGK8Q

Blank, M. B., Mahmood, M., Fox, J. C., & Guterbock, T. (2002). Alternative mental health services: The role of the Black church in the South. *American Journal of Public Health, 92*, 1668–1672. 10.2105/AJPH.92.10.1668

Bronkhorst, B., Tummers, L., Steijn, B., & Vijverberg, D. (2015). Organizational climate and employee mental health outcomes: A systematic review of studies in health care organizations. *Health Care Management Review, 40*(3), 254–271. 10.1097/HMR.0000000000000026

Cobb, T. (2021). *You know so and so is not right: Black women leaders combating mental health stigma within black churches.* (Publication No. 11244/330207) [Doctoral dissertation, University of Oklahoma]. Shareok.

Cobb, T. L. (2022). Destigmatizing black mental health: A black gay woman's experience. In C. Molloy & L. Melonçon (Eds.). *Mental health rhetoric research: Toward strategic interventions.* (pp. 130–149). Taylor and Francis. 10.4324/9781003144854

Cooper, W. P., & Mitra, R. (2018). Religious disengagement and stigma management by African-American young adults. *Journal of Applied Communication Research, 46,* 509–533. 10.1080/00909882.2018.1502462

Eagly, A. H., & Chin, J. L. (2010). Diversity and leadership in a changing world. *The American Psychologist, 65,* 216–224. 10.1037/a0018957

Gray, Senabe, S., Naicker, N., Kgalamono, S., Yassi, A., & Spiegel, J. M. (2019). Workplace-based organizational interventions promoting mental health and happiness among healthcare workers: A realist review. *International Journal of Environmental Research and Public Health, 16*(22), 4396–. 10.3390/ijerph16224396

Hardy, K. M. (2012). Perceptions of African American Christians' attitudes toward religious help-seeking: Results of an exploratory study. *Journal of Religion & Spirituality in Social Work: Social Thought, 31,* 209–225. 10.1080/15426432.2012.679838

Hays, K. (2015). Black churches' capacity to respond to the mental health needs of African Americans. *Social Work and Christianity, 42*(3). 296–312.

Jackson, J. S., Knight, K. M., & Rafferty, J. A. (2010). Race and unhealthy behaviors: Chronic stress, the HPA axis, and physical and mental health disparities over the life course. *American Journal of Public Health, 100,* 933–939. 10.2105/AJPH.2008.143446

Jensen, Pokharel, M., Carcioppolo, N., Upshaw, S., John, K. K., & Katz, R. A. (2020). Cancer information overload: Discriminant validity and relationship to sun safe behaviors. *Patient Education and Counseling, 103*(2), 309–314. 10.1016/j.pec.2019.08.039

King, P. E., & Roeser, R. W. (2009). Religion and spirituality in adolescent development. In R. M. Lerner & L. Steinberg (Eds.), *Handbook of adolescent psychology: Individual bases of adolescent development* (pp. 435–478). John Wiley & Sons Inc. 10.1002/9780470479193.adlpsy001014

Orbe, M. P., Austin, J. T., & Allen, B. J. (2022). "Race matters" in applied communication research: past, present, and future. *Journal of Applied Communication Research: "Race Matters" in Applied Communication Research, 50*(3), 229–235. 10.1080/00909882.2022.2083407

Parker, P. S. (2001). African American women executives' leadership communication within dominant-culture organizations: (Re) conceptualizing notions of collaboration and instrumentality. *Management Communication Quarterly, 15,* 42–82. 10.1177/0893318901151002

Parker (2005). *Race, gender, and leadership re-envisioning organizational leadership from the perspectives of African American women executives.* Lawrence Erlbaum.

Parker, & McDonald, J. (2019). Difference, Diversity, and Inclusion. In *Movements in Organizational Communication Research* (1st ed., pp. 135–154). Routledge. 10.4324/9780203730089-8

Parker-McCullough, B. A. (2020). *Breaking the glass ceiling: African-american clergywomen in the baptist church, a narrative inquiry.* (Order No. 27957639). [Doctoral dissertation, University of Phoenix]. ProQuest.

Porter, J. (2018). In the pastor's study: A grounded theory analysis of African American Baptist ministers' communication on mental health and illness. (Order No. 10743535). Available from ProQuest Dissertations & Theses Global. (2055713442). Retrieved from https://0-search-proquest-com.library.ualr.edu/docview/2055713442?accountid=14482

Samuel, M. (2019). *Mental health concerns in African American churches: Pastoral preparedness in counseling.* (Order No. 22588759). [Doctoral dissertation, Gardner-Webb University]. ProQuest.

Stuijfzand, S., Deforges, C., Sandoz, V., Sajin, C. T., Jaques, C., Elmers, J., & Horsch, A. (2020). Psychological impact of an epidemic/pandemic on the mental health of healthcare professionals: A rapid review. *BMC Public Health, 20*, 1–18. 10.1186/s12889-020-09322-z

Vermaas, J. D., Green, J., Haley, M., & Haddock, L. (2017). Predicting the mental health literacy of clergy: An informational resource for counselors. *Journal of Mental Health Counseling, 39*, 225–241. 10.17744/mehc.39.3.04

Washington (2006). *Medical apartheid: The dark history of medical experimentation on Black Americans from colonial times to the present.* Harlem Moon.

Zoller, H. M. (2010). What are health organizations? Public health and organizational communication. *Management Communication Quarterly, 24*, 482–490. 10.1177/0893318910370273

21

EQUITY-CENTERED LEADERSHIP AND SUSTAINABLE CHANGEMAKING

An Organizational Imperative for Post-Pandemic Leadership and Advancement

Diane Forbes Berthoud

University of Maryland, Baltimore

Learning Objectives

After reading this chapter, you will:

1 Explicate equity principles and practices in leadership and organizational changemaking.
2 Introduce an equity-centered leadership and changemaking model of strategic and sustainable diversity leadership.
3 Identify guidelines for equity-minded post-pandemic workforce development and advancement.

Introduction

Diverse teams and organizations often have increased collaboration, more effective problem-solving, better decision making, and overall, improved morale and increased satisfaction (Chrobot-Mason & Aramovich, 2013; Rock & Grant, 2016; Williams, 2013). Diversity, however, is neither an endpoint nor a single goal or outcome. In the last decade, more attention has been paid to inclusion, equity, belonging, access, and employee engagement. More recently, there has been a greater focus on power, privilege, oppression, justice, and anti-racism. Organizational members and our broader society have more urgently called for authentic and sustainable organizational transformation, one in which persons, especially those from underrepresented and historically marginalized groups, possess the power, resources, and ability to influence the direction of their professional and personal lives.

DOI: 10.4324/9781003333746-24

Institutions have, therefore, been challenged to respond to the organizational and societal pressures to act intently and purposefully to effect meaningful and sustainable organizational changemaking. This changemaking needs to be systemic and sustainable, instead of engaging in what Williams (2020) refers to as the "cheetah" approach, a leadership and organizational approach that is crisis driven, poorly coordinated, has little or no strategic focus, and is characterized by isolated efforts.

Equity—fairness and justice achieved through systematically assessing disparities in opportunities, resources, support, outcomes, and representation—needs to be an organizational priority. Authentic organizational changemaking cannot occur without it. An equity-centered approach takes into account structural factors, historical precedents, and differential outcomes and seeks to address these barriers and disparities (see next section; Bensimon et al., 2016; Kania et al., 2022).

This chapter provides an integrated model of sustainable changemaking that centers equity processes and outcomes and strengthens and enhances leadership in the post-pandemic organization. Drawing on and contextualizing organizational changemaking in the events of 2020 (i.e., the global pandemic), I propose a changemaking model of collective impact that centers equity principles, processes, practices, and outcomes to strengthen and enhance leadership for sustainable organizational change.

The proposed changemaking model is anchored in four major themes: (1) Data and organizational evidence; (2) Review and Reflection; (3) Collective engagement and transformation; and (4) Critical Organizational Praxis (DRCC). The DRCC model provides an integrated model and guide to equity-centered leadership and sustainable changemaking in the post-pandemic organization.

The discussion will first describe organizational challenges associated with the pandemic that have complicated and exacerbated organizational equity, diversity, inclusion, and leadership. Key features of equity centeredness and collective impact will then be explicated to inform transformational organizational changemaking and propose a model of equity-centered leadership and sustainable change. These recommendations are based on my experience leading change initiatives at several organizations at which iterations of this model have been applied, including two large public institutions and a large nonprofit agency.

Background and Context

2020 forever changed our world. Referred to as the triple pandemics in the United States—medical, racial, and economic—the ills of this deadly pandemic, a recession, and a racial reckoning exposed and exacerbated inequities in both U.S. and global societies.

COVID-19 Impacts and Outcomes

The American Psychological Association (2021), a year into the pandemic, found that so-called essential or frontline workers were more likely than other workers to be diagnosed with mental health illnesses. Many workers also experienced job or income loss and other hardships including food and housing loss or insecurity. These social and economic factors help us to understand more fully the systemic forces at work that produce health disparities and inequitable outcomes for marginalized communities. The Household Pulse survey collected data about the ways in which the coronavirus has impacted people's lives. Across almost all measures that included job loss, anxiety, housing insecurity, and depression, Black and Hispanic adults fared worse than white adults when considering social, economic, financial, and psychological experiences and outcomes (Drake & Rudowitz, 2022; Household Pulse Survey, 2022; Maxwell & Solomon, 2020). Studies also showed the disproportionate impact of death and disease among African Americans in the United States during COVID; financial strain, economic and environmental factors, as well as a decline in overall health, were reported at greater rates among African Americans than other populations (Adesogan et al., 2021; Gawthrop, 2022; Golden, 2020).

Women, who make up more than half of the U.S. workforce, have also experienced disproportionate impacts during the pandemic. They experienced professional setbacks that included a reduction in productivity and a departure from the workforce altogether, for example, to take on full-time caregiving responsibilities. Since the pandemic, they have also been more likely than their male counterparts to leave the workforce, which has downstream implications that include significant economic and professional losses (Center for American Progress, 2020; Madgavkar et al., 2020).

The Great Resignation

Another major impact on organizational life since 2020 has been the Great Resignation, also referred to as the Great Reshuffle or Great Attrition—a pattern in which millions of employees are leaving their organizations in the post-pandemic world, after consideration about the purpose and direction of their lives. In some cases, workers have left because of toxic, inflexible, and high-stress environments. In the face of illness, economic downturn and, for some, death, workers have been reconsidering the place work should have in their lives.

Disparities and barriers that existed prior to the pandemic, of mental health and stress, burnout, lack of belonging, and poorer economic and medical outcomes, were exposed and exacerbated during COVID (Adesogan et al., 2021; Bateman & Ross, 2020; Connor et al., 2020). Research revealed that during the pandemic, working women, who typically have more domestic responsibilities (e.g., child and eldercare), left the workforce at higher rates than men and/or reduced their hours to take on full-time home responsibilities (McKinsey, 2020). Organizations that had not been prioritizing equity and the concerns of historically marginalized populations were jolted into a new reality that required our collective attention and action, as well as strategic and critical leadership approaches. This new reality provided opportunities to strengthen organizational processes and examine goals and outcomes to improve employee satisfaction, engagement, morale, and increase retention in the post-pandemic workforce.

Literature Review: Equity-Centered and Sustainable Organizational Changemaking

Scholars have long explored the role of learning and innovation in organizational changemaking and how effective leadership transforms and facilitates organizational cultural change and learning. Organizations committed to learning and continuous improvement are more likely to increase productivity, effectiveness, and collaboration. Furthermore, corporate or for-profit organizations are more likely to increase their competitive advantage in their field or market through continuous improvement and learning (Freifield, 2013; Hao & Yazdanifard, 2015; Park et al., 2014).

Change Processes

A specific focus on equity, diversity, and inclusion (EDI) will, for many organizations, constitute a challenge to the status quo as well as an opportunity for growth. Understanding the nature and value of organizational change and attending to the dynamics of changemaking can create a pathway toward sustainable changemaking. Change processes in organizational and social contexts entail the adjustment or revisiting of norms and customs, ideas, values, beliefs, and practices to create and forge a new reality. Driven by a myriad of political, social, economic, and other factors, change opposes the status quo and can be expressed in different forms (Serrat, 2017). *Discursive change* refers to how people frame and understand an issue. In the case of EDI, at times, issues are framed as siloed and singular, such that diversity becomes synonymous with race, representation, or climate.

Discursively framing EDI holistically and integratively, and not as episodic or specific initiative will support organizational efforts to promote greater understanding and potential engagement in change. *Procedural change* is a change in process management of concerns. This refers to instances in which organizations modify processes for identifying and addressing problems related to *in*equity and inclusion. For example, changing EDI organizational structure and roles from more informal to formal. *Content-based change* refers to changes made in the nature of an issue. In the mid-90s, sensitivity training and diversity management were central to EDI work. During the last decade, the nature of the issues has changed and deepened to include a more critical focus on anti-racism, belonging, cultural humility, justice, and more. *Attitudinal change*, change in approach and perspective about an issue, can lead to *behavioral change,* change in action, speech, procedure, and content, such as telework policies and newly established roles to advance EDI.

These forms of change are not simple nor linear; rather, they are nuanced and complex and require intention, a clear process, strategic alignment, and collective action. The most successful change efforts support and advance the engagement and full participation of groups and communities acting cohesively and jointly to effect change. The collective impact model offers an enriching framework to inform equity-centered leadership and organizational changemaking.

Collective Impact

Collective impact refers to a group's commitment to a common agenda and direction to solve complex social and community problems. Group members from different segments of organizations and society work from the premise that disjointed and isolated initiatives yield little or no real change; rather, change is brought about through a focus on fundamental system change, by addressing policy or improving practice. The five conditions of collective impact that work together for people to create authentic alignment and lead to powerful results are: a common agenda, shared measurement systems, mutually reinforcing activities, continuous communication, and backbone support organizations (Kania & Kramer, 2011). A common agenda refers to collective problem identification and definition, as well as a shared vision to address those problems. We may have a common agenda, but without a sound assessment system in place, progress will be hard to measure and achieve. Therefore, organizations will need shared measurement systems to track progress related to the problems identified. For example, if the underrepresentation of women leaders is identified as an opportunity, a common agenda needs to be established to address the gender disparity in leadership, as is an accessible and shared assessment system to track and measure success. The third element of collective impact is mutually reinforcing activities; or, coordination and synergy across differentiated activities. Organizations at times have isolated and siloed initiatives that lack coherence and common focus. With mutually reinforcing activities, alignment and cohesion across EDI activities are prioritized. Continuous communication is another element—consistent, open, and broad communication to build trust, partnerships, and ongoing collaboration. Finally, the fifth component is the backbone organization, the human and financial resources needed to sponsor, support, and advance planning and change efforts.

Equity-mindedness

Another key framework in changemaking literature is equity-mindedness, which, although applicable to multiple organizational contexts, has been mostly studied/applied in higher education contexts. As a principle and practice in academia, equity-mindedness has centered student success and development. Equity-mindedness seeks to understand the sociohistorical context of exclusionary practices that have come to characterize American education and have had disproportionate impacts on African Americans and Latinos/as/x populations. The framework requires changemakers to reflect on their own assumptions, beliefs, and stereotypes that influence student success. A practice of accountability and an understanding of inequity are needed, as well as a grasp of the social and historical background that shapes practices, outcomes, and inequities in education. Educators need to be both personally and institutionally responsible for student success, rather than applying deficit-based and unjust approaches that problematize students and their outcomes (Bensimon et al., 2016; Bensimon, 2020). Deficit-based models seek to increase academic engagement, performance, and persistence through a focus on student deficit and need. Examples of methods in this approach are remedial courses, and individual, social, and peer programs, which are ineffective when offered in isolation and without a comprehensive organizational and cultural approach (Anderson, 2005; Hunn, 2014).

Drawing on Bensimon's higher education framing, and extending the analyses to organizations more broadly, I propose that equity-centered leadership be concerned with the success and well-being and the opportunity for *all* organizational members to thrive. Equity-centered leadership is the ability to exercise social and organizational influence and inspire organizational members to work toward a common agenda that ensures equivalent processes and outcomes for all organizational members. It requires courage and compassion not only to ensure financial, operational, and managerial success, but to examine and address the organizational and population-specific disparities in opportunities, representation, access, supports, and outcomes. Equity centeredness is not simply a lens; rather, it is an integrative and seamless process and outcome that considers the historical antecedents, structural factors, and foundations that have contributed to our current socioeconomic, political, and social structures. Organizations are influenced by these structures, processes, and outcomes that disproportionately impact historically marginalized groups.

Leaders that commit to learning more about the sociohistorical and structural factors that impact current labor, educational, economic, and political arrangements also need to provide the resources and opportunities to reduce and eliminate those barriers in their organizations. Inequity has been created and sustained by design in economic, political, and social systems. For example, women's exclusion from higher education was built on the premise that they were intellectually inferior and better suited for domestic responsibilities. For almost two centuries, women were denied access to postsecondary opportunities in the United States. Women's colleges and universities were then established to address these barriers and provide opportunities for education, training, and employment (Langdon, 2001; Rudolph, 2021). Many of these institutions are still open and thriving today with a clear mission to educate and empower women and reduce and/or remove barriers to education, economic, political, and professional resources. Similarly, African Americans in the United States were denied access to higher education for centuries, which led to the creation of Historically Black Colleges and Universities (HBCUs). As structures have been designed around inequity, achieving equity, then, must also be by design, that is with targeted strategies and activities that reduce or eliminate systems and structures that (re)produce inequities. Examples of equity-centered leadership would be to provide resources and opportunities for affinity group and cohort model development. These initiatives need key elements such as mentorship, sponsorship, and equal access to organizational, educational, and professional opportunities that specifically support the professional development and career advancement of persons from groups that are underrepresented in leadership or more senior roles (e.g., women and populations of color). Women's leadership programs have been created to address these disparities in opportunities and access to networks, information, mentorship, and advancement and to increase women's sense of belonging and retention. Although the leadership and opportunity barriers for women have not been eliminated, the pipeline in some sectors has slightly improved. Creating such programs and intentionally designing opportunities for increased and equal access produces equivalent and more just outcomes for groups who, by design, were traditionally excluded from full participation and access in organizations.

DRCC Model of Equity-Centered Leadership and Changemaking

Creating equitable conditions and engaging in equity-centered leadership and changemaking requires a keen examination of equity as both process and outcome. As organizations evolve, and as results from any assessments, such as climate surveys and representational data, are analyzed, equity needs to be an organizational priority. How can organizations grow and individuals thrive when there is not fair and just distribution and access to opportunities, networks, and resources? Ensuring equity, which requires understanding and addressing disparities and barriers, can be advanced by first *examining organizational data*, committing to deep *reflection and review*, engaging the organization broadly in the *collective transformation* that is owned by persons at every level of the organization, and committing to consistent and critical inquiry and integration of principle and practice, reflexivity, and positive change—or *critical organizational praxis*. These four components constitute the *Data, Review, Collective Engagement, and Critical Organizational Praxis (DRCC) model*—an integrative framework of sustainable changemaking that centers equity processes and outcomes and aims to strengthen and enhance organizational leadership.

Specifically, the model draws on the work of Bensimon (2016), Williams (2013), and the collective impact model (Kania & Kramer, 2011) to be discussed, which explicate key features of collective engagement, e.g., change, equity-mindedness, and assessment, and organizational transformation, through a case study approach. The model adopts a holistic and integrative approach as it addresses how to engage organizational members, and how to execute planning, implementation, and accountability efforts. Iterations of the model have been applied in two large public institutions and a large nonprofit agency. In each institution, I have had central organizational responsibility and authority to identify, manage, lead, and/or implement organizational strategy to advance institutional diversity, equity, and inclusion.

In addition to scholarship and research related to organizational change and transformation, I also drew on two-plus decades as an academic leader and organizational consultant with key aspects of my portfolio that are closely or directly connected to diversity, equity, and inclusion through program and curricular development and design, assessment, organization development, and student, faculty, and staff diversity. In my most recent role as Vice President and Chief Diversity Officer in a large state institution, this model has been developed and applied to increase opportunities for engagement, development, responsibility, and accountability. In sum, the DRCC Model of equity-centered leadership and sustainable changemaking draws on rich scholarship and the author's extensive experience and expertise in organizational communication and social psychological theory and practice. In the following pages, each component of the model will be explicated, in turn.

Data and Organizational Evidence

The success of EDI initiatives and integration rests partially on collecting, analyzing, and acting on the organizational data that provide information on the state of EDI in the organization. Most common understandings of diversity and available organizational data include composition—that is, who is in the organization in terms of racial and gender identity. At times, "diversity" has been used as a proxy to refer to race, which, while important, simplifies and obscures the multiple diversity dimensions that influence people's experiences and are critical for data collection, analysis, strategic planning, and implementation. Composition in diversity refers to the mix of the groups present in the organization, such as the number of women in the organization, the number of persons of a particular generation (Gen Z, Millennials, etc.), and the racial composition of the workforce. Representation refers to groups' presence across ranks, leadership, decision making, participation and engagement in the organization, the groups' presence overall in the organization, and also in comparison to other groups' presence at that same level (e.g., coordinator, manager, executive, etc.).

Representational and compositional diversity, though important, do not complete our understanding of institutional diversity, equity, and inclusion. Organizations truly dedicated, in word and deed, to the advancement and integration of EDI, will commit the necessary resources and invest in the infrastructure and frameworks to build a strong data arm of the institution. In some cases, this infrastructure exists in Human Resources, a designated Diversity Office, or Institutional Research, depending on the organizational structure, culture, and industry.

What data is important to collect and analyze to be sufficiently equipped to develop and implement change strategies? To advance the D of the DRCC model, this evidence-based foundation needs to be established to support organizational changemaking, effective leadership, and accountability. The following organizational change indicators need to be made available, collated, and synthesized to aptly lay the foundation for EDI examination and advancement. An organization may measure people's entry and experience of growth and development.

Access and success refer to the opportunities to enter and participate and the opportunities to thrive, do well in an organizational or other context that can all be measured by demographic group/social identity (e.g., gender, race, ethnicity, age, disability, sexual orientation, and more).

Measurements of access include the diversity of populations at entry points and the current state of an organization, such as the number and diversity (e.g., racial and gender demographics) of new hires or entrants. In a higher education or program context, an access metric would be the number of persons admitted or enrolled by demographic group/social identity. Tracking representation would involve collecting and analyzing data at all organizational levels by identity group.

Success pertains to organizational members' ability to develop and thrive in a context. Metrics include retention, promotion, advancement, recognition, and rewards, which provide us with opportunities to better understand equity when disaggregated by demographic groups, such as age, gender, and race/ethnicity. Indicators that measure diversity numbers, such as racially diverse hires, are what Williams and Dolkas (2022) refer to as outcome measures, the result of the counts in composition and representation. They also point to the process metrics that may reveal disparities in areas of hiring, mentorship, or salary. Qualitative data is a key component of diversity data collection and analysis as organizational leaders learn more about people's perspectives on organizational culture, structure, and climate. Examples of these are institutional speeches, organizational statements, and other organizational artifacts as well as focus groups. Together with quantitative data, we gain a more comprehensive picture of the experiences of marginalized groups and the organization as a whole.

Review and Reflection

Concrete learning practices and processes such as data collection, interpretation, and sharing information, as well as focused and disciplined analyses to identify and solve problems characterize learning organizations (Garvin et al., 2008). Education and training are also key features that strengthen an organization committed to changemaking and impactful leadership. Areas that could be a focus of capacity building and development include implicit bias, inclusive hiring, and integrating EDI in promotion and tenure processes. Benchmarking and knowledge are also critical here: What are the best and promising practices related to equitable and inclusive hiring? What are the population-specific recruitment and retention trends?

The metrics discussed above, in addition to organizational experience, measures of belonging, morale, respect, and value are important to examine. In the same ways that a special and targeted examination is needed of an organization's or unit's budget operations—practices, procedures, policies, diversity data— representation, composition, and experience need to be collated and integrated into organizational decision and change-making. Data analysis and review are important to inform change and advance organizational EDI.

Collective Engagement and Transformation

While it is important to have leadership buy-in, it is equally important to have active participation and engagement at the mid-level, where managers make hiring, promotion, access, and development decisions. Mid-level managers are influential as they can create or prevent opportunities for career advancement, recognition, and growth for employees. In some organizations, many of the advocates for organizational EDI are employees who are most impacted by inequity, lack of diversity, and exclusion. They typically have the least organizational and political power and tend to be persons from historically marginalized groups, such as racially and ethnically minoritized populations. Organizational efforts cannot rest on their experiences and voices alone; greater accountability and ownership need to be demonstrated and exercised at managerial and leadership levels to ensure impactful changemaking and equity centeredness. For organizational diversity leaders, it is important to consider the level of sponsorship and support at the executive level as organizational goals and outcomes are established related to EDI advancement and leadership. A reactive or symbolic hire of a diversity leader can further thwart and complicate change processes without the necessary elements to support and advance their leadership, collective organizational success, and sustainable change-making. Much of the changemaking process hinges on organizational trust, buy-in, and engagement, which will not be possible without the tangible sponsorship and executive-level support to ensure EDI leadership and integration thrive.

Williams (2017) offers a framework that emphasizes the need for key features that ensure diversity initiatives and leadership succeed: Accountability, Infrastructure, Incentives, and Resources (AIIR). As organizations engage and include multiple areas and levels, the ongoing commitment and sponsorship to these components—both symbolic and material—at the executive level of the organization will be critical to fuel the collective engagement and transformation to effect positive change.

Critical Organizational Praxis

The final part of the framework that formulates and addresses change and is needed to advance the DRCC model is Critical organizational praxis. Critical praxis integrates and combines thought and action for change with consideration for inequities, power relations, access, and historical antecedents of those factors. The process constitutes a reflexive and critical process of inquiry and action for positive change. Typically, strategic planning and change management models are corporate and based on business organization models. One of the final steps is action and implementation—efforts to produce the outcomes that were all outlined in the previous steps (Al-Haddad & Kotnour, 2015; Paton & McCalman, 2008; Teczke et al., 2017; Trainer, 2004).

In the DRCC model, I propose action and implementation; however, this action needs to be integrated and accompanied by critical reflexivity, purpose, and theory. Critical praxis involves focused and consistent efforts to evaluate thought with action, theory, and practice with the goal to increase awareness and effect positive change (Kridel, 2010). Our tendency as organizational actors is to concentrate on our individual or unit experiences, sometimes at the expense of understanding and addressing concerns of the whole. Critical organizational praxis requires systemic and strategic approaches and analyses. Francisco et al. (2021) refer to critical praxis as thought and action with ethical and moral purpose. It involves an analysis of power relations and an exploration of practices, norms, and experiences that may be uncomfortable or cause tension, yet need to be engaged and transformed (Lopez, 2015). As equity centeredness is integrated in diversity leadership and organizational changemaking becomes a greater priority, the following considerations and guidelines can ensure their success and lead to more just and equitable outcomes.

For successful systemic analyses, critical attention is needed to the interconnectedness and interrelatedness of trends, experiences, structures, and outcomes. Therefore, in practical terms, measuring and tracking the representation of women and/or persons of a particular identity group in and across units is part of what may be collected and analyzed to understand representation, power, access, morale, and outcomes related to organizational access and success at a system level. Change is enacted with those considerations of representation, power, and reflexivity. Through critical praxis, we not only ask what and examine systems as they are (e.g., the representation of women and their organizational position and power), but we also ask *why, how,* and what this means— implications and next steps, as we formulate future action and a co-created process and outcome. We explore the ways in which inequity has been designed, structured, and sustained to create exclusive processes and practices, and then work to create ways to redress those disparities and barriers through targeted approaches. In this design process, we simultaneously hold and integrate the historical foundations and the co-created future of equity and justice to accomplish the desired outcomes, particularly for historically marginalized groups.

In the process of critical organizational praxis, we dwell at the critical intersection between organizational principle and practice; a path to co-create a new and different approach that produces social and organizational change informed by thoughtfulness, reflexivity, and critical inquiry. This process is needed for increased awareness and discovery of organizational methods and solutions that lead to symbolic and material change. Policies, practices, and processes, therefore, need to be examined, with collaborative leadership for success.

Questions that can guide the process of critical organizational praxis are:

- What are the current practices that drive access and success in an organization?
- How do they (re)produce, sustain, or challenge oppressive structures and inequity?
- How can I, in my role, or my organizational unit create more equitable conditions and outcomes in my/our sphere of influence?
- As we design and implement these equity-centered programs and initiatives, how will we measure success?
- What is the timeline to assess equity and success for the intended population(s)?

Critical organizational praxis can be interwoven and interconnected across individual, interpersonal, group, organizational, and system levels to effect positive and holistic change.

Practical Applications

Although the DRCC model is presented one step at a time, the components are intersectional and integrative as Figure 21.1 suggests. Decisions, critical inquiry, and reflection need to be informed by data, and so too is data influenced by critical inquiry and collective engagement, where organizational members can provide feedback on all and at every stage of equity-centered leadership and changemaking.

In this chapter, I have advanced a changemaking model, drawing on experience in two universities and a large humanitarian organization, to

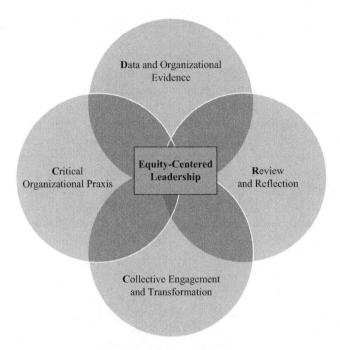

FIGURE 21.1   "DRCC Model".

demonstrate its application and effectiveness. Although the actionable recommendations highlighted in the chapter are presented within the context of higher education, this equity-centered leadership model is applicable across various types of organizations. As such, I encourage leaders to adapt the recommendations above to their own unique organizational contexts.

Conclusion

This chapter provided a review of the most recent political, social, and organizational challenges that, particularly since the pandemic and racial reckoning of 2020, exposed and exacerbated long-standing inequities and disproportionate impacts for racially minoritized groups and women. These factors also complicated and exacerbated organizational equity, diversity, inclusion, and leadership and had profound impacts on work and organizational life.

Drawing on and situating organizational changemaking in the social and political events of the last few years, I proposed an equity-centered leadership and changemaking model with integrative principles, processes, practices, and outcomes to strengthen and enhance leadership to ensure sustainable organizational change.

In sum, the DRCC model—Data and organizational evidence; Review and Reflection; Collective engagement and transformation; and Critical Organizational Praxis—provides an integrated model of equity-centered leadership and sustainable changemaking that centers equity processes and outcomes, strengthens and enhances leadership in the post-pandemic organization. As the pandemic continues to have broad and deep impacts, and as it and other global crises continue to evolve, organizations will be tested, and leaders will be challenged to be more critical in their thinking and acting about transformational and equitable processes. The model presented offers both a framework and a challenge for organizational leadership and sustainable changemaking for the future.

Discussion Questions

1 What key priorities or areas in EDI constitute effective and impactful organizational changemaking in your organizational context?
2 What unique leadership and changemaking challenges does your organization face? And how might the DRCC model proposed here apply in your organizational and professional contexts?
3 How do culture, leadership philosophy, and approach impact organizational changemaking and equity assessments?

Author Bio

Diane Forbes Berthoud (Ph.D., Howard University) is Vice President, Chief Diversity Officer, and Professor at the University of Maryland, Baltimore, and affiliate faculty at George Washington University. Her research focuses on gendered, raced, intersectional processes of organizing and has appeared in peer-reviewed journals and books, such as *Race, Work, and Leadership*, published by Harvard University Press.

References

Adesogan, O., Lavner, J. A., Carter, S. E., & Beach, S. R. (2021). COVID-19 Stress and the health of Black Americans in the rural south. *Clinical Psychological Science, 10*(6), 1111–1128.

Al-Haddad, S., & Kotnour, T. (2015). Integrating the organizational change literature: A model for successful change. *Journal of Organizational Change Management, 28*(2), 234–262.

American Psychological Association. (2021, March). *Essential workers more likely to be diagnosed with a mental health disorder during pandemic.* https://www.apa. org/news/press/releases/stress/2021/one-year-pandemic-stress-essential

Anderson, E. (2005). Strengths-based educating: A concrete way to bring out the best in students and yourself: The confessions of an educator who got it right-finally! *Educational Horizons, 83*(3), 180–189.

Bateman, N. & Ross. M. (2020, October). Why has COVID-19 been especially harmful for working women? *Brookings Gender Equality Series.* https://www. brookings.edu/essay/why-has-covid-19-been-especially-harmful-for-working-women/

Bensimon, E., Dowd, A., & Witham, K. (2016). Five Principles for Enacting Equity by Design, *Diversity and Democracy, Winter 2016,* Vol. 19, No. 1.

Bensimon, E. (2020). *What is Equity-Mindedness?* https://cue.usc.edu/equity/equity-mindedness/#:~:text=The%20term%20%E2%80%9CEuity%2DMindedness% E2%80%9D,of%20inequity%20in%20student%20outcomes.

Center for American Progress (2020). *How COVID-19 Sent Women's Workforce Progress Backward.* https://www.americanprogress.org/article/covid-19-sent-womens-workforce-progress-backward/

Chrobot-Mason, D., & Aramovich, N. P. (2013). The psychological benefits of creating an affirming climate for workplace diversity. *Group & Organization Management, 38*(6), 659–689.

Connor, J., Madhavan, S., Mokashi, M., Amanuel, H., Johnson, N. R., Pace, L. E., & Bartz, D. (2020). Health risks and outcomes that disproportionately affect women during the Covid-19 pandemic: A review. *Social Science & Medicine, 266,* 113364.

Drake, P., & Rudowitz, R. (2022, April 21). *Tracking Social Determinants of Health During the COVID-19 Pandemic.* KFF report. https://www.kff.org/coronavirus-covid-19/issue-brief/tracking-social-determinants-of-health-during-the-covid-19-pandemic/

Francisco, S., Forssten Seiser, A., & Grice, C. (2021). Professional learning that enables the development of critical praxis. *Professional Development in Education,* 1–15.

Freifeld, L. (2013). Emerging training leaders. *Training, 50*(3), 20–31.

Garvin, D. A., Edmondson, A. C., & Gino, F. (2008). Is yours a learning organization? *Harvard Business Review, 86*(3), 109.

Gawthrop, E. (2022, May 10). *The color of coronavirus: COVID-19 deaths by race and ethnicity in the U.S.* AMP Research Lab. https://www.apmresearchlab.org/covid/deaths-by-race

Golden, S. (2020, April 20). *Coronavirus in African Americans and Other People of Color.* https://www.hopkinsmedicine.org/health/conditions-and-diseases/coronavirus/covid19-racial-disparities

Hao, M. J., & Yazdanifard, R. (2015). How effective leadership can facilitate change in organizations through improvement and innovation?. *Global Journal of Management and Business Research, 15*(9), 1–6. Version 1.

Household Pulse Survey (2022). https://www.census.gov/programs-surveys/household-pulse-survey/data.html

Hunn, V. (2014). African American students, retention, and team-based learning: A review of the literature and recommendations for retention at predominately white institutions. *Journal of Black Studies*, *45*(4), 301–314.

Kania, J., & Kramer, M. (2011). Collective impact. *Stanford Social Innovation Review*, *9*(1), 36–41. Retrieved from https://ssir.org/articles/entry/collective_impact

Kania, J., Williams, J., Schmitz, P., Brady, S., Mark Kramer, M., & Splansky Juster, J. (Winter 2022). Centering equity in collective impact. *Stanford Social Innovation Review*, Winter 2022, 38-45.

Kridel, C. (2010). *Encyclopedia of curriculum studies*. San Francisco, CA: Sage Publications.

Langdon, E. A. (2001). Women's colleges then and now: access then, equity now. *Peabody Journal of Education*, *76*(1), 5–30. http://www.jstor.org/stable/1493003

Lopez, A. E. (2015). Navigating cultural borders in diverse contexts: Building capacity through culturally responsive leadership and critical praxis. *Multicultural Education Review*, *7*(3), 171–184.

Madgavkar, A., White, O., Krishnan, M., Mahajan, D., & Azcue, X. (2020). COVID-19 and gender equality: Countering the regressive effects. *McKinsey Global Institute*, *15*, 2020.

Maxwell, C., and Solomon, D. (2020, April 14). *The Economic Fallout of the Coronavirus for People of Color*. Center for American Progress. https://www.americanprogress.org/article/economic-fallout-coronavirus-people-color/

McKinsey (2020). The pandemic's gender effect. https://www.mckinsey.com/featured-insights/diversity-and-inclusion/five-fifty-the-pandemics-gender-effect

Park, Y. K., Song J. H., Yoon S. W., & Kim J. (2014). Learning organization and innovative behavior: The mediating effect of work engagement. *European Journal of Training and Development*, *38* (1/2), 75–94.

Paton, R. A., & McCalman, J. (2008). *Change management: A guide to effective implementation*. Sage.

Rock, D., & Grant, H. (2016). Why diverse teams are smarter. *Harvard Business Review*, *4*(4), 2–5.

Rudolph, F. (2021). *The American college and university: A history*. Plunkett Lake Press.

Serrat, O. (2017). *Knowledge solutions: Tools, methods, and approaches to drive organizational performance*. Springer Nature.

Teczke, M., Sansyzbayevna Bespayeva, R., & Olzhabayevna Bugubayeva, R. (2017). Approaches and models for change management. *Jagiellonian Journal of Management*, *3*(3).

Trainer, J. F. (2004). Models and tools for strategic planning. *New Directions for Institutional Research*, *2004*(123), 129–138.

Williams, D. (2013). *Strategic diversity leadership: Activating change and transformation in higher education*. Stylus Publishing, LLC.

Williams, D. (2017). *Innovating Diversity and Empowering Leaders: Renewing hope through inclusive excellence*. Inclusive Excellence Residency, University of Dayton. https://udayton.edu/diversity/_resources/_doc/dr_ddamon_a_williams_university__dayton_redacted_residency_september_2017_mbedits-ppt.pdf

Williams, D. (2020). *The COVID-19 DEI Crisis action strategy guide: Recommendations to drive inclusive excellence.* Atlanta, GA: Center for Strategic Diversity Leadership & Social Innovation. https://www.northwestern.edu/diversity/resources/diversity-and-inclusion-toolkit/nixla_covid19_dei_strategy-guide.pdf

Williams, J., & Dolkas, (2022, March-April). Data-Driven Diversity: To achieve your inclusion goals, use a metrics-based approach. *Harvard Business Review, 100*(3–4), 74–83.

22

WHITEWASHING THE WALLS

Leading Organizational Change from Cultures of Mistrust to Celebrating Sisterhood

Angela N. Gist-Mackey, Savaughn E. Williams, and Anna Jewell

University of Kansas

Learning Objectives

After reading this chapter, you will:

1 Understand how local community culture and organizational culture influence one another;
2 Analyze the impact of multiple stakeholders in organizational decision making;
3 Evaluate challenges new non-profit organizational leaders have as they change organizational culture; and
4 Develop practical insights into how non-profit practitioners can maintain positive organizational cultures and relationships.

Introduction and Background

It was the 20th anniversary of Lavender Refuge (pseudonym), a non-profit human service organization, which caused staff to reflect on the organization's past, present, and future. Lavender Refuge owns and manages a residential community of apartments for single mothers who are in recovery. The non-profit provides wrap-around services that include, but are not limited to sobriety support, family reunification, family stabilization, affordable housing, and educational or workforce reentry coaching, among other forms of support. In the years leading up to this milestone anniversary, Lavender Refuge experienced a large amount of turnover primarily due to a problematic Executive Director. The Executive Director was an authoritarian and discriminatory leader who cultivated a

DOI: 10.4324/9781003333746-25

problematic organizational culture. The Executive Director retired just before the non-profit's 20th anniversary. Newly hired leadership began by exploring a new vision for the organization.

The past leadership had not been reflexive about how they could enhance the organizational culture to support employees and volunteers. The new leadership took culture seriously. In essence, their organizational culture was in flux. As the new leadership team settled into their roles, they reflected on the history of the organization. The new leadership wanted their anniversary to be marked significantly as a way to communicate their presence to the community, as well as their commitment to change. Hence, the leadership decided part of their celebration would include a new mural commissioned by a local artist of color to illustrate their mission, accomplishments, values, and community as an organization, while working to improve their organizational culture. Lavender Refuge's leaders wanted to meaningfully symbolize their organization's future.

Lavender Refuge's community and offices resided on the historic color line of their Midwestern metropolitan city, which included predominately African American and Hispanic residents. As the anniversary neared, the United States found itself in racial unrest. In fact, the month Lavender Refuge reached its 20-year anniversary, George Floyd was murdered by a police officer in Minneapolis and Black Lives Matter (BLM) protests emerged in response across the nation, as well as in Lavender Refuge's community. The combination of these events led Lavender Refuge's leaders to further explore racial equity in their organizational culture. The hope was to increase the diversity of their clients and make Lavender Refuge a more diverse, inclusive, and equitable place to labor and live. The leadership examined their organizational culture and wondered how racial inequity was manifest in the cultural dynamics of their non-profit work and in the residential community they manage. Hence, this research explores Lavender Refuge's organizational culture focusing on racial equity.

Organizational culture is a complex phenomenon that manifests in physical artifacts, value systems, and implicit assumptions (Keyton, 2011; Schein, 2010). Leaders have been dubbed the creators of culture (Schein, 2010), while other scholars argue that organizational members collectively create and maintain organizational cultures (Keyton, 2011). Martin's (1992) three perspective theory of organizational culture identifies lenses with which organizational culture can be analyzed: integration, differentiation, and fragmentation. Integration focuses on shared values systems and aspects of culture that organizational members have consensus about (Martin, 1992). Differentiation addresses conflict and subcultures (Martin, 1992). Fragmentation centers ambiguity and uncertainty (Martin, 1992). Our study sought to better understand the shift in organizational culture during a major leadership change in a local non-profit organization working to become more racially diverse and inclusive.

This research emerged in collaboration with Lavender Refuge. The first author taught a graduate seminar titled Ethnography and Social Interaction and approached Lavender Refuge leaders asking to partner for a community-engaged class research project so graduate students could learn ethnography experientially. The second and third authors remained with the research team after the class concluded. Three other student researchers decided to depart the project upon completion of the class. Their labor and contributions are much appreciated. Lavender Refuge agreed to be a site for our ethnography and asked for the research to explore issues of racial equity. Our team conducted 24 interviews and 15.5 hours of participant observation with clients and staff/volunteers at Lavender Refuge.

Our interviewees included 24 cis-gender women who were either clients, staff, or volunteers at the organization. Thirteen identified their race as white, six as Black/African American, three as Hispanic/Latinx, one as Asian/Pacific Islander, and one as multi-racial. Their ages ranged from 25 to 56 years. The average age of staff/volunteers interviewed was 45.5 years. The average age of clients interviewed was 36.25 years. Our participant observation included client-oriented events such as craft nights and parenting classes, as well as staff team meetings, program council meetings, and organizational fundraisers.

We analyzed the interview transcripts and field note data using a phronetic iterative approach (Tracy, 2020) assisted by NVivo qualitative analysis software. We first conducted first-cycle coding in NVivo assigning descriptive labels to meaningful sections of text (i.e., interview transcripts or field notes). Then we conducted second-cycle coding by combining first-level codes into categories. Phronetic iterative approaches involve alternating between data analysis and theories or sensitizing concepts that are relevant to the research (Tracy, 2020). The analysis led researchers to focus on the change in the organizational culture (Martin, 1992) as it relates to racial diversity, equity, and inclusion. The analysis below reveals our ethnographic findings.

Findings and Interpretation

The findings are presented in a way that demonstrates the past organizational culture, the change in leadership, and the emergence of a new organizational culture. The past organization's leadership was highly problematic and fostered a harmful organizational culture. Hence, the new leadership worked to create a new and more positive organizational culture. The findings show how the new leadership worked to rebuild the organizational culture and how they leaned into diversity and inclusion as part of that organizational change effort. We close with practical insights for non-profit leaders and practitioners.

Breaking Free: Past Organizational Culture of Mistrust, Prejudice, and Fear

Under former leadership, staff members worked in a problematic organizational culture infused with mistrust, fear, and racism. These problems were upheld and perpetuated by a toxic Executive Director, which fostered an organizational culture where employees withheld information, inequitably applied rules to clients, were overworked, and had job insecurity. The values, norms, and language that illustrated this mistrust were often tied to former leadership, which Clementine, a white, 25-year-old Family Therapist described:

> People's jobs were actively threatened and it was really hard to have any kind of constructive … confrontational conversation with people you know, to address some of these problems without fearing that you are going to be belittled, yelled at, like I said, have your job threatened. And there was a lot of secrets or the illusion of secrets and [exhales] everybody was so paranoid like very, very paranoid. Um who's talking to who, who knows what …

Clementine's account about the former leadership demonstrates the fear of retaliation that employees experienced. Martin's (1992) fragmentation perspective of organizational culture captures the mistrust at Lavender Refuge because it addresses ambiguity and uncertainty. Similar sentiments were echoed by Isabella, a Hispanic, 56-year-old Assistant Director, who struggled to do her job due to being under-resourced and overworked:

> … Whenever I would ask for things like that [to do my job better], what I would get is you're taking from the moms and I believed it …. [Then] I'm gonna [sic] set boundaries and I'm gonna [sic] set self-care. Uh, I will no longer give all of my time and energy to [Lavender Refuge]. 'Cause I was working seven days a week … I was working part-time, but I wasn't working part-time I was …. I was working 50, 60 hours, but they were only paying me 20 hours … because I didn't wanna [sic] take away from the moms …

These data reveal the manipulation staff experienced under the former leader. Former leadership made employees feel guilty, arguing that asking for work necessities would take provisions from clients.

The former director was also discriminatory. Lucky, an African American, 33-year-old Fundraiser, reflected on offensive comments from the Former Director:

> So one time … we had two Black women come in and to be screened and interviewed for acceptance within like a week's time and both of them got accepted and the [Executive Director] literally came out of her office and screamed at the top of her lungs, "We be integratin" [sic] …. Yeah. So, I was like, "What?" Um, everybody was appalled. Like, I remember one- one- one person …. was like, "You cannot say that. Like, that is unacceptable." Um, but then the [Executive Director] would say things like, you know, "We, we can't lose these Black clients because, you know, we- we now have five Black clients, we gotta [sic] do whatever we can to keep them here." You know? …. kinda [sic] thing. So, I, I feel like that was the bias that was playing out, was like we don't wanna [sic] be seen as a program that's like racist or has- is not like inclusive of women of color, so we're gonna [sic] do everything that we can, even if it means ignoring our own rules that, that apply to everyone else, to make sure that they stay.

The cultural mocking by the past Executive Director exaggerating Black English Vernacular that is recounted in Lucky's narrative was one-way racism was manifest in this culture.

Bias was also evident in how mothers of color were treated by former staff members. For instance, Amy, a multi-racial, 35-year-old Wellness Coach shared:

> There was the previous leadership … [who] asked me … if we were hiring at [a local non-profit organization], and I said, "yeah … I know this one mom was looking for a job, a mom of color" and she [the previous executive director] was like yeah "she's not gonna [sic] want it, this other mom needs a job," and it was a White mom you know … like okay, but it was always kind of that way, you know, like yeah don't worry about that one [mother of color] don't bother with that one, do this one [a White mother] instead. There's like an automatic assumption that they [mothers of color] just wouldn't uh follow through or … you know, weren't going to be successful with that so don't bother.

Essentially, there was an implicit racialized assumption that clients of color were not hard workers worthy of job referrals. In reality, mothers of color were treated in a discriminatory manner. Amy's exemplar reveals the past leadership's prejudice and problematic behavior of clients toward clients of color. In addition, there were discriminatory systems keeping Lavender Refuge from becoming more diverse. Patrice, an African American, 35-year-old Events Manager, provided an explanation of this form of systematic racism:

> ... through our referral partners, because we're like "well why aren't we like seeing, like a [Lavender Refuge residential] community that's reflective of the community at large?" Especially like living on [the street that marks the historical color line], you know, like the demographics. There's a certain makeup here that it's just not reflective of our small community. Um and so we found out that we had a reputation for not being inclusive, that moms of color were told not to come here, um we thought that there wasn't an issue with like our referral partners, but the issue is with us, as an organization.

Clients are accepted only by referral from healthcare clinics treating addiction. Lavender Refuge wondered why its clientele was primarily white mothers and realized it was due to their reputation, not referral partners.

Ultimately, past organizational systems were racially biased, operating under an unhealthy organizational culture and leadership. The former Executive Director retired from her role, yet the Board of Directors had so much discontent with her leadership that they aimed to hire a more thoughtful leadership team. As leadership changed and the 20th anniversary drew near, the new leadership worked to develop a collaborative, diverse, and inclusive culture—they wanted the 20th-anniversary celebration to be a new start.

Leading Organizational Change: Painting a Celebration

Lavender Refuge made major changes. Approximately 85% of the leadership and staff turned over, bringing in a new Executive Director and leadership staff. In addition, new hires were much more diverse than the last group of employees, increasing the numbers of Black, Hispanic, and Latinx employees. As the anniversary neared, leaders wanted to celebrate in a big way, yet the pandemic emerged and they were not able to hold celebratory events as they had hoped. It was suggested that painting a mural on the outside of the building would be a way to visually symbolize their community and organizational mission, and communicate their hopes for more diverse clientele that better represented the surrounding community.

One employee, Laura, a Hispanic, 36-year-old Financial Coach explained that before the mural, the media's representation of the community depicted a more homogenous group, and that bothered one client of color:

Yeah so, we had a mom say that she felt she wasn't represented culturally. Um between our web page to everything [Lavender Refuge] was pretty whitewashed. And that bothered her. So, we started having conversations. Um, and then soon that mural was brought to us 'hey, this is what we want to do. This is our idea.'

The mural was an intentional effort to represent the diversity Lavender Refuge wanted to have in their community and to resist the previous "whitewashed" representation by boldly including mothers of color.

The new Executive Director, Kelly, a white, 54-year-old woman, started working in February 2020. She explained the process leadership took to identify the artist and develop the mural:

Well it's our 20th anniversary, and so ... he's [the artist] done several murals up and down [a number of different city streets] and, and so we thought okay that'd be awesome to have him do our mural to celebrate the 20th anniversary .... So, ... he spent some time with us to understand [Lavender Refuge] and you know moms and kids and recovery and hope, and all this good stuff. And um, so then he drew up some pictures and it was it was different, different skin colors, different hairstyles .... you know 'cause staff, first like we had some changes we wanted to make to it. And then I took it to [the residents'] council and said, what do you think? And, and they loved it, I really don't remember that they had any changes to it at all. ... like everybody's in agreement, and so then he painted it.

Kelly outlines the organizational decision-making process in her exemplar. She believed there was consensus about the mural when she says "everybody's in agreement," which we interpret through Martin's (1992) integration perspective of organizational culture. The leadership believed hiring a local artist and having a mural painted that symbolized the mission of the organization seemed like a wonderful way to celebrate the anniversary.

The mural wraps around a main building that is visible on two cross streets. Megan, a white, 45-year-old Volunteer Manager, explained the location of the building that was painted:

Everybody uses that building ... like you need to meet with your case manager, you need to go to therapy ... you're going to a class in that building, or whatever it is um it's where a lot of volunteers are going it's where a lot of our residents are going for services .... I think it's beautiful and it's got a [lavender] background, so it stands out like you know when you're on our campus because the [lavender] building is a landmark .... so we have been like loving the art and we've used it in our new website. We've used it for like marketing campaigns and other things like we've pulled pieces of it out to use all over the place.

Megan's exemplar indicates the mural is in a prominent space. In essence, this new mural and its location changed a central organizational artifact (Schein, 2010). It is a staple location in the community where much of the work is happening for mothers in recovery.

We asked interviewees to describe the mural. Mary, an African American, 58-year-old Office Manager stated:

It's beautiful. It's all different nationalities um and it's just like, on the one side of and its mainly like their backs and they may be like turn halfway to the side, where you're seeing the side of their face. And ... they have their arms around each other, like you know, like sisters and it's just all different races, and it's showing hearts, hope .... love. it's, it's really nice.

The word "beautiful" was repeated across interviews when describing the mural. This common language demonstrates a level of consensus as well (Martin, 1992). For instance, Clementine described the mural, saying:

I think it's beautiful. I think [the artist] did an excellent job ... it's like women's backs, and so you have um there's four or five women and to me they look like women of different races and ethnicities, different skin tones across the board, different hair types and cuts, and then on the front part there is, yeah, there's women, women, women of color. To me a White looking woman and they have like one woman is pregnant and then other women have, have either like a child near them or children, and the children, sometimes have, to me my interpretation of the mural, they may not have the same exact race or ethnicity as their mom so like encompassing that families are multiracial, multicultural now. Um so I think it's beautiful ...

The multi-racial depiction in the art led to some resistance from white clients. In Martin's (1992) theory of organizational culture, the differentiation lens accounts for organizational conflict. Hannah, a white, 32-year-old Director of Resource Development, noted that resistance:

> I love the mural. I think it's beautiful. Um, I was saddened by feedback from a few White moms during an all resident meeting ... saying that they didn't feel represented in it [the mural]. Afterward [Beth, our Senior Empowerment Manager] and I pulled up a picture, together ... the venting moment [between staff] and circled everyone who can be perceived as White in there [the mural].

During data collection, we asked Kelly about this controversy, and she elaborated:

> We had some Caucasian moms who felt like it [the mural] didn't reflect—they didn't see themselves in that mural. Well it's the same number of Caucasian people as it is people of color. ... this one particular mom she was really upset. I mean I talked with her about it and um she just didn't see herself in it, ... even though we have these different ... methods in place to safeguard ourselves and make sure everybody has a voice ... Someone still might feel left out. And, and she did so now she's you know this particular person has just recently moved out .... I don't know that we worked through it, I mean I spent ... time talking with her several times, but I think she just accepted the fact that some people see themselves in it [the mural], and some people don't .... I mean for the most part, people see it, they love it they think it reflects the spirit, they think it reflects um the sisterhood between the moms ...

The racialized conflict that emerged after the mural was completed could reveal a type of demographic counterculture in the organization. However, the multi-cultural depiction of women and children in the mural was intentional.

Patrice explains that the mural intentionally visualized what leadership wanted the future of the community to look like:

> So, this was actually a collaborative effort between what the moms wanted to describe [Lavender Refuge] and then also um what staff wanted to see it become in the future, so we work with [the artist] and on one side of the mural there are a few terms: recovery, community sisterhood, and there are women. You can see their backs only but they're embracing one another and hug you know the front there's mothers and children. Um one of the things that we specifically asked

artists to do was to bring in more diversity in the mural than what was actually present on campus and the reason for doing that is because we wanted to set the tone that this is a welcoming community, and although we are not as reflective of the community around us right now that we are actively working to change that um through our conversations through our policies through the referral partners that we have like just making sure that it's as welcoming and as diverse as possible, because in the past we haven't always had that reputation and we found that out the hard way last summer that we had a reputation for not being as inclusive. Um but we have a whole new staff for the most part ... and so we ... all ... have this mindset that this is a type of place, that we want to be welcoming for everyone. So, um yeah [laughs] so you see more brown faces and more people of color on the mural than, than what is actually on campus.

Despite resistance from some clients, the mural remains. The new leadership felt strongly that it reflected the new culture they were striving for. Lavender Refuge now uses the metaphor of "sisterhood" to convey inclusion and the essence of their new culture.

Building Organizational Culture: Sisterhood of Support

Once the new leadership team joined the organization, they worked to intentionally shift the culture. By racially diversifying the staff, increasing information sharing and collaboration among staff and volunteers, and allowing the clients to have more autonomy and fewer restrictions, they aimed to change the organizational culture. Ultimately, the staff wanted to construct a support system for clients. What unites the staff at Lavender Refuge is their work with clients and their desire to positively impact the community. Note, at the time of our study, all employees and volunteers were cis-gendered women. Their gendered identities influenced cultural changemaking efforts.

We asked interviewees about the new organizational culture. The majority of interviewees mentioned sisterhood. For instance, Jennifer, a Hispanic, 39-year-old mother of five was asked to describe the community, and she replied:

Um, Union, sisterhood, power. Um love, friendship we always look out for each other. I don't think there's thoughts of because I don't ever gossip. And I don't ever don't ever hear that stuff but it's just always we're always looking out for each other, we always making sure we're all okay.

Jennifer describes positive aspects of their community, like friendship and looking out for one another, through a sisterhood metaphor, yet also describes the absence of negative communication, like gossip. The notion of sisterhood crossed racial lines. Similarly, Jane, a white, 36-year-old mother of two shared:

> I really feel like it's kind of um kind of a sisterhood ... I think that it definitely is a community um, a community of support and um there's a lot of fellowship and you know people um leaning on each other for things and stuff like that.

This sisterhood was conveyed by both clients and staff. For instance, veteran staff members identified a culture shift from the old leadership to the new. Beth, an African American, 42-year-old Empowerment Manager stated:

> Um a sisterhood. Um I noticed when I first started there was a lot of like division. Um and mom's knowing their place, but over the past like year I've been there, like they depend on each other a lot so that family um dynamic, like it's a big, uh I think of it as a big family.

Beth marks the shift from the past authoritarian leadership to the new family oriented culture, which she describes as a "sisterhood."

The culture of sisterhood also emerged in organizational practices. For instance, Lavender Refuge started a Facebook page, which was described in Austin's interview, a white, 31-year-old mother of one:

Interviewer: Are you active in the [Lavender Refuge] Facebook group? ...

Austin: Yes, the [Lavender] Sister page, yeah. I'm actually on the ... [residents'] council here at [Lavender Refuge]. So I try to stay pretty active on the sisters' page as far as like posting, you know positive quotes, or you know life hacks or something to make life easier, you know, or information that they might leave on jobs, or just resources.

The sisterhood extended to a digital format through social media. There, clients and alumni of the program can share social support.

Also, Lavender Refuge started a mentoring program to provide social support. Amya, a white, 34-year-old mother of eight, describes this program:

> ... and I really love this because we started it, I don't know, maybe like this year. But we started a big sister program. So basically, like when

you move in, you get one or two big sisters and like they're supposed to help you and answer any questions for you, um, and all that jazz. So, it's actually pretty cool.

The sisterhood is a work in progress, yet there was a shift in the culture. Clementine explained how a new sisterhood made her feel:

Would say that across the board with the residents, there is this idea or theme or underlying maybe a cultural thing of sisterhood um and I feel like each resident has a different level of buy in and trust in that kind of idea, but this idea that you can reach out and rely on your fellow resident, your neighbor, that you have enough shared experience that this is, you know um collaborative were all working together ... to be the best version of ourselves and things like that. And yeah culture in terms of staff? Not sure how to describe that because it's changed. It is changed since I've gotten there .... Uh, I feel like now, with the staff that we have we are in a much better position and are much more likely to follow through the things that we've been saying. And we're hopeful [Lavender Refuge]. I was not hopeful before [laughs].

Organizational change is challenging work. Clementine's expressions of hope demonstrate that at times, positive change is possible, even emerging from a problematic past.

The shared value of sisterhood can be accounted for in Martin's (1992) integration perspective of organizational culture because it allowed the clients and staff to socially construct consensus around a more positive organizational culture that emerged across their organizational artifacts, like the mural, values of sisterhood, and assumptions that human service organizations should foster support (Schein, 2010).

Discussion

The past organizational culture at Lavender Refuge is best characterized by the fragmentation perspective, which accounts for ambiguity and uncertainty (Martin, 1992). The culture of mistrust, paranoia, fear, and racial prejudice that existed both caused and was caused by employees that held secrets, worked in paranoia due to job insecurity, and discriminated against clients of color. As leadership changed, they worked to shift the organizational culture. The new leadership took the opportunity of the 20th anniversary to cultivate a visual organizational artifact in the form of a mural on a prominent building in their community. This visual artifact helped the community identify a new central value of sisterhood, which they used to construct a renewed organizational culture. The mural symbolized the diversity organizational members envisioned for their future.

Artifacts and values are often connected to one another and undergirded by implicit assumptions organizational members hold (Schein, 2010). The few white mothers who resisted the mural revealed assumptions regarding the positionality of whiteness in their culture. Some white mothers felt entitled to representation and expressed resistance to the visual diversity depicted in the mural as a cultural artifact. The organization grappled with assumptions of whiteness and re-asserted its commitment to diversity by re-orienting around the value of sisterhood.

This value of sisterhood served two functions. First, sisterhood as a value is tied to an organizational assumption about support systems, considering others' best interests, and female comradery. Second, the value of sisterhood functioned to obscure the racial bias in organizational culture. This new organizational culture is best understood through Martin's (1992) lens of integration, which accounts for shared values that people have consensus about. Both staff and clients enacted organizational performances around sisterhood to try to move the culture in a more unified direction.

Through organizational change, various stakeholders at Lavender Refuge used communication to constitute a new organizational culture. The 20-year celebration created a positive way for the new leadership at Lavender Refuge to construct its vision of a more diverse future, and the mural was a way to symbolically communicate that vision. Yet, assumptions about mothers of color are obscured through the unifying sisterhood discourse. The new sisterhood discourse finds a common identity, but does not embrace diversity. Few integration-focused studies (Martin, 1992) of organizational culture identify values that are simultaneously unifying yet hegemonic in nature, like the value of sisterhood at Lavender Refuge. By focusing on what seems like an inclusive value of sisterhood and emphasizing the positivity around this value, organizational leaders fail to grapple with the racial inequity that persists in their culture and obscure how whiteness functions throughout the organization. We recommended Lavender Refuge re-examine their past to take accountability of organizational mistakes and trauma, and then work toward a new future where diversity is embraced as part of what makes Lavender Refuge worthwhile. The findings of this ethnographic case study reveal a number of practical insights for non-profit practitioners.

Practical Applications

Our research reveals that non-profit leaders who identify shared values stakeholders can rally around is one way to re-invent organizational culture. However, doing so does not necessarily redress past hurt, pain, and insecurities when an organization is emerging from a destructive past. Changing organizational culture requires an investment from every stakeholder, taking accountability for past hurt, and working through it. We believe the following practical strategies would help non-profit leaders and practitioners effectively engage in culture change. First, leaders should take stock of the past and present organizational culture using culture audits (Wilkins, 1983). Second, leaders and practitioners should engage in trauma stewardship and radical self-care (Lipsky & Burk, 2009). Third, non-profit leaders should lead with humility (Gist, 2020). Each is reviewed below.

Leaders who manage organizations with high turnover have a responsibility to take stock of their past and present organizational cultures. Culture audits are one approach leaders can take to engage this task (Wilkerson, 1983; Testa & Sipe, 2013). Culture audits allow organizational leaders to identify the nuances of an organization's existing culture and function as a tool for determining cultural discrepancies between the real versus ideal organizational culture. Culture audits are often structured through five steps: (1) identifying the organizational vision, mission, values, and strategic goals; (2) developing a cultural narrative that constructs an ideal organizational culture the organization could strive toward; (3) selecting an audit team of people representing diverse units/functions across the organization; (4) collecting a variety of data (quantitative/qualitative); and (5) analyzing and interpreting data and reporting recommendations. Cultural audits should be as holistic as possible, exploring everything from physical characteristics and environment, customs and norms, rituals and ceremonies, rules and policies, assessment and accountability, rewards and punishments, as well as relational dynamics (Testa & Sipe, 2013). This process should engage stakeholder voices at every level. If necessary, an outside party who will guarantee confidentiality can be used to execute a culture audit, so employees and clients can speak freely about experiences. We urge organizational leaders who engage in cultural audits to take the insights provided and develop strategies that can be implemented to move the culture in more positive, equitable, and inclusive directions. Cultural audits may reveal organizational trauma from harmful work conditions or relationships. In that case, we recommend practitioners engage in trauma-informed stewardship (Lipsky & Burk, 2009).

Employees working in human service non-profit organizations often experience vicarious trauma of clients (Jansen, 2004), as well as workplace-induced trauma from problematic workplaces. Dual sources of trauma require enhanced levels of self-care. Lipsky and Burk (2009) outline 16 warning signs of trauma exposure for people engaged in helping professions, which include: feeling helpless and hopeless; a sense that one can never do enough; hypervigilance; diminished creativity; inability to embrace complexity; minimizing others' pain; chronic exhaustion; physical ailments; inability to listen; deliberate avoidance of work; dissociative moments; sense of persecution; guilt; fear; anger and cynicism; inability to empathize; substance abuse; and an inflated sense of the importance of one's work. Non-profit employees that are experiencing multiple forms of trauma need to engage in deep levels of self-care. Bessel van der Kolk (2003) identifies important differences between those who are permanently debilitated versus those who are resilient to trauma, which includes: (1) cultivating a personal sense of control, (2) pursuing personally meaningful tasks, (3) fostering a social support network, and (4) making healthy life choices (i.e., sleep, nutritious foods, and exercise). These action steps should allow employees and leaders to identify when people are experiencing various traumas and when they need to focus on caring for their employees and fostering self-care for those in need. This requires a level of leader humility (Gist, 2020), which is addressed next.

It is recommended that non-profit leaders lead with humility. Gist (2020, p. 2) explains that leader humility is "a tendency to feel and display a deep regard for others' dignity." Leaders who enact humility are able to foster and maintain healthy workplace relationships with all stakeholders where psychological safety and information sharing become the organizational norm (Gist, 2020). There are six best practices for leaders who want to model humility—lead with: (1) a balanced ego, (2) robust integrity, (3) a compelling vision, (4) ethical strategies, (5) generous inclusion, and (6) developmental focus (Gist, 2020). Leaders with balanced egos are aware of their power and authority, but are humble and confident enough to lead in ways where they minimize unnecessary displays of power. Leading with robust integrity means behaving in ways that "reflect a high standard of personal conduct" in both work and non-work domains (Gist, 2020). Leading with compelling vision involves fostering a future for the greater good, a vision that goes beyond the leader's direct responsibilities and personal interests (Gist, 2020). Ethical strategies, such as equitable employee compensation and minimizing waste, are imperative for enacting leader humility (Gist, 2020). Furthermore, leaders with humility also address unethical behavior swiftly and preserve others' dignity while doing so. Leading with generous inclusion makes stakeholders and employees feel seen, heard, and valued for who they are and for what they uniquely contribute. Leaders who are mindful of generous inclusion ask and determine who should be included, on what activities, and in what way. Moreover, this requires leaders to listen and show genuine interest in others' ideas, opinions, and contributions. Finally, leaders with humility enact a developmental focus, meaning they think long-term and holistically about their stakeholders' and employees' growth and trajectory. To lead with developmental focus is to support, empower, uplift, and sponsor people. Ultimately, modeling leader humility upholds the dignity of others at all times.

We encourage non-profit practitioners to consider some practical implications we outlined to foster dignity, equity, and belonging. We recommend that practitioners should take stock of the past and present organizational culture by considering culture audits (Testa & Sipe, 2013), engage in trauma stewardship and self-care (Lipsky & Burk, 2009), and lead with humility (Gist, 2020).

Discussion Questions

1 If you were a new organizational leader at this non-profit, how would you learn about the past organizational culture?
2 What did the mixed reaction about the mural reveal to leaders about the residents' community?
3 How do values of inclusion, like the sisterhood value in this case, overshadow values of diversity?

Author Bios

Angela N. Gist-Mackey, Ph.D. (she/her(s)), is an Associate Professor of Organizational Communication at the University of Kansas. Dr. Gist-Mackey is an interpretive critical scholar who largely researches issues of social mobility and power in organized contexts. Her program of research frequently engages community-based non-profit organizations using ethnographic methods.

Savaughn E. Williams, M.A. (she/her(s)), is currently a Doctoral Candidate in the Communication Studies Department at the University of Kansas. She qualitatively and critically studies interracial friendships and race communication, as well as Blackness across contexts such as sexuality and family communication.

Anna Jewell, (she/her(s)), is a Graduate Student in the Department of Communication Studies at the University of Kansas. Her research looks at the rhetorical significance of counterstories and the ways identity is discursively negotiated.

References

Gist, M. E. (2020). *The extraordinary power of leader humility: Thriving organizations, great results*. Berrett-Koehler Publishers.

Jansen, G. (2004). Vicarious trauma and its impact on advocates, therapists, and friends. *Research & Advocacy Digest, 6*(2), 9–14.

Keyton, J. (2011). *Communication and organizational culture: A key to understanding work experiences.* Sage.

Lipsky, L. & Burk, C. (2009). *Trauma stewardship: An everyday guide to caring for self while caring for others.* Berrett-Koehler Publishers.

Martin, J. (1992). *Cultures in organizations: Three perspectives.* Oxford University Press.

Schein, E. (2010). *Organizational culture and leadership.* (4th ed). Jossey-Bass.

Tracy, S. J. (2020). *Qualitative research methods: Collecting evidence, crafting analysis, communicating impact.* (2nd Edition). Wiley Blackwell.

Testa, M. R., & Sipe, L. J. (2013). The organizational culture audit: Countering cultural ambiguity in the service context. *Open Journal of Leadership, 2*(2), 36–44. 10.4236/ojl.2013.22005

van der Kolk, B. A. (2003). *Psychological trauma.* American Psychiatric Press.

Wilkins, A. L. (1983). The culture audit: A tool for understanding organizations. *Organizational Dynamics, 12*(2), 24–38. 10.1016/0090-2616(83)90031-1

23

ORGANIZING FOR TRANSGENDER INCLUSION

How Control and Resistance Theorizing Serve as Intervention Tools

Alaina C. Zanin and Lore/tta LeMaster

Arizona State University

Learning Objectives

After reading this chapter, you will:

1 Understand and empathize with a transgender athlete's experience.
2 Define and apply organizational theory to issues of exclusion within organizational contexts.
3 Identify and apply practical applications of theory to increase inclusivity within exclusionary organizational structures.

Introduction

This chapter follows Taylor—a youth athlete who happens to be transgender and genderfluid—as they navigate sport contexts. The narratives constituting Taylor's experience are based on a synthesis of experiences and stories retold by transgender and gender non-conforming athletes about turning points within their gender journey across sport contexts. While the narratives reflect a composite of experiences, the identities (i.e., transmasculine and genderfluid) and pronouns (i.e., they/them/theirs) used to describe Taylor reflect a central participant(s)' self-disclosed identity descriptions.

Drawing on organizational theory, this chapter features two interrelated case studies that highlight Taylor's differing experiences in navigating two water polo team's cultures, first in high school and then in college. While the protagonist of these case studies is transgender, the implications of these case studies are intersectionally poignant and reveal ways sport

DOI: 10.4324/9781003333746-26

organizations might work to increase inclusion of groups who have been historically marginalized in sport organizations. The final section of the chapter offers practical recommendations for stakeholders to leverage organizational theory to cultivate inclusivity.

Case 1: Transgender Identity Enactment in the Culture of Sport

Taylor stands in front of the full-length mirror in their bedroom. A single tear rolls out from the edge of their eye to the carpeted floor. Taylor is wearing the requisite and tight one-piece swimsuit allocated to all players on the Centerville women's water polo team. Taylor knew this would be—*had to be*—the last time they would put it on. The heightened body dysmorphia, clashing with their gender dysphoria, was too great a price to bear in exchange for "the privilege" to compete in the sport they loved. In middle school, Taylor played water polo on a mixed-gender team on which they thrived; but in high school, the proverbial "powers that be"—Centerville parents, coaches, teachers, and administrators—forced Taylor to play on an all-women's team. Taylor was 13 years old and still trying to understand gender, to find language for their gendered experience, and to understand why being forced to play on an all-women's team made them so upset, so infuriated, and that made them so depressed they eventually withdrew from their friends, stayed in their room, and wore baggy grey sweats all summer.

Taylor is now 16 years old and has access to a therapist—a resource they utilize. Recently, Taylor has come to understand their gender as fluid, non-binary, and transmasculine. In turn, Taylor has cultivated a sense of healing through their gender journey including transition. Nonetheless, they are hesitant to disclose their trans identity to the Centerville team, and to Coach Miller. Taylor was particularly afraid because, while they knew they were good at water polo—*like team captain and key defender as a freshman good*—they did not want transphobic projections to eclipse their athleticism or their love for athletics. Moreover, they did not want to endure additional pain and turmoil; *and there would be pain*, Taylor knew. There were explicit and implicit rules about who "could" and "could not" compete on Centerville High School's Women's Water Polo team, including strict uniform guidelines coupled with single-gender locker rooms for both home and away matches. Then there were the implied gendered norms that shaped their team's presence on campus—like wearing matching makeup and hair ribbons to school on match days. Coach Miller claimed that the matching gameday attire was to "promote school spirit and show everyone we were a cohesive team." Explicit were the calls for cohesion, and implicit were the calls for adherence to stereotypical feminine gender norms. Taylor did not want to dress that way. *My identity as an athlete,* Taylor reflected, *has nothing to do with wearing make-up and ribbons and everything to do with how I perform in the pool.* Taylor knew they had to quit. It was all so unbearable: the binary sport context, the gendered norms, and the insistent (mis)gendering. The greater their sense of healing, the further from sports they strayed. Taylor threw baggy grey sweats over the requisite and tight one-piece swimsuit and headed to the pool to meet Coach Miller.

***

Taylor looked up at the sign hanging in Coach Miller's office. It read in big, block lettering "**Quitters never win, and Winners never quit.**" The nauseous feeling in the pit of their stomach grew, as Coach Miller chatted excitedly about his plans for the team this year. Taylor couldn't take it any longer.

"I'm not coming back this year, okay!" Taylor blurted out.

Coach Miller was shocked into silence. He had been in the middle of praising Taylor for their accomplishments during their sophomore season—winning all-conference accolades. "Okay, can you tell me why you have had a change of heart with regards to water polo? You know, you are on the track for a college scholarship?"

"I just don't like it anymore. There isn't really much to talk about." Taylor replied directly. They surrendered their uniform, including their captain armband, and walked out of Coach Miller's office in silence. They made it to the parking lot before they burst into tears.

"Taylor, are you okay?" Coach Miller had caught up to Taylor, after jogging from the office. Taylor turned and Coach Miller saw the anguish on their face. "What's going on? Why aren't you joining the team next year?" Taylor remained silent as Coach Miller layered in an empathic gesture, "Whatever it is, you can tell me, I am here for you. In the pool and in life."

Taylor took a tepid breath; they had not anticipated a follow-up gesture of support. From here, things were improvised. Taylor looked cautiously at Coach Miller, who seemed to care about his athletes, and offered, "Well, I have been feeling really down lately."

Coach Miller nodded, listened, and invited Taylor to continue.

Taylor stated directly, "I have been working with a therapist because I feel really down about my body. About puberty and stuff like that." They paused for a moment and softened their gaze before adding, "I'm just so uncomfortable in the women's swimsuit."

Coach Miller nodded again and said, "I hear you, that sounds hard, and it was brave of you to share that with me, but I can work on changing that for you. I know how happy water polo makes you. I have seen those big smiles after a big win. I wouldn't want a uniform to prevent you from experiencing that joy."

Taylor shook their head, and replied, "It's not just that. I don't feel comfortable because I'm not a girl. I mean, I'm not like the other girls. I'm just me. I'm beginning to understand that my gender is fluid or more aligned with masculinity than being a girl. I don't even like when people use 'she' or 'her' to refer to me! And I don't even know where I belong on a so-called 'women's team'!"

Silence hung in the air as Coach Miller processed Taylor's vulnerable words and audible frustration. "Now, *that* was brave, Taylor. I cannot imagine what that is like, but I absolutely hear you and see you. You are right. There is only one Taylor. And that Taylor—you—have been forced into gendered spaces not of your own choosing. And I also hear that I have been part of that process. For that, I am sorry for the harm my gendered assumptions have caused. And thank you for trusting me. Here is the thing, when I said I'm here for you in the pool and in life, I really mean it. You are welcome here. I will do everything in my power to advocate on your behalf and to make this as safe a space as I can—but will you allow me to try and make those changes with you? Will you join me in figuring how to make our team more welcoming of other gender-fluid or trans athletes?"

***

Taylor looks out at the cheering stands surrounding the Centerville High School pool at the regional water polo tournament. They grin as they walk out of the men's locker room, wearing a Centerville men's swimming speed suit, and to join their teammates on the women's water polo team.

Fans cheer as the announcer calls out Taylor's name on the roster but genders them incorrectly. Taylor grimaces as one of their teammates and Coach Miller run over to speak with the announcer. Moments later, the announcer's voice adds, "Excuse me, Taylor Smith's pronouns are they/them, we apologize for the oversight and will use the correct pronouns moving forward." The fans continue to cheer.

The teammate who joined Coach Miller in correcting the announcer returns to the bench where Taylor is now sitting. The teammate jokingly comments, trying to break the thick air, "Jeez, it's not that hard to get it right, announcer guy!" Taylor nods and chortles as the teammate checks, "Are you okay, Taylor?"

Taylor feels seen, supported, and content to focus on the tournament with less internalized transphobia clouding their thoughts or hindering their athletic capacity. Taylor smiles and responds, "Yes, I'm going to be okay."

Theoretical Framing: Unobtrusive Control Theory and Resistance

Within this case, Taylor is negotiating both their liminal gender identity and their identification with the women's water polo team. Past research indicates that organizational members come to know, understand, and enact their multiple, layered identities through group and organizational identities (Zanin et al., 2020). Identification occurs through discourse when people claim *consubstantiality* (i.e., as if they were one with their target of identification, like an organization or identity group) through everyday talk (Gossett, 2002). Mael and Ashforth (1995) defined organizational identification as "the perception of oneness with or belongingness to [a collective], where the individual defines him or herself [*sic*] in terms of the [collective] in which he or she [*sic*] is a member" (p. 104). However, communication scholars argue that this perception can only occur through, and as a result of, discursive interaction (Gossett, 2009). Relatedly, unobtrusive control theory (UCT) (Tompkins & Cheney, 1985) proposes that organizational identification functions to guide member's decision making toward organizational aims. For example, athletes on a team may decide to wear matching uniforms on gameday to demonstrate their belonging and collective identification with their team.

The main premise of UCT is that highly identified members make organizationally relevant decisions by believing and enacting particular organizational premises (Tompkins & Cheney, 1985). New members begin to enact their identity as an organizational member as a result of the inculcation of organizational premises, and through on-going feedback from organizational incumbents. For example, what might the consequences have been for Taylor had they refused to wear ribbons and makeup on match days like their teammates? Taylor might receive sanctioning feedback for "not having team spirit" or for "not being a team player" because they "chose" not to conform to team norms, and because they "chose" not to outwardly demonstrate their identification with the water polo team's gendered choice of dress.

Through these everyday interactions, new members are socialized by incumbent organizational members to take up decisional premises which guide decisions based on organizational beliefs and values. In short, both *what is valued* and *what is perceived* as "true" in an organization becomes implied rather than discussed through these decisional premises.

Highly identified members are expected to make decisions based on these organizational premises. This inculcation process, however, is often "unobtrusive" rather than overt, intentional, or strategic. As a result, many of the current problematic and exclusionary organizational premises are taken-for-granted and sedimented into organizational norms as members change over time. This phenomenon is particularly true for organizations that reside in larger exclusionary systems and structures, for example, the binary gender structures and resultant organizational premises that organize youth, amateur, and professional sport (LeMaster et al., 2023; Travers, 2008, 2018; Zanin & Bisel, 2020).

In Taylor's case, claiming oneness or consubstantiality with their high school women's water polo team barred them from realizing their transgender, masculine, and genderfluid identity. In the case study, Taylor recognized their layered identities (i.e., genderfluid, athlete, and teammate) as no longer fitting into the binary gender structures, nor the subsequent gendered organizational premises, that constituted the women's water polo team. Even though Taylor was a highly identified member of the team—as a star player and team captain—their full identification, particularly their fluid gender identity, was reduced in service of organizational cohesion. As an example, Taylor being mandated to wear a *particularly gendered* swimsuit as requisite for team participation, reinforces a burgeoning gap between their individual identity and the team identity. Simply put, Taylor could not claim oneness with their team while refusing to wear the team garb. When full identification is disallowed, members are likely to leave the organization, similar to Taylor's impulse to leave. In turn, exclusionary premises are likely retained rather than reformed because those who challenge problematic and/or exclusionary organizational premises tend to leave the organization as a result.

Practical Application: Cognitive Gaps and Shared Extra-Organizational Premises

As discussed, organizational members make decisions based on implicit premises (e.g., beliefs, values, and behavioral expectations), which have been instilled by the power holders within the organization (Tompkins & Cheney, 1985). However, as past research has indicated, unobtrusive organizational control is not absolute (e.g., Zanin & Bisel, 2020). One of the ways organizational members can resist unobtrusive control and exclusionary premises is through an understanding of how premises create interpretive gaps that allow for member resistance.

First, organizational premises are multiple, value-laden, and at times contradict one another (Zanin & Bisel, 2020). This inherent quality of premises arises from the fact that organizational and extra-organizational premises often function simultaneously in member decision making. In the case study, Coach Miller reinforced the organizational premises of both team cohesion (e.g., dress, uniforms, team spirit) *and* care for athletes outside of athletics (e.g., "I'm here for you in the pool and in life, I really mean it"). In so doing, Coach Miller showed resistance by developing an extra-organizational premise that challenged the presumption of binary gender contradictions (e.g., ensuring Taylor could wear the men's swimsuit as well as use the men's locker room *while playing on a women's water polo team*).

Second, premises are open to individual interpretation and are often ambiguous (Eisenberg, 1984). As an example, LeMaster et al. (2023) explore the ways trans athletes navigate relational belonging in sport contexts. They found that precisely because gender binarism serves an unstated organizational premise (i.e., masculine and feminine gender are separate, mutually exclusive, and oppositional), trans athletes compete on teams that both do and do not align with their subjective sense of gender. The result is a form of relational ambivalence that enables trans athletes to harness tepid acceptance despite organizational misalignment. As illustration, a transmasculine athlete reflected on the organizational premise of *"empowering women"* in the context of weight lifting: "You have to make the best with what you have which is the two categories, man and woman. I don't think I ever questioned why I was in the woman category because man didn't feel right either. So, it was this thing that I just accepted as truth."

Third, premises function as truncated syllogisms or enthymemes such that members are expected to fill in the conclusion (Tompkins & Cheney, 1985). Traditional syllogisms include a major premise (e.g., *Quitters never win, winners never quit*), a minor premise (e.g., *Water polo players are winners*), and a conclusion (e.g., *Therefore, water polo players never quit*). Enthymemes shorten syllogisms by leaving one of the premises or the conclusion unstated. In the case of organizational premises, highly identified members are expected to fill in their own decisional conclusions. This interpretive gap created by the enthymeme could be exploited to highlight and resist exclusionary practices in organizations (e.g., is it *"empowering"* to require athletes to pray before practice? To stand for the national anthem? To wear uniforms that contradict gender, religious or ethnic identities?).

Finally, past research has demonstrated that if highly identified members perceive there is contradiction between the actions of an organization, and its espoused values, they will resist (Larson & Tompkins, 2005). In the case study, Coach Miller, as a highly identified organizational member within the school and team, perceived a contradiction among the exclusionary policies of gendered uniforms and locker rooms, and the espoused values of inclusion and sport access for all athletes. Coach Miller then chose dissent to reform these contradictions (e.g., advocating for Taylor to play on the women's team as a genderfluid person in men's swim attire). Likewise, organizational stakeholders that are organizing for inclusion could reinforce high-order premises like social justice, equity, and inclusion during the inculcation period for newcomers to the organization (e.g., *our team is made valuable by who we include, rather than who we exclude*) with the goal of exploring what organizational premises and thus practices might need to be re-imagined to increase inclusion in terms that might seem contradictory or impossible at first glance.

Similarly, the case demonstrates how when leaders question organizational policies, this questioning creates contradictions among decisional premises. This questioning enables new premises to be created that can function like spring boards for further member decision making. In the case study, when Taylor's teammate and Coach Miller correct the announcer, there is an instance of reinforcement of a new organizational premise, which future members can now enact to demonstrate their belonging to a relatively more inclusive women's water polo team. However, reforming these exclusionary premises is challenging, given the fact that they are both taken-for-granted, and can be reinforced by misogynistic, homophobic, and transphobic ways of talking in sport cultures as the continued case study in the next section demonstrates (see Travers, 2008, 2018; Zanin & Bisel, 2020).

Case 2: Identity Muting as a Consequence of Exclusionary Organizational Premises

Taylor buried their face in their locker and tried not to wince as Ricky made vulgar hand gestures when talking about his latest "conquest"— Becky, from Middleton State University (MSU) women's water polo team. Ricky slapped Taylor on the back, a little too hard. Ricky sneered, "Right, man? Becky is such a little slut. I saw you looking at her. Have at it, man. I mean, you can have my sloppy seconds." Ricky adds, inferring Taylor, who keeps their face buried in their locker, "I bet this little virgin is too much of pussy to even talk to that slut Becky."

Taylor did not know what to say in response. They thought, *was this locker room talk? What could I say to still fit in?* Becky was Taylor's friend after all. And Taylor wasn't a misogynist. As a genderfluid transmasculine person, Taylor knew exactly what it felt like to be hated for one's own gender difference.

Taylor looked at Ricky, "Fuck off, man. I don't want to get your diseases, asshole." They grabbed their gym bag before run-walking out of the locker room.

Ricky called after Taylor, "This isn't over, you little pussy. I'll find out what kinky shit you're in to, just wait, you little bitch."

Taylor was a sophomore at MSU, and was living their life as a transmasculine person; well, sort of—with people with whom Taylor felt affirmed and safe. On the MSU men's water polo team, Taylor was known as the quiet defender from Centerville HS, but not much else. While Taylor had come out as transgender in high school, they told no one at MSU that they were trans or genderfluid for their own safety. Taylor was competing as a man on a men's sports team; they were living "stealth," which is to say they were living as a regular ol' guy, precisely because they passed as cisgender man in everyday life. Taylor was very well aware of the political privileges that came with passing as a cisgender man. The privilege of passing was the violence of erasure in plain sight. In the hypermasculine, transphobic, and homophobic context of the MSU men's water polo team, Taylor didn't care. Being stealth was about survival as a collegiate athlete.

***

Taylor and Ricky sat in a team meeting prior to the conference tournament against their rival university, Northern State University (NSU). The MSU water polo Head Coach—Coach Johnson—stood at the lectern in the front of the meeting room. Taylor scanned the room, a subtle practice they picked up as they moved across teams as a trans athlete. Everyone in the room, to Taylor's knowledge, were heterosexual non-transgender men, and they were passing as one, too; at least for now.

Coach Johnson cleared his throat, "Alright, men, let's get down to business. Here is the game strategy for our tournament this Friday." Taylor sees Ricky staring them down. Ricky makes the same vulgar gesture as in the locker room and then drags his index finger across his throat. Taylor glares back and flips Ricky the middle finger.

Coach Johnson interjects, "Is there something that is more important than what we're doing right now, Taylor and Ricky? Jesus, if you two want to go screw around, take it outside. We don't have time for your pansy-ass flirting."

Taylor turned bright red, stared at the floor, and nodded. Ricky seemed incensed, but responded with, "Yes, sir." The meeting continued.

***

Later, during a scrimmage at practice, Taylor noticed several of their teammates were treating them differently. On offense, no one was passing to Taylor, even if they were on goal, and could easily score. Even Greg—another player who was the target of Ricky's bullying—kicked Taylor's stomach and pushed their head underwater (illegal fouls in collegiate water polo).

Rather than condemning the illegal fouls, Coach Johnson directs Taylor, "Focus up! Do you want NSU to fucking steamroll us on Saturday?"

After practice, Taylor decides it is no longer safe for them to continue their participation on the team—even though the rules allow them to participate, the team culture does not. Taylor writes an email to Coach Johnson, explaining they can no longer participate on the team due to their challenging coursework in the coming semesters, and turned in their uniform. Unlike Coach Miller, Coach Johnson does not chase after Taylor; rather, Coach Johnson does not question Taylor's reason for quitting the team, thus maintaining the exclusionary team culture.

***

Taylor opened their laptop as morning sunlight flooded in through their New York City loft. Taylor is 35 years old now. They moved to the city after college and began working at a shelter and non-profit aimed at providing safe housing and healthcare services for queer and trans adolescents experiencing homelessness. Drinking coffee and scrolling through morning email, Taylor notices a Facebook message from Greg, his former teammate on the MSU water polo team. Taylor had no interest in "rekindling" a relationship with anyone on the team, given the bullying they had endured. Out of curiosity, Taylor clicked on the message. It read:

Hi Taylor,

I know this may sound weird after all this time, but I really admired your courage in college. I was scrolling and I saw your recent post about trans youth and that you were out as trans now. It brought back so many memories. I just wanted to say I feel really bad for how you were treated and how I treated you. I was starting to understand my queer identities at the time, but I felt that picking on you was the only way I wouldn't be bullied and could fit into the hypermasculine, homophobic team culture. I hope you find it in your heart to forgive me. I find it so inspiring what you're doing for our community. You are amazing. Best wishes for healing and cultivating joy in your future endeavors.

Sincerely—Greg

Taylor closed their laptop and drank another sip of coffee. They felt both validated and hurt. They could not help wondering, *did it have to be this way? What could they have done or do differently to ensure more trans kids and adults have access to sports? How might they create sports orga-nizations that cultivate inclusion rather than exclusion, where queer and other marginalized identities are celebrated rather than muted and bullied?*

Theoretical Framing: Concertive Control and Exclusionary Organizational Premises

One theoretical concept that provides insight into Taylor's vastly different experiences on their high school and collegiate water polo teams is *concertive control*. In traditional organizational settings like the workplace, concertive control refers to collective control that is exercised by organizational peers, according to a set of core organizational values (Barker, 1993; Zanin & Bisel, 2020). Concertive control is a sub-category of unobtrusive control such that it is not readily apparent and observable to organizational members. Moreover, concertive control is a particularly challenging form of control to resist such that highly identified organizational members are enforcing their own "self-prescribed" rules and norms for organizational aims (Barker, 1993).

Within the case study, Taylor experiences concertive control as a sanctioning mechanism for potentially expressing transgender and genderfluid identities in the context of a patriarchal masculine sport culture. This concertive control is related to extra-organizational values that pervade sport culture such as misogyny, homophobia, and transphobia (e.g., Anderson, 2002; Travers, 2008), particularly common within hegemonic masculine sports teams (Cooky & Messner, 2018). Given the organizational premises of performing and valuing cisgender identities over transgender identities, Ricky, Coach Johnson, and importantly Greg, all engage in normative sanctioning of both the actual or potential expression of nonbinary, feminine, or queer identities in sport contexts.

Given this mechanism of concertive control, both Taylor and Greg hid their respective identities in the same sport context (e.g., presenting as "stealth" or "closeted") for their own safety and survival. This muting of identities is problematic for several reasons. First, the muting of identity often leads to member (dis)stress, dissatisfaction, and organizational turnover, thus perpetuating issues of homogeneity in organizational membership (Hollis & McCalla, 2013). For example, while Taylor left the collegiate water polo team to ensure their safety, it is more accurate to suggest the college water polo team violently policed sexual and gender differences such that players are forced to either mute their sexual and/or gender difference (e.g., Greg) and/or depart from the team (e.g., Taylor). The result is an organization made homogenous through disciplinary means. Second, the muting of identity perpetuates exclusionary organizational premises because they are not challenged discursively or materially (e.g., the presence of unique/differing bodies in a space) given the continued homogeneity of the organization. In this case, the muting of transgender and gender non-conforming identities creates the impression of a unified gender identity such that organizational members are discouraged from voicing or embodying difference. In turn, the presumption of "appropriate" organizational behavior (e.g., binary gender) can be understood as a performative accomplishment made secure through disciplinary unobtrusive control. Third, the muting of identity perpetuates specific exclusionary d/Discourse that invalidates the existence of these identities. As a result, binary gender comes to predetermine not only athletic identity but the embodiment of said identities in sport contexts such that men athletes can never be feminine and women athletes can never be more masculine than men athletes. Last, given these organizational premises of exclusion, individuals that do not fit into prescribed organizational identities, both discursively and materially, are unlikely to join future similar organizations, thus perpetuating organization homogeneity rather than diversity.

Practical Application: Organizing for Inclusivity

Given the hidden nature of unobtrusive and concertive control, these forms of control are especially challenging to resist and reform. However, recent organizational scholarship does offer some possibilities for intervention. The following section offers four theory-based recommendations for members at all levels of authority to organize for inclusivity.

First, organizational stakeholders should consider how current organizational premises might be utilized toward fostering inclusivity. Past research has noted that all organizational premises, given their degree of ambiguity, have interpretive gaps that can be utilized for resistance. For example, Zanin and Bisel (2020) documented a football team that had the mantra of "do right," which could be ascribed to a variety of meanings by organizational decision makers. To reframe this already-held organizational premise, organizational leaders might tell a story of "doing right" by being an ally when a teammate was misgendered at a tournament. This storytelling would link the ambiguous organizational premises of "do right" to future decision making for inclusivity. Additional examples can include changing the meaning of: "*Man up!*" to a call for athletes who are men to stand up for teammates regardless of identity—including across intersections of difference and against racism, ableism, and classism, for example, the presumption of binary gender itself might be reconceptualized in terms of multiplicity such that intersectional diversity among athletes is praised as strength.

Second, organizations experiencing change or transition are prime targets for shifting organizational premises toward inclusive interventions. During times of transition, ambiguity and uncertainty are high, which allows for the re-framing and changing of past organizational premises (Larson & Tompkins, 2005). Presently, anti-transgender political leaders are crafting and passing legislation criminalizing trans youth participation in sport across the United States—particularly targeted are trans girls and women athletes. In response, sport organizations are undergoing profound change and transition, even as transgender and gender-expansive athletes bear the violent brunt of these changes. Given that organizations are especially malleable during these times, organizational leaders can articulate new shared values and organizational premises regarding the value of inclusivity—which might be at odds with emergent legislative policy. These new or (re)framed shared values can be articulated in the context of already taken-for-granted organizational premises. For example, if an athletic team already has the organizational premise of "being a good sport," the value of sportsmanship could be expanded to "being a good sport means everyone has a place to play including transgender and gender expansive athletes." The expansion of this organizational premise (gender as binary) connects the past premise ("being a good sport") to the value of inclusivity.

A third recommendation in organizing for inclusivity is idea championing (Cerne et al., 2016) as a means of building allyship within an organization. Past research has documented that one of the ways change and innovation occurs in organizing is through the support of an idea to others within the organization (Cerne et al., 2016). For example, in a meeting where a group member suggests an idea, for the idea to gain traction and consensus, at least one additional group member must advocate for the idea. In the case study, Taylor's teammate demonstrated idea championing through her allyship, the idea being all genders belong and should feel included in sports. The teammate promoted this idea when she went to correct the announcer's misgendering of Taylor. In addition to idea championing, organizational leaders may promote allyship through *identity championing* by advocating on behalf of others' diverse identities within and outside of the organization. This type of allyship has numerous benefits not only for those who reside in diverse identity groups, but also for the organization in terms of member retention, by making visible a variety of diverse identities (e.g., transgender, gender non-conforming, queer, and disabled) as an antidote to identity muting. Some examples can include: investing in trans-affirming diversity training for student athletes and coaches that can evoke a number of ideas that might be championed; reframe gender corrective actions as requisite for team solidarity rather than as a nuisance or as someone else's responsibility; and invite anonymous suggestions and ideas—from team players—for bettering the sport context.

Finally, organizations, particularly organizations that are materially structured by binary gender, must organize new material norms that facilitate inclusivity. In the context of sport, this organizing for inclusivity would include expansions in uniform design, accessible gender-neutral locker rooms, and bathrooms, as well as expansive participation policies that do not include or exclude on the basis of gender difference. These material shifts communicate both symbolic and physical inclusivity for transgender and gender-expansive folks in sport. As Ashcraft et al. (2009) noted, "the body is not simply *made sensible* in talk and symbolism; it is the product of symbolism colliding with various physical limitations" (p. 33). Given that people come to realize and enact their layered, multiple identities through organizational identification, both material and symbolic barriers to identity enactment should be considered when organizing for inclusivity.

Conclusion

Taken together, this case study exemplifies how similar athletic teams might organize in ways that include or exclude individuals who reside in historically marginalized identity groups. Through a lens of UCT and concertive control, this case study exemplified how organizational premises might be utilized as mechanisms of intervention and resistance against exclusionary organizational cultures. Future work might consider testing the efficacy of these recommendations in a variety of organizational contexts.

Discussion Questions

1 Based on the messages exchanged in the case study excerpts, what were the different organizational premises among Taylor's high school and university water polo teams? How were the premises communicated? Were the premises implicit or explicit?

2 To what degree is exclusion intended or unintended as a result of taken-for-granted organizational premises, messages from organizational stakeholders, and formal policies within Taylor's high school and university?

3 Consider your own identity groups, have you ever felt uncomfortable disclosing your full identity in a social setting (e.g., ethnic, religious, health, family, relationship status)? If so, tell the story of what happened.

What was the context or setting? What social forces influenced your own identity muting? If in the context of an organization or group, what implicit or explicit organizational premises might have prevented you from sharing your full identity?

Author Note

The fictional case study presented in this chapter is based on multiple participant narratives from a larger study about transgender, gender non-conforming athlete experiences. To review the empirical research this case is based on see LeMaster et al. (2023) and Zanin et al. (2023).

Author Bios

Alaina C. Zanin (Ph.D., University of Oklahoma) is an associate professor of organizational and health communication at Arizona State University. Her research interests include structuration and identity theories as well as issues surrounding control, and resistance. Her work is published in journals, such as *the Journal of Applied Communication Research, Communication Monographs*, and *Management Communication Quarterly*.

Lore/tta LeMaster, Ph.D. (she/they), lives, loves, and creates on Akimel O'otham and Piipaash land currently called Arizona. Her scholarship engages the intersectional constitution of cultural difference with particular focus on trans of color life, art, and embodiment. She is a full-time care-taker, worldmaker, and avid eater of donuts and tacos.

References

Ashcraft, K. L., Kuhn, T. R., & Cooren, F. (2009). 1 Constitutional amendments: "Materializing" organizational communication. *Academy of Management Annals, 3*(1), 1–64. 10.5465/19416520903047186

Anderson, E. (2002). Openly gay athletes: Contesting hegemonic masculinity in a homophobic environment. *Gender & Society, 16*, 860–877. 10.1177/0891243 0223789

Barker, J. (1993). Tightening the iron cage: Concertive control in self-managing teams. *Administrative Science Quarterly, 38* (3) 408–437. 10.2307/2393374

Cerne, M., Kaše, R., & Skerlavaj, M. (2016). This idea rocks! Idea championing in teams. In M. Škerlavaj, M. Černe, A. Dysvik, & A. Carlsen (Eds.), *Capitalizing on Creativity at work: Fostering the implementation of creative ideas in organizations* (pp. 53–63). Edward Elgar Publishing. 10.4337/9781783476503

Cooky, C., & Messner, M. A. (2018). *No slam dunk: Gender, sport and the unevenness of social change*. Rutgers University Press.

Eisenberg, E. M. (1984). Ambiguity as strategy in organizational communication. *Communication Monographs, 51*(3), 227–242. 10.1080/03637758409390197

Gossett. (2002). Kept at arm's length: Questioning the organizational desirability of member identification. *Communication Monographs, 69*(4), 385–404. 10.1080/03637750216548

Gossett, L. M. (2009). Organizational control theory. In S. W. Littlejohn & K. A. Foss (Eds.) *Encyclopedia of Communication Theory*, 706–710. Sage.

Hollis, L. P., & McCalla, S. A. (2013). Bullied back in the closet: Disengagement of LGBT employees facing workplace bullying. *Journal of Psychological Issues in Organizational Culture, 4*(2), 6–16. 10.1002/jpoc.21109

Larson, G. S. & Tompkins, P. K. (2005). Ambivalence and resistance: A study of management in a concertive control system. *Communication Monographs, 72*(1), 1–21. 10.1080/0363775052000342508

LeMaster, L. T., Zanin, A., Niess, L. C., & Lucero, H. (2023). Trans Relational Ambivalences: A Critical Analysis of Trans and Gender-Nonconforming Relational (Un) Belonging in Sports Contexts. *Women's Studies in Communication, 46* (1), 42–64. 10.1080/07491409.2022.2156418

Mael, F. A., & Ashforth, B. E. (1995). Loyal from day one: Biodata, organizational identification, and turnover among newcomers. *Personnel Psychology, 48*(2), 309–333. 10.1111/j.1744-6570.1995.tb01759.x

Tompkins, P. K., & Cheney. G. (1985). Communication and unobtrusive control in contemporary organizations. In R. D. McPhee & P. K. Tompkins (Eds.), *Organizational communication: Traditional themes and new directions* (pp. 179–210). Sage.

Travers, A. (2008). The sport nexus and gender injustice. *Studies in Social Justice, 2*(1), 79–101. 10.26522/ssj.v2i1.969

Travers, A. (2018). Transgender issues in sport and leisure. In L. Mansfield, J. Caudwell, B. Wheaton, and B. Watson (Eds.), *The palgrave handbook of feminism and sport, leisure and physical education* (pp. 649–665). London: Palgrave Macmillan.

Zanin, A. & Bisel, R. S. (2020). Concertive resistance: How overlapping team identifications enable collective organizational resistance. *Culture and Organization, 26*(3), 231–249. 10.1080/14759551.2019.1566233

Zanin, A. C., LeMaster, L. T., Niess, L. C., & Lucero, H. (2023). Storying the Gender Binary in Sport: Narrative Motifs Among Transgender, Gender Non-Conforming Athletes. Communication & Sport, (Advanced Online Publication) 10.1177/21674795221148815

Zanin, A. C., Shearer, E. T., & Martinez, L. V. (2020). Toward a typology for negotiating layered identities: An oppositional discourse analysis of girls' youth sport. *Communication Monographs, 87*(3), 381–403. 10.1080/03637751.2020.1729993

INDEX

Note: **Bold** page numbers refer to tables and *italic* page numbers refer to figures.

Printed in Great Britain
by Amazon

47623716R00223